GW00598999

Thinner & Richer

Doctor **Ian Shenkin**

Thinner & Richer

The **foodlovers** 365-day calendar **cookbook** to maintain **after-diet** weight loss

Quiller Press
London

Important Warning

If you have a medical condition, or are pregnant, the dictary regime described in this book should not be followed without first consulting your own doctor. All guidelines and warnings should be read carefully, and the author, copyright holder and publisher cannot accept responsibility for injuries or damage arising out of a failure to comply with the same.

First published 1996 by:
Quiller Press Ltd
46 Lillie Road
London SW6 1TN

Copyright © 1996 Linshen Ltd

All rights reserved. No part of this publication may be reproduced by any means without the prior written permission of the publisher and copyright holder.

ISBN 1 899163 26 3

Designed by:
John Mitchell & Jo Lee
Photographs by:
Claire Davies & Stuart McAllister
Printed by:
Colorcraft, Hong Kong

Dedication

This book is the brain child of my friend and mentor Bennie Linden. This quiet man, who shuns publicity, retired to Jersey in 1986 after an extremely successful business career. During that career, his skill and success became the good fortune of numerous charities which he supported throughout the world. Many a successful man, such as Bennie, would have retired to rest upon his laurels – not Bennie! He has continued to exercise his brilliant mind and entrepreneurial skills and shows absolutely no sign of stopping. He took to heart the plight of war torn Rwanda and has given generously towards medical charities there. However, I believe his greatest achievement has been in Jersey where, along with consultant diabetician Dr. Harvey Besterman, he founded and helped finance the Jersey Diabetic Centre, which is now a thriving unit serving all levels of society. Bennie is now turning his attention to 'pain relief', having had a coronary artery by-pass graft, he knows what it is to suffer acute pain. However, chronic pain, often associated with terminal cancer, is Bennie's present target. He has endowed the 'Harry Linden Family Suite' at Eden Hall Hospice, London, in memory of his late brother, who received such skill and sympathetic treatment throughout the final weeks of his life at Eden Hall. The Suite is a unit where relatives can stay in comparative luxury, to be near their loved ones when they are close to death. Not content with this, Bennie has also donated state of the art pain relief beds and equipment to both Eden Hall Hospice and to Jersey Hospice and is in the process of founding a pain relief charity and indeed it is intended that a proportion of the sales of this Thinner & Richer book will go towards funding the new pain relief charity and the Hospices' pain relief equipment. I look forward to working with him for many years to come and hope that much of his boundless enthusiasm will continue to be shared with me.

Ian Shenkin

Acknowledgements

Many thanks to all who have helped create this concept. Firstly to Bennie Linden for his enthusiasm, brave ideas and of course for his sponsorship. I am so grateful to our master chef Peter Marek, photographers Stuart McAllister and Claire Davies and not least to our publisher and editor Jeremy Greenwood of Quiller Press, who, with his designers John Mitchell and Jo Lee, have coped stoically with more changes of direction than 'Spaghetti Junction'. To my partners at Cleveland Clinic and our staff, thanks to you all and sorry for the occasional mood change. To our PR 'Captain' in Jersey, Peter Tabb and to Tony, Susan and all the Midas team. A very big thank you! Our on the ground team of Peter Slater and Anthony and Fiona Linden who provided skillful and appropriate criticism. Once again, thank you all. Finally to Sheryl who started as my secretary and to my son Michael, who took over at short notice from Sheryl and had to suffer my rantings and ravings, we just could not have done it without you! Love to my wife Maureen and all the family – sorry for the mess during the last 2 years, but you can now have the lounge back!

Contents

Man lives on one quarter of
what he eats. On the other
three quarters his doctor lives
A hieroglyphic from ancient Egypt

7

Thinner & Richer

Why I wrote this book

At the beginning I shall tell you what you should be doing. Later on, I shall tell you what you really want to know; how to do it.

Before I start, a digression is in order. Several years ago, I treated Bennie Linden for Obesity. I practise in Jersey, and Bennie is in the happy position of being officially retired to live in our lovely island. He is an expansive fellow, a philanthropist with all the verve and bounce you would expect from an entrepreneur. He is a byword for generosity, often seen in the dining rooms of the islands best hotels, entertaining a party of friends and business associates.

Unfortunately, by the time he came to see me this laudable generosity of character had translated into a generous girth. Bennie was overweight, out of breath, and diabetic. Despite having undergone a double coronary artery by-pass, he was rapidly furring up his new arterial plumbing. He was feeling pretty terrible most of the time.

I gave him a stern warning, as we doctors do (we're very good at that). So did his hospital-based consultant dietitian who put him on a very low calorie, total food replacement diet (TFR), only available on doctor's prescription. Bennie doggedly stuck to it and lost three stone.

And then he asked me how to eat for the rest of his life?

You may find this hard to believe, but this simple question flummoxed me. You see the routine response is "eat sensibly". You send patients away with vague instructions about eating less fat and more carbohydrates and vegetables, and leave them to get on with it.

But Bennie wanted instructions that were both more specific, and more compatible with what he is used to eating. Being Bennie, he knows what he wants and generally gets it. He made me give him precise and workable answers, and that is how I came to write this book.

For the first time I had to draw up a diet calendar that a person could stick to. You see like many people, Bennie lacks nutritional knowledge. He is frankly not interested; as far as his health is concerned, he wants a doctor to tell him what to do, not why he should be doing it. He doesn't know a carbohydrate from a protein and doesn't want to know. Most of all he wants his calories counted by someone else. For people like Bennie, who is none the less anxious never to gain weight, menu plans to be religiously followed are an ideal solution.

I also had to think hard about how to make low-fat, low-sugar food taste as rich and as good as Bennie is used to. There isn't much point in exhorting one's patients to lunch off half a pound of steamed sprouts if they crave chocolate ice-cream with fudge sauce. I had to find some way of changing Bennie's diet, rich as it was in red meat, fried potatoes and brandy-soaked puddings, for a substitute that tasted good but kept his arteries unclogged and his waistline trim.

The result, compiled over months of my own convalescence from an operation, was a list of 365 menu plans. One for each day of the year and with a choice. I was pleased with the recipes. The principles were simple enough. Instead of looking first at what to omit from Bennie's diet, I looked at what substitutions could be made. I found that food manufacturers – far from being co-conspirators in a plot to make us all fatties – turned out to be offering an excellent range of alternatives to the usual high-calorie products.

Fat, the real killer in our diet, is the hardest of all to excise from a recipe – but low-fat versions of many staples are freely available. Instead of cream, one can use fromage frais or in some instances low-fat ice-cream. Instead of searing meat in butter, searing in a pan brushed with olive oil works just as well. A spoonful of coconut milk can be added to a sauce, rather than thickening it with flour and butter roux. Instead of cheddar, one can use low-fat cheese, on sale in every supermarket.*

* Olive oil contains as much fat as any other oil, however it is 'cardiac friendly' as you need to use so little.

I needed an alternative to steaks and roast meat. Persistent searching through the supermarket shelves led me to low-fat alternatives such as venison, calves' liver and Quorn.

Obvious substitutes for sugar and full-cream milk exist in the form of low-calorie sweeteners, low-fat milk and soya milk. I found low-fat ice-cream and chips, fruit canned in juice rather than syrup, and baked beans canned without the usual salt, sugar and fat.

Best of all was the large variety of canned fish high in protein, low in calories and laden with the kind of omega 3 oils which nutritionists advocate.

So I was pretty pleased with the general principles although I hadn't cooked many of the recipes. Bennie's eating plan was I felt ahead of the field.

Until, coming up on the inside against the rails, I noticed my son.

I should explain that Gordon is an amateur National Hunt jockey. Clearly, the less weight his mount is carrying, the better their chances of a win. And just as clearly, there are rules to prevent jockeys from starving themselves to emaciation.

The way it works is this. Flat-race (as opposed to National Hunt) jockeys may weigh as little as 7 stone 10 lbs and apprentices can go right down to 7 stone 3 lbs. This includes silks, saddle, weight cloth, helmet, leathers and whip. A polystyrene back and neck protection jacket weighing up to 2 lbs is usually allowed in addition. A light flat saddle weighs only about 1 lb.

Any weight lower than 8 stone is very low for a young man and can rarely, if ever, be attained without dieting. Sir Gordon Richards, the famous jockey and trainer, struggled in his day to keep down to 8 stone 3 lbs. Lester Piggott, during his celebrated riding career, had to diet constantly in order to stay at 8 stone 7 lbs. Few top jockeys can 'waste' to below 8 stone 5 lbs without feeling faint or giddy. Willie Carson is the exception; he can get down to 7 stone 11 lbs and is as strong as any other leading jockey.

Because of this rigorous weight requirement, many flat jockeys are 'bred' from wiry Irish families with a racing tradition. Many others, with the genetic tendency to stay thin, emerge from the British Racing

School at Newmarket, which takes boys and girls from all walks of life – who will simply not make the grade, however keen they are, unless they can maintain their stamina while rake-thin.

Now my son Gordon is not a flat-race jockey. But even amateur National Hunt jockeys have to stay at the lower end of the permitted weights, which are in their case 10 stone, or 9 stone 7 lbs for amateurs who have ridden less than 25 winners.

As I treated Bennie and other patients for obesity, I hardly noticed that Gordon, as a 5 ft 10 inch amateur, was struggling to reduce to under 10 stone. And he was not alone. National Hunt jockeys traditionally come from hunting-shooting-fishing Anglo-Irish stock, and are not skinny types. Free meals at racecourse canteens tend to be standard British pie and chips with a cola drink chaser, which are the very worst of all the alternatives that they could be offered.*

As a result, these young men starve, dehydrate in the sauna, take appetite suppressants and diuretics (against the rules) or even force themselves to vomit before the weigh out. This is an appalling state of affairs. Drugs can lead to unpleasant mood swings and diuretics eventually deplete the body's store of certain essential minerals. The famous jockey Fred Archer is said to of killed himself in a depression over his weight. Ex-champion National Hunt jockey Richard Dunwoody's celebrated career almost ended due to starvation and saunas in an attempt to be able to ride at 10 stone. Happily he has now come to terms with his weight and no longer risks his health in an effort to ride at an unrealistic weight for his size. He has made a splendid comeback, without the pressures of championship aspirations. Nine National Hunt jockeys have died as a result of injury in the past 21 years in Britain, highlighted recently by the tragic death of Richard Davis at the age of 26. National Hunt racing exceeds motorsports as a cause of fatalities in Britain and is surpassed only by climbing and air sports. Knowing all this, I suddenly became aware that Gordon was suffering. Riding at 9 stone 7 lbs he was faint, giddy and clearly this could not go on. There must be a low weight he could maintain without becoming a short-tempered, wizened, caricature of himself.

Here was my chance to try out my recipes. By trial and error, we found that at 10 stone 4 lbs, Gordon could eat three high protein, low-

* Though on medical advice from the Jockey Club who now have their own nutritionist this is starting to change.

fat meals a day without gaining weight. What is more, once I had made a few improvements, the rest of us were very happy to eat the same meals.

'Once I had made a few improvements' – ah, you noticed. The fact is that low-fat cookery tends to be dull unless you do quite a lot to ginger it up. You can't just add extra seasoning; you need a basic rethink of the way flavourings work. If some of the recipes seem at first to require an odd juxtaposition of ingredients, try them and make up your own mind. The principle is – extra contrast. Taking fat away tends to tone everything down. Flavours and textures become more bland. Eating something slightly sweet with something salt or savoury restores the contrast. That's why so many of my recipes contain tropical fruit with meat or fish.

The discovery was a culinary breakthrough. Yet there was still something missing: convenience. Gradually the meal plans I had originally drawn up for Bennie were modified to fit in with our busy life style. They took less time to prepare and relied on store-cupboard foods. Daily shopping is the ideal but, like most people, we have to put up with tinned food sometimes and can do so with very little loss of flavour, vitamin content or fibre.

I found that low-calorie eating resulted in immediate benefits for the whole family. We all feel and look well and I am heartened to discover from the admirable guru Leslie Kenton, that we stand a better chance of living much longer than we would on a high calorie diet.

So why doesn't everyone do it?

In the following pages, I shall examine some of the reasons why, and show that it is easier than you think.

**One can never be too rich
or too thin**
The Duchess of Windsor

Thinner

Like good sex and triumphant tennis, thinness and riches are all in the mind. Most of us could be both thinner and richer if we stayed focused.

Yet just as an insistent telephone distracts you from gazing straight into each other's eyes, so it is easy to lose track of what you want when everyone else is ordering double whiskies and cream cakes. At such times you may allow yourself to forget that you're eating to stay looking and feeling good – not to be a party animal.

This book is for everyone who knows what they want and for everyone who is looking for a way that will make certain that they will stay thinner. The first rule is – **stay in control**

Control is the essence of 'Thinner and Richer'.

Staying in control also means making your own assessment of reality. If your best friend says 'porridge makes you fat', then get a second opinion. She may be a truly wonderful person, but how does she score as a dietitian? (Abysmally low in my view.) If your mother says 'you are not eating properly' because you don't eat meat, check your vegetarian diet. Does it contain plenty of pulses and grains and nuts and soya and fruit and vegetables, without being over-reliant on cheese? If so it seems likely that you have a healthy diet and just this once you can safely ignore your mother's advice.*

Learn to eat and drink what you want, and when you want, without causing comment. If you're going to a restaurant or party, there is no need to make a big issue of the way you eat. Discussing somebody else's regimen must be the single most boring dinner party topic since the

* Nuts do contain a high proportion of fat and should generally be avoided.

unholy trinity of 'How I Gave Up Smoking', 'How I Want To Give It Up But Can't', and 'Stuff It I'm Going To Keep On Smoking So There.' You can easily consume a healthy meal without drawing attention to yourself; drink spritzers or water, ignore salt, leave fatty sauces on the plate, trim fat off meat, and don't touch your pudding. You don't have to tell the world you're doing this. Nobody will notice. (Well your mother might. If all else fails tell her that you have already had something.)

A warning here. Control is fine. Over-restriction of your food intake is stupid, and anorexia is it's extreme form. Fear of eating is based on the myth that food of any kind makes you put on fat. Of course it does not. An adequate diet is essential for gleaming hair, strong teeth, good skin, fresh breath and lively mind. Without proper nutrition, the internal organs cannot operate as they should, lethargy sets in and, in due course, depression follows. So don't be fanatical; it's dangerous. Learn to enjoy what's good for you.

Once you have learnt to leave food on the plate you can get advanced-level eating control also called thinning. Thinning is very difficult for most of us, brought up as we were to waste not, want not and to find 101 interesting ways of using the leftovers. But as you clear up the serving dishes and your eye lights upon those last spoonfuls of chocolate pudding, just ask yourself do you want it on your hips, or in the bin? Remember that once food is bought and paid for, you can't re-sell it at a profit. Its worth is yours to determine. You can use it to keep you healthy, or you can use it to convert to fat, or you can throw it away.

If by now you are wondering how such single-mindedness is going to make you richer, then you are among the lucky ones who have never had a weight problem. You have probably picked up this book because you've lost weight and want to keep it off. You may think that if you 'eat normally' from now on you'll stay the same. But this isn't the case, your idea of normal eating is what made you fat in the first place. Unless you adjust your idea of what appropriate food intake is the weight will pile back.

Your first task is to tell yourself that you and only you are in control of what you eat. Not your mother, nor the agency with the Mars Bar account, nor the manager of your local take away. You are eating for the sake of your health now and in the future.

There are people who 'never have to diet'. A few of them are nature's bean poles. Most quite obviously are not, yet they seem to be lucky. They don't worry about what they eat. It's not fair; you're always on a diet and they are not. How can this be? This attitude to food seems to be much the same as your own. That is, if it looks, tastes and smells nice, you eat it.

I have news for you. Most slim people don't have your attitude to food at all. If you ask them, they'll say something vague about eating what they like. But if you shine a bright light into their eyes and get to work on their fingernails (you'd be surprised at what goes on in my surgery) – you will find that they have always internalised certain rules. They don't like chocolate, or they say they hate butter, or lunch makes them sleepy. They are generally careful not to eat late at night and they take regular exercise. Certainly they never diet. But they are always watchful.

And theirs is an appropriate attitude, for in this age when everything is available, informed selection is more necessary than ever. If most of us wanted to we could feast on high-fat, high-sugar food all of the day and every day. A few people do, and they become grossly obese. Those who don't are already exerting control to some degree. Maintaining your weight is essentially a matter of increasing the degree of control.

Control isn't 'will power'. If you have to exercise will power, you must be hungry or hankering after the wrong kind of food. If that's the case then you are not eating correctly. And who wants to exercise negative prohibitory 'will power' three times a day, every day of their lives?

Control means learning to prefer food that's good for you and careful not too eat to much of it. That's all.

Unfortunately, at first you may be unaware of what the best food is, or how much of it you should eat. This book will help. If you're in the final weeks of a successful diet, your capacity and your appetite are already retrained to operate efficiently on the moderate amounts of food my recipes require. If you combine any three meals, one drink and one snack from these pages in the course of one day, you won't lose weight, but you will remain at a low weight and you will learn how much to eat and what kind of food. In effect: **You will be learning to be in control.**

Remember... Staying slim is like getting rich, and if you are to succeed you should never be deflected from your goal.

Some have too much, yet still do crave;
I little have, and seek no more.
They are but poor, though much they have,
And I am rich, with little store;
They poor, I rich; they beg, I give;
They lack, I have; they pine, I live.
And he that will his health deny
Down amongst the dead men, let him lie.

Toast – Here's A Health To The King
Edward Dyer, c. 1540–1607

'It is easier for a camel to go through the eye of a needle, than for a rich man to enter into the Kingdom of God' The Gospel according to St Matthew xix 24.

But, here the Gospel was referring to material wealth.

Now, as a doctor, I see patients from all walks of life; those with material wealth and those with spiritual wealth, but surely health is the richest prize of all. Being fat can impoverish your life in many ways. The image of the jolly fat man or woman is almost always no more than that – an image. It's a cliché, but in my experience few fat people, especially those who recognise themselves as being overweight, are jolly. Are you? – when the whole world is telling you that you should be slim!

Being fat means that much of the richness of the diversity that this life offers is denied to you. Fat people tend to have less energy, live less active lives and generally worry about themselves more than leaner, fitter people do. Worry feeds on worry and that can often lead to over-eating (which is costly and thus impoverishing) which leads to more weight and so it goes on.

So as the title says Thinner & Richer.

Now, we have all heard 'early to bed, early to rise; makes a man healthy, wealthy and wise'. I believe that it is never too late to enrich your life. As the famous French sage The Abbe' D'Allain Val said **'L'embarras des richesse'**. In other words, the more alternatives, the more difficult the choice. But, dear reader, you do have a choice; a choice to live a healthy and active life and to enjoy the riches that this would bring to you. I am not talking about money, I am talking about that **feel good factor** which will change your whole outlook upon life.

Just think how wonderful it would be to wear chic and fashionable clothes, to enjoy sport and leisure pursuits, even if you are not particularly adept – reading this book won't make you a champion! – but you can feel like one! This is the richness of life fulfilled; to see, to do, to achieve the goal that seemed so far away before you decided to get down to your target weight. As Julius Caesar said, 'Veni, vedi, vici!' (I came, I saw, I conquered). You have now conquered your weight problem.

This book is all about being able to maintain a healthy weight once you have reached it and to equip you to enjoy your life to the the full, to feel well and to be happy – and with happiness will come a richness of life which you may never have experienced.

Isn't it amazing? Having reached your healthy target weight, all those fashionable clothes really do come in your size! Aircraft seats have become wider and your car doesn't have to be fitted with one of those adjustable steering wheels just to allow you to fit behind it – and indeed a 'super mini' becomes a rational alternative and you don't have to keep now justifying that bigger thirstier car just because nothing smaller can cope with you.

You are richer by far and your self-confidence and self-esteem will rise with every new challenge you meet. Having achieved your target body weight, you have confidence in yourself and of your ability to master your personal destiny.

Just keep thinking positive and enjoy the **feel good factor** of your new and richer life.

From now on: your body is on your side

If everyone of you, housewife, businessman, teenager, sportsman or athlete follows this daily diary and the accompanying recipes, all will be Thinner and Richer. Your life will be enriched with more energy and a sense of well being. Be lean, lithesome and contented with your body and start to enjoy the rest of your life!

Wild animals simply eat the food that's
best for them, and so should we.
Dr Andrew Stanway,
Taking the Rough with the Smooth

I told them once, I told them twice;
They would not listen to advice.
Lewis Carroll, Humpty Dumpty's Song

What's food to you?

If you are going to enrich your life then you must be fit. This means weight maintenance, not weight loss which is dealt with in the chapter 'All Change'. I assume that you want to stay as thin as you are, and don't want to lose any weight. Perhaps you have been getting less exercise lately and have noticed firm muscle turning to flab. Or maybe you're pregnant, concerned that unless you pay particular attention to your figure now, you may never return to your normal slender outline.

Most likely of all, you have successfully dieted and reached your target weight.

It is now well known that most dieters fail to keep weight off. For a doctor who has tried hard to help, seeing vivacious and nimble dieters obstinately reflate to their former zeppelin proportions, is frustrating in the extreme. I would like to say that I can only imagine how depressing it must be for them.

Unfortunately, this is not the case. I can't only imagine it. I see it. Unlike architects, whose failures conveniently collapse, we doctors who advise on weight control have to live with most of our failures. They return. They glower and they weep, demanding to be helped yet again.

When this happens to us for the first time, we allow the patients to creep into our reactions. It is only, we claim, from the heights of our well-balanced profession, a matter of will power. A matter of retraining the appetite. Some of us may become exasperated as this G.P. in his letter to the *Daily Telegraph* says: 'I have learnt to my cost that I am totally wasting my time trying to persuade my patients to lose even a pound in weight. I persist because I am paid to do so, but I have to say that my time could be better employed with those with illnesses that are less obviously self-inflicted.*

After a while we wise up. We learn that once a patient has been fat, he or she will find it much harder to maintain normal weight unless they consume fewer calories than they're used to, possibly for the rest of their lives.**

We try to break it to them gently. 'You'll always have to be careful,' as we say cheerily. 'Cut out sugar and cut down on salt and saturated fat. Eat more vegetables and fibre.' There they go armed with this fashionable wisdom...

and waddle back again, fatter than ever, 6 months later.

Their opening gambit is always the same. 'It's not what I eat, Doctor. I don't eat cakes and I **never eat breakfast.**' If I only had a pound for every time I heard this!

In my observation, the reasons for chronic weight problems like these, whilst they may stem from very real piles of chips and slabs of chocolate, are, in a sense, all in the mind and if these psychological triggers vary, they do so because people vary, and the significance of food varies from person to person and family to family.

In a strict sense, obesity is self-inflicted. The conflicting social pressures and misleading advertising can cause such confusion about how much to eat and what body-image is acceptable that the number of pitiable distressed fat people entering a doctor's surgery is scarcely surprising.

Over the years, doctors interested in weight control learn to classify various obese types. This isn't to say that they don't treat them as individuals; it simply happens to be true that if you have any contact at all with the general public, you start to classify them, After all, shop assistants develop an insight that tells them whether you are just dreaming about that purple satin number, or a big spender with £500 burning a hole in your handbag. Barmen immediately get the measure of the

* Dr James Nelson, Doncaster, 1995.

** Dr Stephen Kreitzman in the Royal College of General Practitioners 1993 Members' Handbook.

maudlin drunk, the aggressive drunk and the merry drunk. Some doctors make a quick, occasionally unfair assessment of patients too. Especially those with weight problem or, more accurately, an eating problem.

I don't, of course, write about those distressing extremes of eating disorder, morbid overeating, bulimia and anorexia. Indeed the behaviour of the people I am about to describe is well within the range of what's considered 'normal'. Far too many of my patients eat the wrong food, in the wrong quantities, at the wrong times, and approach me for help. Of these, three types outweigh – I use the word advisedly – all the others; and I shall, by giving you a 'painting-by-numbers' of each of them, offer an insight into three extremely unhelpful ways of understanding food.

The first patient – let's call him Gerald, a man in his sixties, may never visit his doctor at all. This is a great shame because if he did, he'd be given a dose of preventative medicine. He'd be told to cut down on fat, sugar and alcohol and to walk rather than take the car everywhere.

Instead, Gerald meets his doctor for the first time when he develops symptoms which could have been prevented if he had controlled his diet properly.

But that's the odd thing about Gerald. He controlled every other aspect of his life. His bills are paid and his children educated as they wish. His employees do as they are told and his wife has learnt to accommodate herself to his ways. Yet controlling what he puts into his body has never been high in Gerald's agenda.

As a wartime child Gerald found that there was never enough to eat. He learned, when he was about ten, that plenty is the reward of peace; and as he grew prosperous – he never adjusted his view of food's significance.

Food and drink and generous hospitality are the emollients that smooth Gerald's social and business life. In other words, deals are done over a good lunch. He isn't unusually fat – just well covered. His complexion a little florid perhaps, his breath a little inclined to wheeze in the unlikely event that he has to walk up two flights of stairs.

If you ask Gerald to cut down, he'll scowl. He'll mutter about 'quacks' He'll talk scornfully about food faddists; in short, Gerald finds the whole idea of controlling his food intake slightly redolent of health shops, desiccated women in sandals and worthy cyclists – in Gerald's terms, losers!

I see a lot of Geralds. Generally, I have to say, I see them when they have a mild heart attack, need operations on their poor overworked knees, or have to be treated for late-onset diabetes.

They are chastened men. At long last they realise that while they are healthy, they can keep making things happen. But if their hearts and their livers are beyond repair, life will pass them by, and all the money in the world isn't going to change that.

And here, reading *Slimming* magazine in the corner is Glenda. Glenda is a busy women. Probably just as busy as Gerald in her way, though to far less financial effect. She's fair, fat and forty; her children are at school and she drives (never walks) to a nine to five job. It isn't much fun. She is a lowly secretary, sitting down all day. It's because of the boredom that she eats comfort food at her desk: chocolate biscuits, with cups of tea and coffee. And then a main course and pudding at lunch time, because lunch time is the only time she gets to relax and sit down with her friends and, besides, she's always had a main course and pudding – that's what they gave her at school!

Home is even more of a danger zone for Glenda's waist-line. She keeps ice-cream and biscuits in the house because she says the children expect them. She cooks plenty of meat with chips because her husband expects it, she says. And she worries about getting fat, so she skips meals. She never eats at breakfast time. Then she gets up in the night and raids the fridge!

From time to time she gets painful attacks of gall-bladder colic; she has been complaining of it for years. Fat upsets her. If she continues to eat in this way, the only permanent solution will be to have her gall-bladder removed. But the surgeon she was referred to won't do the operation until she loses weight...!

Glenda is still a relatively young woman with at least two active decades in front of her. In her own perception of herself, she's young enough to want to be slim and attractive to men. On the other hand, forty seems middle-aged, and she could easily sink into becoming a cozy prematurely grey and overweight dumpling.

Glenda is confused. In her confusion, she eats another chocolate biscuit. Her eating pattern is becoming compulsive, and she worries even more about her weight. She weighs herself daily. She counts calories, eats nothing but grapefruit, drinks black coffee, goes to aerobic classes. After just a few weeks she feels terrific: years younger! She plans to take up evening class and starts redecorating. She can nearly squeeze into clothes she bought the last time she was a size 12.

She is in every sense now leading a richer life.

It doesn't last. One day, sitting hungrily at her desk, she is faced with the next twenty years of her boring job. She's thinner, but now that she is no longer using food as a distraction, she perceives that food wasn't the real problem. However, other problems are just too big and difficult. Changing her job really seems scary. She feels bleak. To comfort herself, she eats a chocolate biscuit.

I see Glenda when she has eaten the whole packet and burst into tears!

In many ways Glenda is the saddest victim of the well-known diet and binge syndrome, because not only does food comfort her, but it is unavoidable and deeply symbolic in her life. She is expected to spend time in the kitchen preparing food for the family and in the shops buying it. These tasks, which should be a source of pleasure and a natural demonstration of love, turn into a trial – a kind of torture for a women who is trying to starve herself. The only way out is to buy more ready-meals for the freezer and leave her husband and children to use the microwave.

Unfortunately by doing so poor Glenda deprives herself of part of a role as a mother and nurturer. This makes her more depressed than ever. She goes back to the kitchen, and she starts cooking. At meal times, she eats very little. Most of Glenda's eating happens long after everyone else has finished. She always seems to cook too much, and there are always leftovers. Having had a big lunch at work, she isn't really hungry until late at night.

So when she wakes up at one a.m. to raid the fridge, she is a kind of human dustbin; she'll polish off a slab of cheese, half a pie, the last weetabix in the packet. When she wakes up in the morning she isn't hungry enough for breakfast, but by lunch time she is ready for another two courses in the canteen...

When I am alerted to the existence of the third kind of patient I stop counting in single units these patients who come to see me! It's usually a school visit that draws Jason to my attention. He is the class's fat boy, roly-poly, notably different, often both an unhappy bully and a victim. He may be a victim of fun, yet a deeply tragic character. His mum has booked for him to go on a school activities week in France. He is frightened to go as he is afraid everybody will laugh at his body and his 'boobs'. I immediately suspect that Jason has a fat sister, a fat father and an enormous mother, and I am usually right. In such cases the role of socialisation is plain for all to see: for in this family it's O.K. to graze – to eat whenever you like, wherever you like. And nobody likes anything that isn't saturated in fat, sugar and salt.

You've queued behind this family in the checkout; haven't we all? Fresh fruit becomes a very poor second to giant pizzas, crates of cola and beer, whopping tubs of butter and marge and jam, frozen cakes and burgers, frozen fish in batter and pounds and pounds of sausages.

There is not much point in putting the fat boy on a diet. I really need to tackle the whole family. They may prove quite resistant to this. I am asking the mother to stop buying comfort food and the father to stop drinking beer with his friends. I am asking the children to do something other than watch T.V. and eat crisps.

In a sense I am asking all of them to become different people. Yet if parents don't want to collaborate with me – and they may not be motivated; not everyone sees being overweight as a sign of ill health – there is precious little hope for the children at all.

If you have ever been overweight, were you maintaining a convivial image, consoling yourself, or just avoiding conflict with the family?

Have you ever been told (even by dietitians) that
losing weight is easy because all your patient has
to do is to reduce intake by a few calories per day
over a long enough period that they will reach
desired weight?
This information is completely wrong.
Dr Stephen N. Kreitzman

Why slimmers get fat again

Now, I shall assume that I have treated Gerald, Glenda, and Jason's entire clan. They are all lithe as wands, twinkling into the surgery for their last weigh-in. This is supposed to be the end of the matter, but yet I know that my job as a doctor has only just started.

Because I am looking at a group of people who are statistically likely not only to regain the weight they have lost, but to get even heavier. The reasons are partly psychological and partly physical. The physical reasons are common to everybody and I shall deal with them later in this chapter. The psychological ones, however, as I said at the beginning, vary. As a mere family doctor, I don't see the whole picture. None the less there are certain indicators... Gerald is most likely to be able to stay slim. He has practical advantages. He probably doesn't need to spend time in the kitchen – for one thing – that's his wife's domain. If he's retired, his wife is quite likely to be a housewife, with time and motivation to make sure he eats just what the doctor ordered. If he is still economically active, he and his colleagues will take time off for business lunches much less often than they used to do; it's the way of the world. A bottle of mineral water and a bowl of fruit at the boardroom table are *de rigeur* nowadays and that helps.

Most of all, Gerald is motivated because the sword of Damocles is hanging over him. He is, literally, afraid of dying. Will power, of which he has plenty, will make sure that he never gains weight to a dangerous degree again. Since he'll find life rather grim if its continuance depends on the constant exercise of will power, he may well take up new activities and business interests. Thus distracted, Gerald has a good chance of staying slimmer.

Glenda, elated by having lost weight, is none the less fearful. She has slimmed down before, and because she has always returned to her former cottage-loaf shape, she is now almost fatalistic. She would probably agree that she is programmed to fail.

What's really going on is this. Glenda approached me – the doctor – because she thought she'd find it easier to stick to a diet if an authority figure were monitoring her progress. In other words she wanted a parental figure to take responsibility while she, like an obedient child, did what was good for her. All this worked out fine. I took the part of the stern father and gave her encouragement and approbation as she needed it. However, all good things must come to an end. Glenda's thin enough now. She is a big, grown-up person who's expected to organise her own intake of her own food.

Once again, life is lonely, bleak and fraught with choices. As Glenda leaves the surgery, I see the desperate look in her eye. I know that the temptation to 'be naughty' so that a parental figure will once again take an interest, is greater than ever.

As for Jason's family, now the whole family has reached their target, they're going for a good blow out followed by a big shopping expedition – a couple of trolley loads, just like the old days – 'we've got big bones', his mother says complacently. Jason's father agrees. Yet if there is one thing that he can't stand it's 'rabbit food'. 'My dad was a big fellow, kicked the bucket at fifty-five. I'll go the same way I expect.' Well, if it doesn't bother him… for several generations, no adult in his family has lived beyond seventy. It dawns on me that Jason's family culture is impervious to control. I am asking his parents to make judgments, analyse, and look ahead with trepidation. They're a jolly lot who've never done that before and they're not about to start now. I shall keep trying, fully aware that they may be a lost cause.

As a family doctor, I deal with people's weight and only to a certain extent with their attitude to life. The two are almost inevitably entwined as you can see from my thumbnail sketches of the 'types' who need to lose weight. Glenda, for instance, really needs to take control of her whole adult life, and not just her weight.

Yet I do believe that a permanent cure for a weight problem need not mean years of analysis in order to discover it's source. Sometimes, an obvious solution is best. If there are menu plans to stick to, weight can and will be maintained. The immediate problem resulting in overweight – fear for Gerald, depression for Glenda, social ostracism for Jason – will then melt away so that life can be enjoyed by a confident, healthy person, rather than suffered by one who is disadvantaged by heart disease, diabetes, digestive tract disorders or gall bladder disease.

Now for the theory of weight maintenance. This is less obvious than it seems but I will outline the simple version first, the one we all know.

Food and drink is fuel which converts into energy. The fuel is usually measured in calories, so rather than saying Gerald needs a loaf of bread, a pound of tomatoes and two fishes to keep him going every day, we say Gerald needs 2000 calories to keep him going every day. Gerald, who is a sedentary businessman, needs fewer calories than his younger brother Sam, who is a football coach, because Sam converts more fuel to energy. Now assume that Gerald eats more calories than he needs. These are stored beneath the skin as fat. If he wants to get rid of this fat, he has to eat fewer calories than the 2000 he needs. Like an engine running on an empty tank, his body switches to back-up store – not of petrol, but of adipose tissue – and starts to use that instead. Because the stored fat is getting used up, Gerald regains his trim outline.

Only then does he start the real struggle. He is no longer on a reducing diet, so he thinks he can 'eat normally' from now on. But if he does, he will regain weight and become unhealthy again because he doesn't know what 'normal' eating is. Maybe he's never known. Gerald's idea of good food is likely to contain plenty of high cholesterol, fatty red meat, roast potatoes and cheese. There is nothing wrong with any of these as long as they are served occasionally and in small amounts – and never to people who have lost weight recently. For not only should the 'normal' diet contain as little animal fat as possible, but meals eaten by weight losers have to be rigorously controlled for all time. As this book emphasises, life after successful weight loss is a discipline and this book is aimed at helping you towards self discipline.

This isn't just Dr. Shenkin being nannyish. It is a fact that once you have lost most of the weight you need to lose, you'll find it harder to stay slim than you would if you had never put on the weight in the first place. This is not just because of your poor eating habits, though they are a major factor. Clearly the 2000 calories that kept Gerald going at 13 stone will make him fat at 11 stone. But there is a further factor precipitating weight gain: in the course of a reducing diet, the body adjusts to the new weight thus needing fewer calories. So if you start to eat 'normally' after a diet, you're body won't even use up as many of the surplus calories as it used to. Instead, you will gain weight faster the second time round.

To explain how this happens, it is necessary to understand what happens to a normal healthy body in more detail than the simple 'fuel in, energy out, spare fuel deposited as fat' theory can offer. We have to look at exactly how this potato converts into a ten mile walk – because it's in this conversion process that the slowing up occurs.

Let's say that your weight is stable and your body mass is correct for your height. You eat a potato. The pancreas reacts by secreting insulin. Meanwhile, enzymes are produced by your digestive system which begins to breakdown the potato starch into a sugar, easily absorbed by the blood. This is not much use in your blood, but it would be in your muscles and your liver; all it needs is a converter... and here comes insulin, riding to the rescue. The insulin is released from the pancreas into the blood stream, where it converts the blood sugar to glycogen, which your muscles and liver can use.

If too much glycogen is converted (because the potato was too big for your immediate needs, for instance) it will be stored along with water. This part of your energy store is not hard to lose once you start slimming; your body will use it up in the first week or so. Unfortunately, what you are losing is mostly fluid, which will be quickly replaced. For this reason, those first pounds so dramatically lost on a very low calorie diet are called 'transient weight loss' and will return even faster unless re-feeding is supervised under medical or dietetic advice. This is why those short-sharp-shock diets of the kind peddled in so many women's

28

magazines are ultimately dispiriting and counter-productive.

Real weight loss starts once the glycogen and water deposits have gone and the body has started to convert subcutaneous fat into energy. But this is much harder, because when the body is taking in less food than it needs, it compensates by using less energy *. Its metabolic rate drops by 15%. It's as though instead of getting 30 miles per gallon out of the old thing, you can suddenly get 34.5 to the gallon – 15% more so in order to get down to those surplus tanks, you'll have to wait longer to use up the fuel.

(Here's a health warning. If a Gerald or a Glenda, about to lose their last few pounds, are reading this, I must tell them not to be too depressed by what follows. It is not as bad as it sounds.)

Let's say your normal non-gaining intake is 2000 calories per day, and you think you'll try a gentle diet of 1500 calories per day. Nature immediately plays a mean trick. As you're on diet, which your body 'understands' from the initial loss of glycogen and water, you're metabolic rate slows down by 15% – so instead of needing 2000 calories you only need 1700. To use up a kilo of fat (not the glycogen and water loss of the first few days) you'll have to underfeed yourself by about 7700 calories. So on your 200 calorie a day deficit (below the 1500 you're taking in) you'll take more than 38 days to loose a kilo. Since metabolic rate is related to total body weight, the appropriate slowing of metabolic rate with weight loss, will actually slow down the rate of loss. Dieting, contrary to many rumours, does **not** 'make you fat', and will 'not harm' your metabolism. Extra exercise – unless it is taken more often and more energetically than most people can manage – makes little difference. It is an invaluable aid to keeping the mind off food and for both mental and physical well-being. So the dieter goes grimly on, until the struggle to lose those last few pounds of excess weight seems endless and can take months, or even years. Even if a person could exercise rigid control and count every calorie for such a long time, it's quite likely that he or she might not lose the weight. The reason for this is that the calorie values of every day (fresh) food varies because of different production methods and new strains.

Of course we all know of people who religiously weighed portions, counted calories, and lost surplus flesh and in almost every case they

* Dr Stephen Kreitzman,
 Royal College of General
 Practitioners' Handbook 1993

have regained it. This is only partly because they enjoy food, or eat for comfort, or made an exception for Christmas. It is certainly not because they have 'big bones'; they have the same knobbly knees as when they were thin. The real problem is, as you can see, Physiological, and a person who wants to keep the weight off must keep to a controlled calorie intake.

Not many people know this. Even fewer can count calories with the accuracy required to lose weight. A very obese person who wants to reach a target weight will almost inevitably have to take scientifically formulated meal replacements under medical supervision (more about this in the chapter 'If you need to slim'). To stay at the target weight, the person must continue to eat adequately, though not to excess.

That's why I have devised the menus in this book. They are nutritionally balanced and certainly have been calorie-counted, but they won't help you to lose weight. Any permutation in this book, of breakfast, lunch, and supper, with a snack and a drink, should result in weight maintenance.

Remember... once weight has gone you will need a low-calorie eating pattern that you can follow for life.

Our primitive ancestors survived, not in
spite of problems, but because of them
Manuel J Smith,
When I say no, I feel Guilty

If you want some fresh ideas for
yourself, change them like shirts
Francis Picabia

All change

By the year 2005, according to a recent report, one in five men and one in four women in Britain will be seriously overweight.*

This represents a national crisis. The human and financial costs of obesity are enormous. At a personal level, as we have seen, many of us know what a lie the phrase 'fat and jolly' can be. Overweight people can be unhappy but feel powerless, and very little makes a person less likely to do well than self-dislike and a feeling of helplessness.

A balance must be achieved. We often blame fashion editors for encouraging women, in particular, to become androgynously thin. It's true that emaciated models are often presented as desirable and that their images may contribute to a rise in anorexia amongst the young.

But I would argue that advertisements which depict slender families, stuffing themselves with chips, fried food and cake are just as insidious and – though it can never be statistically proven – probably much more damaging. They represent an ideal which is utterly impossible. You just can't feed a family on high-fat food, which conceals whopping levels of sugar and salt, and expect them to stay fit.

I attribute no evil intent to food manufacturers. It is largely thanks to their commercial efficiency that 55 million people, on a small wet island in Northern Europe, are able to feed themselves at all. Contrary to what some people would have you believe, there is no conspiracy to make us overweight. But those of us who simply buy this 'stuff' must constantly bear in mind what food manufacturers' priorities are. They

* Reversing the level of obesity,
unpublished Department of
Health Report 1994

have to buy their raw materials at the best possible price, preserve the food, make it more attractive than any competitors product on the shelf and get the best price for it in the shop.

Now sugar is a cheap and good bulking agent (which helps to achieve the price) and salt is an excellent preservative. Fat makes anything taste wonderful (think of dry toast – then think about hot toast dripping with melted butter). Unfortunately, food laden with sugar, salt and fat leads to all the ills that the flesh is heir to: heart disease, diabetes and possibly certain kinds of cancer.

Remember Jason? I can tell Jason's mother about the dangers of obesity until I tire of the sound of my own voice, but I promise you that I will still see her filling her supermarket trolley with high-sugar soft drinks, cartons of saturated fat and loads of sliced white bread. So it would be easy for me, exasperated, to dismiss her as stubborn – but it would not be fair.

You see, if we want to change our eating habits, we have to examine what's really going on. Mine is not the only message reaching Jason's mother about her own weight. There is one about men liking 'something to get hold of'. Then there are all the euphemisms for excess flesh which make it acceptable: she may think of herself as 'a big woman', or 'outsize' or even, for heaven's sake, 'rubenesque'. These disguise the facts – that as an obese woman she runs a higher risk from breast cancer and stroke; that the podgy children are already laying the foundations of heart disease and, as for her husband – well, could not their sex life improve if he were not heaving around 40 lbs of excess weight all day and collapsing in his chair in front of the television at night? His snores are enough to waken the next door neighbours!

All these uncomfortable messages are lost in the noise from glossy food advertising and contradictory exhortations (sometimes on the same page); starve for five days and lose 5 lbs; but surely you could argue, apples and salads are advertised too; if advertising is so powerful and she knows the facts, why doesn't Jason's mother choose apples instead of beefburgers?

She doesn't choose them because she, and her whole family, are addicted (I use the word advisedly) to food with a high sugar, salt and a high fat content. They crave it. We've all heard people saying they crave sweets or chocolate, that they 'need' salt and 'couldn't live without' cheese. They have become used to eating food adulterated by the salty preservatives, sugary bulking agents and fatty flavour enhancers used in the manufacture and no longer appreciate the taste of fresh food simply cooked. They really do crave the taste of salt and the energy rush from sugar and fat.

An ideal diet derives no more than 25% of its energy value from fat. It is high in naturally occurring fibre (mainly from grains, fruit and vegetables) and bulky carbohydrate (wholemeal bread, starchy vegetables and grains). It is high in vitamin content, which protects the body against disease.

Fibre and starchy carbohydrates are filling and good for you so, in theory, you shouldn't need to pile extra fat on top of them. Unfortunately it's all so easy to do, if you've become used to mashing potatoes with cream and butter, serving lamb chops with a rim of fat and mushrooms fried in oil. If your weight is to stay the same, you'll need to modify your tastes so that you will come to prefer more frugal but exciting food, in similar quantities.

If you follow the recipes in this book, you will find the process of change much easier than you would think. My recipes represent an adjustment to your eating habits, rather than a sudden, total abstinence from all things you like. But I will come to that later; right now, I want to assure you that you can start the process of healthier eating by jettisoning some of the things on your usual shopping list, in favour of others.

Begin by changing the kind of fat you eat*. All fat isn't equally harmful, which is why people from Southern Europe, where olive oil is a staple and animal fats comparatively rare in the diet, have Europe's lowest rate of heart disease, while Scots and Finns, who prefer butter and bacon and cheese, have heart disease in epidemic proportions (although it is of interest to note that a dietary education campaign by the Finnish Government has greatly improved matters *).

The kind of fat most likely to clog up your arteries is saturated, that is solid at room temperature. Butter, cheese and fatty meat, peanut butter, coconut cream and tahini should all be used sparingly. Polyunsaturated margarine is heavily advertised, but again, it should

* All fats are fattening and are about equal in calorie values. Polyunsaturates and monounsaturates are more heart and body friendly.

* The ABC of Nutrition, Second edition.

be used sparingly. Polyunsaturates are probably not harmful to you but they do put on weight. Olive oil, a monounsaturated fat, actually emerges from some studies as a preventer of heart disease; however that does not mean that if you fry every meal in it you will reduce your risk to nothing. It means that you should use olive oil in accordance with medical advice – which is to reduce the proportion of fat in your diet to 25%.

As for sugar and salt these occur naturally in food. Refined sugar of any kind provides only empty calories, that is calories that come wrapped in no nutritional value of any kind. It is addictive: the more you have, the more you want. It is highly concentrated. If you want something sweet, it makes more sense to eat sultanas or fresh sweet mango than to take sugar in your tea, because by drinking a dose of refined sugar, you're absorbing a high number of calories with no nutrition and no fibre. These will simply flood your system, giving you a 'hit' of energy, followed by a deep low, or come-down – just like a drug high! And just like a drug addict, you will then crave the next hit. If you eat an apple or some sultanas on the other hand, the naturally occurring sugars are absorbed more slowly, and the system doesn't get a shock or try to compensate with a greater craving*.

Only in very hot climates is extra salt necessary to prevent dehydration. A balanced diet in an industrialised country is never likely to be deficient in it, because the manufacturers include it in just about everything from bread to canned fish. Even if your diet consisted entirely of fresh vegetables, nuts and fruit, you would be obtaining some salt (although you'd probably suffer deficiencies in other respects). Too much salt is known to aggravate high blood pressure, and anyone with this condition should avoid it completely or use the potassium substitute salora.

Meals low in fat, salt and sugar need not be dull, as my recipes prove. As Mae West probably said, **'it's not what you've got but the way that you use it that counts.'** I have learnt to rely a great deal on contrasting flavours and textures to make my food more interesting, and so will you.

As for drinks, alcohol, like sugar, is made up of empty calories; tea and coffee are artificial stimulants devoid of nutritional value unless milk is added to them. It is better to substitute herb tea or spring water,

* Miriam Polunin
  The Right Way To Eat.

flavoured if you like with a dash of fruit juice. Water is God's gift. It is free (or almost) and it should be drunk whenever possible. You cannot damage your health by drinking water.

And a last word on exercise. It is of course said that you'd have to climb Ben Nevis in order to lose a pound. This is true and irrelevant. Regular exercise can be clinically proven to improve cardiovascular efficiency and lighten depression. It can make you suppler and increase your stamina. It helps stabilise your metabolism, so that it can cope with exceptional demands. It subtly increases feelings of well being and self-esteem and gets you out of your car, the pub, or the sitting room. Those who exercise regularly are more likely to live longer and the same applies to readers of this book who follow my advice.

Remember... if your weight is to stay the same, your lifestyle and eating habits will have to change.

> **Fat loss, unfortunately, is not the same thing as weight loss and is considerably more difficult and never achieved on some diets.**
> Lipotrim Information Sheet

If you need to slim

The recipes in this book are a weight maintenance plan. They will not help you lose weight but they will help to prevent you from regaining it. Your problem may be that having gained and lost weight again and again over the years, you are obese (that is, having a body mass index above 30) and now find it difficult to lose weight at all. In your heart of hearts, you haven't much hope that you will ever be anything but fat.

That's not true. What you are correct in recognising is that losing weight is harder than it used to be. This is more of a psychological barrier than a physical one.

Why not go along to your G.P, who may have an obesity clinic or offer advice on diet? If your body mass index is above 30*, he may well prescribe for you a total food replacement diet (TFR), made up from special very low calorie drinks (VLCD), very low in fat and giving you about 800 calories per day.

Because losing those last pounds of surplus fat is so difficult, reliance on the ordinary kitchen scales for portion control and calorie counting is not good enough*. A Maris Piper potato may have more or fewer calories than a King Edward, and one kind of cheddar more than another. Besides, although I am all for people taking control of their own lives, I disapprove of the daily grinding boredom and guilt-inducing temptation that calorie-counting ordinary food represents. It is a humiliating reminder, three times a day, for yourself and to the people you love that

* See Page 336

* Study conducted by nutrition scientists at Surrey University quoted in Kreitzman (ibid).

you are overweight. This in itself makes you feel like a person with a problem.

Better by far, in my opinion, to tackle weight loss briskly and accurately like any other physical condition requiring correction. If a precisely measured formula is administered, it will be possible to set a target in time, rather than merely in weight – to say with truth that by December or May or June, Gerald will have reduced to his target weight.

The other dangers of a very low calorie diet self-administered, without a doctor's supervision, are obvious. People get hungry; the slightest backsliding makes them feel guilty and programmed to fail; they succumb to pressure. Removing the overweight person altogether from 'ordinary' food helps them to stay focused, and as for hunger, certain formula foods or drinks available on prescription have a major advantage. They exploit a process in-built into every one of us, which is called ketosis. And one happy side-effect of ketosis is that it reduces hunger.

As I pointed out in an earlier chapter, when the first drastic weight loss associated with glycogen depletion has taken place, the body starts using up its fat stores. Fat has to be converted into various kinds of fuel before it can be used as energy. Among them are substances called ketones. When on a supervised very low calorie diet (nutrient complete VLCD), preferably with normal food replaced by a formulated total food replacement diet (TFR), it becomes possible to measure ketones in the urine three or four days after the diet has begun. Once ketones appear, we know that the body has started to use up its fat store. There are side effects. One is sweet breath, for surplus ketones are expelled in the breath as well as the urine. Another, and more welcome, side-effect is hunger reduction, which in itself makes the diet more likely to succeed.

The last evident side-effect of ketone production is the very fact that it can be measured. You can cheat the scales, or cheat yourself, but you can't cheat the ketone test. If repeated tests by your doctor fail to reveal ketosis, then you are almost certainly taking in something other than the prescribed formula. This may not be as serious as it sounds; even low-calorie drinks or sugar-free gum can slow down ketone production, without making a huge difference to weight loss but they can produce carbohydrate craving and a loss of control. But people whose diets I

38

have supervised have been reassured to know that ketosis is taking place. It means that they are burning up unwanted and potentially harmful fat.

Once you have lost the excess pounds, then you can control your food intake with the delicious recipes from this book.

Your best hope of reducing to a target weight is to diet with help and advice from your doctor and possibly using a scientifically formulated food or drink administered under supervision. This treatment is only for those with a body mass index above 30 (see page 336)

The survey found only one of 18 families it surveyed had detail planned meals in advance. 'For the rest, shortage of time means many eat the first thing that comes to hand', it said.
Guardian account (09/10/95) of 'The Palate of the Nation' Survey by H.M. Government.

Convenience

If you have ever shared a household with teenage children and young adults you will know that no-one seems to keep regular hours. Evenings fill with classes, social events and outings, and weekends go the same way. There is a big temptation to snack.

In the mid-1990's, a team of documentary film-makers set up a static camera in the corner of a domestic kitchen and filmed the family's entrances and exits for a television programme on eating habits. The household was chosen because its two working parents and two teenagers were a typical family of their age and socio-economic group.

Not once in the course of a week did the family eat together. Not even two of them! Instead, one individual would amble into the kitchen, select a ready meal from the fridge or freezer, put it into the microwave, eat it – sometimes straight from the pack, whilst standing up or reading the paper – and then sling the implements into the dishwasher, pull a face at the camera, and leave.

You may feel as I do that a real opportunity for bonding and strengthening relationships is lost if families literally never eat together. But that is the amateur sociologist talking. Not a G.P. As a G.P. my concern about such a way of life is the nature of the food the family was eating. Naturally, it had been bought with one priority in mind: convenience. I had the impression that the family were eating too few fresh green vegetables and too many oven-chips, too little fresh fruit and too many ready-made cakes and sugary cereals.

I can quite understand how this comes about. My wife and I are part of a demographically similar household. We haven't much time, either. However I know the dangers of high-fat, high-sugar and over-salty food. I see the results of it every time Gerald, Glenda or Jason is in the surgery. In our case, nutritional considerations had to precede convenience.

When I began adjusting the recipes that I had drawn up for Bennie Linden to suit our own lifestyle, I wanted to keep our fat intake to 25% and sugar to a minimum, whilst using convenience foods as much as possible. I wandered the aisles of local supermarkets, picking up tins and packets and reading the list of ingredients like an eager browser in a public library. On those Saturday afternoons I had previously spent with my family, I was now to be found lurking suspiciously between the Ryvita and the reconstituted soya protein. I pulled so many packets from deep-freezes that I would emerge from the shop smacking my hands around my body as after a night on a bare mountain. I think I should apologise here and now to the many keen-eyed store detectives whose hunter instincts I must have inadvertently aroused.

I was doing the computing for you, gentle reader, and believe me, mine is a hard act to follow. None of us need find it impossible to eat correctly from any decent supermarket provided we are watchful. But as a doctor, I am very aware that the body's biochemistry is infinitely complex. A diet for life must not simply contain adequate diets of fat, proteins and carbohydrates. It must be so varied as to omit none of the trace elements and vitamins which our immune systems require. It must be practical, affordable, require no finicky and time-consuming measurements. The calories and proportions must be so well judged and tested that you, the person who cooks them, can have faith in them.

And most of all they must taste good.

I have included lists of the equipment a calorie-limited household will need, not because a wok, a lemon zester and a melon baller are indispensable aids to life, but because all these things help you to get from point A (ingredients assembled) to point B (meal cooked and served) with the least possible trouble to the most appetising results. If there is no vast quantity of food, it is all the more important that it should be enticingly presented (as any nouvelle cuisine chef serving a single strawberry in a puddle of raspberry coulis will tell you).

You will find the measurements are metric, with spoons and cups retained. Though at first you may need to consult the tables, which translate them into imperial weights, these will quickly become mental calculations. The same goes for metric weights converted into accessible measures such as cups, wine glasses, tablespoons, and so on. These are also shown in the tables at the back of the book and calculating them easily becomes second nature.

Quantities are for a varying number from one to eight people, because in most households the same number of people don't sit down to every meal. You may simply change the amounts or freeze the final product.

As to cooking and storing, boiling destroys vitamin C and prolonged boiling gets rid of folic acid, which is particularly important for women during pregnancy. Most foods deteriorate eventually in strong sunlight. You will find on page 331 a table of cooking and storing methods which helps you to get the best out of your store cupboard and fridge. Few of us eat apples straight off the (unsprayed) tree or beans from the garden, unpolluted by traffic particles, and we should not waste a single nutrient from the food we bring home from the supermarket.

A friend of mine once told me she had a weight problem until she got less interested in eating and more in cooking. The recipes in this book are certainly challenging enough for anyone who has an interest in cooking, but they are not designed to keep any member of the family slaving over a hot stove. On the contrary, they are meant to be quick and easy to prepare and you, the cook, like me, need not be a cordon bleu chef. Your life is supposed to be concerned with making you feel good; if you are busy, confident and efficient, then these recipes will suit you. Food is a pleasure, but then so are lots of other things. If you eat meals prepared from my recipes, you will have time, health and energy to enrich your life.

Check the tables in this book to get a mental image of what the measurements represent, before you start.

Store Cupboard

The following products are advised to be kept in the store cupboard. They are only a basic guide and numerous variations are acceptable.

Herbs and spices

Salt, peppercorns, stock cubes, dried rosemary, tarragon, dill, basil, thyme, oregano, coriander leaves, cayenne, white and black pepper, garlic salt, garlic pepper, onion salt, onion pepper, cinnamon, ginger, turmeric, chilli, curry powders, mace, cloves, celery salt, etc.

Vinegars

Red and white malt, red and white wine, cider vinegar and balsamic vinegar, which adds subtle splendour to many dishes. Balsamic vinegar is legendary and has been produced in the Modena area of Italy since the early 19th century. It is made from the sweet Trebbiano grapes and is aged in wood barrels following old and traditional methods. It adds a magic splendour to all dishes and in general one pays a price according to quality from £2 to £20. A vintage balsamic vinegar is 20 or more years old and is syrupy and brown.

Oils and Fats

There is no substitute for cold pressed extra virgin olive oil – a fruity green olive taste with a spicy finish makes it ideal for cooking and for salads. Sesame, sunflower and other oils are also essential. To cut down the fat content of frying, my recipes often recommend a reduced-fat spray blend of sunflower and soya oils, high in polyunsaturates and low in saturates. It is sold in the U.K. as Fry Lite. You will also need to keep a pack of butter and some low fat polyunsaturated spread in the fridge. Extra virgin olive oil is made from cold pressed olives, selected by experts to produce the characteristic taste and flavour of the Tuscany region of Italy. It is fruity, green and spicy – ideal for both cooking and salads.

Butter

As mentioned above, keep one small pack of dairy butter in the fridge for occasional use. Pura Light Touch Sunflower Oil with a buttery taste is a superb low-cholesterol butter substitute – but beware, it has an even higher fat content than butter but is more body friendly.

Juices

Cartons and bottles of pasteurised or fresh unsweetened fruit or vegetable juices.

Stock

Cubes available in all supermarkets include chicken, beef, fish, and veg. You may of course make your own stock, provided that ingredients such as bone, meat fish and vegetable are all virtually free from fat. Court Bouillon is actually featured in several of the salmon recipes.

Fish

Sardines and tuna (in brine or drained of oil) and tinned red salmon are a superb source of nourishment. They are the home of the omega 3 oils which lower cholesterol and protect our hearts and arteries.

Thickening agents

Skimmed milk powder, McDougalls Thickening Granules, flour and medium and fine matzo meal (Rakusens). Coconut milk powder, which adds a delicious smoothness to sauces is not in fact made from the liquid inside the coconut but is desiccated powdered coconut. As such it is high in saturates and should be used sparingly.

Fruit and vegetables

These recipes emphasise the use of tropical fruits such as mango, pawpaw, rambutans, lychees, tamarillo, physalis, mangosteins, passion fruit, kumquats, sharron fruits, prickly pair, pineapple, etc… Many of these are available very cheaply in cans and when drained of their syrup make an excellent and immediately available substitute. Canned peaches, apricots, pineapple, etc, and cans of corn, asparagus, plum tomatoes, etc. should be kept.

Dried meats

Keep a couple of packs of dried venison in store; it has a long shelf life, is high in protein and low in fat and cholesterol: it can be substituted for bacon in almost any recipe.

Salad Dressings and spreads

Almost every day sees a new range of salad creams and dressings with very low or nil fat. Buy these.

Equipment apart from usual

A blender and a Wok are essential. A microwave is desirable. Non-stick baking sheets, freezer bags, kitchen foil and melon baller scoop.

When you shop, read the labels and if possible avoid sugar, salt and preservatives, although this is not always possible. You will buy low-fat, no-fat and no-sugar added yoghurt and fromage frais but you may find that the no fat brands are insipid and watery – in general the recipes in this book allow discretion, and in many cases low-fat is preferable to no-fat. You can purchase aerosol cans of low calorie whipped cream substitute. They are tasty as well. They are however quite high in fat but the occasional squirt puts a nice snowy blob on top of sweets and puddings.

The Menus

Over the next 106 pages is your eating diary. Each day you will see your menus set out and whenever possible you should stick to them. There is a reasonable choice. If, however, you want to substitute carefully, this will not harm you in any way but it does defeat the object of the 365 day diet to a certain degree.

Under the Breakfast section you will see each day you have a choice of Quick & Simple, Good old cooked, Why not fish? and Vegetarian. They are permutated so that the same combination of breakfasts does not fall in any one month. Lunch is considered to be the light meal of the day and here there will be a selection of 32 cooked meals, which are meat or fish, 32 vegetarian meals and a choice of picnics. One snack is allowed every 24 hours and a choice of these is displayed later in the book. The evening meal is considered to be the main meal of the day, although there is no reason why the lunch and evening meal cannot be exchanged. Each evening you will have a starter, a choice of meat, fish or vegetarian dishes and a choice of a ready frozen meal, this choice must be low-fat and less than 450 calories per person. Any good supermarket ready frozen meal or Lean Cuisine, Weightwatchers or Healthy Options is suitable for those who are really in a hurry and late home from work. Dessert is also given for the main meal although if you find that you are a few pounds too heavy perhaps it would be a good idea to miss it out.

None of these menus requires you to be a cordon bleu chef and they are basically healthy, quick and simple. To the right of each of the day's suggested dishes, you will find the relevant page number for the recipe. There are no cross-references so you do not have to turn from one page to another. Even sauces, which are frequently used, have directions on the page on which they are used. Two final important points are that these menus, although moderately low in calories, pride themselves on being low in fat. As stated above, readers may use their common sense for variation but it is helpful to stick, as far as possible, to the calendar. The use of very low-fat milk or spread is essential and soya milk is excellent. You can use the sweetened soya milk if you like as the sugar content is very small. Soya milk gives a lovely nutty taste to porridge and cereals. For granulated sweetener we suggest Canderel or Sweet 'n Low. Please try herbal teas. There are so many of them now available at the health food shops, particularly levantiner, rosehip, lemon, raspberry, apple and mango, camomile and passionfruit. The list is almost inexhaustible. In most breakfast menus a glass of fruit juice is suggested. Keep it small, about 100mls, and use any fruit which does not contain sweeteners or sugar. There is a section in the book of beautiful exotic fruit drinks which can be prepared quickly and simply. Before starting your 365 day healthy eating plan just have a look through the preface and some of the menus and make sure your kitchen is well stocked with the ingredients which have a recurring theme throughout this book.

So now you are ready to start your 365 day healthy eating programme. I hope you enjoy eating the meals as much as I have enjoyed preparing and describing them. My sincere thanks, once again, to chef Peter Marek without whose help this book would not have been finished. The dishes were prepared at the Hotel L'Horizon by Peter and I as a mere doctor would not dare to criticise or in any way alter the dishes created by one of the world's leading chefs. Some of the photographs are taken of the dishes prepared by Peter at the hotel. Whole page and additional photographs, often of ingredients, have been taken by Claire Davies. The ingredients are all as in the recipes but the final presentation and trimmings are the work of the Master Chef.

Daily allowances explained
If you follow these delicious calendar menus over a whole year your basic calorie consumption will be about 1600Kcal per day.

	Av.Kcal
Breakfast	400
Lunch	
Picnic	200
Cooked	400
Snack or Drink (only allowed if picnic lunch is chosen)	150
Starter	150
Main Dish	
Meat	500
Fish	400
Vegetarian	350
Frozen	450
Dessert	200

Cooking times
Approximate cooking times and preparation times for each dish is clearly marked.

1

Grapefruit Surprise	156
Chicken Liver Exotique	158
Kipper and Mango Surprise	164
Cherry Tomato, Pineapple and Mango Salad	171

Left-over Turkey	250
Sweet and Sour Amaranth Chinese Lettuce	306
Your choice from Picnic section	196
Your choice from Snacks and Starters section	176

Melon, Kiwi and Grape Surprise	180

Mushroom Flan (contains meat)	231
Red Sockeye Salmon Stir Fry	259
Subtle Kebabs	292
Your choice from a good supermarket	

Super Low Microwaveable Pears	313

2

English Light	155
Start The Day Mixed Grill	159
Sole and Kiwi	169
Banana, Date, Kiwi and Mango	175

Stir Fried Liver	207
Rice Exotique	299
Your choice from Picnic section	196
Your choice from Snacks and Starters section	176

Exotic Red Borscht	194

Schnitzel Exotic	207
Rainbow Trout	264
Vegetable Curry with Lychees	289
Your choice from a good supermarket	

Guava Ice Cream	324

Breakfast bonanza

Quick & simple
Good old cooked
Why not fish?
Vegetarian

Lunch

Good old cooked
Vegetarian
Picnic selection
Snack of the day

Main meal

Starter

Dish of the day – meat
Dish of the day – fish
Dish of the day – vegetarian
Frozen ready meal

Dessert

3

Muesli Treat and Crumpets	153
Bacon and Kiwi Treat	162
Red Salmon Omelette	167
Lemon and Mango Borscht	171

Citrus Chicken	221
Peas Exotique	293
Your choice from Picnic section	196
Your choice from Snacks and Starters section	176

Melon, Orange, Mango and Mint Chantilly	312

Rosemary Lamb	204
Smoked Salmon Expanded a la Thinner & Richer	254
Vegetarian Lasagne	303
Your choice from a good supermarket	

Mango and Peach Brulée	316

4

Continental Breakfast	154
Bagel, Egg and Dried Venison or Bacon	161
Fish with Berries	168
Quick Blend with Simple or Exotic Fruits	174

Kiwi, Mango and Mushroom Soup	206
Crunchy, Kutchie-Fyky	293
Your choice from Picnic section	196
Your choice from Snacks and Starters section	176

Pears, Apple and Ginger Hot Chantilly	315

Tzimmas with Beef, Mango and Prunes	218
Exotic Salmon and Plaice	258
Coconut Rice	301
Your choice	

Honey and Apple Crisp	324

Breakfast bonanza

Quick & simple
Good old cooked
Why not fish?
Vegetarian

Lunch

Good old cooked
Vegetarian
Picnic selection
Snack of the day

Main meal

Starter

Dish of the day – meat
Dish of the day – fish
Dish of the day – vegetarian
Frozen ready meal

Dessert

January

5

Breakfast bonanza

Quick & simple	Light Tabbouleh Breakfast	154
Good old cooked	Thinner & Richer Kebabs	159
Why not fish?	Kipper and Date	166
Vegetarian	Humpty Dumpty	175

Lunch

Good old cooked	Smoked Salmon Expanded a la Thinner & Richer	254
Vegetarian	Budgie Millet Exotique	294
Picnic selection	Your choice from Picnic section	196
Snack of the day	Your choice from Snacks and Starters section	176

Main meal

Starter	Carrot Soup	180
Dish of the day – meat	Chicken Pesto	230
Dish of the day – fish	Sole in Envelopes	254
Dish of the day – vegetarian	Savoury Quorn Puffs	290
Frozen ready meal	Your choice from a good supermarket	
Dessert	Rambutans and Pineapple Chantilly	310

6

Breakfast bonanza

Quick & simple	Highland Variation	153
Good old cooked	Bacon and Eggs	161
Why not fish?	Gefulte Fish	166
Vegetarian	Banana, Date, Kiwi and Mango	175

Lunch

Good old cooked	Chopped Liver	214
Vegetarian	Exotic Leeks	307
Picnic selection	Your choice from Picnic section	196
Snack of the day	Your choice from Snacks and Starters section	176

Main meal

Starter	Watercress, Lychee and Cucumber Soup	181
Dish of the day – meat	Hot Meat or Poultry with Exotic Chunky Sauce	205
Dish of the day – fish	Gefulte Fish	256
Dish of the day – vegetarian	Pumpkin Fritters	294
Frozen ready meal	Your choice from a good supermarket	
Dessert	Pears in Berry Sauce	309

7

Breakfast bonanza

Quick & simple	Choose your own Light Breakfast	155
Good old cooked	Venison Supreme	162
Why not fish?	Smoked Haddock	168
Vegetarian	Egg and Exotic Hot Fruit	174

Lunch

Good old cooked	Plaice and Prawn Creole	282
Vegetarian	Chicory, Pineapple, Kiwi and Mushrooms	304
Picnic selection	Your choice from Picnic section	196
Snack of the day	Your choice from Snacks and Starters section	176

Main meal

Starter	Exotic Welsh Rarebit	187
Dish of the day – meat	Meaty Couscous	239
Dish of the day – fish	Sardine Exotic Surprise	277
Dish of the day – vegetarian	Aubergine Treat	285
Frozen ready meal	Your choice from a good supermarket	
Dessert	Super Low Microwaveable Pears	313

8

Breakfast bonanza

Quick & simple	Exotique Treat Multiple Choice	158
Good old cooked	Mango and Pan Fried Calves Liver	163
Why not fish?	Plaice and Kiwi Surprise	167
Vegetarian	Mushroom Breakfast	172

Lunch

Good old cooked	Cider Chicken Calvados	220
Vegetarian	Mixed Exotic Salad and Yoghurt Dressing	300
Picnic selection	Your choice from Picnic section	196
Snack of the day	Your choice from Snacks and Starters section	176

Main meal

Starter	Devilled Sardines	187
Dish of the day – meat	Veal (or Beef) Roast with Prunes and Rambutans	208
Dish of the day – fish	Oriental Wok Stir Fry	260
Dish of the day – vegetarian	Tofu with Exotic Chunky Sauce	291
Frozen ready meal	Your choice from a good supermarket	
Dessert	Banana Chocolate Treat with Mangoes	316

48

9

Authentic New York Bagel	156
Omelette Exotique of choice	164
Tuna Casserole Exotique	169
Starfruit, Potato and Mushroom	170

Tomato and Tuna Salad Exotique	257
Coconut Vegetables	299
Your choice from Picnic section	196
Your choice from Snacks and Starters section	176

Chicken and Coconut Soup	189

Original Duck a l'Orange	209
Exotic Kedgeree	260
Sesame Seed and Caraway Salad	307
Your choice from a good supermarket	

Mango and Lychee Mousse	313

10

Muesli Treat and Crumpets	153
Thinner & Richer Kebabs	159
Kipper and Mango Surprise	164
Humpty Dumpty	175

Chicken and Peppers	233
Cranberry Rice Salad	303
Your choice from Picnic section	196
Your choice from Snacks and Starters section	176

Stir Fry Vegetables and Chilli	195

Cauliflower au gratin	223
Grapefruit and Red Sockeye Salmon	261
Kiwi, Mango and Lychee Beans	292
Your choice from a good supermarket	

Berry Omelette Exotique	311

Breakfast bonanza
Quick & simple
Good old cooked
Why not fish?
Vegetarian

Lunch
Good old cooked
Vegetarian
Picnic selection
Snack of the day

Main meal
Starter

Dish of the day – meat
Dish of the day – fish
Dish of the day – vegetarian
Frozen ready meal

Dessert

11

English Light	155
Chicken Liver Exotique	158
Fish with Berries	168
Lemon and Mango Borscht	171

Prawn and Exotic Salad	256
Aubergine au Fromage Frais	285
Your choice from Picnic section	196
Your choice from Snacks and Starters section	176

Borscht and Yoghurt	181

Mango and Pan Fried Calves Liver	204
Marinated Red Mullet Exotique	277
Bulghar Wheat Exotique	295
Your choice from a good supermarket	

Pears Grand Marnier	309

12

Grapefruit Surprise	156
Venison Supreme	162
Kipper and Date	166
Cherry Tomato, Pineapple and Mango Salad	171

Chinese Chicken Salad with Lychees	250
Dressed Seasonal Salad	301
Your choice from Picnic section	196
Your choice from Snacks and Starters section	176

Vegetarian Coleslaw	179

Devilled Lamb Steaks	209
Smoked Rainbow Trout with Chunky Sauce	257
Greek Dip Exotique	289
Your choice from a good supermarket	

Stuffed Pineapple	311

Breakfast bonanza
Quick & simple
Good old cooked
Why not fish?
Vegetarian

Lunch
Good old cooked
Vegetarian
Picnic selection
Snack of the day

Main meal
Starter

Dish of the day – meat
Dish of the day – fish
Dish of the day – vegetarian
Frozen ready meal

Dessert

January

13

Breakfast bonanza

Quick & simple	Light Tabbouleh Breakfast	154
Good old cooked	Bagel, Egg and Dried Venison or Bacon	161
Why not fish?	Sole and Kiwi	169
Vegetarian	Quick Blend with Simple or Exotic Fruits	174

Lunch

Good old cooked	Exotic Mackerel	266
Vegetarian	Courgette Exotique	286
Picnic selection	Your choice from Picnic section	196
Snack of the day	Your choice from Snacks and Starters section	176

Main meal

Starter	Leek Soup	184
Dish of the day – meat	Exotic Shepherd's Pie	221
Dish of the day – fish	Plaice and Prawn Creole	282
Dish of the day – vegetarian	Vegetarian Curry with Lychees	289
Frozen ready meal	Your choice from a good supermarket	
Dessert	Ice Cream Grand Marnier	314

14

	Choose your own Light Breakfast	155
	Mango and Pan Fried Calves Liver	163
	Red Salmon Omelette	167
	Hot Fruit Salad	172

	Melon with Dried Wild Venison	214
	Vegetable Curry	296
	Your choice from Picnic section	196
	Your choice from Snacks and Starters section	176

	Fluffy Herb Pâté	179
	Exotique Pintade Rotir (Guinea Fowl)	205
	Salmon for a King	267
	Quorn with Exotic Chunky Sauce	298
	Your choice from a good supermarket	
	Strawberry (or any other fruits) Mousse	320

15

Breakfast bonanza

Quick & simple	Authentic New York Bagel	156
Good old cooked	Omelette Exotique of choice	164
Why not fish?	Plaice and Kiwi Surprise	167
Vegetarian	Starfruit, Potato and Mushroom	170

Lunch

Good old cooked	Avocado Salmon	258
Vegetarian	Cherry Tomato, Pineapple and Mango Salad	300
Picnic selection	Your choice from Picnic section	196
Snack of the day	Your choice from Snacks and Starters section	176

Main meal

Starter	Gefulte Fish	183
Dish of the day – meat	Indonesian Pork Satay	220
Dish of the day – fish	Tuna and Egg Salad Exotique	267
Dish of the day – vegetarian	Baby Parsnips, Breadcrumbs and Corn	302
Frozen ready meal	Your choice from a good supermarket	
Dessert	Quince Thinner & Richer	314

16

	Continental Breakfast	154
	Bacon and Eggs	161
	Tuna Casserole Exotique	169
	Banana, Date, Kiwi and Mango	175

	Rainbow Trout	264
	Wok Quorn	302
	Your choice from Picnic section	196
	Your choice from Snacks and Starters section	176

	Exotic Sardine Pâté	178
	Champagne Quail	222
	White Fish Cous cous	263
	Cauliflower au gratin	305
	Your choice from a good supermarket	
	Kiwango Ice	310

17

18

January

Breakfast bonanza
Quick & simple
Good old cooked
Why not fish?
Vegetarian

Lunch
Good old cooked
Vegetarian
Picnic selection
Snack of the day

Main meal
Starter

Dish of the day – meat
Dish of the day – fish
Dish of the day – vegetarian
Frozen ready meal

Dessert

51

19

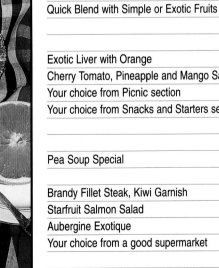

Breakfast bonanza
Quick & simple
Good old cooked
Why not fish?
Vegetarian

Lunch
Good old cooked
Vegetarian
Picnic selection
Snack of the day

Main meal
Starter

Dish of the day – meat
Dish of the day – fish
Dish of the day – vegetarian
Frozen ready meal

Dessert

January

20

Breakfast bonanza

Quick & simple	Grapefruit Surprise	156
Good old cooked	Bagel, Egg and Dried Venison or Bacon	161
Why not fish?	Kipper and Date	166
Vegetarian	Humpty Dumpty	175

Lunch

Good old cooked	Quick Hot Prawns	262
Vegetarian	Kiwi, Mango and Mushroom Treat	304
Picnic selection	Your choice from Picnic section	196
Snack of the day	Your choice from Snacks and Starters section	176

Main meal

Starter	Green Soup	182
Dish of the day – meat	Exotique Lamb and Papaya or Mango	216
Dish of the day – fish	Prawn Exotique	275
Dish of the day – vegetarian	Dressed Seasonal Salad	301
Frozen ready meal	Your choice from a good supermarket	
Dessert	Baked Fruit	318

21

	Light Tabbouleh Breakfast	154
	Bacon and Kiwi Treat	162
	Kipper and Mango Surprise	164
	Starfruit, Potato and Mushroom	170

	Wild Venison with Ratatouille	225
	Dressed Seasonal Salad	301
	Your choice from Picnic section	196
	Your choice from Snacks and Starters section	176

	Devilled Potato Salad and Celery	185
	Mango Cholent	210
	Whole Rainbow Trout a l'Orange	264
	Subtle Kebabs	292
	Your choice from a good supermarket	
	Slimmer Fruit Ice Cream	318

22

Breakfast bonanza

Quick & simple	English Light	155
Good old cooked	Venison Supreme	162
Why not fish?	Sole and Kiwi	169
Vegetarian	Starfruit, Potato and Mushroom	170

Lunch

Good old cooked	Melon and Berries	315
Vegetarian	Courgette Exotique	286
Picnic selection	Your choice from Picnic section	196
Snack of the day	Your choice from Snacks and Starters section	176

Main meal

Starter	Chicken Pâté	183
Dish of the day – meat	Exotique Venison Stew	211
Dish of the day – fish	Smoked Salmon Cous cous	270
Dish of the day – vegetarian	Savoury Quorn Puffs	290
Frozen ready meal	Your choice from a good supermarket	
Dessert	Fruit Flan	317

23

	Continental Breakfast	154
	Bagel, Egg and Dried Venison or Bacon	161
	Red Salmon Omelette	167
	Cherry Tomato, Pineapple and Mango Salad	171

	Exotique Ham and Mango	235
	Vegetable Curry	296
	Your choice from Picnic section	196
	Your choice from Snacks and Starters section	176

	Fish Soup	193
	North American Couscous	226
	Potted Herring	266
	Tofu with Exotic Chunky Sauce	291
	Your choice from a good supermarket	
	Banana Split	325

24

Highland Variations — 153
Mango and Pan Fried Calves Liver — 163
Tuna Casserole Exotique — 169
Quick Blend with Simple or Exotic Fruits — 174

Red Sockeye Salmon Stir Fry — 259
Exotic Leeks — 307
Your choice from Picnic section — 196
Your choice from Snacks and Starters section — 176

Coconut and Beef Satay or Chicken Satay — 195

Exotique Venison Casserole — 233
Plaice, Leek and Lime — 274
Mushroom Flan — 287
Your choice from a good supermarket

Exotique Banana Dessert — 319

25

Muesli Treat and Crumpets — 153
Chicken Liver Exotique — 158
Fish with Berries — 168
Lemon and Mango Borscht — 171

Exotique Turkey and Almonds — 232
Peas Exotique — 293
Your choice from Picnic section — 196
Your choice from Snacks and Starters section — 176

Red Sockeye Salmon Pâté — 194

Veal Goulash with Lychees — 229
Devilled Lobster — 274
Budgie Millet Exotique — 294
Your choice from a good supermarket

Melon, Orange, Mango and Mint Chantilly — 312

26

Exotique Treat Multiple Choice — 158
Start The Day Mixed Grill — 159
Kipper and Mango Surprise — 164
Egg and Exotic Hot Fruit — 174

Smoked Rainbow Trout with Chunky Sauce — 257
Greek Dip Exotique — 289
Your choice from Picnic section — 196
Your choice from Snacks and Starters section — 176

Chopped Herring Chunky Pâté — 178

Exotique Beef Soufflé — 227
Orange Sole — 268
Bulghar Wheat Exotique — 295
Your choice from a good supermarket

Peach and Papaya Chantilly — 319

27

Highland Variations — 153
Thinner & Richer Kebabs — 159
Gefulte Fish — 166
Hot Fruit Salad — 172

Kiwi, Mango and Mushroom Soup — 206
Coconut Rice — 301
Your choice from Picnic section — 196
Your choice from Snacks and Starters section — 176

Lemon and Mango Borscht — 184

Chicken and Aubergine — 232
Pepper, Anchovy and Tomato — 269
Quorn with Exotic Chunky Sauce — 298
Your choice from a good supermarket

Exotic Caramel Custard — 325

January

Breakfast bonanza
Quick & simple
Good old cooked
Why not fish?
Vegetarian

Lunch
Good old cooked
Vegetarian
Picnic selection
Snack of the day

Main meal
Starter

Dish of the day – meat
Dish of the day – fish
Dish of the day – vegetarian
Frozen ready meal

Dessert

53

Breakfast bonanza
Quick & simple
Good old cooked
Why not fish?
Vegetarian

Lunch
Good old cooked
Vegetarian
Picnic selection
Snack of the day

Main meal
Starter

Dish of the day – meat
Dish of the day – fish
Dish of the day – vegetarian
Frozen ready meal

Dessert

January

28

Breakfast bonanza

Quick & simple	Grapefruit Surprise	156
Good old cooked	Venison Supreme	162
Why not fish?	Plaice and Kiwi Surprise	167
Vegetarian	Banana, Date, Kiwi and Mango	175

Lunch

Good old cooked	Salmon Fillet with Hot Exotic Chunky Sauce	259
Vegetarian	Wok Quorn	302
Picnic selection	Your choice from Picnic section	196
Snack of the day	Your choice from Snacks and Starters section	176

Main meal

Starter	Sweet and Sour Amaranth Chinese Lettuce	186
Dish of the day – meat	Chicken and Pasta (cold dish)	236
Dish of the day – fish	Plaice-a-Leekie	278
Dish of the day – vegetarian	Aubergine Exotique au gratin	288
Frozen ready meal	Your choice from a good supermarket	
Dessert	Banana Bake Exotique	323

29

	Authentic New York Bagel	156
	Bacon and Eggs	161
	Sole and Kiwi	169
	Mushroom Breakfast	172

	Wok Beef	213
	Cranberry Rice Salad	303
	Your choice from Picnic section	196
	Your choice from Snacks and Starters section	176

	Cauliflower Soup	193
	Oriental Wok Stir Fry	217
	Lobster Thermidor	272
	Sweet and Sour Amaranth Chinese Lettuce	306
	Your choice from a good supermarket	
	Honey and Apple Crisp	324

30

Breakfast bonanza

Quick & simple	English Light	155
Good old cooked	Bacon and Kiwi Treat	162
Why not fish?	Red Salmon Omelette	167
Vegetarian	Humpty Dumpty	175

Lunch

Good old cooked	Tuna Special	262
Vegetarian	Subtle Kebabs	292
Picnic selection	Your choice from Picnic section	196
Snack of the day	Your choice from Snacks and Starters section	176

Main meal

Starter	Aubergine and Mango Pâté	191
Dish of the day – meat	Chicken Curry with Coconut Milk	237
Dish of the day – fish	Red Salmon Omelette	279
Dish of the day – vegetarian	Vegetarian Quorn Chilli Stir Fry	295
Frozen ready meal	Your choice from a good supermarket	
Dessert	Stuffed Pineapple	311

31

	Continental Breakfast	164
	Omelette Exotique Of Choice	154
	Tuna Casserole Exotique	169
	Quick Blend with Simple or Exotic Fruits	174

	Smoked Trout	261
	Sesame Seed and Caraway Salad	307
	Your choice from Picnic section	196
	Your choice from Snacks and Starters section	176

	Exotic Toast	191
	Pork or Turkey and Apple	206
	Shrimp Pilaf Exotique	273
	Aubergine au Fromage Frais	285
	Your choice from a good supermarket	
	Pears Grand Marnier	309

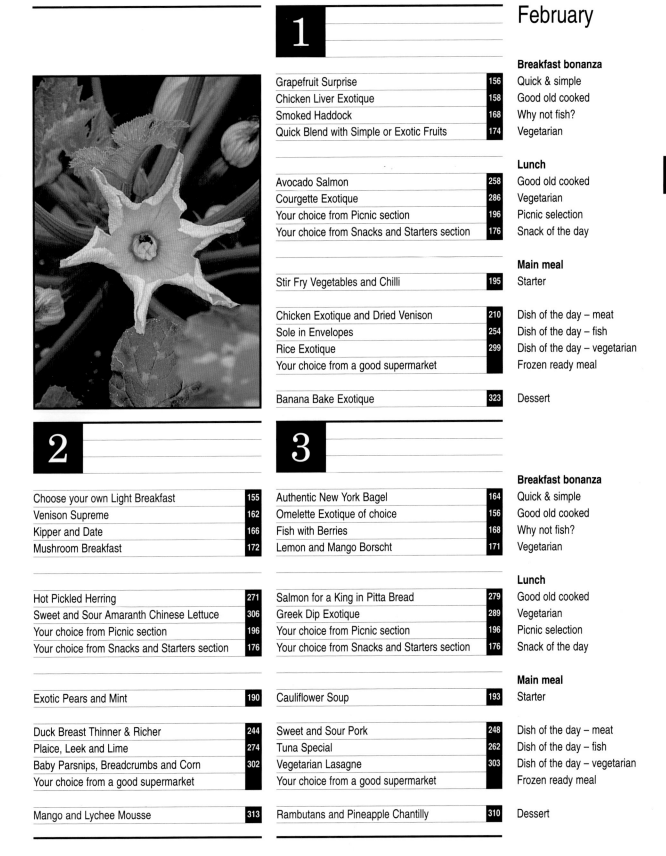

1

2

3

February

4

Breakfast bonanza

Quick & simple	Continental Breakfast	154
Good old cooked	Thinner & Richer Kebabs	159
Why not fish?	Plaice and Kiwi Surprise	167
Vegetarian	Egg and Exotic Hot Fruit	174

Lunch

Good old cooked	Fish Soup	193
Vegetarian	Aubergine Exotique	286
Picnic selection	Your choice from Picnic section	196
Snack of the day	Your choice from Snacks and Starters section	176

Main meal

Starter	Exotic Pears and Mint	190
Dish of the day – meat	Wild Venison and Mango Exotique	228
Dish of the day – fish	Smoked Trout	261
Dish of the day – vegetarian	Peas Exotique	293
Frozen ready meal	Your choice from a good supermarket	
Dessert	Exotique Banana Dessert	319

5

Muesli Treat and Crumpets	153
Start the Day Mixed Grill	159
Gefulte Fish	166
Humpty Dumpty	175

Left-over Turkey	250
Aubergine au Fromage Frais	285
Your choice from Picnic section	196
Your choice from Snacks and Starters section	176

Cauliflower Soup	193
Exotic Liver with Orange	228
White Fish Cous cous	263
Wok Quorn	302
Your choice from a good supermarket	
Exotic Caramel Custard	325

6

Breakfast bonanza

Quick & simple	Exotique Treat Multiple Choice	158
Good old cooked	Bacon and Eggs	161
Why not fish?	Kipper and Mango Surprise	164
Vegetarian	Banana, Date, Kiwi and Mango	175

Lunch

Good old cooked	Coconut Beef Satay or Chicken Satay	245
Vegetarian	Exotic Leeks	307
Picnic selection	Your choice from Picnic section	196
Snack of the day	Your choice from Snacks and Starters section	176

Main meal

Starter	Carrot Soup	180
Dish of the day – meat	Exotique Lamb and Papaya or Mango	216
Dish of the day – fish	Quick Hot Prawns	262
Dish of the day – vegetarian	Subtle Kebabs	292
Frozen ready meal	Your choice from a good supermarket	
Dessert	Baked Fruit	318

7

Highland Variation	153
Mango and Pan Fried Calves Liver	163
Red Salmon Omelette	167
Hot Fruit Salad	172

Aubergine Exotique au gratin	243
Dressed Seasonal Salad	301
Your choice from Picnic section	196
Your choice from Snacks and Starters section	176

Melon with Dried Venison or Parma Ham	177
Cider Chicken Calvados	220
Shrimp Pilaf Exotique	273
Vegetarian Curry with Lychees	289
Your choice from a good supermarket	
Banana Chocolate Treat with Mangoes	316

8

Light Tabbouleh Breakfast	154
Bacon and Kiwi Treat	162
Sole and Kiwi	169
Cherry Tomato, Pineapple and Mango Salad	171

Fish Soup with Sweetcorn and Lychees	255
Peas Exotique	293
Your choice from Picnic section	196
Your choice from Snacks and Starters section	176

Stir Fry Vegetables and Chilli	195

Veal Goulash with Lychees	229
Prawn Exotique	275
Aubergine Treat	285
Your choice from a good supermarket	

Super Low Microwaveable Pears	313

9

Grapefruit Surprise	156
Bagel, Egg and Dried Venison or Bacon	220
Fish with Berries	168
Starfruit, Potato and Mushroom	170

Oriental Wok Stir Fry	217
Cherry Tomato, Pineapple and Mango Salad	300
Your choice from Picnic section	196
Your choice from Snacks and Starters section	176

Watercress, Lychee and Cucumber Soup	181

Original Duck à l'Orange	209
Exotic Kedgeree	260
Cauliflower au gratin	305
Your choice from a good supermarket	

Strawberry (or any other fruits) Mousse	320

February

Breakfast bonanza
Quick & simple
Good old cooked
Why not fish?
Vegetarian

Lunch
Good old cooked
Vegetarian
Picnic selection
Snack of the day

Main meal
Starter

Dish of the day – meat
Dish of the day – fish
Dish of the day – vegetarian
Frozen ready meal

Dessert

10

English Light	164
Omelette Exotique of choice	155
Tuna Casserole Exotique	169
Mushroom Breakfast	172

Plaice and Prawn Creole	282
Coconut Vegetables	299
Your choice from Picnic section	196
Your choice from Snacks and Starters section	176

Chopped Herring Chunky Pâté	178

Steak Diane Exotique	219
Pepper, Anchovy and Tomato	269
Kiwi, Mango and Lychee Beans	292
Your choice from a good supermarket	

Fruit Flan	317

11

Continental Breakfast	154
Mango and Pan Fried Calves Liver	163
Plaice and Kiwi Surprise	167
Hot Fruit Salad	172

Schnitzel Exotic	207
Sesame Seed and Caraway Salad	307
Your choice from Picnic section	196
Your choice from Snacks and Starters section	176

Starfruit, Potato and Mushroom	189

Chicken in Sherry	251
Tuna and Egg Salad Exotique	267
Kiwi, Mango and Mushroom Treat	304
Your choice from a good supermarket	

Guava Ice Cream	324

Breakfast bonanza
Quick & simple
Good old cooked
Why not fish?
Vegetarian

Lunch
Good old cooked
Vegetarian
Picnic selection
Snack of the day

Main meal
Starter

Dish of the day – meat
Dish of the day – fish
Dish of the day – vegetarian
Frozen ready meal

Dessert

February

12

Breakfast bonanza

Quick & simple	Muesli Treat and Crumpets	153
Good old cooked	Bacon and Eggs	161
Why not fish?	Red Salmon Omelette	167
Vegetarian	Lemon and Mango Borscht	171

Lunch

Good old cooked	Hot Pickled Herring	271
Vegetarian	Mixed Exotic Salad and Yoghurt Dressing	300
Picnic selection	Your choice from Picnic section	196
Snack of the day	Your choice from Snacks and Starters section	176

Main meal

Starter	Aubergine and Mango Pâté	191
Dish of the day – meat	North African Couscous	238
Dish of the day – fish	Rainbow Trout	264
Dish of the day – vegetarian	Quorn with Exotic Chunky Sauce	298
Frozen ready meal	Your choice from a good supermarket	
Dessert	Pears, Apple and Ginger Hot Chantilly	315

13

Authentic New York Bagel		156
Thinner & Richer Kebabs		159
Kipper and Date		166
Banana, Date, Kiwi and Mango		175

Kiwi, Mango and Mushroom Soup		206
Budgie Millet Exotique		294
Your choice from Picnic section		196
Your choice from Snacks and Starters section		176

Exotic Toast		191
Chicken, Apricot and Asparagus		249
Starfruit Salmon Salad		271
Mushroom Flan		287
Your choice from a good supermarket		
Stuffed Pineapple		311

14 — St Valentine's Day Special

Breakfast bonanza

Quick & simple	Grapefruit Surprise	156
Good old cooked	Bacon and Kiwi Treat	162
Why not fish?	Fish with Berries	168
Vegetarian	Quick Blend with Simple or Exotic Fruits	174

Lunch

Good old cooked	Smoked Salmon Expanded à la Thinner & Richer	254
Vegetarian	Mixed Exotic Salad and Yoghurt Dressing	300
Picnic selection	Your choice from Picnic section	196
Snack of the day	Your choice from Snacks and Starters section	176

Main meal

Starter	Melon, Kiwi and Grape Surprise	180
Dish of the day – meat	St Valentine's Red Rose Veal Holstein	234
Dish of the day – fish	St Valentine's Red Rose Salmon Fillet	282
Dish of the day – vegetarian	Baby Parsnips, Breadcrumbs and Corn	302
Frozen ready meal	Your choice from a good supermarket	
Dessert	Red Rose Petal Sorbet	326

15

Light Tabbouleh Breakfast		154
Chicken Liver Exotique		158
Smoked Haddock		168
Humpty Dumpty		175

Sardine Exotic Surprise		277
Courgette Exotique		286
Your choice from Picnic section		196
Your choice from Snacks and Starters section		176

Red Sockeye Salmon Pâté		194
Exotique Pintade Rotir (Guinea Fowl)		205
Prawn and Mint Dip		272
Sweet and Sour Amaranth Chinese Lettuce		306
Your choice from a good supermarket		
Berry Omelette Exotique		311

February

16

Breakfast bonanza
Quick & simple	Choose your own Light Breakfast	155
Good old cooked	Start The Day Mixed Grill	159
Why not fish?	Kipper and Mango Surprise	164
Vegetarian	Cherry Tomato, Pineapple and Mango Salad	171

Lunch
Good old cooked	Exotique Chicken Satay	215
Vegetarian	Tuna and Egg Salad Exotique	267
Picnic selection	Your choice from Picnic section	196
Snack of the day	Your choice from Snacks and Starters section	176

Main meal
Starter	Fish Soup	193
Dish of the day – meat	Cold Meat Salad with Exotic Chunky Sauce	236
Dish of the day – fish	Sole in Envelopes	254
Dish of the day – vegetarian	Aubergine Exotique	286
Frozen ready meal	Your choice from a good supermarket	
Dessert	Honey and Apple Crisp	324

17

Highland Variation		153
Venison Supreme		162
Sole and Kiwi		169
Quick Blend with Simple or Exotic Fruits		174

Salmon for a King		267
Dressed Seasonal Salad		301
Your choice from Picnic section		196
Your choice from Snacks and Starters section		176

Grapefruit and Tomato Soup		185
Chicken with Red and Green Peppers		244
Whole Rainbow Trout a l'Orange		264
Vegetable Curry		296
Your choice from a good supermarket		
Mango and Peach Brulée		316

18

Breakfast bonanza
Quick & simple	Continental Breakfast	154
Good old cooked	Bacon and Kiwi Treat	162
Why not fish?	Gefulte Fish	166
Vegetarian	Egg and Exotic Hot Fruit	174

Lunch
Good old cooked	Mixed Kebab	242
Vegetarian	Chicory, Pineapple, Kiwi and Mushrooms	304
Picnic selection	Your choice from Picnic section	196
Snack of the day	Your choice from Snacks and Starters section	176

Main meal
Starter	Exotic Pears and Mint	190
Dish of the day – meat	Exotic Turkey Escalopes	242
Dish of the day – fish	Scallop Seviche	253
Dish of the day – vegetarian	Tofu with Exotic Chunky Sauce	291
Frozen ready meal	Your choice from a good supermarket	
Dessert	Quince Thinner & Richer	314

19

Grapefruit Surprise		156
Omelette Exotique of choice		164
Plaice and Kiwi Surprise		167
Mushroom Breakfast		172

Exotic Mackerel		266
Aubergine Exotique au gratin		288
Your choice from Picnic section		196
Your choice from Snacks and Starters section		176

Leek Soup		184
Tandoori Meat		245
Avocado Salmon		258
Savoury Quorn Puffs		290
Your choice from a good supermarket		
Peach and Papaya Chantilly		319

20

Muesli Treat and Crumpets	153
Bagel, Egg and Dried Venison or Bacon	161
Tuna Casserole Exotique	169
Humpty Dumpty	175

Beef and Lamb Kebabs	201
Cranberry Rice Salad	303
Your choice from Picnic section	196
Your choice from Snacks and Starters section	176

Pea Soup Special	192

Traditional Shepherd's Pie	202
Red Salmon Omelette	279
Pumpkin Fritters	294
Your choice from a good supermarket	

Pears in Berry Sauce	309

21

English Light	155
Mango and Pan Fried Calves Liver	163
Fish with Berries	168
Hot Fruit Salad	172

Steamed Plaice and Mango	278
Rice Exotique	299
Your choice from Picnic section	196
Your choice from Snacks and Starters section	176

Exotic Welsh Rarebit	187

Stuffed Cabbage	235
Orange Sole	268
Bulghar Wheat Exotique	295
Your choice from a good supermarket	

Blackberry, Lychee and Cape Gooseberry	323

February

Breakfast bonanza
Quick & simple
Good old cooked
Why not fish?
Vegetarian

Lunch
Good old cooked
Vegetarian
Picnic selection
Snack of the day

Main meal
Starter

Dish of the day – meat
Dish of the day – fish
Dish of the day – vegetarian
Frozen ready meal

Dessert

22

Exotique Treat Multiple Choice	158
Bacon and Eggs	161
Kipper and Date	166
Lemon and Mango Borscht	171

Exotique Ham and Mango	235
Coconut Rice	301
Your choice from Picnic section	196
Your choice from Snacks and Starters section	176

Devilled Potato Salad and Celery	185

Lamb and Pawpaw Corsican Style	215
Devilled Lobster	274
Crunchy, Kutchie-Fyky	293
Your choice from a good supermarket	

Pears Grand Marnier	309

23

Light Tabbouleh Breakfast	154
Thinner & Richer Kebabs	159
Red Salmon Omelette	167
Banana, Date, Kiwi and Mango	175

Plaice, Leek and Lime	274
Aubergine au Fromage Frais	285
Your choice from Picnic section	196
Your choice from Snacks and Starters section	176

Chicken and Coconut Soup	189

Mushroom Flan (contains meat)	231
Grapefruit and Red Sockeye Salmon	261
Baby Parsnips, Breadcrumbs and Corn	302
Your choice from a good supermarket	

Fruit Jelly	317

Breakfast bonanza
Quick & simple
Good old cooked
Why not fish?
Vegetarian

Lunch
Good old cooked
Vegetarian
Picnic selection
Snack of the day

Main meal
Starter

Dish of the day – meat
Dish of the day – fish
Dish of the day – vegetarian
Frozen ready meal

Dessert

February

24

25

26

27

28

Breakfast bonanza
Quick & simple
Good old cooked
Why not fish?
Vegetarian

Lunch
Good old cooked
Vegetarian
Picnic selection
Snack of the day

Main meal
Starter

Dish of the day – meat
Dish of the day – fish
Dish of the day – vegetarian
Frozen ready meal

Dessert

29   Leap Year Special

Breakfast bonanza
Quick & simple
Good old cooked
Why not fish?
Vegetarian

Lunch
Good old cooked
Vegetarian
Picnic selection
Snack of the day

Main meal
Starter

Dish of the day – meat
Dish of the day – fish
Dish of the day – vegetarian
Frozen ready meal

Dessert

1

Breakfast bonanza

Quick & simple	Exotique Treat Multiple Choice	158
Good old cooked	Thinner & Richer Kebabs	159
Why not fish?	Tuna Casserole Exotique	169
Vegetarian	Banana, Date, Kiwi and Mango	175

Lunch

Good old cooked	Fish Soup à la Thinner & Richer	273
Vegetarian	Rice Exotique	299
Picnic selection	Your choice from Picnic section	196
Snack of the day	Your choice from Snacks and Starters section	176

Main meal

Starter	Sweet and Sour Amaranth Chinese Lettuce	186
Dish of the day – meat	Hot Meat or Poultry with Exotic Chunky Sauce	205
Dish of the day – fish	White Fish Cous cous	263
Dish of the day – vegetarian	Pumpkin Fritters	294
Frozen ready meal	Your choice from a good supermarket	
Dessert	Banana Split	325

2

English Light		155
Omelette Exotique of choice		164
Smoked Haddock		168
Lemon and Mango Borscht		171

Wok Beef		213
Mixed Exotic Salad and Yoghurt Dressing		300
Your choice from Picnic section		196
Your choice from Snacks and Starters section		176

Chicken Pâté		183
Lamb and Pawpaw Corsican Style		215
Lobster Salad		253
Aubergine Exotique		286
Your choice from a good supermarket		
Rambutans and Pineapple Chantilly		310

3

Breakfast bonanza

Quick & simple	Authentic New York Bagel	156
Good old cooked	Bacon and Kiwi Treat	162
Why not fish?	Plaice and Kiwi Surprise	167
Vegetarian	Cherry Tomato, Pineapple and Mango Salad	171

Lunch

Good old cooked	Salmon for a King in Pitta Bread	279
Vegetarian	Tofu with Exotic Chunky Sauce	291
Picnic selection	Your choice from Picnic section	196
Snack of the day	Your choice from Snacks and Starters section	176

Main meal

Starter	Starfruit, Potato and Mushroom	189
Dish of the day – meat	Poultry – Sweet and Sour	217
Dish of the day – fish	Smoked Salmon Cous cous	270
Dish of the day – vegetarian	Mushroom Flan	287
Frozen ready meal	Your choice from a good supermarket	
Dessert	Melon, Orange, Mango and Mint Chantilly	312

4

Highland Variation		153
Chicken Liver Exotique		158
Sole and Kiwi		169
Starfruit, Potato and Mushroom		170

Sweet and Sour Pork		248
Dressed Seasonal Salad		301
Your choice from Picnic section		196
Your choice from Snacks and Starters section		176

Lemon and Mango Borscht		184
Slimmer's Lasagne à la Thinner & Richer		237
Fish Soup with Sweetcorn and Lychees		255
Kiwi, Mango and Lychee Beans		292
Your choice from a good supermarket		
Mango and Lychee Mousse		313

5

Choose your own Light Breakfast	155
Start The Day Mixed Grill	159
Kipper and Mango Surprise	164
Humpty Dumpty	175

Red Sockeye Salmon Stir Fry	259
Coconut Vegetables	299
Your choice from Picnic section	196
Your choice from Snacks and Starters section	176

Melon with Dried Venison or Parma Ham	177

Coconut Beef Satay or Chicken Satay	245
Prawn and Exotic Salad	256
Savoury Quorn Puffs	290
Your choice from a good supermarket	

Super Low Microwaveable Pears	313

6

Continental Breakfast	154
Mango and Pan Fried Calves Liver	163
Fish with Berries	168
Mushroom Breakfast	172

Aubergine Exotique au gratin	243
Chicory, Pineapple, Kiwi and Mushrooms	304
Your choice from Picnic section	196
Your choice from Snacks and Starters section	176

Tuna Pâté	182

Chicken in Sherry	251
Potted Herring	266
Vegetarian Quorn Chilli Stir Fry	295
Your choice from a good supermarket	

Fruit Jelly	317

Breakfast bonanza
Quick & simple
Good old cooked
Why not fish?
Vegetarian

Lunch
Good old cooked
Vegetarian
Picnic selection
Snack of the day

Main meal
Starter

Dish of the day – meat
Dish of the day – fish
Dish of the day – vegetarian
Frozen ready meal

Dessert

65

7

Grapefruit Surprise	156
Venison Supreme	162
Kipper and Date	166
Quick Blend with Simple or Exotic Fruits	174

Red Salmon Omelette	279
Cranberry Rice Salad	303
Your choice from Picnic section	196
Your choice from Snacks and Starters section	176

Borscht and Yoghurt	181

Indonesian Pork Satay	220
Scallop Seviche	253
Cauliflower au gratin	305
Your choice from a good supermarket	

Exotique Banana Dessert	319

8

Muesli Treat and Crumpets	153
Bagel, Egg and Dried Venison or Bacon	161
Gefulte Fish	166
Hot Fruit Salad	172

Exotic Liver with Orange	228
Coconut Rice	301
Your choice from Picnic section	196
Your choice from Snacks and Starters section	176

Coconut and Beef Satay or Chicken Satay	195

Rosemary Lamb	204
Quick Hot Prawns	262
Aubergine au Fromage Frais	285
Your choice from a good supermarket	

Baked Fruit	318

Breakfast bonanza
Quick & simple
Good old cooked
Why not fish?
Vegetarian

Lunch
Good old cooked
Vegetarian
Picnic selection
Snack of the day

Main meal
Starter

Dish of the day – meat
Dish of the day – fish
Dish of the day – vegetarian
Frozen ready meal

Dessert

9

Breakfast bonanza

Quick & simple	Exotique Treat Multiple Choice	158
Good old cooked	Omelette Exotique of choice	164
Why not fish?	Tuna Casserole Exotique	169
Vegetarian	Egg and Exotic Hot Fruit	174

Lunch

Good old cooked	Exotic Kedgeree	260
Vegetarian	Budgie Millet Exotique	294
Picnic selection	Your choice from Picnic section	196
Snack of the day	Your choice from Snacks and Starters section	176

Main meal

Starter	Watercress, Lychee and Cucumber Soup	181
Dish of the day – meat	Wild Venison and Mango Exotique	228
Dish of the day – fish	Avocado Salmon	258
Dish of the day – vegetarian	Mushroom Flan	287
Frozen ready meal	Your choice from a good supermarket	
Dessert	Honey and Apple Crisp	324

10

Light Tabbouleh Breakfast	154
Bacon and Eggs	161
Smoked Haddock	168
Lemon and Mango Borscht	171

Chicken Pâté	248
Aubergine Exotique au gratin	288
Your choice from Picnic section	196
Your choice from Snacks and Starters section	176

Stir Fry Vegetables and Chilli	195
Duck Breast Thinner & Richer	244
Salmon à la Greque	268
Sesame Seed and Caraway Salad	307
Your choice from a good supermarket	
Fruit Flan	317

11

Breakfast bonanza

Quick & simple	Highland Variation	153
Good old cooked	Thinner & Richer Kebabs	159
Why not fish?	Red Salmon Omelette	167
Vegetarian	Banana, Date, Kiwi and Mango	175

Lunch

Good old cooked	Exotic Mackerel	266
Vegetarian	Baby Parsnips, Breadcrumbs and Corn	302
Picnic selection	Your choice from Picnic section	196
Snack of the day	Your choice from Snacks and Starters section	176

Main meal

Starter	Cauliflower Soup	193
Dish of the day – meat	Exotique Chicken Satay	215
Dish of the day – fish	Sole in Envelopes	254
Dish of the day – vegetarian	Bulghar Wheat Exotique	295
Frozen ready meal	Your choice from a good supermarket	
Dessert	Guava Ice Cream	324

12

Authentic New York Bagel	156
Chicken Liver Exotique	158
Fish with Berries	168
Humpty Dumpty	175

Exotique Turkey and Almonds	232
Sweet and Sour Amaranth Chinese Lettuce	306
Your choice from Picnic section	196
Your choice from Snacks and Starters section	176

Fish Soup	193

North African Couscous	226
Prawn and Mint Dip	272
Quorn with Exotic Chunky Sauce	298
Your choice from a good supermarket	

Mango and Peach Brulée	316

13

English Light	155
Bacon and Kiwi Treat	162
Sole and Kiwi	169
Cherry Tomato, Pineapple and Mango Salad	171

Exotique Turkey and Almonds	232
Sweet and Sour Amaranth Chinese Lettuce	306
Your choice from Picnic section	196
Your choice from Snacks and Starters section	176

Fish Soup	193

North American Couscous	226
Prawn and Mint Dip	272
Quorn with Exotic Chunky Sauce	298
Your choice from a good supermarket	

Mango and Peach Brulée	316

Breakfast bonanza
Quick & simple
Good old cooked
Why not fish?
Vegetarian

Lunch
Good old cooked
Vegetarian
Picnic selection
Snack of the day

Main meal
Starter

Dish of the day – meat
Dish of the day – fish
Dish of the day – vegetarian
Frozen ready meal

Dessert

14

Continental Breakfast	154
Venison Supreme	162
Kipper and Mango Surprise	164
Starfruit, Potato and Mushroom	170

Mango and Pan Fried Calves Liver	204
Mixed Exotic Salad and Yoghurt Dressing	300
Your choice from Picnic section	196
Your choice from Snacks and Starters section	176

Exotic Pears and Mint	190

Veal (or Beef) Roast with Prunes & Rambutans	208
Fish Soup with Sweetcorn and Lychees	255
Vegetarian Curry with Lychees	289
Your choice from a good supermarket	

Berry Omelette Exotique	311

15

Choose your own Light Breakfast	155
Mango and Pan Fried Calves Liver	163
Plaice and Kiwi Surprise	167
Quick Blend with Simple or Exotic Fruits	174

Quick Hot Prawns	262
Kiwi, Mango and Mushroom Treat	304
Your choice from Picnic section	196
Your choice from Snacks and Starters section	176

Exotic Welsh Rarebit	187

Traditional Shepherd's Pie	202
Smoked Rainbow Trout with Chunky Sauce	257
Aubergine Exotique	286
Your choice from a good supermarket	

Pears, Apple and Ginger Hot Chantilly	315

Breakfast bonanza
Quick & simple
Good old cooked
Why not fish?
Vegetarian

Lunch
Good old cooked
Vegetarian
Picnic selection
Snack of the day

Main meal
Starter

Dish of the day – meat
Dish of the day – fish
Dish of the day – vegetarian
Frozen ready meal

Dessert

March

68

16

Breakfast bonanza
Quick & simple	Grapefruit Surprise	156
Good old cooked	Start The Day Mixed Grill	159
Why not fish?	Gefulte Fish	166
Vegetarian	Hot Fruit Salad	172

Lunch
Good old cooked	Kiwi, Mango and Mushroom Soup	206
Vegetarian	Cherry Tomato, Pineapple and Mango Salad	300
Picnic selection	Your choice from Picnic section	196
Snack of the day	Your choice from Snacks and Starters section	176

Main meal
Starter	Pumpkin Soup with Prawns	192
Dish of the day – meat	Chicken and Peppers	233
Dish of the day – fish	Grapefruit and Red Sockeye Salmon	261
Dish of the day – vegetarian	Courgette Exotique	286
Frozen ready meal	Your choice from a good supermarket	
Dessert	Banana Bake Exotique	323

17

Breakfast bonanza
	Exotique Treat Multiple Choice	158
	Bagel, Egg and Dried Venison or Bacon	161
	Kipper and Date	166
	Mushroom Breakfast	172

	Orange Sole	268
	Rice Exotique	299
	Your choice from Picnic section	196
	Your choice from Snacks and Starters section	176

	Devilled Potato Salad and Celery	185
	Mango Cholent	210
	Steamed Plaice and Mango	278
	Tofu with Exotic Chunky Sauce	291
	Your choice from a good supermarket	
	Ice Cream Grand Marnier	314

18

Breakfast bonanza
Quick & simple	Muesli Treat and Crumpets	153
Good old cooked	Omelette Exotique of choice	164
Why not fish?	Tuna Casserole Exotique	169
Vegetarian	Lemon and Mango Borscht	171

Lunch
Good old cooked	Mixed Kebab	242
Vegetarian	Crunchy, Kutchie-Fyky	293
Picnic selection	Your choice from Picnic section	196
Snack of the day	Your choice from Snacks and Starters section	176

Main meal
Starter	Chicken and Coconut Soup	189
Dish of the day – meat	Chicken, Apricot and Asparagus	249
Dish of the day – fish	Rainbow Trout	264
Dish of the day – vegetarian	Cauliflower au gratin	305
Frozen ready meal	Your choice from a good supermarket	
Dessert	Strawberry (or any other fruits) Mousse	320

19

Breakfast bonanza
	Light Tabbouleh Breakfast	154
	Venison Supreme	162
	Red Salmon Omelette	167
	Banana, Date, Kiwi and Mango	175

	Oriental Wok Stir Fry	217
	Budgie Millet Exotique	294
	Your choice from Picnic section	196
	Your choice from Snacks and Starters section	176

	Exotic Sardine Pâté	178
	Meaty Couscous	239
	Lobster Salad	253
	Chicory, Pineapple, Kiwi and Mushrooms	304
	Your choice from a good supermarket	
	Stuffed Pineapple	311

20

Authentic New York Bagel	156
Bacon and Kiwi Treat	162
Smoked Haddock	168
Egg and Exotic Hot Fruit	174

Tandoori Meat	245
Sesame Seed and Caraway Salad	307
Your choice from Picnic section	196
Your choice from Snacks and Starters section	176

Red Sockeye Salmon Pâté	194

Melon with Dried Wild Venison	214
Shrimp Pilaf Exotique	273
Pumpkin Fritters	294
Your choice from a good supermarket	

Peach and Papaya Chantilly	319

22

Highland Variation	153
Chicken Liver Exotique	158
Fish with Berries	168
Starfruit, Potato and Mushroom	170

Chinese Chicken Salad with Lychees	250
Peas Exotique	293
Your choice from Picnic section	196
Your choice from Snacks and Starters section	176

Lemon and Mango Borscht	184

Ginger Turkey	240
Salmon Fillet with Hot Exotic Chunky Sauce	259
Aubergine Treat	285
Your choice from a good supermarket	

Slimmer Fruit Ice Cream	318

21

English Light	155
Thinner & Richer Kebabs	159
Sole and Kiwi	169
Cherry Tomato, Pineapple and Mango Salad	171

Scallop Seviche	253
Coconut Vegetables	299
Your choice from Picnic section	196
Your choice from Snacks and Starters section	176

Aubergine and Mango Pâté	191

Cider Chicken Calvados	220
Plaice and Prawn Creole	282
Kiwi, Mango and Lychee Beans	292
Your choice from a good supermarket	

Pears in Berry Sauce	309

23

Choose your own Light Breakfast	155
Bacon and Eggs	161
Kipper and Mango Surprise	164
Humpty Dumpty	175

Exotic Kedgeree	260
Vegetarian Quorn Chilli Stir Fry	295
Your choice from Picnic section	196
Your choice from Snacks and Starters section	176

Melon, Kiwi and Grape Surprise	180

Exotique Venison Stew	211
Devilled Lobster	274
Savoury Quorn Puffs	290
Your choice from a good supermarket	

Rambutans and Pineapple Chantilly	310

March

Breakfast bonanza
Quick & simple
Good old cooked
Why not fish?
Vegetarian

Lunch
Good old cooked
Vegetarian
Picnic selection
Snack of the day

Main meal
Starter

Dish of the day – meat
Dish of the day – fish
Dish of the day – vegetarian
Frozen ready meal

Dessert

Breakfast bonanza
Quick & simple
Good old cooked
Why not fish?
Vegetarian

Lunch
Good old cooked
Vegetarian
Picnic selection
Snack of the day

Main meal
Starter

Dish of the day – meat
Dish of the day – fish
Dish of the day – vegetarian
Frozen ready meal

Dessert

24

Continental Breakfast	154
Start The Day Mixed Grill	159
Plaice and Kiwi Surprise	167
Hot Fruit Salad	172

Chicken Pâté	248
Chicory, Pineapple, Kiwi and Mushrooms	304
Your choice from Picnic section	196
Your choice from Snacks and Starters section	176

Devilled Sardines	187

Brandy Fillet Steak, Kiwi Garnish	216
Quick Salmon Steak for One	269
Vegetarian Lasagne	303
Your choice from a good supermarket	

Melon and Berries	315

25

Grapefruit Surprise	156
Mango and Pan Fried Calves Liver	163
Gefulte Fish	166
Quick Blend with Simple or Exotic Fruits	174

Prawn and Mint Dip	272
Baby Parsnips, Breadcrumbs and Corn	302
Your choice from Picnic section	196
Your choice from Snacks and Starters section	176

Sweet and Sour Amaranth Chinese Lettuce	186

Tzimmas with Beef, Mango and Prunes	218
Lobster Salad	253
Vegetarian Quorn Chilli Stir Fry	295
Your choice from a good supermarket	

Quince Thinner & Richer	314

March

Breakfast bonanza
Quick & simple
Good old cooked
Why not fish?
Vegetarian

Lunch
Good old cooked
Vegetarian
Picnic selection
Snack of the day

Main meal
Starter

Dish of the day – meat
Dish of the day – fish
Dish of the day – vegetarian
Frozen ready meal

Dessert

26

Muesli Treat and Crumpets	153
Venison Supreme	162
Tuna Casserole Exotique	169
Lemon and Mango Borscht	171

Coconut Beef Satay or Chicken Satay	245
Kiwi, Mango and Mushroom Treat	304
Your choice from Picnic section	196
Your choice from Snacks and Starters section	176

Leek Soup	184

Chicken in Sherry	251
Plaice-a-Leekie	278
Aubergine Exotique	286
Your choice from a good supermarket	

Cranberry Ice Cream	312

27

Light Tabbouleh Breakfast	154
Omelette Exotique of choice	164
Kipper and Date	166
Mushroom Breakfast	172

Fish Soup à la Thinner & Richer	273
Tofu with Exotic Chunky Sauce	291
Your choice from Picnic section	196
Your choice from Snacks and Starters section	176

Starfruit, Potato and Mushroom	189

Schnitzel Exotic	207
White Fish Couscous	263
Vegetarian Curry with Lychees	289
Your choice from a good supermarket	

Melon, Orange, Mango and Mint Chantilly	312

Breakfast bonanza
Quick & simple
Good old cooked
Why not fish?
Vegetarian

Lunch
Good old cooked
Vegetarian
Picnic selection
Snack of the day

Main meal
Starter

Dish of the day – meat
Dish of the day – fish
Dish of the day – vegetarian
Frozen ready meal

Dessert

March

28

Breakfast bonanza

Quick & simple	Exotique Treat Multiple Choice	158
Good old cooked	Bagel, Egg and Dried Venison or Bacon	161
Why not fish?	Red Salmon Omelette	167
Vegetarian	Egg and Exotic Hot Fruit	174

Lunch

Good old cooked	Chicken Curry with Coconut Milk	237
Vegetarian	Exotic Leeks	307
Picnic selection	Your choice from Picnic section	196
Snack of the day	Your choice from Snacks and Starters section	176

Main meal

Starter	Chicken Pâté	183
Dish of the day – meat	Exotique Beef Soufflé	227
Dish of the day – fish	Potted Herring	266
Dish of the day – vegetarian	Quorn with Exotic Chunky Sauce	298
Frozen ready meal	Your choice from a good supermarket	
Dessert	Banana Split	325

29

English Light	155
Bacon and Eggs	161
Kipper and Mango Surprise	164
Banana, Date, Kiwi and Mango	175

Prawn Exotique	275
Cauliflower au gratin	305
Your choice from Picnic section	196
Your choice from Snacks and Starters section	176

Pea Soup Special	192
Exotique Venison Casserole	233
Lobster Thermidor	272
Bulghar Wheat Exotique	295
Your choice from a good supermarket	
Fruit Flan	317

30

Breakfast bonanza

Quick & simple	Authentic New York Bagel	156
Good old cooked	Chicken Liver Exotique	158
Why not fish?	Sole and Kiwi	169
Vegetarian	Humpty Dumpty	175

Lunch

Good old cooked	Exotique Ham and Mango	235
Vegetarian	Coconut Rice	301
Picnic selection	Your choice from Picnic section	196
Snack of the day	Your choice from Snacks and Starters section	176

Main meal

Starter	Exotic Red Borscht	194
Dish of the day – meat	Slimmers' Lasagne à la Thinner & Richer	237
Dish of the day – fish	Tuna and Egg Salad Exotique	267
Dish of the day – vegetarian	Tofu with Exotic Chunky Sauce	291
Frozen ready meal	Your choice from a good supermarket	
Dessert	Kiwango Ice	310

31

Highland Variation	153
Thinner & Richer Kebabs	159
Smoked Haddock	168
Starfruit, Potato and Mushroom	170

Oriental Wok Stir Fry	217
Mixed Exotic Salad and Yoghurt Dressing	300
Your choice from Picnic section	196
Your choice from Snacks and Starters section	176

Vegetarian Coleslaw	179
Lamb and Pawpaw Corsican Style	215
Gefulte Fish	256
Aubergine Exotique au gratin	288
Your choice from a good supermarket	
Pears, Apple and Ginger Hot Chantilly	315

1

Continental Breakfast	154
Bacon and Kiwi Treat	162
Fish with Berries	168
Cherry Tomato, Pineapple and Mango Salad	171

Citrus Chicken	221
Kiwi, Mango and Lychee Beans	292
Your choice from Picnic section	196
Your choice from Snacks and Starters section	176

Grapefruit and Tomato Soup	185

Indonesian Pork Satay	220
Marinated Red Mullet Exotique	277
Mushroom Flan	287
Your choice from a good supermarket	

Exotic Caramel Custard	325

2

Grapefruit Surprise	156
Mango and Pan Fried Calves Liver	163
Tuna Casserole Exotique	169
Quick Blend with Simple or Exotic Fruits	174

Salmon for a King in Pitta Bread	279
Cranberry Rice Salad	303
Your choice from Picnic section	196
Your choice from Snacks and Starters section	176

Green Soup	182

Exotic Shepherd's Pie	221
Smoked Salmon Couscous	270
Crunchy, Kutchie-Fyky	293
Your choice from a good supermarket	

Super Low Microwaveable Pears	313

April

Breakfast bonanza
Quick & simple
Good old cooked
Why not fish?
Vegetarian

Lunch
Good old cooked
Vegetarian
Picnic selection
Snack of the day

Main meal
Starter

Dish of the day – meat
Dish of the day – fish
Dish of the day – vegetarian
Frozen ready meal

Dessert

3

Choose your own Light Breakfast	155
Venison Supreme	162
Gefulte Fish	166
Lemon and Mango Borscht	171

Chicken Pesto	230
Coconut Vegetables	299
Your choice from Picnic section	196
Your choice from Snacks and Starters section	176

Pumpkin Soup with Prawns	192

Sweet and Sour Pork	248
Salmon and Rice	255
Aubergine au Fromage Frais	285
Your choice from a good supermarket	

Blackberry, Lychee and Cape Gooseberry	323

4

Light Tabbouleh Breakfast	154
Start The Day Mixed Grill	159
Kipper and Mango Surprise	164
Hot Fruit Salad	172

Plaice and Prawn Creole	282
Greek Dip Exotique	289
Your choice from Picnic section	196
Your choice from Snacks and Starters section	176

Exotic Toast	191

Chicken and Aubergine	232
Tomato and Tuna Salad Exotique	257
Cauliflower au gratin	305
Your choice from a good supermarket	

Ice Cream Grand Marnier	314

Breakfast bonanza
Quick & simple
Good old cooked
Why not fish?
Vegetarian

Lunch
Good old cooked
Vegetarian
Picnic selection
Snack of the day

Main meal
Starter

Dish of the day – meat
Dish of the day – fish
Dish of the day – vegetarian
Frozen ready meal

Dessert

5

Breakfast bonanza

Quick & simple	Muesli Treat and Crumpets	153
Good old cooked	Bagel, Egg and Dried Venison or Bacon	161
Why not fish?	Red Salmon Omelette	167
Vegetarian	Egg and Exotic Hot Fruit	174

Lunch

Good old cooked	Tandoori Meat	245
Vegetarian	Wok Quorn	302
Picnic selection	Your choice from Picnic section	196
Snack of the day	Your choice from Snacks and Starters section	176

Main meal

Starter	Chopped Herring Chunky Pâté	178
Dish of the day – meat	Pork or Turkey and Apple	206
Dish of the day – fish	Salmon Fillet with Hot Exotic Chunky Sauce	259
Dish of the day – vegetarian	Aubergine Treat	285
Frozen ready meal	Your choice from a good supermarket	
Dessert	Peach and Papaya Chantilly	319

6

Breakfast bonanza

English Light	155
Omelette Exotique of choice	164
Kipper and Date	166
Mushroom Breakfast	172

Lunch

Rainbow Trout	264
Courgette Exotique	286
Your choice from Picnic section	196
Your choice from Snacks and Starters section	176

Main meal

Fluffy Herb Pâté	179
Stuffed Cabbage	235
Pepper, Anchovy and Tomato	269
Subtle Kebabs	292
Your choice from a good supermarket	
Baked Fruit	318

7

Breakfast bonanza

Quick & simple	Exotique Treat Multiple Choice	158
Good old cooked	Thinner & Richer Kebabs	159
Why not fish?	Fish with Berries	168
Vegetarian	Starfruit, Potato and Mushroom	170

Lunch

Good old cooked	Coconut Beef Satay or Chicken Satay	245
Vegetarian	Cherry Tomato, Pineapple and Mango Salad	300
Picnic selection	Your choice from Picnic section	196
Snack of the day	Your choice from Snacks and Starters section	176

Main meal

Starter	Borscht and Yoghurt	181
Dish of the day – meat	Exotic Turkey Escalopes	242
Dish of the day – fish	Exotic Salmon and Plaice	258
Dish of the day – vegetarian	Budgie Millet Exotique	294
Frozen ready meal	Your choice from a good supermarket	
Dessert	Banana Split	325

8

9

April

Breakfast bonanza
Quick & simple
Good old cooked
Why not fish?
Vegetarian

Lunch
Good old cooked
Vegetarian
Picnic selection
Snack of the day

Main meal
Starter

Dish of the day – meat
Dish of the day – fish
Dish of the day – vegetarian
Frozen ready meal

Dessert

10

11

Breakfast bonanza
Quick & simple
Good old cooked
Why not fish?
Vegetarian

Lunch
Good old cooked
Vegetarian
Picnic selection
Snack of the day

Main meal
Starter

Dish of the day – meat
Dish of the day – fish
Dish of the day – vegetarian
Frozen ready meal

Dessert

April

12

13

14

15

76

16

Highland Variation	153
Chicken Liver Exotique	158
Fish with Berries	168
Mushroom Breakfast	172

Steamed Plaice and Mango	278
Tofu with Exotic Chunky Sauce	291
Your choice from Picnic section	196
Your choice from Snacks and Starters section	176

Fish Soup	193

Champagne Quail	222
Red Salmon Omelette	279
Bulghar Wheat Exotique	295
Your choice from a good supermarket	

Guava Ice Cream	324

17

Authentic New York Bagel	156
Thinner & Richer Kebabs	159
Smoked Haddock	168
Starfruit, Potato and Mushroom	170

Devilled Lamb Steaks	209
Mixed Exotic Salad and Yoghurt Dressing	300
Your choice from Picnic section	196
Your choice from Snacks and Starters section	176

Exotic Welsh Rarebit	187

North African Couscous	238
Salmon for a King	267
Vegetarian Curry with Lychees	289
Your choice from a good supermarket	

Strawberry (or any other fruits) Mousse	320

April

Breakfast bonanza
Quick & simple
Good old cooked
Why not fish?
Vegetarian

Lunch
Good old cooked
Vegetarian
Picnic selection
Snack of the day

Main meal
Starter

Dish of the day – meat
Dish of the day – fish
Dish of the day – vegetarian
Frozen ready meal

Dessert

77

18

Exotique Treat Multiple Choice	158
Bacon and Eggs	161
Kipper and Mango Surprise	164
Banana, Date, Kiwi and Mango	175

Red Sockeye Salmon Stir Fry	259
Coconut Vegetables	299
Your choice from Picnic section	196
Your choice from Snacks and Starters section	176

Watercress, Lychee and Cucumber Soup	181

Chopped Liver	214
Smoked Trout	261
Baby Parsnips, Breadcrumbs and Corn	302
Your choice from a good supermarket	

Melon and Berries	315

19

Grapefruit Surprise	156
Bacon and Kiwi Treat	162
Tuna Casserole Exotique	169
Cherry Tomato, Pineapple and Mango Salad	171

Mixed Kebab	242
Greek Dip Exotique	289
Your choice from Picnic section	196
Your choice from Snacks and Starters section	176

Sweet and Sour Amaranth Chinese Lettuce	186

Chicken Exotique and Dried Venison	210
Smoked Rainbow Trout with Chunky Sauce	257
Savoury Quorn Puffs	
Your choice from a good supermarket	290

Melon, Orange, Mango and Mint Chantilly	312

Breakfast bonanza
Quick & simple
Good old cooked
Why not fish?
Vegetarian

Lunch
Good old cooked
Vegetarian
Picnic selection
Snack of the day

Main meal
Starter

Dish of the day – meat
Dish of the day – fish
Dish of the day – vegetarian
Frozen ready meal

Dessert

20

Breakfast bonanza

Quick & simple	Continental Breakfast	154
Good old cooked	Venison Supreme	162
Why not fish?	Sole and Kiwi	169
Vegetarian	Lemon and Mango Borscht	171

Lunch

Good old cooked	Quick Hot Prawns	262
Vegetarian	Crunchy, Kutchie-Fyky	293
Picnic selection	Your choice from Picnic section	196
Snack of the day	Your choice from Snacks and Starters section	176

Main meal

Starter	Devilled Potato Salad and Celery	185
Dish of the day – meat	Cauliflower au Gratin	223
Dish of the day – fish	Starfruit Salmon Salad	271
Dish of the day – vegetarian	Cranberry Rice Salad	303
Frozen ready meal	Your choice from a good supermarket	
Dessert	Slimmer Fruit Ice Cream	318

21

Breakfast bonanza

	Choose your own Light Breakfast	155
	Bagel, Egg and Dried Venison or Bacon	161
	Kipper and Date	166
	Quick Blend with Simple or Exotic Fruits	174

	Chicken and Pasta (cold dish)	236
	Courgette Exotique	286
	Your choice from Picnic section	196
	Your choice from Snacks and Starters section	176

	Starfruit, Potato and Mushroom	189
	Mango Cholent	210
	Lobster Salad	253
	Aubergine Exotique	286
	Your choice from a good supermarket	
	Lemon and Mango Borscht	184

22

Breakfast bonanza

Quick & simple	English Light	155
Good old cooked	Mango and Pan Fried Calves Liver	163
Why not fish?	Plaice and Kiwi Surprise	167
Vegetarian	Humpty Dumpty	175

Lunch

Good old cooked	Quick Salmon Steak for One	269
Vegetarian	Peas Exotique	293
Picnic selection	Your choice from Picnic section	196
Snack of the day	Your choice from Snacks and Starters section	176

Main meal

Starter	Chopped Herring Chunky Pâté	178
Dish of the day – meat	Chicken Pâté	248
Dish of the day – fish	Salmon à la Greque	268
Dish of the day – vegetarian	Mushroom Flan	287
Frozen ready meal	Your choice from a good supermarket	
Dessert	Quince Thinner & Richer	314

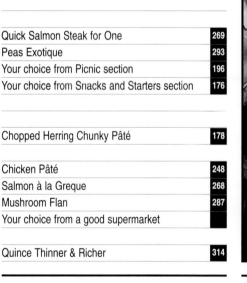

23

Muesli Treat and Crumpets	153
Chicken Liver Exotique	158
Red Salmon Omelette	167
Hot Fruit Salad	172

Chicken Curry with Coconut Milk	237
Kiwi, Mango and Mushroom Treat	304
Your choice from Picnic section	196
Your choice from Snacks and Starters section	176

Fluffy Herb Pâté	179

Cold Meat Salad with Exotic Chunky Sauce	236
Orange Sole	268
Cherry Tomato, Pineapple and Mango Salad	300
Your choice from a good supermarket	

Pears Grand Marnier	309

24

Light Tabbouleh Breakfast	154
Omelette Exotique Of Choice	164
Fish with Berries	168
Egg and Exotic Hot Fruit	174

Salmon for a King in Pitta Bread	279
Subtle Kebabs	292
Your choice from Picnic section	196
Your choice from Snacks and Starters section	176

Exotic Red Borscht	194

Steak Diane Exotique	219
Plaice-a-Leekie	278
Budgie Millet Exotique	294
Your choice from a good supermarket	

Rambutans and Pineapple Chantilly	310

Breakfast bonanza
Quick & simple
Good old cooked
Why not fish?
Vegetarian

Lunch
Good old cooked
Vegetarian
Picnic selection
Snack of the day

Main meal
Starter

Dish of the day – meat
Dish of the day – fish
Dish of the day – vegetarian
Frozen ready meal

Dessert

25

Exotique Treat Multiple Choice	158
Start The Day Mixed Grill	159
Gefulte Fish	166
Mushroom Breakfast	172

Sweet and Sour Pork	248
Coconut Rice	301
Your choice from Picnic section	196
Your choice from Snacks and Starters section	176

Green Soup	182

North American Couscous	226
Exotic Salmon and Plaice	258
Kiwi, Mango and Lychee Beans	292
Your choice from a good supermarket	

Cranberry Ice Cream	312

26

Muesli Treat and Crumpets	153
Bacon and Eggs	161
Kipper and Mango Surprise	164
Banana, Date, Kiwi and Mango	175

Prawn Exotique	275
Aubergine Exotique au gratin	288
Your choice from Picnic section	196
Your choice from Snacks and Starters section	176

Borscht and Yoghurt	181

Chicken, Apricot and Asparagus	249
Marinated Red Mullet Exotique	277
Vegetarian Lasagne	303
Your choice from a good supermarket	

Banana Chocolate Treat with Mangoes	316

Breakfast bonanza
Quick & simple
Good old cooked
Why not fish?
Vegetarian

Lunch
Good old cooked
Vegetarian
Picnic selection
Snack of the day

Main meal
Starter

Dish of the day – meat
Dish of the day – fish
Dish of the day – vegetarian
Frozen ready meal

Dessert

27

Breakfast bonanza

Quick & simple	Authentic New York Bagel	156
Good old cooked	Thinner & Richer Kebabs	159
Why not fish?	Smoked Haddock	168
Vegetarian	Starfruit, Potato and Mushroom	170

Lunch

Good old cooked	Stir Fried Liver	207
Vegetarian	Sesame Seed and Caraway Salad	307
Picnic selection	Your choice from Picnic section	196
Snack of the day	Your choice from Snacks and Starters section	176

Main meal

Starter	Vegetarian Coleslaw	179
Dish of the day – meat	Original Duck à l'Orange	209
Dish of the day – fish	Gefulte Fish	256
Dish of the day – vegetarian	Cauliflower au gratin	305
Frozen ready meal	Your choice from a good supermarket	
Dessert	Exotic Caramel Custard	325

28

Continental Breakfast	154
Venison Supreme	162
Tuna Casserole Exotique	169
Cherry Tomato, Pineapple and Mango Salad	171

Exotic Mackerel	266
Sweet and Sour Amaranth Chinese Lettuce	306
Your choice from Picnic section	196
Your choice from Snacks and Starters section	176

Melon, Kiwi and Grape Surprise	180
Veal Goulash with Lychees	229
Red Sockeye Salmon Stir Fry	259
Bulghar Wheat Exotique	295
Your choice from a good supermarket	
Peach and Papaya Chantilly	319

80

29

Breakfast bonanza

Quick & simple	Choose your own Light Breakfast	155
Good old cooked	Bagel, Egg and Dried Venison or Bacon	161
Why not fish?	Plaice and Kiwi Surprise	167
Vegetarian	Quick Blend with Simple or Exotic Fruits	174

Lunch

Good old cooked	Exotique Chicken Satay	215
Vegetarian	Quorn with Exotic Chunky Sauce	298
Picnic selection	Your choice from Picnic section	196
Snack of the day	Your choice from Snacks and Starters section	176

Main meal

Starter	Melon with Dried Venison or Parma Ham	177
Dish of the day – meat	Exotique Pintade Rotir (Guinea Fowl)	205
Dish of the day – fish	Tuna and Egg Salad Exotique	267
Dish of the day – vegetarian	Quorn with Exotic Chunky Sauce	298
Frozen ready meal	Your choice from a good supermarket	
Dessert	Banana Split	325

30

Grapefruit Surprise	156
Bacon and Kiwi Treat	162
Sole and Kiwi	169
Humpty Dumpty	175

Salmon Fillet with Hot Exotic Chunky Sauce	259
Chicory, Pineapple, Kiwi and Mushrooms	304
Your choice from Picnic section	196
Your choice from Snacks and Starters section	176

Pumpkin Soup with Prawns	192
Aubergine Exotique au gratin	243
Smoked Salmon Couscous	270
Vegetarian Curry with Lychees	289
Your choice from a good supermarket	
Blackberry, Lychee and Cape Gooseberry	323

May

1

Light Tabbouleh Breakfast	154
Omelette Exotique of choice	164
Kipper and Date	166
Lemon and Mango Borscht	171

Beef and Lamb Kebabs	201
Exotic Leeks	307
Your choice from Picnic section	196
Your choice from Snacks and Starters section	176

| Exotic Pears and Mint | 190 |

Slimmers' Lasagne à la Thinner & Richer	237
Plaice, Leek and Lime	274
Wok Quorn	302
Your choice from a good supermarket	

| Kiwango Ice | 310 |

2

English Light	155
Start The Day Mixed Grill	159
Fish with Berries	168
Egg and Exotic Hot Fruit	174

Hot Pickled Herring	271
Mixed Exotic Salad and Yoghurt Dressing	300
Your choice from Picnic section	196
Your choice from Snacks and Starters section	176

| Chicken Pâté | 183 |

Stuffed Cabbage	235
Devilled Lobster	274
Aubergine au Fromage Frais	285
Your choice from a good supermarket	

| Mango and Peach Brulée | 316 |

Breakfast bonanza
Quick & simple
Good old cooked
Why not fish?
Vegetarian

Lunch
Good old cooked
Vegetarian
Picnic selection
Snack of the day

Main meal
Starter

Dish of the day – meat
Dish of the day – fish
Dish of the day – vegetarian
Frozen ready meal

Dessert

3

Muesli Treat and Crumpets	153
Chicken Liver Exotique	158
Red Salmon Omelette	167
Hot Fruit Salad	172

Chicken with Red and Green Peppers	244
Coconut Vegetables	299
Your choice from Picnic section	196
Your choice from Snacks and Starters section	176

| Leek Soup | 184 |

Exotique Turkey and Almonds	232
White Fish Cous cous	263
Tofu with Exotic Chunky Sauce	291
Your choice from a good supermarket	

| Super Low Microwaveable Pears | 313 |

4

Highland Variation	153
Mango and Pan Fried Calves Liver	163
Kipper and Mango Surprise	164
Mushroom Breakfast	172

Fish Soup à la Thinner & Richer	273
Rice Exotique	299
Your choice from Picnic section	196
Your choice from Snacks and Starters section	176

| Red Sockeye Salmon Pâté | 194 |

Pork or Turkey and Apple	206
Prawn and Mint Dip	272
Savoury Quorn Puffs	290
Your choice from a good supermarket	

| Exotique Banana Dessert | 319 |

Breakfast bonanza
Quick & simple
Good old cooked
Why not fish?
Vegetarian

Lunch
Good old cooked
Vegetarian
Picnic selection
Snack of the day

Main meal
Starter

Dish of the day – meat
Dish of the day – fish
Dish of the day – vegetarian
Frozen ready meal

Dessert

5

Breakfast bonanza

Quick & simple	Authentic New York Bagel	156
Good old cooked	Bacon and Eggs	161
Why not fish?	Gefulte Fish	166
Vegetarian	Starfruit, Potato and Mushroom	170

Lunch

Good old cooked	Chicken in Sherry	251
Vegetarian	Cranberry Rice Salad	303
Picnic selection	Your choice from Picnic section	196
Snack of the day	Your choice from Snacks and Starters section	176

Main meal

Starter	Grapefruit and Tomato Soup	185
Dish of the day – meat	Wok Beef	213
Dish of the day – fish	Salmon for a King	267
Dish of the day – vegetarian	Aubergine Treat	285
Frozen ready meal	Your choice from a good supermarket	
Dessert	Melon and Berries	315

6

Exotique Treat Multiple Choice	158
Thinner & Richer Kebabs	159
Tuna Casserole Exotique	169
Banana, Date, Kiwi and Mango	175

Quick Hot Prawns	262
Vegetarian Quorn Chilli Stir Fry	295
Your choice from Picnic section	196
Your choice from Snacks and Starters section	176

Carrot Soup	180
Brandy Fillet Steak, Kiwi Garnish	216
Plaice and Prawn Creole	282
Pumpkin Fritters	294
Your choice from a good supermarket	
Ice Cream Grand Marnier	314

7

Breakfast bonanza

Quick & simple	Grapefruit Surprise	156
Good old cooked	Start The Day Mixed Grill	159
Why not fish?	Smoked Haddock	168
Vegetarian	Cherry Tomato, Pineapple and Mango Salad	171

Lunch

Good old cooked	Wild Venison with Ratatouille	225
Vegetarian	Greek Dip Exotique	289
Picnic selection	Your choice from Picnic section	196
Snack of the day	Your choice from Snacks and Starters section	176

Main meal

Starter	Gefulte Fish	183
Dish of the day – meat	Melon with Dried Wild Venison or Parma Ham	214
Dish of the day – fish	Smoked Salmon Cous cous	270
Dish of the day – vegetarian	Vegetable Curry	296
Frozen ready meal	Your choice from a good supermarket	
Dessert	Pears in Berry Sauce	309

8

Choose your own Light Breakfast	155
Venison Supreme	162
Sole and Kiwi	169
Lemon and Mango Borscht	171

Avocado Salmon	258
Aubergine au Fromage Frais	285
Your choice from Picnic section	196
Your choice from Snacks and Starters section	176

Coconut and Beef Satay or Chicken Satay	195
Ginger Turkey	240
Whole Rainbow Trout à l'Orange	264
Dressed Seasonal Salad	301
Your choice from a good supermarket	
Mango and Lychee Mousse	313

9

Breakfast bonanza

Quick & simple	Continental Breakfast	154
Good old cooked	Bacon and Kiwi Treat	162
Why not fish?	Fish with Berries	168
Vegetarian	Humpty Dumpty	175

Lunch

Good old cooked	Citrus Chicken	221
Vegetarian	Courgette Exotique	286
Picnic selection	Your choice from Picnic section	196
Snack of the day	Your choice from Snacks and Starters section	176

Main meal

Starter	Exotic Toast	191
Dish of the day – meat	Hot Meat or Poultry with Exotic Chunky Sauce	205
Dish of the day – fish	Potted Herring	266
Dish of the day – vegetarian	Mushroom Flan	287
Frozen ready meal	Your choice from a good supermarket	
Dessert	Guava Ice Cream	324

10

Quick & simple	Highland Variation	153
Good old cooked	Bagel, Egg and Dried Venison or Bacon	161
Why not fish?	Plaice and Kiwi Surprise	167
Vegetarian	Quick Blend with Simple or Exotic Fruits	174

Good old cooked	Sardine Exotic Surprise	277
Vegetarian	Kiwi, Mango and Mushroom Treat	304
Picnic selection	Your choice from Picnic section	196
Snack of the day	Your choice from Snacks and Starters section	176

Starter	Devilled Sardines	187
Dish of the day – meat	Exotique Beef Soufflé	227
Dish of the day – fish	Smoked Salmon Expanded à la Thinner & Richer	254
Dish of the day – vegetarian	Subtle Kebabs	292
Frozen ready meal	Your choice from a good supermarket	
Dessert	Berry Omelette Exotique	311

11

Breakfast bonanza

Quick & simple	English Light	155
Good old cooked	Chicken Liver Exotique	158
Why not fish?	Kipper and Date	166
Vegetarian	Egg and Exotic Hot Fruit	174

Lunch

Good old cooked	Chicken Pesto	230
Vegetarian	Cherry Tomato, Pineapple and Mango Salad	300
Picnic selection	Your choice from Picnic section	196
Snack of the day	Your choice from Snacks and Starters section	176

Main meal

Starter	Pea Soup Special	192
Dish of the day – meat	Traditional Shepherd's Pie	202
Dish of the day – fish	Oriental Wok Stir Fry	260
Dish of the day – vegetarian	Aubergine Exotique au gratin	288
Frozen ready meal	Your choice from a good supermarket	
Dessert	Stuffed Pineapple	311

12

Quick & simple	Light Tabbouleh Breakfast	154
Good old cooked	Omelette Exotique of choice	164
Why not fish?	Fish with Berries	168
Vegetarian	Lemon and Mango Borscht	171

Good old cooked	Scallop Seviche	253
Vegetarian	Coconut Rice	301
Picnic selection	Your choice from Picnic section	196
Snack of the day	Your choice from Snacks and Starters section	176

Starter	Exotic Sardine Pâté	178
Dish of the day – meat	Tzimmas with Beef, Mango and Prunes	218
Dish of the day – fish	Lobster Thermidor	272
Dish of the day – vegetarian	Aubergine Treat	285
Frozen ready meal	Your choice from a good supermarket	
Dessert	Strawberry (or any other fruits) Mousse	320

13

Muesli Treat and Crumpets	153
Start The Day Mixed Grill	159
Red Salmon Omelette	167
Hot Fruit Salad	172

Mango and Pan Fried Calves Liver	204
Budgie Millet Exotique	294
Your choice from Picnic section	196
Your choice from Snacks and Starters section	176

Watercress, Lychee and Cucumber Soup	181

Poultry – Sweet and Sour	217
Steamed Plaice and Mango	278
Quorn with Exotic Chunky Sauce	298
Your choice from a good supermarket	

Pears, Apple and Ginger Hot Chantilly	315

14

Grapefruit Surprise	156
Mango and Pan Fried Calves Liver	163
Gefulte Fish	166
Starfruit, Potato and Mushroom	170

Pepper, Anchovy and Tomato	269
Wok Quorn	302
Your choice from Picnic section	196
Your choice from Snacks and Starters section	176

Lemon and Mango Borscht	184

Exotique Venison Casserole	233
Starfruit Salmon Salad	271
Crunchy, Kutchie-Fyky	293
Your choice from a good supermarket	

Fruit Jelly	317

May

Breakfast bonanza
Quick & simple
Good old cooked
Why not fish?
Vegetarian

Lunch
Good old cooked
Vegetarian
Picnic selection
Snack of the day

Main meal
Starter

Dish of the day – meat
Dish of the day – fish
Dish of the day – vegetarian
Frozen ready meal

Dessert

15

Exotique Treat Multiple Choice	158
Start The Day Mixed Grill	159
Kipper and Mango Surprise	164
Mushroom Breakfast	172

Oriental Wok Stir Fry	217
Coconut Vegetables	299
Your choice from Picnic section	196
Your choice from Snacks and Starters section	176

Aubergine and Mango Pâté	191

Lamb and Pawpaw Corsican Style	215
Plaice and Prawn Creole	282
Vegetarian Lasagne	303
Your choice from a good supermarket	

Banana Bake Exotique	323

16

Authentic New York Bagel	156
Thinner & Richer Kebabs	159
Smoked Haddock	168
Cherry Tomato, Pineapple and Mango Salad	171

Red Salmon Omelette	279
Sesame Seed and Caraway Salad	307
Your choice from Picnic section	196
Your choice from Snacks and Starters section	176

Cauliflower Soup	193

Exotique Ham and Mango	235
Tomato and Tuna Salad Exotique	257
Vegetarian Curry with Lychees	289
Your choice from a good supermarket	

Baked Fruit	318

Breakfast bonanza
Quick & simple
Good old cooked
Why not fish?
Vegetarian

Lunch
Good old cooked
Vegetarian
Picnic selection
Snack of the day

Main meal
Starter

Dish of the day – meat
Dish of the day – fish
Dish of the day – vegetarian
Frozen ready meal

Dessert

17

Breakfast bonanza

Quick & simple	Continental Breakfast	154
Good old cooked	Bacon and Eggs	161
Why not fish?	Tuna Casserole Exotique	169
Vegetarian	Banana, Date, Kiwi and Mango	175

Lunch

Good old cooked	Schnitzel Exotic	207
Vegetarian	Baby Parsnips, Breadcrumbs and Corn	302
Picnic selection	Your choice from Picnic section	196
Snack of the day	Your choice from Snacks and Starters section	176

Main meal

Starter	Chicken and Coconut Soup	189
Dish of the day – meat	Chinese Chicken Salad with Lychees	250
Dish of the day – fish	Prawn and Exotic Salad	256
Dish of the day – vegetarian	Kiwi, Mango and Lychee Beans	292
Frozen ready meal	Your choice from a good supermarket	
Dessert	Fruit Flan	317

18

Highland Variation		153
Bacon and Kiwi Treat		162
Sole and Kiwi		169
Humpty Dumpty		175

Sole in Envelopes		254
Sweet and Sour Amaranth Chinese Lettuce		306
Your choice from Picnic section		196
Your choice from Snacks and Starters section		176

Exotic Welsh Rarebit		187
Chicken and Aubergine		232
Rainbow Trout		264
Aubergine Exotique		286
Your choice from a good supermarket		
Slimmer Fruit Ice Cream		318

19

Breakfast bonanza

Quick & simple	Choose your own Light Breakfast	155
Good old cooked	Venison Supreme	162
Why not fish?	Plaice and Kiwi Surprise	167
Vegetarian	Egg and Exotic Hot Fruit	174

Lunch

Good old cooked	Mango and Pan Fried Calves Liver	204
Vegetarian	Exotic Leeks	307
Picnic selection	Your choice from Picnic section	196
Snack of the day	Your choice from Snacks and Starters section	176

Main meal

Starter	Stir Fry Vegetables and Chilli	195
Dish of the day – meat	Mushroom Flan (contains meat)	231
Dish of the day – fish	Salmon and Rice	255
Dish of the day – vegetarian	Cauliflower au gratin	305
Frozen ready meal	Your choice from a good supermarket	
Dessert	Honey and Apple Crisp	324

20

Light Tabbouleh Breakfast		154
Chicken Liver Exotique		158
Fish with Berries		168
Quick Blend with Simple or Exotic Fruits		174

Exotic Kedgeree		260
Peas Exotique		293
Your choice from Picnic section		196
Your choice from Snacks and Starters section		176

Fish Soup		193
Tandoori Meat		245
Shrimp Pilaf Exotique		273
Bulghar Wheat Exotique		295
Your choice from a good supermarket		
Pears Grand Marnier		309

21

22

23

May

Breakfast bonanza

Quick & simple
Good old cooked
Why not fish?
Vegetarian

Lunch

Good old cooked
Vegetarian
Picnic selection
Snack of the day

Main meal

Starter

Dish of the day – meat
Dish of the day – fish
Dish of the day – vegetarian
Frozen ready meal

Dessert

Breakfast bonanza

Quick & simple
Good old cooked
Why not fish?
Vegetarian

Lunch

Good old cooked
Vegetarian
Picnic selection
Snack of the day

Main meal

Starter

Dish of the day – meat
Dish of the day – fish
Dish of the day – vegetarian
Frozen ready meal

Dessert

May

24

Breakfast bonanza

Quick & simple	Authentic New York Bagel	156
Good old cooked	Start The Day Mixed Grill	159
Why not fish?	Kipper and Mango Surprise	164
Vegetarian	Cherry Tomato, Pineapple and Mango Salad	171

Lunch

Good old cooked	Tuna Special	262
Vegetarian	Chicory, Pineapple, Kiwi and Mushrooms	304
Picnic selection	Your choice from Picnic section	196
Snack of the day	Your choice from Snacks and Starters section	176

Main meal

Starter	Pumpkin Soup with Prawns	192
Dish of the day – meat	Indonesian Pork Satay	220
Dish of the day – fish	Gefulte Fish	256
Dish of the day – vegetarian	Cranberry Rice Salad	303
Frozen ready meal	Your choice from a good supermarket	
Dessert	Kiwango Ice	310

25

Grapefruit Surprise		156
Bacon and Kiwi Treat		162
Tuna Casserole Exotique		169
Banana, Date, Kiwi and Mango		175

Cider Chicken Calvados		220
Mixed Exotic Salad and Yoghurt Dressing		300
Your choice from Picnic section		196
Your choice from Snacks and Starters section		176

Chicken and Coconut Soup		189
Meaty Cous cous		239
Marinated Red Mullet Exotique		277
Quorn with Exotic Chunky Sauce		298
Your choice from a good supermarket		
Melon, Orange, Mango and Mint Chantilly		312

26

Breakfast bonanza

Quick & simple	Highland Variation	153
Good old cooked	Thinner & Richer Kebabs	159
Why not fish?	Smoked Haddock	168
Vegetarian	Mushroom Breakfast	172

Lunch

Good old cooked	Hot Pickled Herring	271
Vegetarian	Coconut Rice	301
Picnic selection	Your choice from Picnic section	196
Snack of the day	Your choice from Snacks and Starters section	176

Main meal

Starter	Dandelion Summer Starter	177
Dish of the day – meat	Rosemary Lamb	204
Dish of the day – fish	Salmon à la Greque	268
Dish of the day – vegetarian	Aubergine au Fromage Frais	285
Frozen ready meal	Your choice from a good supermarket	
Dessert	Banana Chocolate Treat with Mangoes	316

27

Choose your own Light Breakfast		155
Bacon and Eggs		161
Plaice and Kiwi Surprise		167
Egg and Exotic Hot Fruit		174

Exotic Liver with Orange		228
Cherry Tomato, Pineapple and Mango Salad		300
Your choice from Picnic section		196
Your choice from Snacks and Starters section		176

Devilled Potato Salad and Celery		185
Cauliflower au gratin		223
Exotic Mackerel		266
Mushroom Flan		287
Your choice from a good supermarket		
Berry Omelette Exotique		311

28

Continental Breakfast	154
Bagel, Egg and Dried Venison or Bacon	161
Sole and Kiwi	169
Humpty Dumpty	175

Salmon for a King in Pitta Bread	279
Crunchy, Kutchie-Fyky	293
Your choice from Picnic section	196
Your choice from Snacks and Starters section	176

Exotic Red Borscht	194

Coconut Beef Satay or Chicken Satay	245
Potted Herring	266
Vegetarian Curry with Lychees	289
Your choice from a good supermarket	

Pears in Berry Sauce	309

29

Muesli Treat and Crumpets	153
Chicken Liver Exotique	158
Kipper and Date	166
Lemon and Mango Borscht	171

Chicken and Peppers	233
Aubergine Exotique	286
Your choice from Picnic section	196
Your choice from Snacks and Starters section	176

Leek Soup	184

Exotic Turkey Escalopes	242
Tomato and Tuna Salad Exotique	257
Tofu with Exotic Chunky Sauce	291
Your choice from a good supermarket	

Super Low Microwaveable Pears	313

May

Breakfast bonanza
Quick & simple
Good old cooked
Why not fish?
Vegetarian

Lunch
Good old cooked
Vegetarian
Picnic selection
Snack of the day

Main meal
Starter

Dish of the day – meat
Dish of the day – fish
Dish of the day – vegetarian
Frozen ready meal

Dessert

30

Light Tabbouleh Breakfast	154
Mango and Pan Fried Calves Liver	163
Fish with Berries	168
Quick Blend with Simple or Exotic Fruits	174

Lobster Salad	253
Dressed Seasonal Salad	301
Your choice from Picnic section	196
Your choice from Snacks and Starters section	176

Red Sockeye Salmon Pâté	194

Duck Breast Thinner & Richer	244
Smoked Salmon Cous cous	270
Subtle Kebabs	292
Your choice from a good supermarket	

Mango and Peach Brulée	316

31

English Light	155
Venison Supreme	162
Red Salmon Omelette	167
Cherry Tomato, Pineapple and Mango Salad	171

Stir Fried Liver	207
Greek Dip Exotique	289
Your choice from Picnic section	196
Your choice from Snacks and Starters section	176

Pea Soup Special	192

Exotique Lamb and Papaya or Mango	216
Sardine Exotic Surprise	277
Cauliflower au gratin	305
Your choice from a good supermarket	

Mango and Lychee Mousse	313

Breakfast bonanza
Quick & simple
Good old cooked
Why not fish?
Vegetarian

Lunch
Good old cooked
Vegetarian
Picnic selection
Snack of the day

Main meal
Starter

Dish of the day – meat
Dish of the day – fish
Dish of the day – vegetarian
Frozen ready meal

Dessert

June

1

Breakfast bonanza

Quick & simple	Exotique Treat Multiple Choice	158
Good old cooked	Omelette Exotique of choice	164
Why not fish?	Kipper and Mango Surprise	164
Vegetarian	Hot Fruit Salad	172

Lunch

Good old cooked	Fish Soup à la Thinner & Richer	273
Vegetarian	Sesame Seed and Caraway Salad	307
Picnic selection	Your choice from Picnic section	196
Snack of the day	Your choice from Snacks and Starters section	176

Main meal

Starter	Dandelion Summer Starter	177
Dish of the day – meat	Veal (or Beef) Roast with Prunes and Rambutans	208
Dish of the day – fish	Salmon and Rice	255
Dish of the day – vegetarian	Vegetarian Lasagne	303
Frozen ready meal	Your choice from a good supermarket	
Dessert	Guava Ice Cream	324

2

Breakfast bonanza

Authentic New York Bagel		156
Bacon and Kiwi Treat		162
Gefulte Fish		166
Starfruit, Potato and Mushroom		170

Lunch

Chicken and Pasta (cold dish)		236
Chicory, Pineapple, Kiwi and Mushrooms		304
Your choice from Picnic section		196
Your choice from Snacks and Starters section		176

Main meal

Chopped Herring Chunky Pâté		178
Cold Meat Salad with Exotic Chunky Sauce		236
Whole Rainbow Trout a l'Orange		264
Pumpkin Fritters		294
Your choice from a good supermarket		
Melon, Orange, Mango and Mint Chantilly		312

3

Breakfast bonanza

Quick & simple	Muesli Treat and Crumpets	153
Good old cooked	Start The Day Mixed Grill	159
Why not fish?	Plaice and Kiwi Surprise	167
Vegetarian	Mushroom Breakfast	172

Lunch

Good old cooked	Salmon Fillet with Hot Exotic Chunky Sauce	259
Vegetarian	Vegetable Curry	296
Picnic selection	Your choice from Picnic section	196
Snack of the day	Your choice from Snacks and Starters section	176

Main meal

Starter	Borscht and Yoghurt	181
Dish of the day – meat	Steak Diane Exotique	219
Dish of the day – fish	Starfruit Salmon Salad	271
Dish of the day – vegetarian	Exotic Leeks	307
Frozen ready meal	Your choice from a good supermarket	
Dessert	Cranberry Ice Cream	312

4

Breakfast bonanza

Highland Variation		153
Bacon and Eggs		161
Tuna Casserole Exotique		169
Egg and Exotic Hot Fruit		174

Lunch

Original Duck à l'Orange		209
Kiwi, Mango and Mushroom Treat		304
Your choice from Picnic section		196
Your choice from Snacks and Starters section		176

Main meal

Exotic Pears and Mint		190
Chicken Exotique and Dried Venison		210
Exotic Salmon and Plaice		258
Bulghar Wheat Exotique		295
Your choice from a good supermarket		
Mango and Peach Brulée		316

5

Grapefruit Surprise	156
Thinner & Richer Kebabs	159
Smoked Haddock	168
Banana, Date, Kiwi and Mango	175

Salmon for a King	267
Courgette Exotique	286
Your choice from Picnic section	196
Your choice from Snacks and Starters section	176

Carrot Soup	180

North American Cous cous	226
Plaice, Leek and Lime	274
Kiwi, Mango and Lychee Beans	292
Your choice from a good supermarket	

Ice Cream Grand Marnier	314

Breakfast bonanza
Quick & simple
Good old cooked
Why not fish?
Vegetarian

Lunch
Good old cooked
Vegetarian
Picnic selection
Snack of the day

Main meal
Starter

Dish of the day – meat
Dish of the day – fish
Dish of the day – vegetarian
Frozen ready meal

Dessert

6

Choose your own Light Breakfast	155
Chicken Liver Exotique	158
Fish with Berries	168
Lemon and Mango Borscht	171

Left-over Turkey	250
Budgie Millet Exotique	294
Your choice from Picnic section	196
Your choice from Snacks and Starters section	176

Devilled Sardines	187

Exotique Venison Stew	211
Devilled Lobster	274
Wok Quorn	302
Your choice from a good supermarket	

Melon and Berries	315

7

Continental Breakfast	154
Mango and Pan Fried Calves Liver	163
Kipper and Date	166
Humpty Dumpty	175

Prawn Exotique	275
Coconut Vegetables	299
Your choice from Picnic section	196
Your choice from Snacks and Starters section	176

Stir Fry Vegetables and Chilli	195

Exotic Shepherd's Pie	221
Orange Sole	268
Quorn with Exotic Chunky Sauce	298
Your choice from a good supermarket	

Slimmer Fruit Ice Cream	318

Breakfast bonanza
Quick & simple
Good old cooked
Why not fish?
Vegetarian

Lunch
Good old cooked
Vegetarian
Picnic selection
Snack of the day

Main meal
Starter

Dish of the day – meat
Dish of the day – fish
Dish of the day – vegetarian
Frozen ready meal

Dessert

June

8

Breakfast bonanza

Quick & simple	Light Tabbouleh Breakfast	154
Good old cooked	Bagel, Egg and Dried Venison or Bacon	161
Why not fish?	Sole and Kiwi	169
Vegetarian	Quick Blend with Simple or Exotic Fruits	174

Lunch

Good old cooked	Citrus Chicken	221
Vegetarian	Baby Parsnips, Breadcrumbs and Corn	302
Picnic selection	Your choice from Picnic section	196
Snack of the day	Your choice from Snacks and Starters section	176

Main meal

Starter	Gefulte Fish	183
Dish of the day – meat	Chicken Pesto	230
Dish of the day – fish	Tuna and Egg Salad Exotique	267
Dish of the day – vegetarian	Aubergine Exotique au gratin	288
Frozen ready meal	Your choice from a good supermarket	
Dessert	Pears Grand Marnier	309

9

Breakfast bonanza

Authentic New York Bagel	156
Bacon and Kiwi Treat	162
Gefulte Fish	166
Hot Fruit Salad	172

Lunch

Tuna Special	262
Vegetarian Quorn Chilli Stir Fry	295
Your choice from Picnic section	196
Your choice from Snacks and Starters section	176

Main meal

Green Soup	182
Exotique Pintade Rotir (Guinea Fowl)	205
Smoked Rainbow Trout with Chunky Sauce	257
Peas Exotique	293
Your choice from a good supermarket	
Fruit Flan	317

10

Breakfast bonanza

Quick & simple	English Light	155
Good old cooked	Start The Day Mixed Grill	159
Why not fish?	Kipper and Mango Surprise	164
Vegetarian	Cherry Tomato, Pineapple and Mango Salad	171

Lunch

Good old cooked	Exotique Turkey and Almonds	232
Vegetarian	Sweet and Sour Amaranth Chinese Lettuce	306
Picnic selection	Your choice from Picnic section	196
Snack of the day	Your choice from Snacks and Starters section	176

Main meal

Starter	Tuna Pâté	182
Dish of the day – meat	Tzimmas with Beef, Mango and Prunes	218
Dish of the day – fish	Lobster Thermidor	272
Dish of the day – vegetarian	Savoury Quorn Puffs	290
Frozen ready meal	Your choice from a good supermarket	
Dessert	Banana Split	325

11

Breakfast bonanza

Exotique Treat Multiple Choice	158
Venison Supreme	162
Plaice and Kiwi Surprise	167
Starfruit, Potato and Mushroom	170

Lunch

Quick Salmon Steak for One	269
Mixed Exotic Salad and Yoghurt Dressing	300
Your choice from Picnic section	196
Your choice from Snacks and Starters section	176

Main meal

Lemon and Mango Borscht	184
Exotique Venison Casserole	233
Prawn and Mint Dip	272
Aubergine Treat	285
Your choice from a good supermarket	
Exotic Caramel Custard	325

12

Highland Variation	153
Omelette Exotique of choice	164
Red Salmon Omelette	167
Egg and Exotic Hot Fruit	174

Beef and Lamb Kebabs	201
Rice Exotique	299
Your choice from Picnic section	196
Your choice from Snacks and Starters section	176

Starfruit, Potato and Mushroom	189

Mango Cholent	210
Prawn and Exotic Salad	256
Greek Dip Exotique	289
Your choice from a good supermarket	

Exotique Banana Dessert	319

13

Grapefruit Surprise	156
Thinner & Richer Kebabs	159
Fish with Berries	168
Banana, Date, Kiwi and Mango	175

Fish Soup with Sweetcorn and Lychees	255
Coconut Rice	301
Your choice from Picnic section	196
Your choice from Snacks and Starters section	176

Melon with Dried Venison or Parma Ham	177

Oriental Wok Stir Fry	217
Scallop Seviche	253
Vegetarian Quorn Chilli Stir Fry	295
Your choice from a good supermarket	

Blackberry, Lychee and Cape Gooseberry	323

Breakfast bonanza
Quick & simple
Good old cooked
Why not fish?
Vegetarian

Lunch
Good old cooked
Vegetarian
Picnic selection
Snack of the day

Main meal
Starter

Dish of the day – meat
Dish of the day – fish
Dish of the day – vegetarian
Frozen ready meal

Dessert

93

14

Muesli Treat and Crumpets	153
Bacon and Eggs	161
Tuna Casserole Exotique	169
Mushroom Breakfast	172

Aubergine Exotique au gratin	288
Cranberry Rice Salad	303
Your choice from Picnic section	196
Your choice from Snacks and Starters section	176

Sweet and Sour Amaranth Chinese Lettuce	186

Melon with Dried Wild Venison or Parma Ham	214
Plaice-a-Leekie	278
Subtle Kebabs	292
Your choice from a good supermarket	

Banana Bake Exotique	323

15

Light Tabbouleh Breakfast	154
Chicken Liver Exotique	158
Smoked Haddock	168
Quick Blend with Simple or Exotic Fruits	174

Red Salmon Omelette	279
Crunchy, Kutchie-Fyky	293
Your choice from Picnic section	196
Your choice from Snacks and Starters section	176

Coconut and Beef Satay or Chicken Satay	195

Slimmers' Lasagne à la Thinner & Richer	237
Pepper, Anchovy and Tomato	269
Vegetarian Curry with Lychees	289
Your choice from a good supermarket	

Baked Fruit	318

Breakfast bonanza
Quick & simple
Good old cooked
Why not fish?
Vegetarian

Lunch
Good old cooked
Vegetarian
Picnic selection
Snack of the day

Main meal
Starter

Dish of the day – meat
Dish of the day – fish
Dish of the day – vegetarian
Frozen ready meal

Dessert

16

Choose your own Light Breakfast	155
Bagel, Egg and Dried Venison or Bacon	161
Gefulte Fish	166
Lemon and Mango Borscht	171

Chicken Curry with Coconut Milk	237
Aubergine au Fromage Frais	285
Your choice from Picnic section	196
Your choice from Snacks and Starters section	176

Exotic Sardine Pâté	178

Chicken, Apricot and Asparagus	249
Plaice and Prawn Creole	282
Mushroom Flan	287
Your choice from a good supermarket	

Strawberry (or any other fruits) Mousse	320

17

Continental Breakfast	154
Start The Day Mixed Grill	159
Kipper and Date	166
Humpty Dumpty	175

Salmon for a King in Pitta Bread	279
Dressed Seasonal Salad	301
Your choice from Picnic section	196
Your choice from Snacks and Starters section	176

Exotic Toast	191

Hot Meat or Poultry with Exotic Chunky Sauce	205
Marinated Red Mullet Exotique	277
Tofu with Exotic Chunky Sauce	291
Your choice from a good supermarket	

Rambutans and Pineapple Chantilly	310

June

Breakfast bonanza
Quick & simple
Good old cooked
Why not fish?
Vegetarian

Lunch
Good old cooked
Vegetarian
Picnic selection
Snack of the day

Main meal
Starter

Dish of the day – meat
Dish of the day – fish
Dish of the day – vegetarian
Frozen ready meal

Dessert

18

Exotique Treat Multiple Choice	158
Mango and Pan Fried Calves Liver	163
Sole and Kiwi	169
Cherry Tomato, Pineapple and Mango Salad	171

Exotique Chicken Satay	215
Aubergine Exotique	286
Your choice from Picnic section	196
Your choice from Snacks and Starters section	176

Chicken Pâté	183

Brandy Fillet Steak, Kiwi Garnish	216
Avocado Salmon	258
Savoury Quorn Puffs	290
Your choice from a good supermarket	

Banana Chocolate Treat with Mangoes	316

19

Highland Variation	153
Bacon and Kiwi Treat	162
Kipper and Mango Surprise	164
Hot Fruit Salad	172

Fish Soup à la Thinner & Richer	273
Cherry Tomato, Pineapple and Mango Salad	300
Your choice from Picnic section	196
Your choice from Snacks and Starters section	176

Cauliflower Soup	193

Veal Goulash with Lychees	229
Tuna Special	262
Budgie Millet Exotique	294
Your choice from a good supermarket	

Super Low Microwaveable Pears	313

Breakfast bonanza
Quick & simple
Good old cooked
Why not fish?
Vegetarian

Lunch
Good old cooked
Vegetarian
Picnic selection
Snack of the day

Main meal
Starter

Dish of the day – meat
Dish of the day – fish
Dish of the day – vegetarian
Frozen ready meal

Dessert

20

Breakfast bonanza

Quick & simple	Authentic New York Bagel	156
Good old cooked	Thinner & Richer Kebabs	159
Why not fish?	Red Salmon Omelette	167
Vegetarian	Starfruit, Potato and Mushroom	170

Lunch

Good old cooked	Chicken with Red and Green Peppers	244
Vegetarian	Coconut Vegetables	299
Picnic selection	Your choice from Picnic section	196
Snack of the day	Your choice from Snacks and Starters section	176

Main meal

Starter	Red Sockeye Salmon Pâté	194
Dish of the day – meat	Exotique Beef Soufflé	227
Dish of the day – fish	White Fish Cous cous	263
Dish of the day – vegetarian	Bulghar Wheat Exotique	295
Frozen ready meal	Your choice from a good supermarket	
Dessert	Kiwango Ice	310

21

Breakfast bonanza

English Light	155
Omelette Exotique of choice	164
Plaice and Kiwi Surprise	167
Mushroom Breakfast	172

Lunch

Smoked Salmon Expanded à la Thinner & Richer	254
Courgette Exotique	286
Your choice from Picnic section	196
Your choice from Snacks and Starters section	176

Main meal

Lemon and Mango Borscht	184
Duckling with Crystallised Flowers and Nettles	203
Poached Whole Salmon with Flowers	283
Cauliflower au gratin	305
Your choice from a good supermarket	
Midsummer Fruits with Flowers	322

22

Breakfast bonanza

Quick & simple	Muesli Treat and Crumpets	153
Good old cooked	Venison Supreme	162
Why not fish?	Tuna Casserole Exotique	169
Vegetarian	Egg and Exotic Hot Fruit	174

Lunch

Good old cooked	Mixed Kebab	242
Vegetarian	Kiwi, Mango and Mushroom Treat	304
Picnic selection	Your choice from Picnic section	196
Snack of the day	Your choice from Snacks and Starters section	176

Main meal

Starter	Pumpkin Soup with Prawns	192
Dish of the day – meat	Pork or Turkey and Apple	206
Dish of the day – fish	Rainbow Trout	264
Dish of the day – vegetarian	Vegetable Curry	296
Frozen ready meal	Your choice from a good supermarket	
Dessert	Quince Thinner & Richer	314

23

Breakfast bonanza

Light Tabbouleh Breakfast	154
Chicken Liver Exotique	158
Fish with Berries	168
Banana, Date, Kiwi and Mango	175

Lunch

Shrimp Pilaf Exotique	273
Exotic Leeks	307
Your choice from Picnic section	196
Your choice from Snacks and Starters section	176

Main meal

Fish Soup	193
North African Cous cous	238
Exotic Mackerel	266
Aubergine Treat	285
Your choice from a good supermarket	
Honey and Apple Crisp	324

24

Choose your own Light Breakfast	155
Bacon and Eggs	161
Smoked Haddock	168
Lemon and Mango Borscht	171

Exotic Liver with Orange	228
Rice Exotique	299
Your choice from Picnic section	196
Your choice from Snacks and Starters section	176

Devilled Potato Salad and Celery	185

Exotique Venison Stew	211
Smoked Salmon Cous cous	270
Quorn with Exotic Chunky Sauce	298
Your choice from a good supermarket	

Peach and Papaya Chantilly	319

25

Grapefruit Surprise	156
Bagel, Egg and Dried Venison or Bacon	161
Kipper and Date	166
Quick Blend with Simple or Exotic Fruits	174

Oriental Wok Stir Fry	260
Mixed Exotic Salad and Yoghurt Dressing	300
Your choice from Picnic section	196
Your choice from Snacks and Starters section	176

Fluffy Herb Pâté	179

Exotique Lamb and Papaya or Mango	216
Potted Herring	266
Kiwi, Mango and Lychee Beans	292
Your choice from a good supermarket	

Fruit Jelly	317

June

Breakfast bonanza
Quick & simple
Good old cooked
Why not fish?
Vegetarian

Lunch
Good old cooked
Vegetarian
Picnic selection
Snack of the day

Main meal
Starter

Dish of the day – meat
Dish of the day – fish
Dish of the day – vegetarian
Frozen ready meal

Dessert

26

Continental Breakfast	154
Mango and Pan Fried Calves Liver	163
Gefulte Fish	166
Humpty Dumpty	175

Devilled Lamb Steaks	209
Baby Parsnips, Breadcrumbs and Corn	302
Your choice from Picnic section	196
Your choice from Snacks and Starters section	176

Vegetarian Coleslaw	179

Meaty Cous cous	239
Steamed Plaice and Mango	278
Aubergine Exotique au gratin	288
Your choice from a good supermarket	

Pears, Apple and Ginger Hot Chantilly	315

27

Exotique Treat Multiple Choice	158
Start The Day Mixed Grill	159
Kipper and Mango Surprise	164
Hot Fruit Salad	172

Hot Pickled Herring	271
Peas Exotique	293
Your choice from Picnic section	196
Your choice from Snacks and Starters section	176

Chicken and Coconut Soup	189

Veal (or Beef) Roast with Prunes and Rambutans	208
Grapefruit and Red Sockeye Salmon	261
Pumpkin Fritters	294
Your choice from a good supermarket	

Pears in Berry Sauce	309

Breakfast bonanza
Quick & simple
Good old cooked
Why not fish?
Vegetarian

Lunch
Good old cooked
Vegetarian
Picnic selection
Snack of the day

Main meal
Starter

Dish of the day – meat
Dish of the day – fish
Dish of the day – vegetarian
Frozen ready meal

Dessert

28

Breakfast bonanza

Quick & simple	Authentic New York Bagel	156
Good old cooked	Bacon and Kiwi Treat	162
Why not fish?	Sole and Kiwi	169
Vegetarian	Cherry Tomato, Pineapple and Mango Salad	171

Lunch

Good old cooked	Schnitzel Exotic	207
Vegetarian	Chicory, Pineapple, Kiwi and Mushrooms	304
Picnic selection	Your choice from Picnic section	196
Snack of the day	Your choice from Snacks and Starters section	176

Main meal

Starter	Aubergine and Mango Pâté	191
Dish of the day – meat	Poultry – Sweet and Sour	217
Dish of the day – fish	Smoked Trout	261
Dish of the day – vegetarian	Sweet and Sour Amaranth Chinese Lettuce	306
Frozen ready meal	Your choice from a good supermarket	
Dessert	Berry Omelette Exotique	311

29

Highland Variation		153
Thinner & Richer Kebabs		159
Plaice and Kiwi Surprise		167
Mushroom Breakfast		172

Smoked Salmon Expanded à la Thinner & Richer		254
Courgette Exotique		286
Your choice from Picnic section		196
Your choice from Snacks and Starters section		176

Lemon and Mango Borscht		184
Stuffed Cabbage		235
Lobster Salad		253
Cauliflower au gratin		305
Your choice from a good supermarket		
Stuffed Pineapple		311

30

Breakfast bonanza

Quick & simple	Muesli Treat and Crumpets	153
Good old cooked	Venison Supreme	162
Why not fish?	Red Salmon Omelette	167
Vegetarian	Starfruit, Potato and Mushroom	170

Lunch

Good old cooked	Kiwi, Mango and Mushroom Soup	206
Vegetarian	Coconut Rice	301
Picnic selection	Your choice from Picnic section	196
Snack of the day	Your choice from Snacks and Starters section	176

Main meal

Starter	Tuna Pâté	182
Dish of the day – meat	Rosemary Lamb	204
Dish of the day – fish	Gefulte Fish	256
Dish of the day – vegetarian	Vegetarian Lasagne	303
Frozen ready meal	Your choice from a good supermarket	
Dessert	Melon, Orange, Mango and Mint Chantilly	312

1

English Light	155
Bacon and Eggs	161
Kipper and Date	166
Egg and Exotic Hot Fruit	174

Quick Hot Prawns	262
Wok Quorn	302
Your choice from Picnic section	196
Your choice from Snacks and Starters section	176

| Starfruit, Potato and Mushroom | 189 |

Cider Chicken Calvados	220
Plaice, Leek and Lime	274
Cranberry Rice Salad	303
Your choice from a good supermarket	

| Pears Grand Marnier | 309 |

2

Grapefruit Surprise	156
Bagel, Egg and Dried Venison or Bacon	161
Fish with Berries	168
Lemon and Mango Borscht	171

Chicken and Peppers	233
Greek Dip Exotique	289
Your choice from Picnic section	196
Your choice from Snacks and Starters section	176

| Gefulte Fish | 183 |

Exotique Ham and Mango	235
Sole in Envelopes	254
Aubergine Treat	285
Your choice from a good supermarket	

| Exotic Caramel Custard | 325 |

Breakfast bonanza
Quick & simple
Good old cooked
Why not fish?
Vegetarian

Lunch
Good old cooked
Vegetarian
Picnic selection
Snack of the day

Main meal
Starter

Dish of the day – meat
Dish of the day – fish
Dish of the day – vegetarian
Frozen ready meal

Dessert

3

Choose your own Light Breakfast	155
Chicken Liver Exotique	158
Smoked Haddock	168
Banana, Date, Kiwi and Mango	175

Exotic Salmon and Plaice	258
Sesame Seed and Caraway Salad	307
Your choice from Picnic section	196
Your choice from Snacks and Starters section	176

| Dandelion Summer Starter | 177 |

Chicken and Aubergine	232
Pepper, Anchovy and Tomato	269
Budgie Millet Exotique	294
Your choice from a good supermarket	

| Cranberry Ice Cream | 312 |

4 Independence Day Special

Exotique Treat Multiple Choice	158
Mango and Pan Fried Calves Liver	163
Kipper and Mango Surprise	164
Banana, Date, Kiwi and Mango	175

Duck Breast Thinner & Richer	244
Sweet and Sour Amaranth Chinese Lettuce	306
Your choice from Picnic section	196
Your choice from Snacks and Starters section	176

| Watercress, Lychee and Cucumber Soup | 181 |

Turkey and Lychees	249
Lobster Thermidor	272
Subtle Kebabs	292
Your choice from a good supermarket	

| Sweet Dessert Flag | 326 |

Breakfast bonanza
Quick & simple
Good old cooked
Why not fish?
Vegetarian

Lunch
Good old cooked
Vegetarian
Picnic selection
Snack of the day

Main meal
Starter

Dish of the day – meat
Dish of the day – fish
Dish of the day – vegetarian
Frozen ready meal

Dessert

5

Breakfast bonanza

Quick & simple	Authentic New York Bagel	156
Good old cooked	Bacon and Kiwi Treat	162
Why not fish?	Sole and Kiwi	169
Vegetarian	Hot Fruit Salad	172

Lunch

Good old cooked	Rosemary Lamb	204
Vegetarian	Tofu with Exotic Chunky Sauce	291
Picnic selection	Your choice from Picnic section	196
Snack of the day	Your choice from Snacks and Starters section	176

Main meal

Starter	Melon, Kiwi and Grape Surprise	180
Dish of the day – meat	Chicken Exotique and Dried Venison	210
Dish of the day – fish	Tomato and Tuna Salad Exotique	257
Dish of the day – vegetarian	Savoury Quorn Puffs	290
Frozen ready meal	Your choice from a good supermarket	
Dessert	Mango and Lychee Mousse	313

6

	Continental Breakfast	154
	Start The Day Mixed Grill	159
	Gefulte Fish	166
	Cherry Tomato, Pineapple and Mango Salad	171

	Sardine Exotic Surprise	277
	Mixed Exotic Salad and Yoghurt Dressing	300
	Your choice from Picnic section	196
	Your choice from Snacks and Starters section	176

	Exotic Pears and Mint	190
	Tzimmas with Beef, Mango and Prunes	218
	White Fish Cous cous	263
	Coconut Rice	301
	Your choice from a good supermarket	
	Melon and Berries	315

7

Breakfast bonanza

Quick & simple	Light Tabbouleh Breakfast	154
Good old cooked	Omelette Exotique of choice	164
Why not fish?	Tuna Casserole Exotique	169
Vegetarian	Humpty Dumpty	175

Lunch

Good old cooked	Left-over Turkey	250
Vegetarian	Coconut Vegetables	299
Picnic selection	Your choice from Picnic section	196
Snack of the day	Your choice from Snacks and Starters section	176

Main meal

Starter	Pea Soup Special	192
Dish of the day – meat	Wild Venison and Mango Exotique	228
Dish of the day – fish	Gefulte Fish	256
Dish of the day – vegetarian	Exotic Leeks	307
Frozen ready meal	Your choice from a good supermarket	
Dessert	Mango and Peach Brulée	316

8

	Muesli Treat and Crumpets	153
	Bacon and Eggs	161
	Kipper and Date	166
	Egg and Exotic Hot Fruit	174

	Exotic Kedgeree	260
	Rice Exotique	299
	Your choice from Picnic section	196
	Your choice from Snacks and Starters section	176

	Stir Fry Vegetables and Chilli	195
	Exotic Shepherd's Pie	221
	Avocado Salmon	258
	Vegetarian Lasagne	303
	Your choice from a good supermarket	
	Guava Ice Cream	324

9

Highland Variation	153
Venison Supreme	162
Red Salmon Omelette	167
Mushroom Breakfast	172

Stir Fried Liver	207
Vegetarian Quorn Chilli Stir Fry	295
Your choice from Picnic section	196
Your choice from Snacks and Starters section	176

Exotic Welsh Rarebit	187

Cauliflower au gratin	223
Salmon à la Greque	268
Courgette Exotique	286
Your choice from a good supermarket	

Banana Split	325

10

Choose your own Light Breakfast	155
Thinner & Richer Kebabs	159
Plaice and Kiwi Surprise	167
Starfruit, Potato and Mushroom	170

Red Sockeye Salmon Stir Fry	259
Dressed Seasonal Salad	301
Your choice from Picnic section	196
Your choice from Snacks and Starters section	176

Grapefruit and Tomato Soup	185

Original Duck à l'Orange	209
Salmon Fillet with Hot Exotic Chunky Sauce	259
Cherry Tomato, Pineapple and Mango Salad	300
Your choice from a good supermarket	

Fruit Flan	317

Breakfast bonanza
Quick & simple
Good old cooked
Why not fish?
Vegetarian

Lunch
Good old cooked
Vegetarian
Picnic selection
Snack of the day

Main meal
Starter

Dish of the day – meat
Dish of the day – fish
Dish of the day – vegetarian
Frozen ready meal

Dessert

11

Grapefruit Surprise	156
Chicken Liver Exotique	158
Smoked Haddock	168
Banana, Date, Kiwi and Mango	175

Exotique Turkey and Almonds	232
Cherry Tomato, Pineapple and Mango Salad	300
Your choice from Picnic section	196
Your choice from Snacks and Starters section	176

Leek Soup	184

Indonesian Pork Satay	220
Smoked Salmon Cous cous	270
Vegetarian Quorn Chilli Stir Fry	295
Your choice from a good supermarket	

Blackberry, Lychee and Cape Gooseberry	323

12

English Light	155
Mango and Pan Fried Calves Liver	163
Fish with Berries	168
Lemon and Mango Borscht	171

Salmon Fillet with Hot Exotic Chunky Sauce	259
Kiwi, Mango and Mushroom Treat	304
Your choice from Picnic section	196
Your choice from Snacks and Starters section	176

Devilled Sardines	187

North American Cous cous	226
Prawn Exotique	275
Aubergine Exotique	286
Your choice from a good supermarket	

Slimmer Fruit Ice Cream	318

Breakfast bonanza
Quick & simple
Good old cooked
Why not fish?
Vegetarian

Lunch
Good old cooked
Vegetarian
Picnic selection
Snack of the day

Main meal
Starter

Dish of the day – meat
Dish of the day – fish
Dish of the day – vegetarian
Frozen ready meal

Dessert

13

Breakfast bonanza

Quick & simple	Continental Breakfast	154
Good old cooked	Bagel, Egg and Dried Venison or Bacon	161
Why not fish?	Gefulte Fish	166
Vegetarian	Quick Blend with Simple or Exotic Fruits	174

Lunch

Good old cooked	Tandoori Meat	245
Vegetarian	Mixed Exotic Salad and Yoghurt Dressing	300
Picnic selection	Your choice from Picnic section	196
Snack of the day	Your choice from Snacks and Starters section	176

Main meal

Starter	Carrot Soup	180
Dish of the day – meat	Cold Meat Salad with Exotic Chunky Sauce	236
Dish of the day – fish	Devilled Lobster	274
Dish of the day – vegetarian	Cranberry Rice Salad	303
Frozen ready meal	Your choice from a good supermarket	
Dessert	Exotique Banana Dessert	319

14

Breakfast bonanza

Quick & simple	Exotique Treat Multiple Choice	158
Good old cooked	Omelette Exotique of choice	164
Why not fish?	Kipper and Mango Surprise	164
Vegetarian	Cherry Tomato, Pineapple and Mango Salad	171

Lunch

Good old cooked	Prawn Exotique	275
Vegetarian	Subtle Kebabs	292
Picnic selection	Your choice from Picnic section	196
Snack of the day	Your choice from Snacks and Starters section	176

Main meal

Starter	Tuna Pâté	182
Dish of the day – meat	Beef and Lamb Kebabs	201
Dish of the day – fish	Salmon à la Greque	268
Dish of the day – vegetarian	Pumpkin Fritters	294
Frozen ready meal	Your choice from a good supermarket	
Dessert	Stuffed Pineapple	311

15

Authentic New York Bagel	156
Start The Day Mixed Grill	159
Sole and Kiwi	169
Humpty Dumpty	175

Wok Beef	213
Crunchy, Kutchie-Fyky	293
Your choice from Picnic section	196
Your choice from Snacks and Starters section	176

Coconut and Beef Satay or Chicken Satay	195
Sweet and Sour Pork	248
Rainbow Trout	264
Kiwi, Mango and Lychee Beans	292
Your choice from a good supermarket	
Kiwango Ice	310

16

Highland Variation	153
Bacon and Eggs	161
Kipper and Date	166
Hot Fruit Salad	172

Avocado Salmon	258
Peas Exotique	293
Your choice from Picnic section	196
Your choice from Snacks and Starters section	176

Exotic Toast	191

Lamb and Pawpaw Corsican Style	215
Lobster Thermidor	272
Bulghar Wheat Exotique	295
Your choice from a good supermarket	

Rambutans and Pineapple Chantilly	310

17

Muesli Treat and Crumpets	153
Bacon and Kiwi Treat	162
Red Salmon Omelette	167
Mushroom Breakfast	172

Chicken and Pasta (cold dish)	236
Chicory, Pineapple, Kiwi and Mushrooms	304
Your choice from Picnic section	196
Your choice from Snacks and Starters section	176

Chicken Pâté	183

Steak Diane Exotique	219
Prawn and Mint Dip	272
Vegetarian Curry with Lychees	289
Your choice from a good supermarket	

Pears in Berry Sauce	309

July

Breakfast bonanza
Quick & simple
Good old cooked
Why not fish?
Vegetarian

Lunch
Good old cooked
Vegetarian
Picnic selection
Snack of the day

Main meal
Starter

Dish of the day – meat
Dish of the day – fish
Dish of the day – vegetarian
Frozen ready meal

Dessert

18

Light Tabbouleh Breakfast	154
Thinner & Richer Kebabs	159
Tuna Casserole Exotique	169
Egg and Exotic Hot Fruit	174

Smoked Trout	261
Baby Parsnips, Breadcrumbs and Corn	302
Your choice from Picnic section	196
Your choice from Snacks and Starters section	176

Melon with Dried Venison or Parma Ham	177

Chicken and Aubergine	232
Plaice-a-Leekie	278
Quorn with Exotic Chunky Sauce	298
Your choice from a good supermarket	

Ice Cream Grand Marnier	314

19

Grapefruit Surprise	156
Venison Supreme	162
Smoked Haddock	168
Starfruit, Potato and Mushroom	170

Mango and Pan Fried Calves Liver	204
Wok Quorn	302
Your choice from Picnic section	196
Your choice from Snacks and Starters section	176

Exotic Red Borscht	194

Chinese Chicken Salad with Lychees	250
Orange Sole	268
Aubergine Exotique au gratin	288
Your choice from a good supermarket	

Pears, Apple and Ginger Hot Chantilly	315

Breakfast bonanza
Quick & simple
Good old cooked
Why not fish?
Vegetarian

Lunch
Good old cooked
Vegetarian
Picnic selection
Snack of the day

Main meal
Starter

Dish of the day – meat
Dish of the day – fish
Dish of the day – vegetarian
Frozen ready meal

Dessert

July

104

20

Breakfast bonanza

Quick & simple	English Light	155
Good old cooked	Chicken Liver Exotique	158
Why not fish?	Fish with Berries	168
Vegetarian	Quick Blend with Simple or Exotic Fruits	174

Lunch

Good old cooked	Oriental Wok Stir Fry	260
Vegetarian	Sweet and Sour Amaranth Chinese Lettuce	306
Picnic selection	Your choice from Picnic section	196
Snack of the day	Your choice from Snacks and Starters section	176

Main meal

Starter	Watercress, Lychee and Cucumber Soup	181
Dish of the day – meat	Exotique Pintade Rotir (Guinea Fowl)	205
Dish of the day – fish	Gefulte Fish	256
Dish of the day – vegetarian	Vegetable Curry	296
Frozen ready meal	Your choice from a good supermarket	
Dessert	Quince Thinner & Richer	314

21

Continental Breakfast	154
Bagel, Egg and Dried Venison or Bacon	161
Plaice and Kiwi Surprise	167
Banana, Date, Kiwi and Mango	175

Citrus Chicken	221
Aubergine au Fromage Frais	285
Your choice from Picnic section	196
Your choice from Snacks and Starters section	176

Chopped Herring Chunky Pâté	178
Chopped Liver	214
Smoked Rainbow Trout with Chunky Sauce	257
Mushroom Flan	287
Your choice from a good supermarket	
Strawberry (or any other fruits) Mousse	320

22

Breakfast bonanza

Quick & simple	Choose your own Light Breakfast	155
Good old cooked	Start The Day Mixed Grill	159
Why not fish?	Kipper and Mango Surprise	164
Vegetarian	Lemon and Mango Borscht	171

Lunch

Good old cooked	Tuna Special	262
Vegetarian	Tofu with Exotic Chunky Sauce	291
Picnic selection	Your choice from Picnic section	196
Snack of the day	Your choice from Snacks and Starters section	176

Main meal

Starter	Starfruit, Potato and Mushroom	189
Dish of the day – meat	Chicken Pesto	230
Dish of the day – fish	Rainbow Trout	264
Dish of the day – vegetarian	Savoury Quorn Puffs	290
Frozen ready meal	Your choice from a good supermarket	
Dessert	Fruit Jelly	317

23

Authentic New York Bagel	156
Omelette Exotique of choice	164
Gefulte Fish	166
Humpty Dumpty	175

Chicken in Sherry	251
Budgie Millet Exotique	294
Your choice from Picnic section	196
Your choice from Snacks and Starters section	176

Green Soup	182
Mango Cholent	210
Salmon for a King	267
Aubergine Treat	285
Your choice from a good supermarket	
Honey and Apple Crisp	324

24

Exotique Treat Multiple Choice	158
Mango and Pan Fried Calves Liver	163
Sole and Kiwi	169
Hot Fruit Salad	172

Red Sockeye Salmon Stir Fry	259
Sesame Seed and Caraway Salad	307
Your choice from Picnic section	196
Your choice from Snacks and Starters section	176

Exotic Sardine Pâté	178

Exotique Venison Casserole	233
Prawn Exotique	275
Vegetarian Lasagne	303
Your choice from a good supermarket	

Baked Fruit	318

25

Muesli Treat and Crumpets	153
Bacon and Kiwi Treat	162
Tuna Casserole Exotique	169
Cherry Tomato, Pineapple and Mango Salad	171

Kiwi, Mango and Mushroom Soup	206
Coconut Rice	301
Your choice from Picnic section	196
Your choice from Snacks and Starters section	176

Gefulte Fish	183

Champagne Quail	222
Whole Rainbow Trout à l'Orange	264
Pumpkin Fritters	294
Your choice from a good supermarket	

Banana Bake Exotique	323

July

Breakfast bonanza
Quick & simple
Good old cooked
Why not fish?
Vegetarian

Lunch
Good old cooked
Vegetarian
Picnic selection
Snack of the day

Main meal
Starter

Dish of the day – meat
Dish of the day – fish
Dish of the day – vegetarian
Frozen ready meal

Dessert

26

Light Tabbouleh Breakfast	154
Thinner & Richer Kebabs	159
Kipper and Date	166
Egg and Exotic Hot Fruit	174

Exotic Kedgeree	260
Cranberry Rice Salad	303
Your choice from Picnic section	196
Your choice from Snacks and Starters section	176

Exotic Welsh Rarebit	187

Exotic Turkey Escalopes	242
Steamed Plaice and Mango	278
Cauliflower au gratin	305
Your choice from a good supermarket	

Peach and Papaya Chantilly	319

27

Highland Variation	153
Bacon and Eggs	161
Red Salmon Omelette	167
Mushroom Breakfast	172

Schnitzel Exotic	207
Greek Dip Exotique	289
Your choice from Picnic section	196
Your choice from Snacks and Starters section	176

Chicken and Coconut Soup	189

Traditional Shepherd's Pie	202
Quick Hot Prawns	262
Kiwi, Mango and Mushroom Treat	304
Your choice from a good supermarket	

Berry Omelette Exotique	311

Breakfast bonanza
Quick & simple
Good old cooked
Why not fish?
Vegetarian

Lunch
Good old cooked
Vegetarian
Picnic selection
Snack of the day

Main meal
Starter

Dish of the day – meat
Dish of the day – fish
Dish of the day – vegetarian
Frozen ready meal

Dessert

28

Breakfast bonanza

Quick & simple	Grapefruit Surprise	156
Good old cooked	Venison Supreme	162
Why not fish?	Fish with Berries	168
Vegetarian	Starfruit, Potato and Mushroom	170

Lunch

Good old cooked	Hot Pickled Herring	271
Vegetarian	Dressed Seasonal Salad	301
Picnic selection	Your choice from Picnic section	196
Snack of the day	Your choice from Snacks and Starters section	176

Main meal

Starter	Borscht and Yoghurt	181
Dish of the day – meat	Chicken Pâté	248
Dish of the day – fish	Grapefruit and Red Sockeye Salmon	261
Dish of the day – vegetarian	Chicory, Pineapple, Kiwi and Mushrooms	304
Frozen ready meal	Your choice from a good supermarket	
Dessert	Mango and Lychee Mousse	313

29

English Light	155
Chicken Liver Exotique	158
Smoked Haddock	168
Quick Blend with Simple or Exotic Fruits	174

Devilled Lamb Steaks	209
Mixed Exotic Salad and Yoghurt Dressing	300
Your choice from Picnic section	196
Your choice from Snacks and Starters section	176

Vegetarian Coleslaw	179
Mushroom Flan (contains meat)	231
Pepper, Anchovy and Tomato	269
Exotic Leeks	307
Your choice from a good supermarket	
Melon, Orange, Mango and Mint Chantilly	312

30

Breakfast bonanza

Quick & simple	Continental Breakfast	154
Good old cooked	Start The Day Mixed Grill	159
Why not fish?	Gefulte Fish	166
Vegetarian	Humpty Dumpty	175

Lunch

Good old cooked	Wild Venison with Ratatouille	225
Vegetarian	Subtle Kebabs	292
Picnic selection	Your choice from Picnic section	196
Snack of the day	Your choice from Snacks and Starters section	176

Main meal

Starter	Sweet and Sour Amaranth Chinese Lettuce	186
Dish of the day – meat	Exotique Ham and Mango	235
Dish of the day – fish	Starfruit Salmon Salad	271
Dish of the day – vegetarian	Kiwi, Mango and Lychee Beans	292
Frozen ready meal	Your choice from a good supermarket	
Dessert	Cranberry Ice Cream	312

31

Choose your own Light Breakfast	155
Omelette Exotique of choice	164
Kipper and Mango Surprise	164
Lemon and Mango Borscht	171

Quick Salmon Steak for One	269
Sesame Seed and Caraway Salad	307
Your choice from Picnic section	196
Your choice from Snacks and Starters section	176

Carrot Soup	180
Ginger Turkey	240
Potted Herring	266
Coconut Rice	301
Your choice from a good supermarket	
Super Low Microwaveable Pears	313

August

1

Breakfast bonanza
Quick & simple	Authentic New York Bagel	156
Good old cooked	Bagel, Egg and Dried Venison or Bacon	161
Why not fish?	Plaice and Kiwi Surprise	167
Vegetarian	Banana, Date, Kiwi and Mango	175

Lunch
Good old cooked	Chicken and Peppers	233
Vegetarian	Peas Exotique	293
Picnic selection	Your choice from Picnic section	196
Snack of the day	Your choice from Snacks and Starters section	176

Main meal
Starter	Melon, Kiwi and Grape Surprise	180
Dish of the day – meat	Duck Breast Thinner & Richer	244
Dish of the day – fish	Prawn and Exotic Salad	256
Dish of the day – vegetarian	Wok Quorn	302
Frozen ready meal	Your choice from a good supermarket	
Dessert	Banana Chocolate Treat with Mangoes	316

2

Breakfast bonanza
Muesli Treat and Crumpets	153
Bacon and Kiwi Treat	162
Tuna Casserole Exotique	169
Cherry Tomato, Pineapple and Mango Salad	171

Lunch
Smoked Salmon Expanded à la Thinner & Richer	254
Coconut Vegetables	299
Your choice from Picnic section	196
Your choice from Snacks and Starters section	176

Main meal
Chicken and Coconut Soup	189
Cider Chicken Calvados	220
Plaice and Prawn Creole	282
Aubergine Exotique au gratin	288
Your choice from a good supermarket	
Exotic Caramel Custard	325

3

Breakfast bonanza
Quick & simple	Exotique Treat Multiple Choice	158
Good old cooked	Thinner & Richer Kebabs	159
Why not fish?	Kipper and Date	166
Vegetarian	Hot Fruit Salad	172

Lunch
Good old cooked	Coconut Beef Satay or Chicken Satay	245
Vegetarian	Rice Exotique	299
Picnic selection	Your choice from Picnic section	196
Snack of the day	Your choice from Snacks and Starters section	176

Main meal
Starter	Fluffy Herb Pâté	179
Dish of the day – meat	North American Cous cous	226
Dish of the day – fish	Marinated Red Mullet Exotique	277
Dish of the day – vegetarian	Vegetarian Lasagne	303
Frozen ready meal	Your choice from a good supermarket	
Dessert	Pears Grand Marnier	309

4

Breakfast bonanza
Light Tabbouleh Breakfast	154
Mango and Pan Fried Calves Liver	163
Sole and Kiwi	169
Egg and Exotic Hot Fruit	174

Lunch
Exotic Salmon and Plaice	258
Baby Parsnips, Breadcrumbs and Corn	302
Your choice from Picnic section	196
Your choice from Snacks and Starters section	176

Main meal
Devilled Potato Salad and Celery	185
Veal Goulash with Lychees	229
Salmon and Rice	255
Vegetarian Quorn Chilli Stir Fry	295
Your choice from a good supermarket	
Rambutans and Pineapple Chantilly	310

108

5

English Light	155
Bacon and Eggs	161
Fish with Berries	168
Starfruit, Potato and Mushroom	170

Melon with Dried Wild Venison or Parma Ham	214
Exotic Leeks	307
Your choice from Picnic section	196
Your choice from Snacks and Starters section	176

Fish Soup	193

Exotique Beef Soufflé	227
Tuna and Egg Salad Exotique	267
Cherry Tomato, Pineapple and Mango Salad	300
Your choice from a good supermarket	

Mango and Peach Brulée	316

6

Grapefruit Surprise	156
Venison Supreme	162
Red Salmon Omelette	167
Quick Blend with Simple or Exotic Fruits	174

Tuna Special	262
Sweet and Sour Amaranth Chinese Lettuce	306
Your choice from Picnic section	196
Your choice from Snacks and Starters section	176

Dandelion Summer Starter	177

Exotique Lamb and Papaya or Mango	216
Plaice, Leek and Lime	274
Cauliflower au gratin	305
Your choice from a good supermarket	

Guava Ice Cream	324

109

Breakfast bonanza
Quick & simple
Good old cooked
Why not fish?
Vegetarian

Lunch
Good old cooked
Vegetarian
Picnic selection
Snack of the day

Main meal
Starter

Dish of the day – meat
Dish of the day – fish
Dish of the day – vegetarian
Frozen ready meal

Dessert

7

Highland Variation	153
Chicken Liver Exotique	158
Smoked Haddock	168
Mushroom Breakfast	172

Chicken with Red and Green Peppers	244
Courgette Exotique	286
Your choice from Picnic section	196
Your choice from Snacks and Starters section	176

Lemon and Mango Borscht	184

Exotique Venison Stew	211
Devilled Lobster	274
Vegetable Curry	296
Your choice from a good supermarket	

Pears in Berry Sauce	309

8

Choose your own Light Breakfast	155
Omelette Exotique of choice	164
Plaice and Kiwi Surprise	167
Lemon and Mango Borscht	171

Scallop Seviche	253
Cranberry Rice Salad	303
Your choice from Picnic section	196
Your choice from Snacks and Starters section	176

Red Sockeye Salmon Pâté	194

Veal (or Beef) Roast with Prunes and Rambutans	208
Prawn and Mint Dip	272
Aubergine Exotique	286
Your choice from a good supermarket	

Stuffed Pineapple	311

Breakfast bonanza
Quick & simple
Good old cooked
Why not fish?
Vegetarian

Lunch
Good old cooked
Vegetarian
Picnic selection
Snack of the day

Main meal
Starter

Dish of the day – meat
Dish of the day – fish
Dish of the day – vegetarian
Frozen ready meal

Dessert

9

Breakfast bonanza

Quick & simple	Muesli Treat and Crumpets	153
Good old cooked	Bacon and Kiwi Treat	162
Why not fish?	Kipper and Mango Surprise	164
Vegetarian	Cherry Tomato, Pineapple and Mango Salad	171

Lunch

Good old cooked	Mixed Kebab	242
Vegetarian	Dressed Seasonal Salad	301
Picnic selection	Your choice from Picnic section	196
Snack of the day	Your choice from Snacks and Starters section	176

Main meal

Starter	Sweet and Sour Amaranth Chinese Lettuce	186
Dish of the day – meat	Exotic Shepherd's Pie	221
Dish of the day – fish	Red Salmon Omelette	279
Dish of the day – vegetarian	Budgie Millet Exotique	294
Frozen ready meal	Your choice from a good supermarket	
Dessert	Fruit Jelly	317

10

Breakfast bonanza

Authentic New York Bagel	156
Bagel, Egg and Dried Venison or Bacon	161
Tuna Casserole Exotique	169
Humpty Dumpty	175

Lunch

Fish Soup à la Thinner & Richer	273
Kiwi, Mango and Mushroom Treat	304
Your choice from Picnic section	196
Your choice from Snacks and Starters section	176

Main meal

Chopped Herring Chunky Pâté	178
Chicken Curry with Coconut Milk	237
Plaice-a-Leekie	278
Quorn with Exotic Chunky Sauce	298
Your choice from a good supermarket	
Strawberry (or any other fruits) Mousse	320

11

Breakfast bonanza

Quick & simple	Continental Breakfast	154
Good old cooked	Start The Day Mixed Grill	159
Why not fish?	Gefulte Fish	166
Vegetarian	Banana, Date, Kiwi and Mango	175

Lunch

Good old cooked	Chicken Pâté	248
Vegetarian	Greek Dip Exotique	289
Picnic selection	Your choice from Picnic section	196
Snack of the day	Your choice from Snacks and Starters section	176

Main meal

Starter	Cauliflower Soup	193
Dish of the day – meat	North African Cous cous	238
Dish of the day – fish	Salmon Fillet with Hot Exotic Chunky Sauce	259
Dish of the day – vegetarian	Mushroom Flan	287
Frozen ready meal	Your choice from a good supermarket	
Dessert	Peach and Papaya Chantilly	319

110

12

English Light	155
Mango and Pan Fried Calves Liver	163
Sole and Kiwi	169
Egg and Exotic Hot Fruit	174

Red Sockeye Salmon Stir Fry	259
Aubergine au Fromage Frais	285
Your choice from Picnic section	196
Your choice from Snacks and Starters section	176

Aubergine and Mango Pâté	191

Stuffed Cabbage	235
Smoked Salmon Cous cous	270
Bulghar Wheat Exotique	295
Your choice from a good supermarket	

Banana Bake Exotique	323

13

Exotique Treat Multiple Choice	158
Bacon and Eggs	161
Fish with Berries	168
Starfruit, Potato and Mushroom	170

Exotique Chicken Satay	215
Tofu with Exotic Chunky Sauce	291
Your choice from Picnic section	196
Your choice from Snacks and Starters section	176

Pumpkin Soup with Prawns	192

Chicken, Apricot and Asparagus	249
Exotic Mackerel	266
Chicory, Pineapple, Kiwi and Mushrooms	304
Your choice from a good supermarket	

Honey and Apple Crisp	324

August

Breakfast bonanza
Quick & simple
Good old cooked
Why not fish?
Vegetarian

111

Lunch
Good old cooked
Vegetarian
Picnic selection
Snack of the day

Main meal
Starter

Dish of the day – meat
Dish of the day – fish
Dish of the day – vegetarian
Frozen ready meal

Dessert

14

Light Tabbouleh Breakfast	154
Venison Supreme	162
Kipper and Date	166
Hot Fruit Salad	172

Salmon for a King in Pitta Bread	279
Mixed Exotic Salad and Yoghurt Dressing	300
Your choice from Picnic section	196
Your choice from Snacks and Starters section	176

Vegetarian Coleslaw	179

Meaty Cous cous	239
Sole in Envelopes	254
Savoury Quorn Puffs	290
Your choice from a good supermarket	

Kiwango Ice	310

15

Choose your own Light Breakfast	155
Thinner & Richer Kebabs	159
Smoked Haddock	168
Mushroom Breakfast	172

Aubergine Exotique au gratin	243
Crunchy, Kutchie-Fyky	293
Your choice from Picnic section	196
Your choice from Snacks and Starters section	176

Watercress, Lychee and Cucumber Soup	181

Mango Cholent	210
Tomato and Tuna Salad Exotique	257
Vegetarian Curry with Lychees	289
Your choice from a good supermarket	

Quince Thinner & Richer	314

Breakfast bonanza
Quick & simple
Good old cooked
Why not fish?
Vegetarian

Lunch
Good old cooked
Vegetarian
Picnic selection
Snack of the day

Main meal
Starter

Dish of the day – meat
Dish of the day – fish
Dish of the day – vegetarian
Frozen ready meal

Dessert

16

Breakfast bonanza

Quick & simple	Continental Breakfast	154
Good old cooked	Omelette Exotique of choice	164
Why not fish?	Red Salmon Omelette	167
Vegetarian	Quick Blend with Simple or Exotic Fruits	174

Lunch

Good old cooked	Fish Soup with Sweetcorn and Lychees	255
Vegetarian	Cherry Tomato, Pineapple and Mango Salad	300
Picnic selection	Your choice from Picnic section	196
Snack of the day	Your choice from Snacks and Starters section	176

Main meal

Starter	Tuna Pâté	182
Dish of the day – meat	Poultry – Sweet and Sour	217
Dish of the day – fish	Salmon à la Greque	268
Dish of the day – vegetarian	Pumpkin Fritters	294
Frozen ready meal	Your choice from a good supermarket	
Dessert	Exotique Banana Dessert	319

17

Grapefruit Surprise	156
Chicken Liver Exotique	158
Plaice and Kiwi Surprise	167
Lemon and Mango Borscht	171

Cold Meat Salad with Exotic Chunky Sauce	236
Aubergine Exotique	286
Your choice from Picnic section	196
Your choice from Snacks and Starters section	176

Melon with Dried Venison or Parma Ham	177
Cauliflower au gratin	223
Lobster Thermidor	272
Aubergine Treat	285
Your choice from a good supermarket	
Ice Cream Grand Marnier	314

18

Breakfast bonanza

Quick & simple	Continental Breakfast	154
Good old cooked	Start The Day Mixed Grill	159
Why not fish?	Gefulte Fish	166
Vegetarian	Humpty Dumpty	175

Lunch

Good old cooked	Sardine Exotic Surprise	277
Vegetarian	Sesame Seed and Caraway Salad	307
Picnic selection	Your choice from Picnic section	196
Snack of the day	Your choice from Snacks and Starters section	176

Main meal

Starter	Pumpkin Soup with Flowers	190
Dish of the day – meat	Hot Meat or Poultry with Exotic Chunky Sauce	205
Dish of the day – fish	Pepper, Anchovy and Tomato	269
Dish of the day – vegetarian	Courgette Exotique	286
Frozen ready meal	Your choice from a good supermarket	
Dessert	Melon and Berries	315

19

Authentic New York Bagel	156
Bagel, Egg and Dried Venison or Bacon	161
Tuna Casserole Exotique	169
Cherry Tomato, Pineapple and Mango Salad	171

Chicken and Pasta (cold dish)	236
Peas Exotique	293
Your choice from Picnic section	196
Your choice from Snacks and Starters section	176

Starfruit, Potato and Mushroom	189
Brandy Fillet Steak, Kiwi Garnish	216
Gefulte Fish	256
Cauliflower au gratin	305
Your choice from a good supermarket	
Slimmer Fruit Ice Cream	318

August

20

Muesli Treat and Crumpets	153
Bacon and Kiwi Treat	162
Sole and Kiwi	169
Banana, Date, Kiwi and Mango	175

Rainbow Trout	264
Greek Dip Exotique	289
Your choice from Picnic section	196
Your choice from Snacks and Starters section	176

Red Sockeye Salmon Pâté	194

Ginger Turkey	240
Grapefruit and Red Sockeye Salmon	261
Subtle Kebabs	292
Your choice from a good supermarket	

Pears, Apple and Ginger Hot Chantilly	315

21

Light Tabbouleh Breakfast	154
Bacon and Eggs	161
Kipper and Mango Surprise	164
Hot Fruit Salad	172

Oriental Wok Stir Fry	217
Sweet and Sour Amaranth Chinese Lettuce	306
Your choice from Picnic section	196
Your choice from Snacks and Starters section	176

Coconut and Beef Satay or Chicken Satay	195

Mushroom Flan (contains meat)	231
White Fish Cous cous	263
Exotic Leeks	307
Your choice from a good supermarket	

Blackberry, Lychee and Cape Gooseberry	323

Breakfast bonanza
Quick & simple
Good old cooked
Why not fish?
Vegetarian

Lunch
Good old cooked
Vegetarian
Picnic selection
Snack of the day

Main meal
Starter

Dish of the day – meat
Dish of the day – fish
Dish of the day – vegetarian
Frozen ready meal

Dessert

22

Choose your own Light Breakfast	155
Venison Supreme	162
Fish with Berries	168
Egg and Exotic Hot Fruit	174

Oriental Wok Stir Fry	260
Aubergine Exotique au gratin	288
Your choice from Picnic section	196
Your choice from Snacks and Starters section	176

Grapefruit and Tomato Soup	185

Pork or Turkey and Apple	206
Quick Salmon Steak for One	269
Baby Parsnips, Breadcrumbs and Corn	302
Your choice from a good supermarket	

Banana Split	325

23

Exotique Treat Multiple Choice	158
Mango and Pan Fried Calves Liver	163
Smoked Haddock	168
Starfruit, Potato and Mushroom	170

Sweet and Sour Pork	248
Coconut Rice	301
Your choice from Picnic section	196
Your choice from Snacks and Starters section	176

Pea Soup Special	192

Traditional Shepherd's Pie	202
Whole Rainbow Trout a l'Orange	264
Vegetarian Quorn Chilli Stir Fry	295
Your choice from a good supermarket	

Fruit Flan	317

Breakfast bonanza
Quick & simple
Good old cooked
Why not fish?
Vegetarian

Lunch
Good old cooked
Vegetarian
Picnic selection
Snack of the day

Main meal
Starter

Dish of the day – meat
Dish of the day – fish
Dish of the day – vegetarian
Frozen ready meal

Dessert

August

24

Breakfast bonanza

Quick & simple	English Light	155
Good old cooked	Omelette Exotique of choice	164
Why not fish?	Kipper and Date	166
Vegetarian	Mushroom Breakfast	172

Lunch

Good old cooked	Quick Hot Prawns	262
Vegetarian	Wok Quorn	302
Picnic selection	Your choice from Picnic section	196
Snack of the day	Your choice from Snacks and Starters section	176

Main meal

Starter	Exotic Sardine Pâté	178
Dish of the day – meat	Champagne Quail	222
Dish of the day – fish	Orange Sole	268
Dish of the day – vegetarian	Vegetarian Lasagne	303
Frozen ready meal	Your choice from a good supermarket	
Dessert	Melon, Orange, Mango and Mint Chantilly	312

25

Continental Breakfast		154
Chicken Liver Exotique		158
Plaice and Kiwi Surprise		167
Lemon and Mango Borscht		171

Tandoori Meat		245
Cranberry Rice Salad		303
Your choice from Picnic section		196
Your choice from Snacks and Starters section		176

Exotic Red Borscht		194
Chicken Pesto		230
Salmon for a King		267
Kiwi, Mango and Lychee Beans		292
Your choice from a good supermarket		
Mango and Lychee Mousse		313

26

Breakfast bonanza

Quick & simple	Grapefruit Surprise	156
Good old cooked	Thinner & Richer Kebabs	159
Why not fish?	Red Salmon Omelette	167
Vegetarian	Quick Blend with Simple or Exotic Fruits	174

Lunch

Good old cooked	Prawn Exotique	275
Vegetarian	Aubergine au Fromage Frais	285
Picnic selection	Your choice from Picnic section	196
Snack of the day	Your choice from Snacks and Starters section	176

Main meal

Starter	Gefulte Fish	183
Dish of the day – meat	Chopped Liver	214
Dish of the day – fish	Lobster Salad	253
Dish of the day – vegetarian	Coconut Vegetables	299
Frozen ready meal	Your choice from a good supermarket	
Dessert	Baked Fruit	318

27

Highland Variation		153
Bagel, Egg and Dried Venison or Bacon		161
Gefulte Fish		166
Cherry Tomato, Pineapple and Mango Salad		171

Wok Beef		213
Chicory, Pineapple, Kiwi and Mushrooms		304
Your choice from Picnic section		196
Your choice from Snacks and Starters section		176

Leek Soup		184
Left-over Turkey		250
Smoked Rainbow Trout with Chunky Sauce		257
Bulghar Wheat Exotique		295
Your choice from a good supermarket		
Berry Omelette Exotique		311

28

Light Tabbouleh Breakfast	154
Bacon and Kiwi Treat	162
Sole and Kiwi	169
Humpty Dumpty	175

Avocado Salmon	258
Budgie Millet Exotique	294
Your choice from Picnic section	196
Your choice from Snacks and Starters section	176

Stir Fry Vegetables and Chilli	195

Wild Venison and Mango Exotique	228
Exotic Kedgeree	260
Tofu with Exotic Chunky Sauce	291
Your choice from a good supermarket	

Cranberry Ice Cream	312

29

Muesli Treat and Crumpets	153
Start The Day Mixed Grill	159
Tuna Casserole Exotique	169
Banana, Date, Kiwi and Mango	175

Exotic Liver with Orange	228
Dressed Seasonal Salad	301
Your choice from Picnic section	196
Your choice from Snacks and Starters section	176

Devilled Sardines	187

Original Duck à l'Orange	209
Hot Pickled Herring	271
Savoury Quorn Puffs	290
Your choice from a good supermarket	

Super Low Microwaveable Pears	313

30

Choose your own Light Breakfast	155
Venison Supreme	162
Fish with Berries	168
Egg and Exotic Hot Fruit	174

Smoked Trout	261
Crunchy, Kutchie-Fyky	293
Your choice from Picnic section	196
Your choice from Snacks and Starters section	176

Exotic Welsh Rarebit	187

Exotique Turkey and Almonds	232
Salmon for a King	267
Pumpkin Fritters	294
Your choice from a good supermarket	

Mango and Peach Brulée	316

31

Exotique Treat Multiple Choice	158
Bacon and Eggs	161
Smoked Haddock	168
Starfruit, Potato and Mushroom	170

Kiwi, Mango and Mushroom Soup	206
Rice Exotique	299
Your choice from Picnic section	196
Your choice from Snacks and Starters section	176

Aubergine and Mango Pâté	191

Devilled Lamb Steaks	209
Marinated Red Mullet Exotique	277
Aubergine Treat	285
Your choice from a good supermarket	

Guava Ice Cream	324

August

Breakfast bonanza
Quick & simple
Good old cooked
Why not fish?
Vegetarian

Lunch
Good old cooked
Vegetarian
Picnic selection
Snack of the day

Main meal
Starter

Dish of the day – meat
Dish of the day – fish
Dish of the day – vegetarian
Frozen ready meal

Dessert

Breakfast bonanza
Quick and simple
Good old cooked
Why not fish?
Vegetarian

Lunch
Good old cooked
Vegetarian
Picnic selection
Snack of the day

Main meal
Starter

Dish of the day – meat
Dish of the day – fish
Dish of the day – vegetarian
Frozen ready meal

Dessert

1

Breakfast bonanza

Quick & simple	Choose your own Light Breakfast	155
Good old cooked	Mango and Pan Fried Calves Liver	163
Why not fish?	Kipper and Mango Surprise	164
Vegetarian	Hot Fruit Salad	172

Lunch

Good old cooked	Salmon for a King in Pitta Bread	279
Vegetarian	Mixed Exotic Salad and Yoghurt Dressing	300
Picnic selection	Your choice from Picnic section	196
Snack of the day	Your choice from Snacks and Starters section	176

Main meal

Starter	Pumpkin Soup with Prawns	192
Dish of the day – meat	Chicken Exotique and Dried Venison	210
Dish of the day – fish	Exotic Salmon and Plaice	258
Dish of the day – vegetarian	Vegetarian Curry with Lychees	289
Frozen ready meal	Your choice from a good supermarket	
Dessert	Pears in Berry Sauce	309

2

Continental Breakfast		154
Venison Supreme		162
Plaice and Kiwi Surprise		167
Lemon and Mango Borscht		171

Stir Fried Liver		207
Kiwi, Mango and Mushroom Treat		304
Your choice from Picnic section		196
Your choice from Snacks and Starters section		176

Devilled Potato Salad and Celery		185
Schnitzel Exotic		207
Smoked Salmon Expanded à la Thinner & Richer		254
Mushroom Flan		287
Your choice from a good supermarket		
Rambutans and Pineapple Chantilly		310

3

Breakfast bonanza

Quick & simple	Grapefruit Surprise	156
Good old cooked	Chicken Liver Exotique	158
Why not fish?	Gefulte Fish	166
Vegetarian	Mushroom Breakfast	172

Lunch

Good old cooked	Grapefruit and Red Sockeye Salmon	261
Vegetarian	Subtle Kebabs	292
Picnic selection	Your choice from Picnic section	196
Snack of the day	Your choice from Snacks and Starters section	176

Main meal

Starter	Dandelion Summer Starter	177
Dish of the day – meat	Exotique Pintade Rotir (Guinea Fowl)	205
Dish of the day – fish	Plaice and Prawn Creole	282
Dish of the day – vegetarian	Quorn with Exotic Chunky Sauce	298
Frozen ready meal	Your choice from a good supermarket	
Dessert	Pears, Apple and Ginger Hot Chantilly	315

4

English Light		155
Omelette Exotique of choice		164
Red Salmon Omelette		167
Quick Blend with Simple or Exotic Fruits		174

Chinese Chicken Salad with Lychees		250
Exotic Leeks		307
Your choice from Picnic section		196
Your choice from Snacks and Starters section		176

Fluffy Herb Pâté		179
Indonesian Pork Satay		220
Tuna Special		262
Vegetable Curry		296
Your choice from a good supermarket		
Strawberry (or any other fruits) Mousse		320

5

Light Tabbouleh Breakfast	154
Thinner & Richer Kebabs	159
Kipper and Date	166
Humpty Dumpty	175

Salmon Fillet with Hot Exotic Chunky Sauce	259
Sesame Seed and Caraway Salad	307
Your choice from Picnic section	196
Your choice from Snacks and Starters section	176

Pumpkin Soup with Flowers	190

Lamb and Pawpaw Corsican Style	215
Starfruit Salmon Salad	271
Aubergine Exotique	286
Your choice from a good supermarket	

Pears Grand Marnier	309

6

Muesli Treat and Crumpets	153
Bacon and Kiwi Treat	162
Tuna Casserole Exotique	169
Cherry Tomato, Pineapple and Mango Salad	171

Beef and Lamb Kebabs	201
Vegetarian Quorn Chilli Stir Fry	295
Your choice from Picnic section	196
Your choice from Snacks and Starters section	176

Exotic Toast	191

Slimmers' Lasagne à la Thinner & Richer	237
Devilled Lobster	274
Cauliflower au gratin	305
Your choice from a good supermarket	

Honey and Apple Crisp	324

Breakfast bonanza
Quick & simple
Good old cooked
Why not fish?
Vegetarian

Lunch
Good old cooked
Vegetarian
Picnic selection
Snack of the day

Main meal
Starter

Dish of the day – meat
Dish of the day – fish
Dish of the day – vegetarian
Frozen ready meal

Dessert

7

Highland Variation	153
Bagel, Egg and Dried Venison or Bacon	161
Sole and Kiwi	169
Banana, Date, Kiwi and Mango	175

Fish Soup à la Thinner & Richer	273
Cranberry Rice Salad	303
Your choice from Picnic section	196
Your choice from Snacks and Starters section	176

Exotic Pears and Mint	190

Chicken and Aubergine	232
Smoked Salmon Cous cous	270
Sweet and Sour Amaranth Chinese Lettuce	306
Your choice from a good supermarket	

Slimmer Fruit Ice Cream	318

8

Exotique Treat Multiple Choice	158
Start The Day Mixed Grill	159
Kipper and Mango Surprise	164
Egg and Exotic Hot Fruit	174

Chicken in Sherry	251
Baby Parsnips, Breadcrumbs and Corn	302
Your choice from Picnic section	196
Your choice from Snacks and Starters section	176

Melon and Dried Venison or Parma Ham	177

Steak Diane Exotique	219
Prawn and Mint Dip	272
Wok Quorn	302
Your choice from a good supermarket	

Blackberry, Lychee and Cape Gooseberry	323

Breakfast bonanza
Quick & simple
Good old cooked
Why not fish?
Vegetarian

Lunch
Good old cooked
Vegetarian
Picnic selection
Snack of the day

Main meal
Starter

Dish of the day – meat
Dish of the day – fish
Dish of the day – vegetarian
Frozen ready meal

Dessert

9

Choose your own Light Breakfast	155
Bacon and Eggs	161
Fish with Berries	168
Hot Fruit Salad	172

Shrimp Pilaf Exotique	273
Coconut Rice	301
Your choice from Picnic section	196
Your choice from Snacks and Starters section	176

Sweet and Sour Amaranth Chinese Lettuce	186

Exotique Turkey Escalopes	242
Red Salmon Omelette	279
Peas Exotique	293
Your choice from a good supermarket	

Banana Bake Exotique	323

10

Grapefruit Surprise	156
Mango and Pan Fried Calves Liver	163
Smoked Haddock	168
Starfruit, Potato and Mushroom	170

Citrus Chicken	221
Greek Dip Exotique	289
Your choice from Picnic section	196
Your choice from Snacks and Starters section	176

Chopped Herring Chunky Pâté	178

Rosemary Lamb	204
Scallop Seviche	253
Kiwi, Mango and Lychee Beans	292
Your choice from a good supermarket	

Fruit Flan	317

Breakfast bonanza
Quick & simple
Good old cooked
Why not fish?
Vegetarian

Lunch
Good old cooked
Vegetarian
Picnic selection
Snack of the day

Main meal
Starter

Dish of the day – meat
Dish of the day – fish
Dish of the day – vegetarian
Frozen ready meal

Dessert

11

Continental Breakfast	154
Venison Supreme	162
Red Salmon Omelette	167
Lemon and Mango Borscht	171

Exotic Mackerel	266
Rice Exotique	299
Your choice from Picnic section	196
Your choice from Snacks and Starters section	176

Devilled Sardines	187

Tzimmas with Beef, Mango and Prunes	218
Prawn and Exotic Salad	256
Coconut Vegetables	299
Your choice from a good supermarket	

Banana Chocolate Treat with Mangoes	316

12

English Light	155
Omelette Exotique of choice	164
Gefulte Fish	166
Quick Blend with Simple or Exotic Fruits	174

Mango and Pan Fried Calves Liver	204
Aubergine Exotique au gratin	288
Your choice from Picnic section	196
Your choice from Snacks and Starters section	176

Melon, Kiwi and Grape Surprise	180

Exotique Venison Casserole	233
Salmon à la Greque	268
Vegetarian Lasagne	303
Your choice from a good supermarket	

Kiwango Ice	310

Breakfast bonanza
Quick & simple
Good old cooked
Why not fish?
Vegetarian

Lunch
Good old cooked
Vegetarian
Picnic selection
Snack of the day

Main meal
Starter

Dish of the day – meat
Dish of the day – fish
Dish of the day – vegetarian
Frozen ready meal

Dessert

13

Breakfast bonanza

Quick & simple	Authentic New York Bagel	156
Good old cooked	Chicken Liver Exotique	158
Why not fish?	Plaice and Kiwi Surprise	167
Vegetarian	Mushroom Breakfast	172

Lunch

Good old cooked	Fish Soup with Sweetcorn and Lychees	255
Vegetarian	Courgette Exotique	286
Picnic selection	Your choice from Picnic section	196
Snack of the day	Your choice from Snacks and Starters section	176

Main meal

Starter	Watercress, Lychee and Cucumber Soup	181
Dish of the day – meat	Meaty Cous cous	239
Dish of the day – fish	Salmon and Rice	255
Dish of the day – vegetarian	Mushroom Flan	287
Frozen ready meal	Your choice from a good supermarket	
Dessert	Stuffed Pineapple	311

14

Muesli Treat and Crumpets		153
Bacon and Kiwi Treat		162
Tuna Casserole Exotique		169
Cherry Tomato, Pineapple and Mango Salad		171

Melon with Dried Wild Venison		214
Cherry Tomato, Pineapple and Mango Salad		300
Your choice from Picnic section		196
Your choice from Snacks and Starters section		176

Lemon and Mango Borscht		184
Cauliflower au gratin		223
Tuna and Egg Salad Exotique		267
Vegetable Curry		296
Your choice from a good supermarket		
Ice Cream Grand Marnier		314

15

Breakfast bonanza

Quick & simple	Light Tabbouleh Breakfast	154
Good old cooked	Start The Day Mixed Grill	159
Why not fish?	Sole and Kiwi	169
Vegetarian	Banana, Date, Kiwi and Mango	175

Lunch

Good old cooked	Sardine Exotic Surprise	277
Vegetarian	Aubergine Exotique	286
Picnic selection	Your choice from Picnic section	196
Snack of the day	Your choice from Snacks and Starters section	176

Main meal

Starter	Red Sockeye Salmon Pâté	194
Dish of the day – meat	Exotique Lamb and Papaya or Mango	216
Dish of the day – fish	Potted Herring	266
Dish of the day – vegetarian	Savoury Quorn Puffs	290
Frozen ready meal	Your choice from a good supermarket	
Dessert	Quince Thinner & Richer	314

16

Exotique Treat Multiple Choice		158
Thinner & Richer Kebabs		159
Kipper and Date		166
Humpty Dumpty		175

Chicken Curry with Coconut Milk		237
Crunchy, Kutchie-Fyky		293
Your choice from Picnic section		196
Your choice from Snacks and Starters section		176

Cauliflower Soup		193
Exotique Venison Stew		211
Plaice, Leek and Lime		274
Aubergine Treat		285
Your choice from a good supermarket		
Baked Fruit		318

17

Highland Variation	153
Bagel, Egg and Dried Venison or Bacon	161
Fish with Berries	168
Hot Fruit Salad	172

Quick Salmon Steak for One	269
Budgie Millet Exotique	294
Your choice from Picnic section	196
Your choice from Snacks and Starters section	176

Sweet and Sour Amaranth Chinese Lettuce	186

Veal Goulash with Lychees	229
Sole in Envelopes	254
Quorn with Exotic Chunky Sauce	298
Your choice from a good supermarket	

Peach and Papaya Chantilly	319

18

Choose your own Light Breakfast	155
Mango and Pan Fried Calves Liver	163
Smoked Haddock	168
Starfruit, Potato and Mushroom	170

Aubergine Exotique au gratin	243
Aubergine au Fromage Frais	285
Your choice from Picnic section	196
Your choice from Snacks and Starters section	176

Coconut and Beef Satay or Chicken Satay	195

Chicken with Red and Green Peppers	244
Gefulte Fish	256
Vegetarian Curry with Lychees	289
Your choice from a good supermarket	

Exotic Caramel Custard	325

Breakfast bonanza
Quick & simple
Good old cooked
Why not fish?
Vegetarian

Lunch
Good old cooked
Vegetarian
Picnic selection
Snack of the day

Main meal
Starter

Dish of the day – meat
Dish of the day – fish
Dish of the day – vegetarian
Frozen ready meal

Dessert

19

Continental Breakfast	154
Venison Supreme	162
Kipper and Mango Surprise	164
Egg and Exotic Hot Fruit	174

Oriental Wok Stir Fry	260
Mixed Exotic Salad and Yoghurt Dressing	300
Your choice from Picnic section	196
Your choice from Snacks and Starters section	176

Fish Soup	193

Exotique Beef Soufflé	227
Tomato and Tuna Salad Exotique	257
Bulghar Wheat Exotique	295
Your choice from a good supermarket	

Melon and Berries	315

20

English Light	155
Bacon and Eggs	161
Gefulte Fish	166
Quick Blend with Simple or Exotic Fruits	174

Exotique Chicken Satay	215
Chicory, Pineapple, Kiwi and Mushrooms	304
Your choice from Picnic section	196
Your choice from Snacks and Starters section	176

Chicken Pâté	183

North African Cous cous	238
Smoked Rainbow Trout with Chunky Sauce	257
Pumpkin Fritters	294
Your choice from a good supermarket	

Exotique Banana Dessert	319

Breakfast bonanza
Quick & simple
Good old cooked
Why not fish?
Vegetarian

Lunch
Good old cooked
Vegetarian
Picnic selection
Snack of the day

Main meal
Starter

Dish of the day – meat
Dish of the day – fish
Dish of the day – vegetarian
Frozen ready meal

Dessert

September

21

Breakfast bonanza

Quick & simple	Grapefruit Surprise	156
Good old cooked	Omelette Exotique of choice	164
Why not fish?	Plaice and Kiwi Surprise	167
Vegetarian	Mushroom Breakfast	172

Lunch

Good old cooked	Quick Hot Prawns	262
Vegetarian	Dressed Seasonal Salad	301
Picnic selection	Your choice from Picnic section	196
Snack of the day	Your choice from Snacks and Starters section	176

Main meal

Starter	Exotic Red Borscht	194
Dish of the day – meat	Mushroom Flan (contains meat)	231
Dish of the day – fish	White Fish Cous cous	263
Dish of the day – vegetarian	Courgette Exotique	286
Frozen ready meal	Your choice from a good supermarket	
Dessert	Fruit Jelly	317

22

Light Tabbouleh Breakfast	154
Bacon and Kiwi Treat	162
Red Salmon Omelette	167
Lemon and Mango Borscht	171

Cold Meat Salad with Exotic Chunky Sauce	236
Kiwi, Mango and Mushroom Treat	304
Your choice from Picnic section	196
Your choice from Snacks and Starters section	176

Carrot Soup	180
Slimmers' Lasagne à la Thinner & Richer	237
Smoked Trout	261
Cauliflower au gratin	305
Your choice from a good supermarket	
Mango and Lychee Mousse	313

23

Breakfast bonanza

Quick & simple	Muesli Treat and Crumpets	153
Good old cooked	Chicken Liver Exotique	158
Why not fish?	Sole and Kiwi	169
Vegetarian	Banana, Date, Kiwi and Mango	175

Lunch

Good old cooked	Hot Pickled Herring	271
Vegetarian	Sesame Seed and Caraway Salad	307
Picnic selection	Your choice from Picnic section	196
Snack of the day	Your choice from Snacks and Starters section	176

Main meal

Starter	Exotic Sardine Pâté	178
Dish of the day – meat	Chicken, Apricot and Asparagus	249
Dish of the day – fish	Whole Rainbow Trout à l'Orange	264
Dish of the day – vegetarian	Coconut Rice	301
Frozen ready meal	Your choice from a good supermarket	
Dessert	Banana Split	325

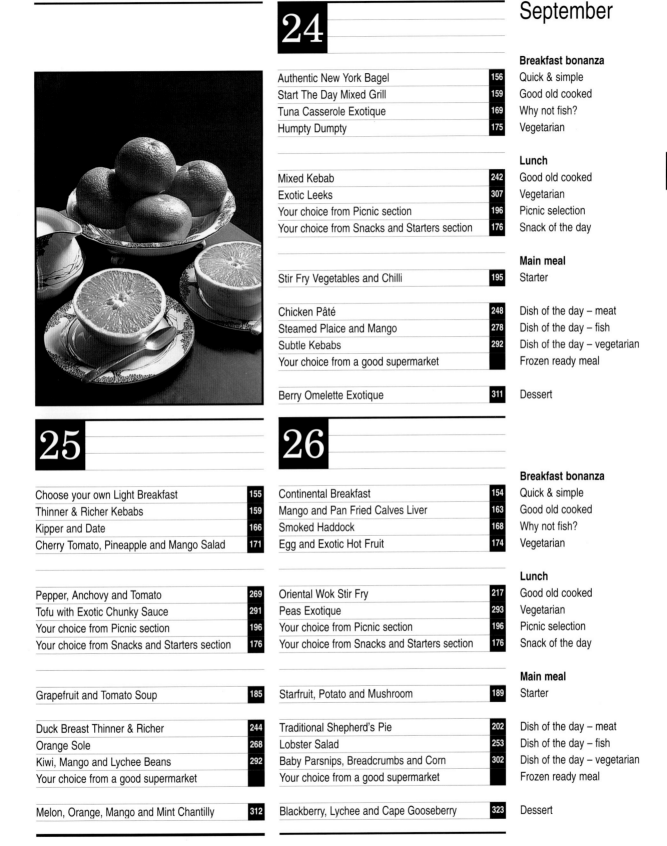

24

Authentic New York Bagel	156
Start The Day Mixed Grill	159
Tuna Casserole Exotique	169
Humpty Dumpty	175

Mixed Kebab	242
Exotic Leeks	307
Your choice from Picnic section	196
Your choice from Snacks and Starters section	176

Stir Fry Vegetables and Chilli	195

Chicken Pâté	248
Steamed Plaice and Mango	278
Subtle Kebabs	292
Your choice from a good supermarket	

Berry Omelette Exotique	311

Breakfast bonanza
Quick & simple
Good old cooked
Why not fish?
Vegetarian

Lunch
Good old cooked
Vegetarian
Picnic selection
Snack of the day

Main meal
Starter

Dish of the day – meat
Dish of the day – fish
Dish of the day – vegetarian
Frozen ready meal

Dessert

25

Choose your own Light Breakfast	155
Thinner & Richer Kebabs	159
Kipper and Date	166
Cherry Tomato, Pineapple and Mango Salad	171

Pepper, Anchovy and Tomato	269
Tofu with Exotic Chunky Sauce	291
Your choice from Picnic section	196
Your choice from Snacks and Starters section	176

Grapefruit and Tomato Soup	185

Duck Breast Thinner & Richer	244
Orange Sole	268
Kiwi, Mango and Lychee Beans	292
Your choice from a good supermarket	

Melon, Orange, Mango and Mint Chantilly	312

26

Continental Breakfast	154
Mango and Pan Fried Calves Liver	163
Smoked Haddock	168
Egg and Exotic Hot Fruit	174

Oriental Wok Stir Fry	217
Peas Exotique	293
Your choice from Picnic section	196
Your choice from Snacks and Starters section	176

Starfruit, Potato and Mushroom	189

Traditional Shepherd's Pie	202
Lobster Salad	253
Baby Parsnips, Breadcrumbs and Corn	302
Your choice from a good supermarket	

Blackberry, Lychee and Cape Gooseberry	323

Breakfast bonanza
Quick & simple
Good old cooked
Why not fish?
Vegetarian

Lunch
Good old cooked
Vegetarian
Picnic selection
Snack of the day

Main meal
Starter

Dish of the day – meat
Dish of the day – fish
Dish of the day – vegetarian
Frozen ready meal

Dessert

27

Breakfast bonanza

Quick & simple	Highland Variation	153
Good old cooked	Bagel, Egg and Dried Venison or Bacon	161
Why not fish?	Fish with Berries	168
Vegetarian	Starfruit, Potato and Mushroom	170

Lunch

Good old cooked	Shrimp Pilaf Exotique	273
Vegetarian	Greek Dip Exotique	289
Picnic selection	Your choice from Picnic section	196
Snack of the day	Your choice from Snacks and Starters section	176

Main meal

Starter	Exotic Pears and Mint	190
Dish of the day – meat	Pork or Turkey and Apple	206
Dish of the day – fish	Plaice-a-Leekie	278
Dish of the day – vegetarian	Coconut Vegetables	299
Frozen ready meal	Your choice from a good supermarket	
Dessert	Baked Fruit	318

28

Exotique Treat Multiple Choice	158
Bacon and Eggs	161
Plaice and Kiwi Surprise	167
Hot Fruit Salad	172

Wok Beef	213
Wok Quorn	302
Your choice from Picnic section	196
Your choice from Snacks and Starters section	176

Gefulte Fish	183
Ginger Turkey	240
Exotic Kedgeree	260
Vegetarian Lasagne	303
Your choice from a good supermarket	
Pears Grand Marnier	309

29

Breakfast bonanza

Quick & simple	Grapefruit Surprise	156
Good old cooked	Omelette Exotique of choice	164
Why not fish?	Gefulte Fish	166
Vegetarian	Mushroom Breakfast	172

Lunch

Good old cooked	Red Sockeye Salmon Stir Fry	259
Vegetarian	Vegetarian Quorn Chilli Stir Fry	295
Picnic selection	Your choice from Picnic section	196
Snack of the day	Your choice from Snacks and Starters section	176

Main meal

Starter	Green Soup	182
Dish of the day – meat	Stuffed Cabbage	235
Dish of the day – fish	Prawn Exotique	275
Dish of the day – vegetarian	Cranberry Rice Salad	303
Frozen ready meal	Your choice from a good supermarket	
Dessert	Cranberry Ice Cream	312

30

English Light	155
Venison Supreme	162
Kipper and Mango Surprise	164
Quick Blend with Simple or Exotic Fruits	174

Wild Venison with Ratatouille	225
Sweet and Sour Amaranth Chinese Lettuce	306
Your choice from Picnic section	196
Your choice from Snacks and Starters section	176

Tuna Pâté	182
Poultry – Sweet and Sour	217
Avocado Salmon	258
Cherry Tomato, Pineapple and Mango Salad	300
Your choice from a good supermarket	
Pears in Berry Sauce	309

124

1

Light Tabbouleh Breakfast	154
Chicken Liver Exotique	158
Sole and Kiwi	169
Banana, Date, Kiwi and Mango	175

Exotic Salmon and Plaice	258
Chicory, Pineapple, Kiwi and Mushrooms	304
Your choice from Picnic section	196
Your choice from Snacks and Starters section	176

Exotic Welsh Rarebit	187

Chicken Pesto	230
Rainbow Trout	264
Savoury Quorn Puffs	290
Your choice from a good supermarket	

Berry Omelette Exotique	311

2

Authentic New York Bagel	156
Thinner & Richer Kebabs	159
Red Salmon Omelette	167
Lemon and Mango Borscht	171

Stir Fried Liver	207
Tofu with Exotic Chunky Sauce	291
Your choice from Picnic section	196
Your choice from Snacks and Starters section	176

Borscht and Yoghurt	181

Devilled Lamb Steaks	209
Marinated Red Mullet Exotique	277
Bulghar Wheat Exotique	295
Your choice from a good supermarket	

Stuffed Pineapple	311

Breakfast bonanza
Quick & simple
Good old cooked
Why not fish?
Vegetarian

Lunch
Good old cooked
Vegetarian
Picnic selection
Snack of the day

Main meal
Starter

Dish of the day – meat
Dish of the day – fish
Dish of the day – vegetarian
Frozen ready meal

Dessert

3

Continental Breakfast	154
Bacon and Eggs	161
Smoked Haddock	168
Egg and Exotic Hot Fruit	174

Left-over Turkey	250
Dressed Seasonal Salad	301
Your choice from Picnic section	196
Your choice from Snacks and Starters section	176

Pumpkin Soup with Flowers	190

Brandy Fillet Steak, Kiwi Garnish	216
Scallop Seviche	253
Mushroom Flan	287
Your choice from a good supermarket	

Exotic Caramel Custard	325

4

Highland Variation	153
Bagel, Egg and Dried Venison or Bacon	161
Fish with Berries	168
Cherry Tomato, Pineapple and Mango Salad	171

Shrimp Pilaf Exotique	273
Kiwi, Mango and Mushroom Treat	304
Your choice from Picnic section	196
Your choice from Snacks and Starters section	176

Starfruit, Potato and Mushroom	189

Exotique Pintade Rotir (Guinea Fowl)	205
Lobster Salad	253
Vegetable Curry	296
Your choice from a good supermarket	

Mango and Peach Brulée	316

Breakfast bonanza
Quick & simple
Good old cooked
Why not fish?
Vegetarian

Lunch
Good old cooked
Vegetarian
Picnic selection
Snack of the day

Main meal
Starter

Dish of the day – meat
Dish of the day – fish
Dish of the day – vegetarian
Frozen ready meal

Dessert

5

Breakfast bonanza

Quick & simple	Choose your own Light Breakfast	155
Good old cooked	Mango and Pan Fried Calves Liver	163
Why not fish?	Kipper and Date	166
Vegetarian	Starfruit, Potato and Mushroom	170

Lunch

Good old cooked	Citrus Chicken	221
Vegetarian	Coconut Vegetables	299
Picnic selection	Your choice from Picnic section	196
Snack of the day	Your choice from Snacks and Starters section	176

Main meal

Starter	Lemon and Mango Borscht	184
Dish of the day – meat	Schnitzel Exotic	207
Dish of the day – fish	Pepper, Anchovy and Tomato	269
Dish of the day – vegetarian	Kiwi, Mango and Lychee Beans	292
Frozen ready meal	Your choice from a good supermarket	
Dessert	Banana Chocolate Treat with Mangoes	316

6

Grapefruit Surprise	156
Venison Supreme	162
Gefulte Fish	166
Mushroom Breakfast	172

Fish Soup à la Thinner & Richer	273
Sesame Seed and Caraway Salad	307
Your choice from Picnic section	196
Your choice from Snacks and Starters section	176

Melon and Dried Venison or Parma Ham	177
Hot Meat or Poultry with Exotic Chunky Sauce	205
Tuna and Egg Salad Exotique	267
Courgette Exotique	286
Your choice from a good supermarket	
Rambutans and Pineapple Chantilly	310

7

Breakfast bonanza

Quick & simple	Exotique Treat Multiple Choice	158
Good old cooked	Omelette Exotique of choice	164
Why not fish?	Plaice and Kiwi Surprise	167
Vegetarian	Quick Blend with Simple or Exotic Fruits	174

Lunch

Good old cooked	Chicken and Pasta (cold dish)	236
Vegetarian	Sweet and Sour Amaranth Chinese Lettuce	306
Picnic selection	Your choice from Picnic section	196
Snack of the day	Your choice from Snacks and Starters section	176

Main meal

Starter	Pea Soup Special	192
Dish of the day – meat	Meaty Cous cous	239
Dish of the day – fish	Oriental Wok Stir Fry	260
Dish of the day – vegetarian	Aubergine Treat	285
Frozen ready meal	Your choice from a good supermarket	
Dessert	Peach and Papaya Chantilly	319

8

English Light	155
Bacon and Kiwi Treat	162
Kipper and Mango Surprise	164
Hot Fruit Salad	172

Prawn Exotique	275
Mixed Exotic Salad and Yoghurt Dressing	300
Your choice from Picnic section	196
Your choice from Snacks and Starters section	176

Coconut and Beef Satay or Chicken Satay	195
Mushroom Flan (contains meat)	231
Orange Sole	268
Budgie Millet Exotique	294
Your choice from a good supermarket	
Fruit Jelly	317

Breakfast bonanza
Quick & simple
Good old cooked
Why not fish?
Vegetarian

Lunch
Good old cooked
Vegetarian
Picnic selection
Snack of the day

Main meal
Starter

Dish of the day – meat
Dish of the day – fish
Dish of the day – vegetarian
Frozen ready meal

Dessert

11

Breakfast bonanza
Quick & simple
Good old cooked
Why not fish?
Vegetarian

Lunch
Good old cooked
Vegetarian
Picnic selection
Snack of the day

Main meal
Starter

Dish of the day – meat
Dish of the day – fish
Dish of the day – vegetarian
Frozen ready meal

Dessert

October

12

Breakfast bonanza
Quick & simple	Highland Variation	153
Good old cooked	Chicken Liver Exotique	158
Why not fish?	Sole and Kiwi	169
Vegetarian	Banana, Date, Kiwi and Mango	175

Lunch
Good old cooked	Red Sockeye Salmon Stir Fry	259
Vegetarian	Cranberry Rice Salad	303
Picnic selection	Your choice from Picnic section	196
Snack of the day	Your choice from Snacks and Starters section	176

Main meal
Starter	Melon, Kiwi and Grape Surprise	180
Dish of the day – meat	Mango Cholent	210
Dish of the day – fish	Potted Herring	266
Dish of the day – vegetarian	Quorn with Exotic Chunky Sauce	298
Frozen ready meal	Your choice from a good supermarket	
Dessert	Fruit Flan	317

13

Breakfast bonanza
	Choose your own Light Breakfast	155
	Mango and Pan Fried Calves Liver	163
	Kipper and Date	166
	Starfruit, Potato and Mushroom	170

Lunch
	Exotique Ham and Mango	235
	Baby Parsnips, Breadcrumbs and Corn	302
	Your choice from Picnic section	196
	Your choice from Snacks and Starters section	176

Main meal
	Aubergine and Mango Pâté	191
	Exotique Venison Stew	211
	Starfruit Salmon Salad	271
	Cauliflower au gratin	305
	Your choice from a good supermarket	
	Slimmer Fruit Ice Cream	318

14

Breakfast bonanza
Quick and simple	Continental Breakfast	154
Good old cooked	Start the Day Mixed Grill	159
Why not fish?	Red Salmon Omelette	167
Vegetarian	Lemon and Mango Borscht	171

Lunch
Good old cooked	Chicken and Pasta (cold dish)	236
Vegetarian	Aubergine Exotique	286
Picnic selection	Your choice from Picnic section	196
Snack of the day	Your choice from Snacks and Starters section	176

Main meal
Starter	Pumpkin Soup with Flowers	190
Dish of the day – meat	Brandy Fillet Steat with Kiwi Garnish	216
Dish of the day – fish	Rainbow Trout	264
Dish of the day – vegetarian	Cauliflower au Gratin	305
Frozen ready meal	Your choice from a good supermarket	
Dessert	Exotique Banana Dessert	319

15

Breakfast bonanza
	English Light	155
	Bagel, Egg and Dried Venison or Bacon	161
	Gefulte Fish	166
	Mushroom Breakfast	172

Lunch
	Chicken and Peppers	233
	Coconut Rice	301
	Your choice from Picnic section	196
	Your choice from Snacks and Starters section	176

Main meal
	Exotic Pears and Mint	190
	North American Cous cous	226
	Tomato and Tuna Salad Exotique	257
	Wok Quorn	302
	Your choice from a good supermarket	
	Kiwango Ice	310

16

Exotique Treat Multiple Choice	158
Bacon and Kiwi Treat	162
Fish with Berries	168
Hot Fruit Salad	172

Plaice and Prawn Creole	282
Greek Dip Exotique	289
Your choice from Picnic section	196
Your choice from Snacks and Starters section	176

Chicken Pâté	183

Champagne Quail	222
Smoked Salmon Expanded à la Thinner & Richer	254
Courgette Exotique	286
Your choice from a good supermarket	

Honey and Apple Crisp	324

17

Grapefruit Surprise	156
Omelette Exotique of choice	164
Kipper and Mango Surprise	164
Starfruit, Potato and Mushroom	170

Exotique Liver with Orange	228
Peas Exotique	293
Your choice from Picnic section	196
Your choice from Snacks and Starters section	176

Fish Soup	193

Cauliflower au gratin	223
Gefulte Fish	256
Aubergine Exotique au gratin	288
Your choice from a good supermarket	

Pears, Apple and Ginger Hot Chantilly	315

October

Breakfast bonanza
Quick & simple
Good old cooked
Why not fish?
Vegetarian

Lunch
Good old cooked
Vegetarian
Picnic selection
Snack of the day

Main meal
Starter

Dish of the day – meat
Dish of the day – fish
Dish of the day – vegetarian
Frozen ready meal

Dessert

18

Authentic New York Bagel	156
Thinner & Richer Kebabs	159
Smoked Haddock	168
Humpty Dumpty	175

Tuna Special	262
Sesame Seed and Caraway Salad	307
Your choice from Picnic section	196
Your choice from Snacks and Starters section	176

Tuna Pâté	182

Veal Goulash with Lychees	229
Sole in Envelopes	254
Rice Exotique	299
Your choice from a good supermarket	

Guava Ice Cream	324

19

Highland Variation	153
Chicken Liver Exotique	158
Sole and Kiwi	169
Egg and Exotic Hot Fruit	174

Rosemary Lamb	204
Baby Parsnips, Breadcrumbs and Corn	302
Your choice from Picnic section	196
Your choice from Snacks and Starters section	176

Leek Soup	184

Tzimmas with Beef, Mango and Prunes	218
Steamed Plaice and Mango	278
Savoury Quorn Puffs	290
Your choice from a good supermarket	

Melon and Berries	315

Breakfast bonanza
Quick & simple
Good old cooked
Why not fish?
Vegetarian

Lunch
Good old cooked
Vegetarian
Picnic selection
Snack of the day

Main meal
Starter

Dish of the day – meat
Dish of the day – fish
Dish of the day – vegetarian
Frozen ready meal

Dessert

20

Breakfast bonanza

Quick & simple	Light Tabbouleh Breakfast	154
Good old cooked	Start The Day Mixed Grill	159
Why not fish?	Red Salmon Omelette	167
Vegetarian	Lemon and Mango Borscht	171

130

Lunch

Good old cooked	Prawn and Mint Dip	272
Vegetarian	Sweet and Sour Amaranth Chinese Lettuce	306
Picnic selection	Your choice from Picnic section	196
Snack of the day	Your choice from Snacks and Starters section	176

Main meal

Starter	Fluffy Herb Pâté	179
Dish of the day – meat	Indonesian Pork Satay	220
Dish of the day – fish	Devilled Lobster	274
Dish of the day – vegetarian	Kiwi, Mango and Lychee Beans	292
Frozen ready meal	Your choice from a good supermarket	
Dessert	Banana Split	325

21

Muesli Treat and Crumpets	153
Bacon and Eggs	161
Tuna Casserole Exotique	169
Cherry Tomato, Pineapple and Mango Salad	171

Wild Venison and Mango Exotique	228
Aubergine au Fromage Frais	285
Your choice from Picnic section	196
Your choice from Snacks and Starters section	176

Stir Fry Vegetables and Chilli	195
Exotique Lamb and Papaya or Mango	216
Plaice-a-Leekie	278
Bulghar Wheat Exotique	295
Your choice from a good supermarket	
Stuffed Pineapple	311

22

Breakfast bonanza

Quick & simple	Continental Breakfast	154
Good old cooked	Venison Supreme	162
Why not fish?	Kipper and Date	166
Vegetarian	Banana, Date, Kiwi and Mango	175

Lunch

Good old cooked	Red Salmon Omelette	279
Vegetarian	Chicory, Pineapple, Kiwi and Mushrooms	304
Picnic selection	Your choice from Picnic section	196
Snack of the day	Your choice from Snacks and Starters section	176

Main meal

Starter	Chicken and Coconut Soup	189
Dish of the day – meat	Exotique Beef Soufflé	227
Dish of the day – fish	Whole Rainbow Trout à l'Orange	264
Dish of the day – vegetarian	Vegetarian Curry with Lychees	289
Frozen ready meal	Your choice from a good supermarket	
Dessert	Pears Grand Marnier	309

23

Choose your own Light Breakfast	155
Bagel, Egg and Dried Venison or Bacon	161
Gefulte Fish	166
Mushroom Breakfast	172

Cider Chicken Calvados	220
Greek Dip Exotique	289
Your choice from Picnic section	196
Your choice from Snacks and Starters section	176

Grapefruit and Tomato Soup	185
Chopped Liver	214
Smoked Rainbow Trout with Chunky Sauce	257
Vegetarian Lasagne	303
Your choice from a good supermarket	
Baked Fruit	318

October

24

Breakfast bonanza

Quick & simple	Exotique Treat Multiple Choice	158
Good old cooked	Mango and Pan Fried Calves Liver	163
Why not fish?	Plaice and Kiwi Surprise	167
Vegetarian	Starfruit, Potato and Mushroom	170

Lunch

Good old cooked	Fish Soup with Sweetcorn and Lychees	255
Vegetarian	Aubergine Exotique au gratin	288
Picnic selection	Your choice from Picnic section	196
Snack of the day	Your choice from Snacks and Starters section	176

Main meal

Starter	Gefulte Fish	183
Dish of the day – meat	Exotique Venison Casserole	233
Dish of the day – fish	Salmon à la Greque	268
Dish of the day – vegetarian	Vegetarian Quorn Chilli Stir Fry	295
Frozen ready meal	Your choice from a good supermarket	
Dessert	Blackberry, Lychee and Cape Gooseberry	323

25

English Light	155
Omelette Exotique of choice	164
Fish with Berries	168
Quick Blend with Simple or Exotic Fruits	174

Oriental Wok Stir Fry	217
Cranberry Rice Salad	303
Your choice from Picnic section	196
Your choice from Snacks and Starters section	176

Devilled Potato Salad and Celery	185
Chicken and Aubergine	232
Grapefruit and Red Sockeye Salmon	261
Coconut Rice	301
Your choice from a good supermarket	
Mango and Lychee Mousse	313

26

Breakfast bonanza

Quick & simple	Grapefruit Surprise	156
Good old cooked	Bacon and Kiwi Treat	162
Why not fish?	Kipper and Mango Surprise	164
Vegetarian	Hot Fruit Salad	172

Lunch

Good old cooked	Salmon for a King in Pitta Bread	279
Vegetarian	Peas Exotique	293
Picnic selection	Your choice from Picnic section	196
Snack of the day	Your choice from Snacks and Starters section	176

Main meal

Starter	Chopped Herring Chunky Pâté	178
Dish of the day – meat	Melon with Dried Wild Venison	214
Dish of the day – fish	White Fish Cous cous	263
Dish of the day – vegetarian	Budgie Millet Exotique	294
Frozen ready meal	Your choice from a good supermarket	
Dessert	Cranberry Ice Cream	312

27

Highland Variation	153
Bacon and Eggs	161
Sole and Kiwi	169
Egg and Exotic Hot Fruit	174

Wok Beef	213
Subtle Kebabs	292
Your choice from Picnic section	196
Your choice from Snacks and Starters section	176

Sweet and Sour Amaranth Chinese Lettuce	186
Chicken Curry with Coconut Milk	237
Quick Salmon Steak for One	269
Aubergine Treat	285
Your choice from a good supermarket	
Melon, Orange, Mango and Mint Chantilly	312

28

Light Tabbouleh Breakfast	154
Thinner & Richer Kebabs	159
Red Salmon Omelette	167
Lemon and Mango Borscht	171

Hot Pickled Herring	271
Coconut Vegetables	299
Your choice from Picnic section	196
Your choice from Snacks and Starters section	176

Exotic Red Borscht	194

Stuffed Cabbage	235
Plaice, Leek and Lime	274
Tofu with Exotic Chunky Sauce	291
Your choice from a good supermarket	

Pears in Berry Sauce	309

29

Muesli Treat and Crumpets	153
Start The Day Mixed Grill	159
Smoked Haddock	168
Humpty Dumpty	175

Chicken in Sherry	251
Wok Quorn	302
Your choice from Picnic section	196
Your choice from Snacks and Starters section	176

Watercress, Lychee and Cucumber Soup	181

Aubergine Exotique au gratin	243
Smoked Salmon Cous cous	270
Crunchy, Kutchie-Fyky	293
Your choice from a good supermarket	

Mango and Peach Brulée	316

Breakfast bonanza
Quick & simple
Good old cooked
Why not fish?
Vegetarian

Lunch
Good old cooked
Vegetarian
Picnic selection
Snack of the day

Main meal
Starter

Dish of the day – meat
Dish of the day – fish
Dish of the day – vegetarian
Frozen ready meal

Dessert

30

Authentic New York Bagel	156
Chicken Liver Exotique	158
Kipper and Date	166
Banana, Date, Kiwi and Mango	175

Avocado Salmon	258
Dressed Seasonal Salad	301
Your choice from Picnic section	196
Your choice from Snacks and Starters section	176

Exotic Sardine Pâté	178

Chicken Pâté	248
Smoked Trout	261
Courgette Exotique	286
Your choice from a good supermarket	

Guava Ice Cream	324

31 Halloween Special

Grapefruit Surprise	156
Pumpkin and Bacon	163
Witches Plaice	170
Hot Fruit Salad	172

Prawn Exotique	275
Baby Parsnips, Breadcrumbs and Corn	302
Your choice from Picnic section	196
Your choice from Snacks and Starters section	176

Watercress, Lychee and Cucumber Soup	181

Mango and Pan Fried Calves Liver	204
Orange Sole	268
Pumpkin Fritters	294
Your choice from a good supermarket	

Witches Blackberry Sorbet	320

Breakfast bonanza
Quick & simple
Good old cooked
Why not fish?
Vegetarian

Lunch
Good old cooked
Vegetarian
Picnic selection
Snack of the day

Main meal
Starter

Dish of the day – meat
Dish of the day – fish
Dish of the day – vegetarian
Frozen ready meal

Dessert

November

1

Breakfast bonanza
Quick & simple	Continental Breakfast	154
Good old cooked	Venison Supreme	162
Why not fish?	Tuna Casserole Exotique	169
Vegetarian	Cherry Tomato, Pineapple and Mango Salad	171

Lunch
Good old cooked	Exotique Chicken Satay	215
Vegetarian	Kiwi, Mango and Mushroom Treat	304
Picnic selection	Your choice from Picnic section	196
Snack of the day	Your choice from Snacks and Starters section	176

Main meal
Starter	Pumpkin Soup with Flowers	190
Dish of the day – meat	Steak Diane Exotique	219
Dish of the day – fish	Tomato and Tuna Salad Exotique	257
Dish of the day – vegetarian	Vegetable Curry	296
Frozen ready meal	Your choice from a good supermarket	
Dessert	Super Low Microwaveable Pears	313

2

Breakfast bonanza
Quick & simple	Exotique Treat Multiple Choice	158
Good old cooked	Mango and Pan Fried Calves Liver	163
Why not fish?	Fish with Berries	168
Vegetarian	Starfruit, Potato and Mushroom	170

Lunch
Good old cooked	Plaice and Prawn Creole	282
Vegetarian	Aubergine Exotique	286
Picnic selection	Your choice from Picnic section	196
Snack of the day	Your choice from Snacks and Starters section	176

Main meal
Starter	Red Sockeye Salmon Pâté	194
Dish of the day – meat	Mixed Kebab	242
Dish of the day – fish	Devilled Lobster	274
Dish of the day – vegetarian	Mushroom Flan	287
Frozen ready meal	Your choice from a good supermarket	
Dessert	Rambutans and Pineapple Chantilly	310

3

English Light	155
Bagel, Egg and Dried Venison or Bacon	161
Gefulte Fish	166
Quick Blend with Simple or Exotic Fruits	174

Sweet and Sour Pork	248
Mixed Exotic Salad and Yoghurt Dressing	300
Your choice from Picnic section	196
Your choice from Snacks and Starters section	176

Pumpkin Soup with Prawns	192
Duck Breast Thinner & Richer	244
Plaice-a-Leekie	278
Cauliflower au gratin	305
Your choice from a good supermarket	
Banana Chocolate Treat with Mangoes	316

4

Choose your own Light Breakfast	155
Omelette Exotique of choice	164
Plaice and Kiwi Surprise	167
Mushroom Breakfast	172

Salmon for a King in Pitta Bread	279
Exotic Leeks	307
Your choice from Picnic section	196
Your choice from Snacks and Starters section	176

Exotic Toast	191

North African Cous cous	238
Pepper, Anchovy and Tomato	269
Pumpkin Fritters	294
Your choice from a good supermarket	

Strawberry (or any other fruits) Mousse	320

5

Muesli Treat and Crumpets	153
Chicken Liver Exotique	158
Kipper and Date	166
Banana, Date, Kiwi and Mango	175

Rosemary Lamb	204
Tofu with Exotic Chunky Sauce	291
Your choice from Picnic section	196
Your choice from Snacks and Starters section	176

Melon, Kiwi and Grape Surprise	180

Veal (or Beef) Roast with Prunes and Rambutans	208
Rainbow Trout	264
Savoury Quorn Puffs	290
Your choice from a good supermarket	

Kiwango Ice	310

Breakfast bonanza
Quick & simple
Good old cooked
Why not fish?
Vegetarian

Lunch
Good old cooked
Vegetarian
Picnic selection
Snack of the day

Main meal
Starter

Dish of the day – meat
Dish of the day – fish
Dish of the day – vegetarian
Frozen ready meal

Dessert

6

Highland Variation	153
Bacon and Eggs	161
Sole and Kiwi	169
Hot Fruit Salad	172

Tandoori Meat	245
Rice Exotique	299
Your choice from Picnic section	196
Your choice from Snacks and Starters section	176

Pea Soup Special	192

Exotique Turkey Escalopes	242
Scallop Seviche	253
Quorn with Exotic Chunky Sauce	298
Your choice from a good supermarket	

Honey and Apple Crisp	324

7

Grapefruit Surprise	156
Bacon and Kiwi Treat	162
Kipper and Mango Surprise	164
Lemon and Mango Borscht	171

Fish Soup à la Thinner & Richer	273
Cherry Tomato, Pineapple and Mango Salad	300
Your choice from Picnic section	196
Your choice from Snacks and Starters section	176

Borscht and Yoghurt	181

Chicken Exotique and Dried Venison	210
Red Salmon Omelette	279
Tofu with Exotic Chunky Sauce	291
Your choice from a good supermarket	

Banana Bake Exotique	323

Breakfast bonanza
Quick & simple
Good old cooked
Why not fish?
Vegetarian

Lunch
Good old cooked
Vegetarian
Picnic selection
Snack of the day

Main meal
Starter

Dish of the day – meat
Dish of the day – fish
Dish of the day – vegetarian
Frozen ready meal

Dessert

November

8

Breakfast bonanza
Quick & simple	Light Tabbouleh Breakfast	154
Good old cooked	Start The Day Mixed Grill	159
Why not fish?	Smoked Haddock	168
Vegetarian	Egg and Exotic Hot Fruit	174

Lunch
Good old cooked	Kiwi, Mango and Mushroom Soup	206
Vegetarian	Greek Dip Exotique	289
Picnic selection	Your choice from Picnic section	196
Snack of the day	Your choice from Snacks and Starters section	176

Main meal
Starter	Aubergine and Mango Pâté	191
Dish of the day – meat	Veal (or Beef) Roast with Prunes and Rambutans	208
Dish of the day – fish	Salmon Fillet with Hot Exotic Chunky Sauce	259
Dish of the day – vegetarian	Subtle Kebabs	292
Frozen ready meal	Your choice from a good supermarket	
Dessert	Peach and Papaya Chantilly	319

9

Breakfast bonanza
Authentic New York Bagel	156
Thinner & Richer Kebabs	159
Red Salmon Omelette	167
Cherry Tomato, Pineapple and Mango Salad	171

Lunch
Sardine Exotic Surprise	277
Vegetarian Quorn Chilli Stir Fry	295
Your choice from Picnic section	196
Your choice from Snacks and Starters section	176

Main meal
Melon and Dried Venison or Parma Ham	177
Wild Venison with Ratatouille	225
Exotic Salmon and Plaice	258
Baby Parsnips, Breadcrumbs and Corn	302
Your choice from a good supermarket	
Slimmer Fruit Ice Cream	318

10

Breakfast bonanza
Quick & simple	Muesli Treat and Crumpets	153
Good old cooked	Chicken Liver Exotique	158
Why not fish?	Kipper and Date	166
Vegetarian	Banana, Date, Kiwi and Mango	175

Lunch
Good old cooked	Beef and Lamb Kebabs	201
Vegetarian	Mixed Exotic Salad and Yoghurt Dressing	300
Picnic selection	Your choice from Picnic section	196
Snack of the day	Your choice from Snacks and Starters section	176

Main meal
Starter	Devilled Potato Salad and Celery	185
Dish of the day – meat	Chicken and Aubergine	232
Dish of the day – fish	Prawn and Exotic Salad	256
Dish of the day – vegetarian	Vegetarian Curry with Lychees	289
Frozen ready meal	Your choice from a good supermarket	
Dessert	Fruit Flan	317

11

Breakfast bonanza
Continental Breakfast	154
Mango and Pan Fried Calves Liver	163
Fish with Berries	168
Humpty Dumpty	175

Lunch
Exotic Mackerel	266
Chicory, Pineapple, Kiwi and Mushrooms	304
Your choice from Picnic section	196
Your choice from Snacks and Starters section	176

Main meal
Fluffy Herb Pâté	179
Traditional Shepherd's Pie	202
Smoked Salmon Expanded à la Thinner & Richer	254
Bulghar Wheat Exotique	295
Your choice from a good supermarket	
Quince Thinner & Richer	314

12

English Light	155
Venison Supreme	162
Tuna Casserole Exotique	169
Starfruit, Potato and Mushroom	170

Coconut Beef Satay or Chicken Satay	245
Cranberry Rice Salad	303
Your choice from Picnic section	196
Your choice from Snacks and Starters section	176

Vegetarian Coleslaw	179

Pork or Turkey and Apple	206
Tuna and Egg Salad Exotique	267
Mushroom Flan	287
Your choice from a good supermarket	

Ice Cream Grand Marnier	314

13

Exotique Treat Multiple Choice	158
Omelette Exotique of choice	164
Gefulte Fish	166
Mushroom Breakfast	172

Tuna Special	262
Tofu with Exotic Chunky Sauce	291
Your choice from Picnic section	196
Your choice from Snacks and Starters section	176

Leek Soup	184

Ginger Turkey	240
Starfruit Salmon Salad	271
Savoury Quorn Puffs	290
Your choice from a good supermarket	

Exotic Caramel Custard	325

Breakfast bonanza
Quick & simple
Good old cooked
Why not fish?
Vegetarian

Lunch
Good old cooked
Vegetarian
Picnic selection
Snack of the day

Main meal
Starter

Dish of the day – meat
Dish of the day – fish
Dish of the day – vegetarian
Frozen ready meal

Dessert

14

Choose your own Light Breakfast	155
Bagel, Egg and Dried Venison or Bacon	161
Plaice and Kiwi Surprise	167
Quick Blend with Simple or Exotic Fruits	174

Stir Fried Liver	207
Rice Exotique	299
Your choice from Picnic section	196
Your choice from Snacks and Starters section	176

Chicken Pâté	183

Chinese Chicken Salad with Lychees	250
Potted Herring	266
Vegetarian Lasagne	303
Your choice from a good supermarket	

Banana Split	325

15

Highland Variation	153
Thinner & Richer Kebabs	159
Smoked Haddock	168
Egg and Exotic Hot Fruit	174

Quick Salmon Steak for One	269
Wok Quorn	302
Your choice from Picnic section	196
Your choice from Snacks and Starters section	176

Fish Soup	193

Brandy Fillet Steak, Kiwi Garnish	216
Marinated Red Mullet Exotique	277
Aubergine Exotique au gratin	288
Your choice from a good supermarket	

Fruit Jelly	317

Breakfast bonanza
Quick & simple
Good old cooked
Why not fish?
Vegetarian

Lunch
Good old cooked
Vegetarian
Picnic selection
Snack of the day

Main meal
Starter

Dish of the day – meat
Dish of the day – fish
Dish of the day – vegetarian
Frozen ready meal

Dessert

16

Breakfast bonanza

Quick & simple	Light Tabbouleh Breakfast	154
Good old cooked	Bacon and Kiwi Treat	162
Why not fish?	Kipper and Mango Surprise	164
Vegetarian	Hot Fruit Salad	172

Lunch

Good old cooked	Schnitzel Exotic	207
Vegetarian	Aubergine au Fromage Frais	285
Picnic selection	Your choice from Picnic section	196
Snack of the day	Your choice from Snacks and Starters section	176

Main meal

Starter	Red Sockeye Salmon Pâté	194
Dish of the day – meat	Mango Cholent	210
Dish of the day – fish	Salmon à la Greque	268
Dish of the day – vegetarian	Kiwi, Mango and Lychee Beans	292
Frozen ready meal	Your choice from a good supermarket	
Dessert	Pears, Apple and Ginger Hot Chantilly	315

17

Authentic New York Bagel	156
Start The Day Mixed Grill	159
Sole and Kiwi	169
Lemon and Mango Borscht	171

Fish Soup with Sweetcorn and Lychees	255
Sweet and Sour Amaranth Chinese Lettuce	306
Your choice from Picnic section	196
Your choice from Snacks and Starters section	176

Stir Fry Vegetables and Chilli	195
Champagne Quail	222
Salmon and Rice	255
Exotic Leeks	307
Your choice from a good supermarket	
Kiwango Ice	310

18

Breakfast bonanza

Quick & simple	Grapefruit Surprise	156
Good old cooked	Bacon and Eggs	161
Why not fish?	Fish with Berries	168
Vegetarian	Humpty Dumpty	175

Lunch

Good old cooked	Chicken and Peppers	233
Vegetarian	Crunchy, Kutchie-Fyky	293
Picnic selection	Your choice from Picnic section	196
Snack of the day	Your choice from Snacks and Starters section	176

Main meal

Starter	Melon, Kiwi and Grape Surprise	180
Dish of the day – meat	Indonesian Pork Satay	220
Dish of the day – fish	Plaice, Leek and Lime	274
Dish of the day – vegetarian	Aubergine Treat	285
Frozen ready meal	Your choice from a good supermarket	
Dessert	Mango and Peach Brulée	316

19

Continental Breakfast	154
Mango and Pan Fried Calves Liver	163
Red Salmon Omelette	167
Banana, Date, Kiwi and Mango	175

Shrimp Pilaf Exotique	273
Peas Exotique	293
Your choice from Picnic section	196
Your choice from Snacks and Starters section	176

Carrot Soup	180
Chicken Pesto	230
Lobster Thermidor	272
Budgie Millet Exotique	294
Your choice from a good supermarket	
Banana Chocolate Treat with Mangoes	316

20

English Light	155
Chicken Liver Exotique	158
Kipper and Date	166
Starfruit, Potato and Mushroom	170

Steak Diane Exotique	219
Coconut Rice	301
Your choice from Picnic section	196
Your choice from Snacks and Starters section	176

Sweet and Sour Amaranth Chinese Lettuce	186

Veal Goulash with Lychees	229
Prawn and Mint Dip	272
Quorn with Exotic Chunky Sauce	298
Your choice from a good supermarket	

Cranberry Ice Cream	312

21

Muesli Treat and Crumpets	153
Venison Supreme	162
Tuna Casserole Exotique	169
Cherry Tomato, Pineapple and Mango Salad	171

Red Salmon Omelette	279
Dressed Seasonal Salad	301
Your choice from Picnic section	196
Your choice from Snacks and Starters section	176

Exotic Pears and Mint	190

Exotique Beef Soufflé	227
Plaice-a-Leekie	278
Vegetable Curry	296
Your choice from a good supermarket	

Rambutans and Pineapple Chantilly	310

22

Choose your own Light Breakfast	155
Bagel, Egg and Dried Venison or Bacon	161
Plaice and Kiwi Surprise	167
Quick Blend with Simple or Exotic Fruits	174

Exotique Chicken Satay	215
Kiwi, Mango and Mushroom Treat	304
Your choice from Picnic section	196
Your choice from Snacks and Starters section	176

Lemon and Mango Borscht	184

Slimmers' Lasagne à la Thinner & Richer	237
Salmon for a King	267
Aubergine Exotique	286
Your choice from a good supermarket	

Melon, Orange, Mango and Mint Chantilly	312

Breakfast bonanza
Quick & simple
Good old cooked
Why not fish?
Vegetarian

Lunch
Good old cooked
Vegetarian
Picnic selection
Snack of the day

Main meal
Starter

Dish of the day – meat
Dish of the day – fish
Dish of the day – vegetarian
Frozen ready meal

Dessert

Breakfast bonanza
Quick & simple
Good old cooked
Why not fish?
Vegetarian

Lunch
Good old cooked
Vegetarian
Picnic selection
Snack of the day

Main meal
Starter

Dish of the day – meat
Dish of the day – fish
Dish of the day – vegetarian
Frozen ready meal

Dessert

November

23

Breakfast bonanza

Quick & simple	Exotique Treat Multiple Choice	158
Good old cooked	Bacon and Kiwi Treat	162
Why not fish?	Gefulte Fish	166
Vegetarian	Mushroom Breakfast	172

Lunch

Good old cooked	Smoked Trout	261
Vegetarian	Aubergine au Fromage Frais	285
Picnic selection	Your choice from Picnic section	196
Snack of the day	Your choice from Snacks and Starters section	176

Main meal

Starter	Coconut and Beef Satay or Chicken Satay	195
Dish of the day – meat	Exotique Venison Casserole	233
Dish of the day – fish	White Fish Cous cous	263
Dish of the day – vegetarian	Courgette Exotique	286
Frozen ready meal	Your choice from a good supermarket	
Dessert	Super Low Microwaveable Pears	313

24

Highland Variation		153
Omelette Exotique of choice		164
Kipper and Mango Surprise		164
Hot Fruit Salad		172

Aubergine Exotique au gratin		243
Sesame Seed and Caraway Salad		307
Your choice from Picnic section		196
Your choice from Snacks and Starters section		176

Grapefruit and Tomato Soup		185
Chicken, Apricot and Asparagus		249
Salmon Fillet with Hot Exotic Chunky Sauce		259
Cauliflower au gratin		305
Your choice from a good supermarket		
Exotique Banana Dessert		319

25 Thanksgiving Day Special

Breakfast bonanza

Quick & simple	Continental Breakfast	154
Good old cooked	Chicken Liver Exotique	158
Why not fish?	Plaice and Kiwi Surprise	167
Vegetarian	Humpty Dumpty	175

Lunch

Good old cooked	Kiwi, Mango and Mushroom Soup	206
Vegetarian	Baby Parsnips, Breadcrumbs and Corn	302
Picnic selection	Your choice from Picnic section	196
Snack of the day	Your choice from Snacks and Starters section	176

Main meal

Starter	Carrot Soup	180
Dish of the day – meat	Turkey and Lychees	249
Dish of the day – fish	Whole Poached Salmon with Nettles	281
Dish of the day – vegetarian	Savoury Quorn Puffs	290
Frozen ready meal	Your choice from a good supermarket	
Dessert	Pears Grand Marnier	309

26

Authentic New York Bagel		156
Thinner & Richer Kebabs		159
Smoked Haddock		168
Egg and Exotic Hot Fruit		174

Quick Hot Prawns		262
Baby Parsnips, Breadcrumbs and Corn		302
Your choice from Picnic section		196
Your choice from Snacks and Starters section		176

Exotic Welsh Rarebit		187
Mushroom Flan (contains meat)		231
Smoked Rainbow Trout with Chunky Sauce		257
Pumpkin Fritters		294
Your choice from a good supermarket		
Melon and Berries		315

27

Grapefruit Surprise	156
Bacon and Eggs	161
Fish with Berries	168
Humpty Dumpty	175

Wok Beef	213
Coconut Vegetables	299
Your choice from Picnic section	196
Your choice from Snacks and Starters section	176

Watercress, Lychee and Cucumber Soup	181

Pork or Turkey and Apple	206
Sole in Envelopes	254
Vegetarian Quorn Chilli Stir Fry	295
Your choice from a good supermarket	

Blackberry, Lychee and Cape Gooseberry	323

28

Light Tabbouleh Breakfast	154
Mango and Pan Fried Calves Liver	163
Red Salmon Omelette	167
Lemon and Mango Borscht	171

Red Sockeye Salmon Stir Fry	259
Quince Thinner & Richer	314
Your choice from Picnic section	196
Your choice from Snacks and Starters section	176

Exotic Sardine Pâté	178

Stuffed Cabbage	235
Gefulte Fish	256
Bulghar Wheat Exotique	295
Your choice from a good supermarket	

Honey and Apple Crisp	324

November

Breakfast bonanza
Quick & simple
Good old cooked
Why not fish?
Vegetarian

Lunch
Good old cooked
Vegetarian
Picnic selection
Snack of the day

Main meal
Starter

Dish of the day – meat
Dish of the day – fish
Dish of the day – vegetarian
Frozen ready meal

Dessert

29

English Light	155
Start The Day Mixed Grill	159
Sole and Kiwi	169
Cherry Tomato, Pineapple and Mango Salad	171

Tandoori Meat	245
Greek Dip Exotique	289
Your choice from Picnic section	196
Your choice from Snacks and Starters section	176

Devilled Sardines	187

Exotique Turkey Escalopes	242
Rainbow Trout	264
Subtle Kebabs	292
Your choice from a good supermarket	

Quince Thinner & Richer	314

30

Muesli Treat and Crumpets	153
Venison Supreme	162
Tuna Casserole Exotique	169
Starfruit, Potato and Mushroom	170

Steamed Plaice and Mango	278
Chicory, Pineapple, Kiwi and Mushrooms	304
Your choice from Picnic section	196
Your choice from Snacks and Starters section	176

Green Soup	182

Exotique Ham and Mango	235
Salmon à la Greque	268
Vegetarian Curry with Lychees	289
Your choice from a good supermarket	

Berry Omelette Exotique	311

Breakfast bonanza
Quick & simple
Good old cooked
Why not fish?
Vegetarian

Lunch
Good old cooked
Vegetarian
Picnic selection
Snack of the day

Main meal
Starter

Dish of the day – meat
Dish of the day – fish
Dish of the day – vegetarian
Frozen ready meal

Dessert

1

Continental Breakfast	154
Bagel, Egg and Dried Venison or Bacon	161
Kipper and Date	166
Banana, Date, Kiwi and Mango	175

Chicken and Pasta (cold dish)	236
Cranberry Rice Salad	303
Your choice from Picnic section	196
Your choice from Snacks and Starters section	176

Starfruit, Potato and Mushroom	189

Exotique Turkey and Almonds	232
Salmon and Rice	255
Courgette Exotique	286
Your choice from a good supermarket	

Pears in Berry Sauce	309

2

Highland Variation	153
Chicken Liver Exotique	158
Gefulte Fish	166
Mushroom Breakfast	172

Tuna Special	262
Aubergine Exotique	286
Your choice from Picnic section	196
Your choice from Snacks and Starters section	176

Chicken and Coconut Soup	189

Traditional Shepherd's Pie	202
Tuna and Egg Salad Exotique	267
Kiwi, Mango and Lychee Beans	292
Your choice from a good supermarket	

Guava Ice Cream	324

Breakfast bonanza
Quick & simple
Good old cooked
Why not fish?
Vegetarian

Lunch
Good old cooked
Vegetarian
Picnic selection
Snack of the day

Main meal
Starter

Dish of the day – meat
Dish of the day – fish
Dish of the day – vegetarian
Frozen ready meal

Dessert

3

Exotique Treat Multiple Choice	158
Bacon and Kiwi Treat	162
Plaice and Kiwi Surprise	167
Quick Blend with Simple or Exotic Fruits	174

Left-over Turkey	250
Rice Exotique	299
Your choice from Picnic section	196
Your choice from Snacks and Starters section	176

Melon and Dried Venison or Parma Ham	177

Mixed Kebab	242
Smoked Salmon Cous cous	270
Mushroom Flan	287
Your choice from a good supermarket	

Mango and Lychee Mousse	313

4

Authentic New York Bagel	156
Omelette Exotique of choice	164
Kipper and Mango Surprise	164
Hot Fruit Salad	172

Hot Pickled Herring	271
Crunchy, Kutchie-Fyky	293
Your choice from Picnic section	196
Your choice from Snacks and Starters section	176

Pumpkin Soup with Prawns	192

Duck Breast Thinner & Richer	244
Whole Rainbow Trout a l'Orange	264
Savoury Quorn Puffs	290
Your choice from a good supermarket	

Pears Grand Marnier	309

Breakfast bonanza
Quick & simple
Good old cooked
Why not fish?
Vegetarian

Lunch
Good old cooked
Vegetarian
Picnic selection
Snack of the day

Main meal
Starter

Dish of the day – meat
Dish of the day – fish
Dish of the day – vegetarian
Frozen ready meal

Dessert

December

5

Breakfast bonanza

Quick & simple	Choose your own Light Breakfast	155
Good old cooked	Bacon and Eggs	161
Why not fish?	Fish with Berries	168
Vegetarian	Humpty Dumpty	175

Lunch

Good old cooked	Chicken in Sherry	251
Vegetarian	Peas Exotique	293
Picnic selection	Your choice from Picnic section	196
Snack of the day	Your choice from Snacks and Starters section	176

Main meal

Starter	Aubergine and Mango Pâté	191
Dish of the day – meat	North African Cous cous	238
Dish of the day – fish	Potted Herring	266
Dish of the day – vegetarian	Tofu with Exotic Chunky Sauce	291
Frozen ready meal	Your choice from a good supermarket	
Dessert	Melon and Berries	315

6

Light Tabbouleh Breakfast	154
Thinner & Richer Kebabs	159
Smoked Haddock	168
Cherry Tomato, Pineapple and Mango Salad	171

Prawn Exotique	275
Coconut Rice	301
Your choice from Picnic section	196
Your choice from Snacks and Starters section	176

Exotic Toast	191
Beef and Lamb Kebabs	201
Plaice, Leek and Lime	274
Sweet and Sour Amaranth Chinese Lettuce	306
Your choice from a good supermarket	
Exotique Banana Dessert	319

7

Breakfast bonanza

Quick & simple	Grapefruit Surprise	156
Good old cooked	Start The Day Mixed Grill	159
Why not fish?	Sole and Kiwi	169
Vegetarian	Egg and Exotic Hot Fruit	174

Lunch

Good old cooked	Wok Beef	213
Vegetarian	Aubergine au Fromage Frais	285
Picnic selection	Your choice from Picnic section	196
Snack of the day	Your choice from Snacks and Starters section	176

Main meal

Starter	Sweet and Sour Amaranth Chinese Lettuce	186
Dish of the day – meat	Chicken and Aubergine	232
Dish of the day – fish	Plaice and Prawn Creole	282
Dish of the day – vegetarian	Vegetarian Lasagne	303
Frozen ready meal	Your choice from a good supermarket	
Dessert	Fruit Flan	317

8

English Light	155
Mango and Pan Fried Calves Liver	163
Red Salmon Omelette	167
Lemon and Mango Borscht	171

Exotic Mackerel	266
Sesame Seed and Caraway Salad	307
Your choice from Picnic section	196
Your choice from Snacks and Starters section	176

Cauliflower Soup	193
Cold Meat Salad with Exotic Chunky Sauce	236
Oriental Wok Stir Fry	260
Budgie Millet Exotique	294
Your choice from a good supermarket	
Exotic Caramel Custard	325

9

Continental Breakfast	154
Bagel, Egg and Dried Venison or Bacon	161
Kipper and Date	166
Mushroom Breakfast	172

Sweet and Sour Pork	248
Exotic Leeks	307
Your choice from Picnic section	196
Your choice from Snacks and Starters section	176

Devilled Potato Salad and Celery	185

Chicken Pâté	248
Avocado Salmon	258
Tofu with Exotic Chunky Sauce	291
Your choice from a good supermarket	

Peach and Papaya Chantilly	319

10

Exotique Treat Multiple Choice	158
Chicken Liver Exotique	158
Tuna Casserole Exotique	169
Banana, Date, Kiwi and Mango	175

Sardine Exotic Surprise	277
Aubergine Exotique au gratin	288
Your choice from Picnic section	196
Your choice from Snacks and Starters section	176

Gefulte Fish	183

Lamb and Pawpaw Corsican Style	215
Marinated Red Mullet Exotique	277
Vegetarian Quorn Chilli Stir Fry	295
Your choice from a good supermarket	

Pears, Apple and Ginger Hot Chantilly	315

Breakfast bonanza
Quick & simple
Good old cooked
Why not fish?
Vegetarian

Lunch
Good old cooked
Vegetarian
Picnic selection
Snack of the day

Main meal
Starter

Dish of the day – meat
Dish of the day – fish
Dish of the day – vegetarian
Frozen ready meal

Dessert

11

Muesli Treat and Crumpets	153
Venison Supreme	162
Gefulte Fish	166
Starfruit, Potato and Mushroom	170

Kiwi, Mango and Mushroom Soup	206
Cranberry Rice Salad	303
Your choice from Picnic section	196
Your choice from Snacks and Starters section	176

Chicken and Coconut Soup	189

Veal (or Beef) Roast with Prunes and Rambutans	208
Grapefruit and Red Sockeye Salmon	261
Quorn with Exotic Chunky Sauce	298
Your choice from a good supermarket	

Strawberry (or any other fruits) Mousse	320

12

Highland Variation	153
Bacon and Kiwi Treat	162
Plaice and Kiwi Surprise	167
Quick Blend with Simple or Exotic Fruits	174

Exotic Kedgeree	260
Dressed Seasonal Salad	301
Your choice from Picnic section	196
Your choice from Snacks and Starters section	176

Exotic Welsh Rarebit	187

Chinese Chicken Salad with Lychees	250
Pepper, Anchovy and Tomato	269
Vegetable Curry	296
Your choice from a good supermarket	

Stuffed Pineapple	311

Breakfast bonanza
Quick & simple
Good old cooked
Why not fish?
Vegetarian

Lunch
Good old cooked
Vegetarian
Picnic selection
Snack of the day

Main meal
Starter

Dish of the day – meat
Dish of the day – fish
Dish of the day – vegetarian
Frozen ready meal

Dessert

13

Breakfast bonanza

Quick & simple	Choose your own Light Breakfast	155
Good old cooked	Bacon and Eggs	161
Why not fish?	Fish with Berries	168
Vegetarian	Humpty Dumpty	175

Lunch

Good old cooked	Exotique Liver with Orange	228
Vegetarian	Kiwi, Mango and Mushroom Treat	304
Picnic selection	Your choice from Picnic section	196
Snack of the day	Your choice from Snacks and Starters section	176

Main meal

Starter	Carrot Soup	180
Dish of the day – meat	Wild Venison with Ratatouille	225
Dish of the day – fish	Orange Sole	268
Dish of the day – vegetarian	Cauliflower au gratin	305
Frozen ready meal	Your choice from a good supermarket	
Dessert	Fruit Jelly	317

14

Light Tabbouleh Breakfast	154
Thinner & Richer Kebabs	159
Kipper and Mango Surprise	164
Cherry Tomato, Pineapple and Mango Salad	171

Exotic Salmon and Plaice	258
Cherry Tomato, Pineapple and Mango Salad	300
Your choice from Picnic section	196
Your choice from Snacks and Starters section	176

Exotic Pears and Mint	190
North American Cous cous	226
Starfruit Salmon Salad	271
Mushroom Flan	287
Your choice from a good supermarket	
Ice Cream Grand Marnier	314

15

Breakfast bonanza

Quick & simple	Authentic New York Bagel	156
Good old cooked	Omelette Exotique of choice	164
Why not fish?	Smoked Haddock	168
Vegetarian	Hot Fruit Salad	172

Lunch

Good old cooked	Cider Chicken Calvados	220
Vegetarian	Wok Quorn	302
Picnic selection	Your choice from Picnic section	196
Snack of the day	Your choice from Snacks and Starters section	176

Main meal

Starter	Pea Soup Special	192
Dish of the day – meat	Exotique Venison Stew	211
Dish of the day – fish	Steamed Plaice and Mango	278
Dish of the day – vegetarian	Bulghar Wheat Exotique	295
Frozen ready meal	Your choice from a good supermarket	
Dessert	Baked Fruit	318

16

English Light	155
Mango and Pan Fried Calves Liver	163
Red Salmon Omelette	167
Mushroom Breakfast	172

Salmon for a King in Pitta Bread	279
Coconut Vegetables	299
Your choice from Picnic section	196
Your choice from Snacks and Starters section	176

Lemon and Mango Borscht	184
Exotique Lamb and Papaya or Mango	216
Smoked Salmon Cous cous	270
Quorn with Exotic Chunky Sauce	298
Your choice from a good supermarket	
Slimmer Fruit Ice Cream	318

17

Continental Breakfast	154
Start The Day Mixed Grill	159
Kipper and Date	166
Egg and Exotic Hot Fruit	174

Mango and Pan Fried Calves Liver	204
Exotic Leeks	307
Your choice from Picnic section	196
Your choice from Snacks and Starters section	176

| Cauliflower Soup | 193 |

Original Duck a l'Orange	209
Lobster Thermidor	272
Vegetarian Curry with Lychees	289
Your choice from a good supermarket	

| Strawberry (or any other fruits) Mousse | 320 |

18

Grapefruit Surprise	156
Chicken Liver Exotique	158
Sole and Kiwi	169
Lemon and Mango Borscht	171

Smoked Salmon Expanded à la Thinner & Richer	254
Mixed Exotic Salad and Yoghurt Dressing	300
Your choice from Picnic section	196
Your choice from Snacks and Starters section	176

| Red Sockeye Salmon Pâté | 194 |

Tzimmas with Beef, Mango and Prunes	218
Tomato and Tuna Salad Exotique	257
Baby Parsnips, Breadcrumbs and Corn	302
Your choice from a good supermarket	

| Banana Bake Exotique | 323 |

Breakfast bonanza
Quick & simple
Good old cooked
Why not fish?
Vegetarian

Lunch
Good old cooked
Vegetarian
Picnic selection
Snack of the day

Main meal
Starter

Dish of the day – meat
Dish of the day – fish
Dish of the day – vegetarian
Frozen ready meal

Dessert

19

Muesli Treat and Crumpets	153
Bagel, Egg and Dried Venison or Bacon	161
Gefulte Fish	166
Humpty Dumpty	175

Citrus Chicken	221
Greek Dip Exotique	289
Your choice from Picnic section	196
Your choice from Snacks and Starters section	176

| Fish Soup | 193 |

Exotic Shepherd's Pie	221
Prawn and Mint Dip	272
Kiwi, Mango and Lychee Beans	292
Your choice from a good supermarket	

| Kiwango Ice | 310 |

20

Exotique Treat Multiple Choice	158
Bacon and Kiwi Treat	162
Plaice and Kiwi Surprise	167
Quick Blend with Simple or Exotic Fruits	174

Fish Soup à la Thinner & Richer	273
Crunchy, Kutchie-Fyky	293
Your choice from Picnic section	196
Your choice from Snacks and Starters section	176

| Coconut and Beef Satay or Chicken Satay | 195 |

Original Duck a l'Orange	209
Scallop Seviche	253
Aubergine Treat	285
Your choice from a good supermarket	

| Super Low Microwaveable Pears | 313 |

Breakfast bonanza
Quick & simple
Good old cooked
Why not fish?
Vegetarian

Lunch
Good old cooked
Vegetarian
Picnic selection
Snack of the day

Main meal
Starter

Dish of the day – meat
Dish of the day – fish
Dish of the day – vegetarian
Frozen ready meal

Dessert

21

Breakfast bonanza

Quick & simple	Highland Variation	153
Good old cooked	Venison Supreme	162
Why not fish?	Tuna Casserole Exotique	169
Vegetarian	Starfruit, Potato and Mushroom	170

Lunch

Good old cooked	Devilled Lamb Steaks	209
Vegetarian	Tofu with Exotic Chunky Sauce	291
Picnic selection	Your choice from Picnic section	196
Snack of the day	Your choice from Snacks and Starters section	176

Main meal

Starter	Green Soup	182
Dish of the day – meat	Chopped Liver	214
Dish of the day – fish	Red Salmon Omelette	279
Dish of the day – vegetarian	Subtle Kebabs	292
Frozen ready meal	Your choice from a good supermarket	
Dessert	Banana Split	325

22

Light Tabbouleh Breakfast	154
Omelette Exotique of choice	164
Kipper and Mango Surprise	164
Banana, Date, Kiwi and Mango	175

Smoked Trout	261
Sweet and Sour Amaranth Chinese Lettuce	306
Your choice from Picnic section	196
Your choice from Snacks and Starters section	176

Tuna Pâté	182
Meaty Cous cous	239
Pepper, Anchovy and Tomato	269
Vegetarian Lasagne	303
Your choice from a good supermarket	
Peach and Papaya Chantilly	319

23

Breakfast bonanza

Quick & simple	English Light	155
Good old cooked	Thinner & Richer Kebabs	159
Why not fish?	Smoked Haddock	168
Vegetarian	Hot Fruit Salad	172

Lunch

Good old cooked	Wild Venison and Mango Exotique	228
Vegetarian	Aubergine au Fromage Frais	285
Picnic selection	Your choice from Picnic section	196
Snack of the day	Your choice from Snacks and Starters section	176

Main meal

Starter	Vegetarian Coleslaw	179
Dish of the day – meat	Veal (or Beef) Roast with Prunes and Rambutans	208
Dish of the day – fish	Devilled Lobster	274
Dish of the day – vegetarian	Courgette Exotique	286
Frozen ready meal	Your choice from a good supermarket	
Dessert	Baked Fruit	318

24

Authentic New York Bagel	156
Bacon and Eggs	161
Fish with Berries	168
Cherry Tomato, Pineapple and Mango Salad	171

Fish Soup with Sweetcorn and Lychees	255
Kiwi, Mango and Mushroom Treat	304
Your choice from Picnic section	196
Your choice from Snacks and Starters section	176

Fluffy Herb Pâté	179
Hot Meat or Poultry with Exotic Chunky Sauce	205
Whole Rainbow Trout a l'Orange	264
Vegetable Curry	296
Your choice from Picnic section	
Rambutans and Pineapple Chantilly	310

December

25 Christmas Day Special

Exotique Treat Multiple Choice	158
Venison Supreme	162
Kipper and Mango Surprise	164
Starfruit, Potato and Mushroom	170

Exotic Sardine Pâté	178

Turkey and Lychees	249
Whole Poached Salmon with Nettles	281
Savoury Quorn Puffs	290
Your choice from a good supermarket	

Cranberry Ice Cream	312

Wild Venison with Ratatouille	225
Chicory, Pineapple, Kiwi and Mushrooms	304
Your choice from Picnic section	196
Your choice from Snacks and Starters section	176

Breakfast bonanza
Quick & simple
Good old cooked
Why not fish?
Vegetarian

Lunch
Starter

Dish of the day – meat
Dish of the day – fish
Dish of the day – vegetarian
Frozen ready meal

Dessert

Snack evening meal
Good old cooked
Vegetarian
Picnic selection
Snack of the day

26

Choose your own Light Breakfast	155
Start The Day Mixed Grill	159
Kipper and Date	166
Mushroom Breakfast	172

Brandy Fillet Steak, Kiwi Garnish	216
Aubergine Exotique	286
Your choice from Picnic section	196
Your choice from Snacks and Starters section	176

Stir Fry Vegetables and Chilli	195

Cauliflower au gratin	223
Salmon à la Greque	268
Cauliflower au gratin	305
Your choice from a good supermarket	

Pears in Berry Sauce	309

27

Grapefruit Surprise	156
Mango and Pan Fried Calves Liver	163
Gefulte Fish	166
Lemon and Mango Borscht	171

Tuna Special	262
Dressed Seasonal Salad	301
Your choice from Picnic section	196
Your choice from Snacks and Starters section	176

Exotic Red Borscht	194

Left-over Turkey	250
Marinated Red Mullet Exotique	277
Coconut Rice	301
Your choice from a good supermarket	

Guava Ice Cream	324

Breakfast bonanza
Quick & simple
Good old cooked
Why not fish?
Vegetarian

Lunch
Good old cooked
Vegetarian
Picnic selection
Snack of the day

Main meal
Starter

Dish of the day – meat
Dish of the day – fish
Dish of the day – vegetarian
Frozen ready meal

Dessert

December

28

Breakfast bonanza

Quick & simple	Muesli Treat and Crumpets	153
Good old cooked	Chicken Liver Exotique	158
Why not fish?	Red Salmon Omelette	167
Vegetarian	Egg and Exotic Hot Fruit	174

Lunch

Good old cooked	Melon with Dried Wild Venison	214
Vegetarian	Cherry Tomato, Pineapple and Mango Salad	300
Picnic selection	Your choice from Picnic section	196
Snack of the day	Your choice from Snacks and Starters section	176

Main meal

Starter	Devilled Sardines	187
Dish of the day – meat	Exotique Pintade Rotir (Guinea Fowl)	205
Dish of the day – fish	Gefulte Fish	256
Dish of the day – vegetarian	Wok Quorn	302
Frozen ready meal	Your choice from a good supermarket	
Dessert	Banana Chocolate Treat with Mangoes	316

29

Breakfast bonanza

	Continental Breakfast	154
	Bacon and Kiwi Treat	162
	Sole and Kiwi	169
	Quick Blend with Simple or Exotic Fruits	174

Lunch

	Quick Hot Prawns	262
	Peas Exotique	293
	Your choice from Picnic section	196
	Your choice from Snacks and Starters section	176

Main meal

	Melon, Kiwi and Grape Surprise	180
	Cold Meat Salad with Exotic Chunky Sauce	236
	White Fish Cous cous	263
	Aubergine Treat	285
	Your choice from a good supermarket	
	Cranberry Ice Cream	312

30

Breakfast bonanza

Quick & simple	Exotique Treat Multiple Choice	158
Good old cooked	Bagel, Egg and Dried Venison or Bacon	161
Why not fish?	Plaice and Kiwi Surprise	167
Vegetarian	Humpty Dumpty	175

Lunch

Good old cooked	Coconut Beef Satay or Chicken Satay	245
Vegetarian	Budgie Millet Exotique	294
Picnic selection	Your choice from Picnic section	196
Snack of the day	Your choice from Snacks and Starters section	176

Main meal

Starter	Watercress, Lychee and Cucumber Soup	181
Dish of the day – meat	Ginger Turkey	240
Dish of the day – fish	Salmon Fillet with Hot Exotic Chunky Sauce	259
Dish of the day – vegetarian	Exotic Leeks	307
Frozen ready meal	Your choice from a good supermarket	
Dessert	Mango and Peach Brulée	316

31 — New Years Eve Special

Breakfast bonanza

	Authentic New York Bagel	156
	Omelette Exotique of choice	164
	Smoked Haddock	168
	Starfruit, Potato and Mushroom	170

Lunch

	Scallop Seviche	253
	Mixed Exotic Salad and Yoghurt Dressing	300
	Your choice from Picnic section	196
	Your choice from Snacks and Starters section	176

Main meal

	Exotic Pears and Mint		190
	Quail or Venison, Caviar and Champagne	246	247
	Poached Salmon, Caviar and Champagne		280
	Mushroom Flan		287
	Your choice from a good supermarket		
	Hot Winter Fruits and Champagne		322

A very happy Thinner & Richer New Year

Muesli Treat and Crumpets

Highland Variation

Breakfast

30 minutes (veg)

To serve one person, you will need:

1 x 100ml glass any fruit or vegetable juice of your choice – why not try cranberry?

1 good portion (breakfast bowl) any muesli with few or no nuts

150ml skimmed or soya milk, sweetened or unsweetened (soya milk produces a lovely nutty flavour without using any fattening nuts)

1 crumpet

Very low-fat spread

Tea, coffee or lemon tea

Preparation:

Enjoy your glass of fruit or vegetable juice chilled. Enjoy your bowl of muesli served with the skimmed or soya milk. Toast the crumpet. Spread with very low-fat spread and, if required, 1 teaspoon of jam or honey. Drink your tea or coffee with a slice of lemon or dash of milk. Why not try herbal tea? Today's suggestion is camomile.

Approximate calories per serving: 400

30 minutes (veg)

To serve one person, you will need:

1 x 150ml glass any fruit or vegetable juice of your choice (Safeway produce a massive range)

Porridge – you may use the traditional way of steeping oats overnight or it is probably quicker to use the instant porridge which can be bought from any supermarket

1 carton soya milk, sweetened or unsweetened

1 eggcup raisins or craisins (dried cranberries) or pieces of any dried fruit, but do not use nuts, they contain too much fat

1 teaspoon sea salt

2 teaspoons clear honey

Tea, coffee or herbal tea

Preparation:

Enjoy your glass of fruit or vegetable juice chilled. Prepare your porridge either in the traditional way or following the manufacturer's instructions on the packet. It only takes about 90 seconds to make it in the microwave. Use soya milk as this gives a lovely nutty taste. Once cooked mix in the raisins or craisins. Add salt to taste. Top with 2 teaspoons of clear honey and enjoy. Drink tea or coffee with a slice of lemon or dash of milk and granulated sweetener. Why not try herbal tea? Today's suggestion is mango and apple.

Approximate calories per serving: 300

Highland Variation

Breakfast

Continental Breakfast

30 minutes (veg)

To serve one person, you will need:

1 x 100ml glass unsweetened, chilled apple and mango, or any other fruit juice (the Safeway brand is excellent and is relatively unsweetened)

2 thin slices large loaf bread, any colour

1 portion very low-fat spread

1 small portion jam, honey, marmalade or diabetic preserve

Tea, coffee or herbal tea

Preparation:

Enjoy your glass of fruit juice.
Toast your bread and spread with low-fat spread and preserve. Enjoy your tea or coffee with a slice of lemon or dash of milk. Add granulated sugar, if required. Why not try a herbal tea?

Approximate calories per serving: 300

Light Tabbouleh Breakfast

1 hour (veg)

To serve four people, you will need:

125g bulgar wheat (supermarket or health food shop)

2 tablespoons extra virgin olive oil

1 tablespoon lime juice

1 tablespoon lemon juice

3 large spring onions, sliced julienne (longways)

1/2 tablespoon chopped mint

2 tablespoons chopped parsley

2 medium tomatoes, diced

2 chopped dried apricots

4 dried prunes, stoned and chopped

6 stoneless olives, quartered

1 small chicory

1 little gem lettuce

Salt and ground black pepper

Preparation:

Cover the bulgar wheat with boiling water. Cover and leave for 20 minutes. Drain and squeeze in kitchen roll. Add the lemon and lime juices and olive oil and mix well. Stand for 20 minutes. Add the spring onions, mint, parsley, apricot and prunes and mix well and season. Serve on a bed of lettuce and chicory topped with olives. Serve each portion with a large 200ml glass of fruit juice, preferably unsweetened, black tea or coffee with a splash of milk or lemon. Add granulated sweetener if required. Why not try herbal tea? Camomile, levantier, mango and apple or other.

Approximate calories per serving: 400

English Light

30 minutes (veg)

To serve one person, you will need:

1 x 100ml glass juice of any type (why not try unsweetened orange, prune, grape, pineapple, carrot or vegetable of your choice)

1 cup (200mls) Kelloggs Corn Flakes, Quaker Puffed Wheat or other non-sugar cereal

2 teaspoons clear honey

150ml skimmed milk

1 thin slice, large loaf bread, any colour

1 portion very low-fat spread

Small portion jam, honey, marmalade or diabetic preserve

Tea, coffee or herbal tea

Preparation:

Enjoy your glass of fruit juice chilled. Enjoy your cereal topped with clear honey and milk. Toast your bread and spread thinly with low-fat spread and small portion of preserve. Enjoy your tea or coffee with a slice of lemon or dash of milk. Why not try a herbal tea? Today's suggestion is camomile, levantier or rosehip.

Approximate calories per serving: 250

Choose your own Light Breakfast

30 minutes (veg)

To serve one person, you will need:

1 x 100ml glass of any fruit or vegetable juice

Your choice of a medium breakfast bowl (large cup) of any cereal or muesli but avoid the sugar coated ones and those containing nuts

150ml skimmed milk or soya milk (sweetened or unsweetened) which gives a lovely nutty taste

1 crumpet or 1/2 teacake or 1 medium slice of bread or 1/2 bagel

Low-fat fromage frais, any flavour

Very low-fat spread

1 banana

A little brown sugar

1 portion jam, honey or marmalade or other preserve

Preparation:

Enjoy your chilled glass of fruit or vegetable juice. Enjoy your choice of cereal made with skimmed or soya milk. Toast your crumpet or 1/2 teacake or slice of bread or 1/2 bagel and spread with either a heaped teaspoon of fromage frais (any flavour) or, alternatively, a portion of very low-fat spread. Top this with a few slices of banana and a sprinkling of brown sugar or, alternatively, you can use a portion of any jam, honey, preserve or diabetic preserve. Finish off with tea or coffee with a slice of lemon or a dash of milk with granulated sweetener or why not try your choice of any herbal tea.

Approximate calories per serving: 350

Breakfast

Grapefruit Surprise

30 minutes (veg)

To serve one person, you will need:

1/2 grapefruit

1 glacé cherry

Candarel, or similar granulated sweetener

1 large thin slice brown or white bread

Very low-fat spread

1 portion jam, honey or diabetic preserve

1 Shapers (Boots) apricot and chocolate chip cereal bar or similar

Tea, coffee or herbal tea

Preparation:
Cut the grapefruit in half. Using a grapefruit knife divide it into sections and top with a glacé cherry. Chill if required. Spread bread thinly with low-fat spread and a portion of preserve. Enjoy your chocolate chip cereal bar. Make tea or coffee served black or with a slice of lemon or dash of milk. Add granulated sweetener if required. Why not try herbal tea? There's camomile, levantine, rosehip, mango and apple, raspberry etc.

Approximate calories per serving: 250

Authentic New York Bagel
with a vegetarian option

30 minutes

To serve one person, you will need:

1 whole bagel, any colour or flavour or texture (I suggest Authentic New York Bagels). Each bagel will probably be sliced in half

A portion of very low-fat spread, if required

Suggested fillings: low-fat fromage frais; 1 egg scrambled in Fry Light cooking spray; low-fat salami; dried meat or venison; low-fat thick cream cheese; 1 rasher of lean bacon; 1 low-fat sausage or piece of ham; any exotic fruit, eg mango, or traditional fruit, eg banana, or berries of choice; drained tuna, sardine or salmon; smoked salmon; prawns and a little slimline mayonnaise; smoked salmon and some low-fat cheese, low or no fat fromage frais; sliced mushrooms and peppers; sliced chicken or turkey (no skin or fat); lean steak; lean venison (freshly cooked or smoked); cinnamon, apple or raisins; mixed colour grapes and low-fat cream cheese; Kiwi, mango, banana, strawberry and fromage frais; any salad mixture of choice with only one nut element; any jam, relish, honey or preserve

Preparation: Bagels are a super base for your breakfast. They contain no cholesterol or added fat and they are healthy and wholesome. Toast your half bagel in a pop-up toaster until it is just brown and then spread it with one of the fantastic range of fillings suggested above. Do not worry too much about the calorie content if you stick to the above range, even a slice of venison or steak will only be around 120 calories. Enjoy your half bagel with 100ml glass of chilled fruit juice, tea or coffee with a dash of milk or why not try a herbal tea. You can, if you wish, have a whole bagel but, in this case, please miss out the fruit juice.

Approximate calories per half Bagel fully dressed with a glass of fruit juice: 250. A whole Bagel fully dressed: 350

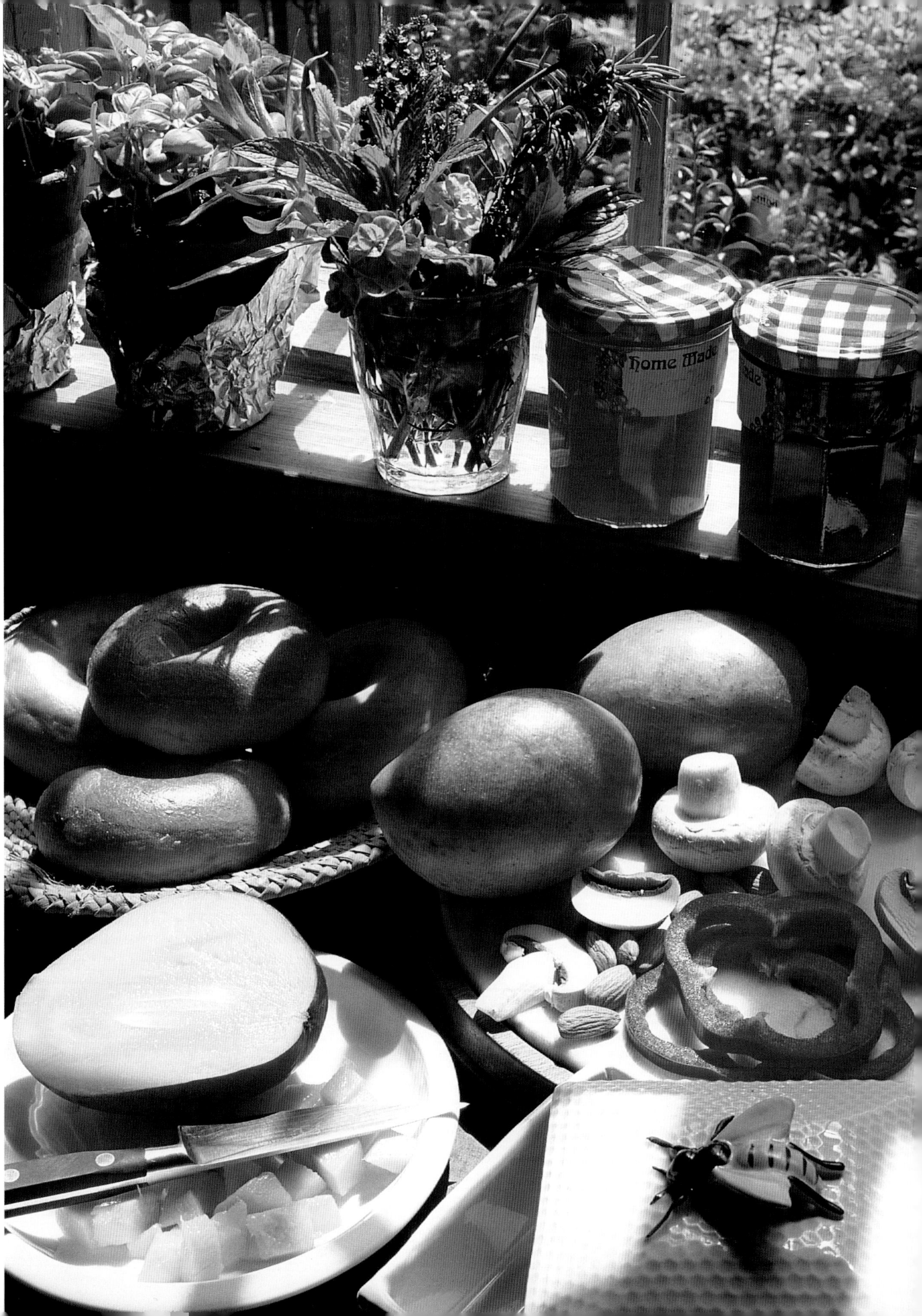
Home Made

Breakfast

Exotique Treat Multiple Choice

30 minutes (veg)

To serve one person, you will need:

1 x 100ml glass of any fruit or vegetable juice (why not try Safeway Banana Nectar)

Make up a choice of any of the following combinations to fill a normal size breakfast cereal bowl. These can be fresh or canned provided you drain off the syrup (Safeway produce a range of most of the fruits canned):

Mango, coconut milk (but not coconut), banana, lychees, paw paw (papaya), starfruit (carambola), pomello, pomegranate, custard apple, passion fruit, guava, physalis (cape gooseberry), granadilla, pineapple, kiwango, kumquat, prickly pear, rambutans, sharon fruit and mangosteen

Tea, coffee or herbal tea

Preparation:

Enjoy your chilled fruit or vegetable juice. Make up a big breakfast bowl of any combination of the exotic fruits and enjoy them. Have a cup of tea or coffee with a slice of lemon or a dash of milk and granulated sweetener if required but why not try a herbal tea. Today's suggestion is mango and apple.

Approximate calories per portion: 300

Good old Cooked

Chicken Liver Exotique

30 minutes

To serve two people, you will need:

225g frozen or fresh chicken liver (well defrosted)

Fry Light non-stick cooking spray

1 tablespoon virgin olive oil

Ground ginger

Ground black pepper

3 heaped teaspoons coarse cut marmalade (any fruit)

1 head chicory or lettuce

1 medium tomato – thinly sliced

6 stoned lychees – fresh or drained from can

2 teaspoons coconut milk powder

Salt

1 Kiwi fruit, peeled and thinly sliced

Preparation:

Coat a hot non-stick pan or wok with 4 applications of Fry Light and 1 tablespoon of virgin olive oil. Season with salt and fry the livers gently for 6 minutes turning frequently to prevent burning. Remove from the heat and baste the liver with the juices. Sprinkle on black pepper, ground ginger and coconut milk powder. Top each liver with marmalade and add lychees. Cook in a pan under a hot grill for 2 minutes. Serve on a bed of chicory or lettuce and sliced tomato and Kiwi. Serve each portion with 1 large slice of wholemeal bread, lightly toasted. Enjoy with a 100ml glass of chilled fruit or vegetable juice, tea, coffee or herbal tea with a slice of lemon or dash of milk.

Approximate calories per serving: 450

Start The Day Mixed Grill

30 minutes

To serve one person, you will need:

5 small tomatoes

50g lean rump steak (with all the fat cut off) cut into 3 pieces

1 boned lamb chop (with the fat taken off) cut in half

2 low-fat or vegetarian sausages

1 pepper, green or red, thinly sliced and deseeded

8 button mushrooms

1 small onion, finely chopped

Fry Light non-stick cooking spray

1 tablespoon extra virgin olive oil

Salt and ground black pepper

Dried rosemary

Parsley

Preparation:

Spray a hot non-stick pan, frying pan or wok with 2 applications of Fry Light. Add the olive oil. Heat and add the pepper and onions. After 1 minute add the steak, lamb, sausage and pricked tomatoes. Sprinkle with rosemary and season with salt and pepper. Keep turning and cook for 5 minutes, stirring and turning all the time. Add the mushrooms whole and cook for a further 2 minutes. Stir well, put under a very hot grill for 90 seconds, garnish with parsley and serve. This breakfast should be accompanied with a 100ml glass of fruit or vegetable juice of your choice and tea, coffee or herbal tea

Approximate calories per serving: 500

Thinner & Richer Kebabs

1 hour

To serve one person, you will need:

225g raw skinless, boneless chicken or turkey breast

100g lean rump or fillet steak or veal

150g button mushrooms

1 red pepper, deseeded and cut into chunks

1 green pepper, deseeded and cut into chunks

8 large spring onions, cut in half

3 tablespoons extra virgin olive oil

1 clove garlic, crushed

4 teaspoons lime juice

3 teaspoons tomato purée

Dried rosemary

Salt and ground black pepper

Maggi liquid seasoning or soy sauce

Preparation:

On 8 long steel skewers arrange chunks of chicken, peppers, meat, spring onion, mushrooms as decoratively as possible. Season with salt and black pepper. Mix in a bowl the olive oil, garlic, lime juice, tomato purée and Maggi. Brush this lavishly over the skewered kebabs and sprinkle with dried rosemary. Cook at 180 degrees centigrade in a grill pan lined and covered with foil. Cooking time is approximately 1 hour with frequent basting with the juices during cooking. Serve as your breakfast with 1 medium slice of bread, toasted and covered with very low-fat spread. Start with 100ml glass of chilled fruit or vegetable juice, tea, coffee or herbal tea of your choice.

Approximate calories per serving: 450

Bagel, Egg and Dried Venison or Quorn

Bacon and Eggs or Quorn

30 minutes

To serve two people, you will need:
2 Authentic New York Bagels, sliced in half, from a good supermarket
100g (6 slices) wild dried venison, supermarket own brand, or 2 rashers very lean bacon, or 100g Quorn
2 medium eggs
Very low-fat spread
Skimmed milk
Fry Light non-stick spray

Preparation:
Toast the bagels and lightly spread with very low-fat spread. Coat a hot non-stick pan with 4 applications of Fry Light and fry the venison for 60 seconds, turning once, or fry the bacon for 3 minutes. Alternatively, the bacon can be grilled. Crack 2 eggs into a bowl and discard 1 yolk. Add 1 tablespoon of skimmed milk and scramble in a non-stick pan coated with Fry Light. Serve the bagel as a sandwich with the venison or bacon and egg in the middle. This breakfast should be accompanied by 100ml glass of fruit or vegetable juice of your choice and tea, coffee or herbal tea.

Approximate calories per serving: 375

NB Quorn is a vegetable substitute for bacon or venison

30 minutes

To serve one person, you will need:
2 rashers (40g) lean streaky bacon, or 100g Quorn
2 small eggs
1 slice of large loaf, any colour, toasted, with a thin covering of very low-fat spread
Salt and ground black pepper

Preparation:
Weigh the bacon to 40g and trim off any fat. Grill under a medium heat for 3 minutes each side. Crack 2 small eggs into a bowl and discard 1 yolk. Add 25mls of skimmed milk and whisk gently. Add salt and pepper to taste. Spray a small non-stick pan with 3 sprays of Fry Light non-stick cooking spray. Add the eggs, stirring all the time, until nicely scrambled. Place the cooked bacon on the toast and top with the egg and a fresh halved tomato. Put under a hot grill for 30 seconds and serve. This breakfast should be accompanied by a 100ml glass of any fruit or vegetable juice of your choice and tea, coffee or herbal tea.

Approximate calories per serving: 450

Breakfast

Bacon or Quorn and Kiwi Treat

can be Beef or Beefburger instead of Quorn

30 minutes

To serve one person, you will need:

2 lean rashers of bacon (50g) or lean rump steak or
1 low-fat beefburger, or 100g Quorn

1 Kiwi fruit, sliced (the skin can be left on or off)

1 peeled banana, sliced

Unsweetened lemon juice

2 medium tomatoes, cut in half

100g (1/5 small tin) Heinz baked beans, preferably
Weight Watcher with no added sugar

Salt and ground black pepper

Preparation:

Grill the bacon (steak or beefburger) for a few minutes each side. Top with the sliced fruit and the tomatoes. Grill for 2 further minutes. Season and sprinkle with lemon juice. Serve with hot baked beans. This breakfast should be accompanied by a 100ml glass of any fruit or vegetable juice of your choice, preferably from the large Safeway range. You could also have tea, coffee or herbal tea with a slice of lemon or dash of milk, if required.

Approximate calories per serving: 350

Venison Supreme

30 minutes

To serve two people, you will need:

A supermarket vacuum packed venison steak (8 ounces or 200g)

Fry Light non-stick spray oil

2 teaspoons extra virgin olive oil

1 teaspoon Pura Light-touch sunflower oil with Buttery Taste

1 large tomato

Garlic salt

Ground black pepper

1 x 400g can sliced mango (half reserved or freeze and use the other half)

1 satsuma, leaved and peeled

Lettuce

Preparation:

Coat a hot non-stick pan or wok with 4 applications of Fry Light and add the olive oil and Pura Light-touch oil. When very hot add the venison. Fry, turning frequently for 3 minutes for rare, 4 minutes for medium, 5 minutes for well done and 6 minutes for over done. Meanwhile heat half the mango slices and juices in a microwave for 1 minute. Serve the venison topped with satsuma and half a tomato and surrounded with 2 or 3 mango slices. Allow 1 dark Ryvita, water biscuit or cream cracker spread with very low-fat spread. This breakfast should be accompanied by 100ml glass of any vegetable or fruit juice of your choice. Why not try apricot, prune, carrot, mango, tangerine or cranberry? You could also have black tea or coffee with a dash of milk or slice of lemon or any herbal tea of your choice.

Approximate calories per serving: 450

Mango and Pan Fried Calves Liver

30 minutes

To serve two people, you will need:

2 x 75g fresh calves liver (2 portions)

Fry Light non-stick spray oil

2 teaspoons extra virgin olive oil

1/2 level teaspoon dairy butter

6 shallots or small pickling onions, chopped

1/4 of 400g can sliced mangoes (the rest will keep in fridge or freeze)

Garlic salt

Ground black pepper

Salt

Preparation:

Coat a hot non-stick pan with 4 applications of Fry Light. Add the olive oil, butter and the salt. Sauté the onions for 4 minutes over a medium heat stirring all the time. Remove the onions with a spoon and reserve. Lightly sprinkle each liver with garlic salt and black pepper. Sauté in the pan for 6 minutes, turning frequently. Reintroduce the onions and sauté for 3 minutes stirring all the time over a medium heat. Serve with a seasonal salad or 1 thin slice of toast spread with very low-fat spread. This breakfast should be accompanied be a 100ml glass of chilled fruit or vegetable juice of your choice and tea, coffee or herbal tea.

Approximate calories per serving: 400

Pumpkin and Quorn or Bacon

30 minutes

To serve four people, you will need:

4 lean rashers bacon, all fat cut off and chopped, or 200g Quorn

800g pumpkin, deseeded and cut into 3 inch x 1/2 inch oblongs

2 medium onions, finely chopped

2 cloves garlic, finely chopped

2 tablespoons extra virgin olive oil

100g can chopped tomatoes

3 tablespoons tomato purée

1/2 teaspoon each of dried coriander, rosemary and thyme

75g low-fat cheddar cheese, grated

Fry Light cooking spray

Parsley to garnish

Salt and ground black pepper

Preparation:

Coat a large hot non-stick pan with 4 applications of Fry Light and add the olive oil. Put in the bacon, garlic and onions and sauté for 5 minutes, stirring frequently. Add tomato purée, tomatoes and herbs and then add the pumpkin. Bring to the boil and simmer for 25 minutes, stirring frequently. Add half the cheese and simmer for 60 seconds. Put in a bowl and sprinkle with the rest of the cheese and the parsley. Toast under a hot grill for 30 seconds and serve. This breakfast may be enjoyed with a 100ml glass of chilled fruit or vegetable juice and tea, coffee or herbal tea of your choice.

Approximate calories per serving: 450

Breakfast | Omelette Exotique of choice | Kipper and Mango Surprise

164

30 minutes

To serve one person, you will need:

Fry Light spray cooking oil

2 teaspoons extra virgin olive oil

3 small eggs, cracked into a bowl, discard one yolk

2 tablespoons skimmed milk

Salt and pepper

2 teaspoons skimmed milk powder

1 Kiwi fruit, sliced and unpeeled

Parsley

Filling of choice: either 1 ounce grated cheese; 1 ounce diced smoked salmon; 2 ounces diced, strained, tinned salmon, tuna, sardine or mackerel; 1 ounce ham or dried venison; 2 ounces vegetable mix of choice; 2 ounces baked beans; 1 ounce flaked almonds mixed with herbs and onions, or really whatever you choose

Preparation:

Coat a hot non-stick omelette pan with 4 applications of Fry Light and add the olive oil. Sauté the filling for 2 to 3 minutes, stirring all the time. Beat together the eggs, milk, milk powder and season. Pour over the filling and cook over a moderate heat until the egg begins to set. Sprinkle with cheese if using cheese. Turn the omelette if you so wish. Garnish with parsley and serve topped with Kiwi slices and 1 thin slice of a large loaf of bread, any colour, toasted and spread with very low-fat spread. This breakfast can be accompanied by a 100ml glass of chilled fruit or vegetable juice of your choice, coffee, tea or herbal tea

Approximate calories per serving: 400

Omelette Exotique of choice

Kipper and Mango Surprise

30 minutes

To serve one person, you will need:

1 tin sliced mango

1 tin grapefruit segments

1 tin mandarin segments

100g fresh boneless kipper or 100g boil in the bag boneless kipper (wt. approx)

1 aerosol pack low calorie whipped cream substitute (Anchor or Delissimo)

Preparation:

Discard any juices and syrup from the fruit. Mix equal portions of the fruits in a glass bowl to a total of 125 grams per person. Top with a portion of low calorie spray aerosol cream substitute and serve as a super starter. Boil the kipper in the bag for 15 minutes or grill without added fat for 3 minutes each side under a medium heat. Drain off all the juices on a kitchen roll. Serve on 1 thin slice of bread, toasted, thinly spread, if required, with very low-fat spread. Garnish with 2 slices of drained mango and a small sliced tomato, if available. Return to the grill for 15 seconds on a maximum heat and serve. As you had a fruit starter today you cannot have fruit juice but you may still have tea, coffee or herbal tea of your choice.

Approximate calories per serving: 350

NB Boil-in-the-bag kippers vary from 100-250g and may serve 2 people. They can be kept in the fridge, defrosted and grilled as fresh, or boiled in the bag, as directed

Smoked Kippers

Breakfast

Gefullte Fish

2 hours +

To serve four people, you will need:

2 small carrots

2 medium onions

1lb fresh skinned and boneless haddock fillets (keep the skin, bones and head, if available)

4 teaspoons extra virgin olive oil

1 ½ teaspoons caster sugar

Salt and white pepper

2 eggs with 1 yolk discarded

3 tablespoons matzo meal (crumbs, if not available)

1 tablespoon ground almonds

Preparation:

Mince the fish, onion and 1 carrot together. Add the eggs, ground almonds, olive oil, sugar, 1 teaspoon salt and a pinch of pepper. Add matzo meal and shape into balls or patties. In a separate pan bring to the boil 750mls of water along with the fish skins, bones and heads, the other carrot and a sliced onion. Season with a little salt and pepper and simmer for 30 minutes and then strain. Pour the strained liquid over the patties in a deep pan and boil gently for 45 minutes. Serve hot or chilled from the fridge, each portion with 2 dark Ryvita spread with very low-fat spread. Enjoy your breakfast with a 100ml glass of chilled fruit or vegetable juice and tea, coffee or herbal tea.

Approximate calories per serving: 350

Kipper and Dates

30 minutes

To serve one person, you will need:

100g (wt. approx) boned kipper fillet or boil-in-the-bag kipper

6 dates, stoned

6 seedless grapes, halved

1 slice thin large loaf, brown or white bread

Lemon juice

Very low-fat spread

Preparation:

Lightly toast the bread and spread with low-fat spread. Grill the kipper (no fat added) under a medium grill, turning twice until cooked (about 10 minutes) or boil in the bag. Alternatively the boil in the bag kipper can be removed and grilled. Do not use the juices. Put the cooked kipper on toast and cover with stoned dates and halved grapes. Cook under a hot grill for 40 seconds, sprinkle with lemon juice and serve. Enjoy this breakfast with a 100ml glass of chilled fruit or vegetable juice of your choice and tea, coffee or herbal tea.

Approximate calories per serving: 450

Plaice and Kiwi Surprise

30 minutes

To serve one person, you will need:

2 small 75g (wt. approx) fillets boneless plaice

2 teaspoons dairy butter

Salt and ground black pepper

1 Kiwi fruit, unpeeled and thinly sliced

2 oatmeal biscuits

Preparation:

Season the plaice in a non-stick grill pan. Put a knob of butter on each and grill under a medium heat for 2 minutes each side. Top with Kiwi and grill under a hot grill for 1 minute and serve each on an oatmeal biscuit. You can enjoy this breakfast with a 100ml glass of fruit or vegetable juice and tea, coffee or herbal tea.

Approximate calories per serving: 350

Red Salmon Omelette

30 minutes

To serve one person, you will need:

1 x 105g can red salmon, drained and flaked

2 small eggs with 1 yolk discarded

2 tablespoons low-fat fromage frais

Salt and ground black pepper

1/2 teaspoon freshly chopped tarragon, chives or spring onions

Fry Light spray cooking oil

1 teaspoon dairy butter

Preparation:

Coat a hot non-stick omelette pan with 4 applications of Fry Light and add the butter. Beat the eggs, fromage frais and the herbs together and season. Cook over a moderate heat until the bottom begins to set. Remove from the heat, flake salmon over and put under a moderate grill in the pan until it sets. Fold over and serve. This breakfast can be enjoyed with a 100ml glass of chilled fruit or vegetable juice of your choice and tea, coffee or herbal tea.

Approximate calories per serving: 400

Breakfast

Fish with Berries

Smoked Haddock

30 minutes

1 hour

To serve two people, you will need:

2 fillets white fish (trout, salmon, herring, plaice, mackerel, sole)

1 tablespoon fine oatmeal

Salt and ground black pepper

25g dairy butter

100g berries of your choice eg. gooseberries, rasp-berries, blackberries, cranberries

1 teaspoon soft brown sugar

Pinch of nutmeg

1 tablespoon apple juice

To serve one person, you will need:

1 medium onion, sliced in rings

125g boneless smoked haddock (or mackerel or cod) or 125g pack of boil in the bag smoked haddock or fish of your choice

Very low-fat spread (good supermarket own brand)

Salt and ground black pepper

125mls skimmed milk

8 small tomatoes

Parsley or chives

1 thin slice of large wholemeal loaf or rye bread

Preparation:

Sprinkle cleaned fish with oatmeal, salt and pepper. Dot with butter and cook under a medium grill for 12 minutes. Simmer the berries, the sugar, the nutmeg and the apple juice until soft (about 10 to 15 minutes). Blend, pour over the fish and serve. You could enjoy this breakfast with a 100ml glass of chilled fruit or vegetable juice of your choice, preferably from the Safeway range, and tea, coffee or herbal tea. One half slice of toast or 1 dark Ryvita spread with very low-fat spread is also permitted.

Approximate calories per serving: 400

Preparation:

Either boil in the bag, or bake the fish in a hot oven in an oven proof dish at 190 degrees centigrade with a level tea-spoon of low-fat spread for 45 minutes. Once cooked, add the milk, the sliced onion and 4 tomatoes halved and sea-son to taste. Continue to cook until the fish is tender and succulent. Slice the 4 remaining tomatoes. Surround the had-dock with the raw sliced tomato. Garnish with parsley or chives and a dash of low-fat spread. Serve with 1 thin slice of large wholemeal or rye bread lightly spread with low-fat spread. This breakfast can be enjoyed with a 100ml glass of chilled fruit or vegetable juice of your choice. Why not try the Safeway range, eg apple, banana, grape, carrot, mandarin, apple and mango, mixed vegetable, prune, the choice is endless. You can also have tea, coffee or one of the large range of herbal teas.

Approximate calories per serving: 400

168

Fish with Berries

Smoked Haddock

Tuna Casserole Exotique

Sole and Kiwi

30 minutes

To serve four people, you will need:

2 x 200g can tuna chunks in brine or water

1 x 300g can Campbells Condensed Chicken Soup, or similar

2 x 200g can creamed sweetcorn

1 red pepper, chopped

1 large red onion, chopped

1 x 400g can lychees, drained (good supermarket own brand)

Salt and ground black pepper

30 minutes

To serve four people, you will need:

4 x 100g fillets skinned and boneless sole (or white fish of choice)

1 small red onion, finely chopped

4 teaspoons extra virgin olive oil

2 teaspoons lemon juice

2 teaspoons lime juice

2 teaspoons balsamic vinegar

1 teaspoon sea salt

1/2 teaspoon ground black pepper

4 peeled Kiwi fruit

1/4 cucumber, sliced

Parsley, chopped

Sole and Kiwi

Preparation:

Combine in a casserole dish all the ingredients. Bake at 190 degrees centigrade for 25 minutes and serve with a little seasonal salad. This breakfast can be enjoyed with a 100ml glass of chilled fruit or vegetable juice and tea, coffee or herbal tea.

Approximate calories per serving: 350

Preparation:

Cut and liquidise 1 Kiwi and set aside.

A. In a large bowl combine 3 chopped Kiwis, onion, cucumber, 1 teaspoon olive oil, 1 teaspoon lemon juice, half the salt and all the pepper. Set aside...

B. Lightly oil the grill pan with olive oil. Whisk the remaining lemon juice, lime juice, salt and a pinch of pepper. Coat the fish with this mixture and grill for 3 minutes each side, turning and brushing with the whisked juices.

Serve topped with A and then B. Serve each portion with 2 dark Ryvita spread with very low-fat spread or 1 medium slice large loaf, toasted. This breakfast can be enjoyed with a 100ml glass of chilled fruit or vegetable juice and tea, coffee or herbal tea.

Approximate calories per serving: 350

Breakfast

Witches Plaice

Starfruit, Potato and Mushroom

1 hour

To serve four people, you will need:

8 small plaice fillets and 8 blackberries

3 tablespoons chopped chives

Salt and ground black pepper

4 tablespoons sunflower margarine

2 tablespoons plain flour

250ml dry white wine

2 tablespoons lime juice

2 red roses

Preparation:

Place on each fillet chopped chives, rose petals and 8 blackberries and half a teaspoon of margarine. Roll up the fillets and secure each with a cocktail stick or string. Line a shallow oven-proof dish with a little margarine to grease. Arrange the fillets and season again. In a hot non-stick pan melt the remaining 2 tablespoons of margarine. Stir in the flour and cook for 50 seconds, stirring all the time. Pour in the wine until the mixture thickens and add the lime juice. Pour over the plaice fillets and cover with foil. Bake in the oven at 180 degrees centigrade for 30 minutes. Remove the foil and sprinkle with remaining blackberries and rose petals. Serve for breakfast with 2 dark Ryvita or 1 medium slice of bread, toasted, each spread with very low-fat spread. You may also enjoy with this breakfast 1 small glass of chilled fruit or vegetable juice, for instance from the large Safeway range. Why not try Prune Juice or Banana Nectar? This breakfast should also be accompanied by tea, coffee or a choice of any of the lovely herbal teas. Why not try camomile or rosehip?

Approximate calories per serving: 450

30 minutes (veg)

To serve four people, you will need:

500g scrubbed small new potatoes, cut in half

2 medium onions, sliced

100g small button mushrooms, whole

50ml vegetable stock (supermarket own brand cube)

2 teaspoons sherry or balsamic vinegar

2 tablespoons chopped chives

100ml low-fat Greek yoghurt

Salt and ground white pepper

1 Florida starfruit

Preparation:

Put the potatoes and onions in a large microwave dish and sprinkle over the stock and the vinegar. Cover with Stretch 'n Seal (no vent) and cook on the maximum for 4 minutes in a microwave. Cut away the Stretch 'n Seal but be careful – do not get scalded by the steam. Stir and season with salt and pepper. Now cover with Stretch 'n Seal with a vent (slit). Microwave for another 4 minutes until soft. Allow to stand for 5 or 10 minutes, stirring occasionally. Slice the starfruit into 8 slices and spoon the mixture over each and garnish with yoghurt and chives. Serve each portion with 1 large slice of toast covered, if necessary, with very low-fat spread. Enjoy this breakfast with a 100ml glass of chilled vegetable or fruit juice and tea, coffee or herbal tea.

Approximate calories per serving: 300

Cherry Tomato, Pineapple and Mango Salad

30 minutes (veg)

To serve four people, you will need:

500g cherry tomatoes (green, red or yellow)

1 x 400g can mango slices

1 x 400g can pineapple chunks

2 Kiwi fruit

2 satsumas, leaved

12 berries (strawberry, raspberry, gooseberry, logan-berry etc)

3 tablespoons (50ml) low-fat fromage frais

1 bunch calabrese (sprouting broccoli)

2 tablespoons sherry vinegar

1 tablespoon natural yoghurt

Worcester Sauce

Coleman's Old English mustard powder

2 teaspoons soft brown sugar

Preparation:

Put in a liquidiser and blend together half of the mango slices and the juices from the mango and pineapple. Add the fromage frais, yoghurt, sherry vinegar, a dash of Worcester Sauce and a pinch of mustard powder. Blend until smooth, add sugar, blend again and refrigerate. Arrange on a platter tomatoes, mangoes (the other half of the can), pineapple chunks and Kiwi balls made with the melon baller scoop. Cut off the stalks of the calabrese and add the heads to the platter. Add the berries and the satsumas. Pour over the mango sauce and serve each portion with 2 dark Ryvita spread, if necessary, with very low-fat spread. This breakfast can be enjoyed with a 100ml glass of chilled fruit or vegetable juice of your choice and tea, coffee or herbal tea.

Approximate calories per serving: 350

Lemon and Mango Borscht

30 minutes (veg)

To serve four people, you will need:

1 stalk lemon grass (the outer 2 layers removed), very finely chopped – if none available a teaspoon of lemon and 2 teaspoons of lime juice will suffice

6 medium cooked beetroot (home or ready cooked from the supermarket but not pickled)

3 teaspoons Dijon mustard

1 x 400g can tinned supermarket mangoes

150-200ml cultured buttermilk or nil percent fat fromage frais

1 tablespoon balsamic or sherry vinegar

1/2 teaspoon dried tarragon

1/2 teaspoon dried mixed herbs

Salt and ground black pepper

McDougalls Thickening Granules

Preparation:

Liquidise all the ingredients and season to taste. If too thin gently simmer with McDougalls granules. If too thick add water or skimmed milk. Chill. Serve cold for breakfast with 2 dark Ryvita or 1 large slice of medium bread, toasted and spread with very low-fat spread. Enjoy this breakfast with a 100ml glass of vegetable or fruit juice, chilled, and tea, coffee or herbal tea.

Approximate calories per serving: 300

NB This breakfast can be served hot on a cold day. Heat, preferably, in a microwave in a soup bowl.

Breakfast

Hot Fruit Salad

Mushroom Breakfast

30 minutes (veg)

To serve four people, you will need:

50g dried apricots

75g dried pears

75g dried figs

2 medium bananas, peeled and sliced

1/2 tin sliced mango, drained

75g green grapes, seedless

2 sticks cinnamon

Very low-fat spread (good supermarket own brand)

2 medium oranges, peeled and segmented

10ml (2 level teaspoons) cornflour

200ml apple juice

Preparation:

Cut the dried apricots, pears and figs into 1/2 inch squares or chunks. Put in a saucepan with cinnamon and apple juice and boil. Simmer for 10 minutes stirring occasionally. Mix the cornflour with 2 to 3 teaspoons of water and add to the mixture and stir until it begins to thicken. Remove the cinnamon sticks. Add the banana, orange and the grapes. Stir and heat for 3 minutes and serve hot. Enjoy this breakfast with a 100ml glass of unsweetened, chilled fruit or vegetable juice of your choice, a Boots 28 calorie rice cake and tea, coffee or herbal tea.

Approximate calories per serving: 350

Hot Fruit Salad

Assorted Mushrooms

30 minutes (veg)

To serve four people, you will need:

Fry Light spray cooking oil

2 teaspoons extra virgin olive oil

500g any type of mushroom or edible fungus

120ml vegetable stock made from supermarket cube

1 teaspoon Maggi mixed seasoning or soy sauce

1 teaspoon Lea and Perrins Worcester Sauce

4 spring onions, chopped

1 medium red onion, chopped

2 teaspoons Dijon mustard

1 teaspoon dried tarragon

120ml white wine or dry sherry or vermouth or white apple juice

Salt and ground black pepper

McDougalls Thickening Granules

Preparation:

Coat a hot large non-stick saucepan with 4 applications of Fry Light and add the olive oil. Sauté the onions and the spring onions for 2 minutes, stirring. Add the mushrooms, stock, Maggi, Lea and Perrins and wine and simmer and stir until it reduces and thickens. Now season with salt and pepper and add the tarragon and Dijon mustard. Simmer until the ingredients are soft and the sauce is thick. If necessary add McDougalls granules. Serve each of the 4 portions heaped onto 2 thin toasted slices of large loaf bread, finely spread, if necessary, with very low-fat spread. This breakfast can be enjoyed with a 100ml glass of chilled fruit or vegetable juice and tea, coffee or herbal tea.

Approximate calories per serving: 350

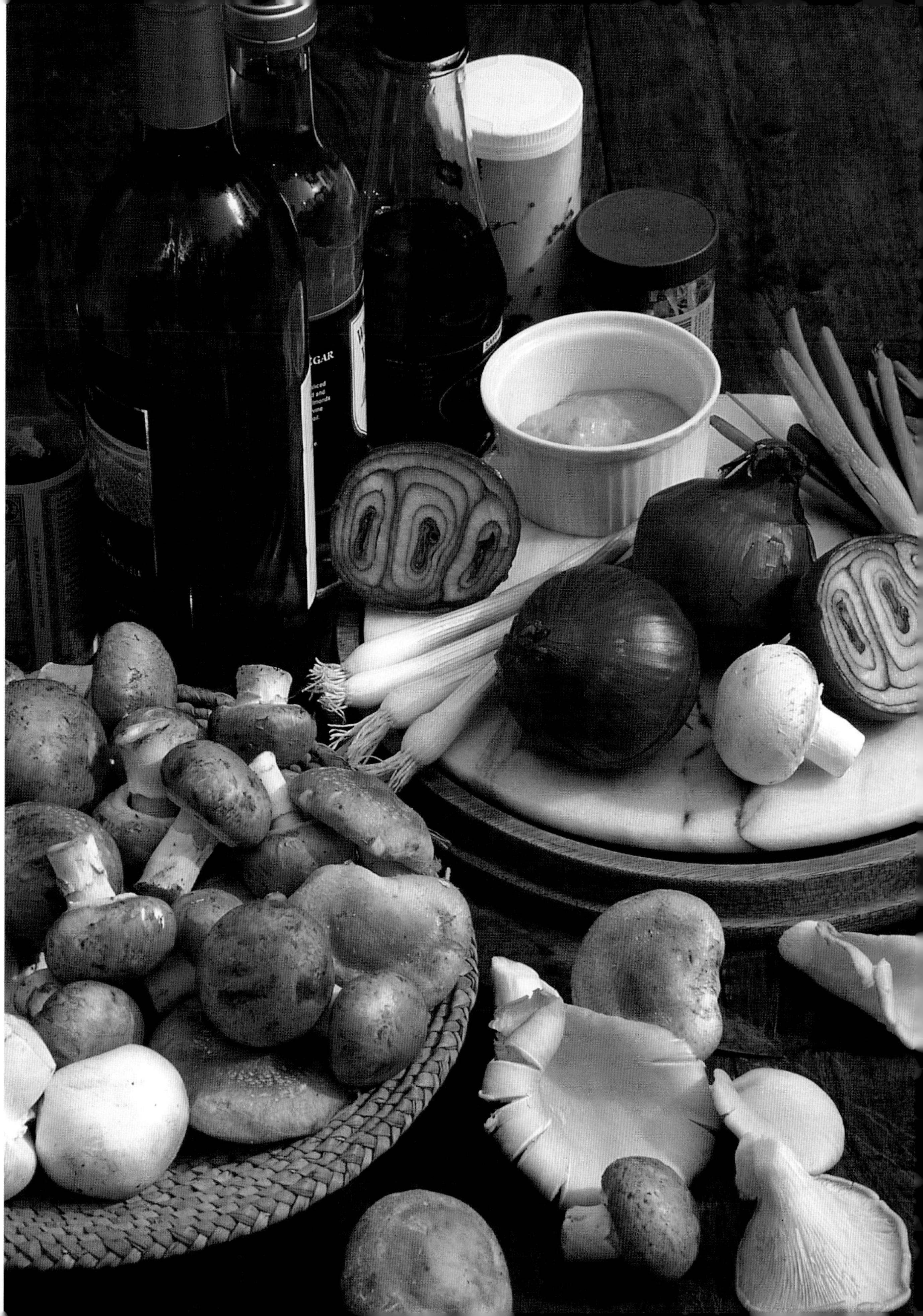

Ingredients for Mushroom Breakfast

Breakfast

Quick Blend Breakfast with Simple or Exotic Fruits

30 minutes (veg)

To serve one person, you will need:

1 soft banana

2 oranges, squeezed (use the juices and a little of the pulp but no skin, pips or pith)

3 tablespoons low-fat fromage frais or natural yoghurt

1 peach or nectarine, diced with the skin on

1 soft pear, diced with the skin on

1/2 mango, diced with the skin removed or 3 slices from a can of mangoes

6 or 8 seasonal berries eg. strawberries, raspberries or blackberries

Preparation:
Blend and serve, chilled or at room temperature. Enjoy with 2 dark Ryvita spread with very low-fat spread, 100ml glass of chilled fruit or vegetable juice and tea, coffee or herbal tea.

Approximate calories per serving: 350

Egg and Exotic Hot Fruit

30 minutes (veg)

To serve one person, you will need:

1 medium egg

1 large thin slice of bread, any colour

Very low-fat spread

1 small Kiwi fruit, sliced with the skin off or on

4 slices tinned mango

1/2 small banana cut into 1 half moon crescent

Salt and ground black pepper

Preparation:
Toast the bread and spread thinly with low-fat spread. Poach the egg for 4 minutes until ready. Season with salt and pepper. Put the egg on the toast and circle with banana on one side and Kiwi slices on the other and top with mango. Put under a hot grill for 40 seconds and serve. This breakfast should be enjoyed with a 100ml glass of chilled fruit or vegetable juice and tea, coffee or herbal tea.

Approximate calories per serving: 300

Banana, Date, Kiwi and Mango

30 minutes (veg)

To serve one person, you will need:

1 medium banana, peeled

3 stoned dates

1 large Kiwi fruit

1 tin sliced mango (supermarket own brand)

1 Anchor, or similar, aerosol pack whipped cream substitute

Preparation:

Cut the banana into 2 new moons. Slice the Kiwi, peeled or unpeeled, into 10 small slices and surround the banana on the outside of a large plate. Drain the juice from the mangoes and arrange 75g within the banana crescents. Top the mangoes with dates and apply 1 serving of whipped cream substitute. This breakfast can be enjoyed with a 100ml glass of any chilled vegetable or fruit juice of your choice and tea, coffee or herbal tea. As an extra treat, 1 Boots 28 calorie rice cake goes beautifully with this breakfast.

Approximate calories per serving: 350

Humpty Dumpty

30 minutes (veg)

To serve one person, you will need:

1 medium brown egg

1 large thin slice of bread, any colour

Very low-fat spread

Preparation:

Boil a fresh brown egg for about 4 minutes or a little more if you want it firmly set. Serve with toast soldiers which can be dipped into the yolk. Enjoy this breakfast with a 100ml glass of chilled fruit or vegetable juice of your choice. Why not try Safeway Banana Nectar, Tangerine Juice or Mixed Vegetable Juice? You can also have tea, coffee or herbal tea of your choice, why not try raspberry, rosehip, levantine, lemon, camomile, apple or mango.

Approximate calories per serving: 300

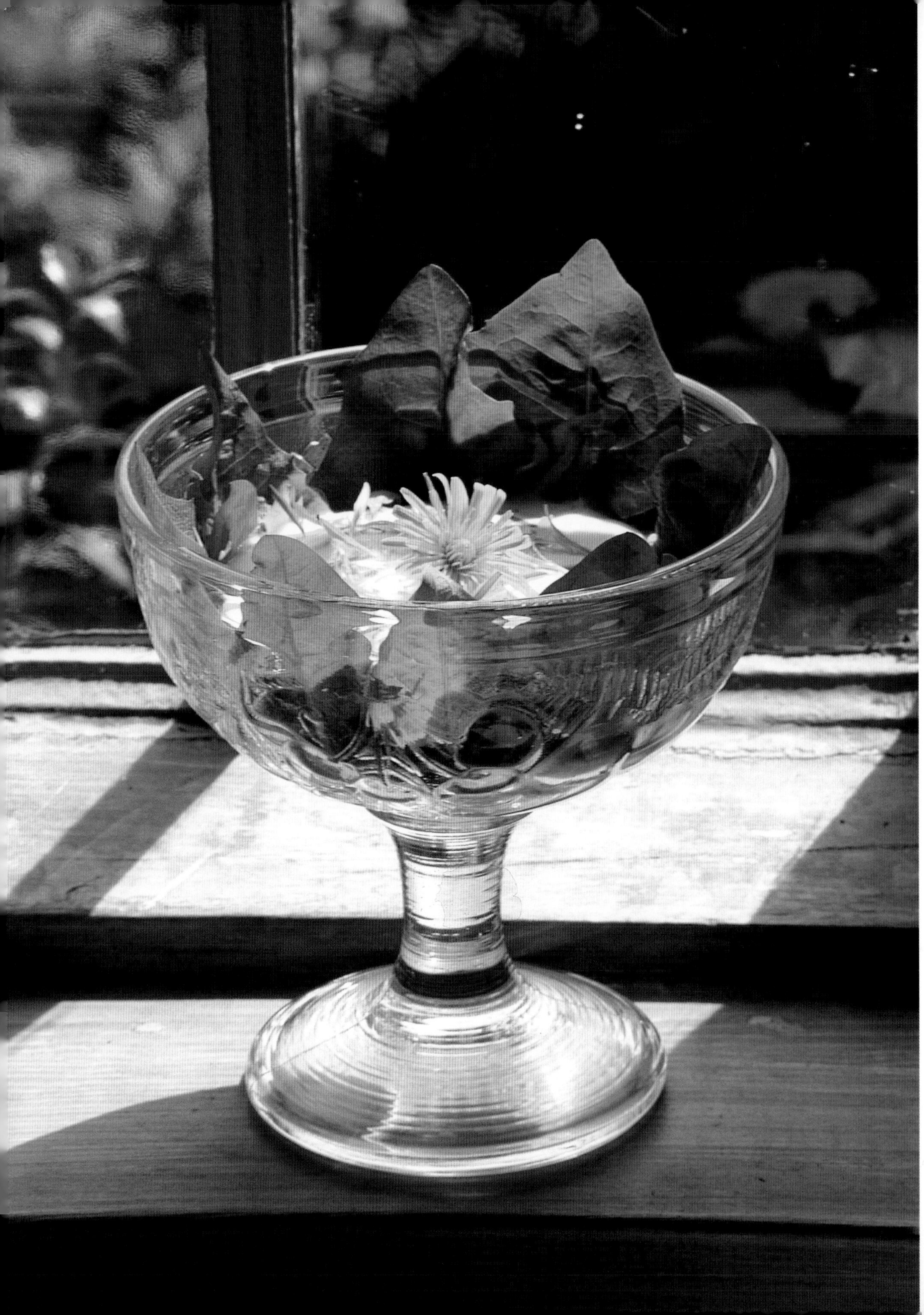

Dandelion Summer Starter

Dandelion Summer Starter

Melon with Dried Venison or Parma Ham

30 minutes (veg)

To serve four people, you will need:

8 dandelions, preferably young ones with young leaves and fresh flowers

4 small lettuce hearts

1 x 200g carton Greek low-fat yoghurt

Salt and ground black pepper

30 minutes

To serve two people, you will need:

1 sweet ogen melon

100g dried wild venison (supermarket own brand) or parma ham

Preparation:

Halve and deseed the melon.

Serve each half with 50 grams parma ham or dried wild venison. Chill before serving.

Approximate calories per serving: 150
(with Venison)

Approximate calories per serving: 200
(with Parma Ham)

NB Wild venison comes packaged in a 6 slice 100g supermarket pack with approximately 207 calories in total. It is made by Rannoch Smokery, various other outlets and supermarkets, such as Safeway, do their own brand.

Preparation:

Line a grapefruit dish with young dandelion leaves. If they are a little tough, blanch them in hot water first. Shred the lettuce hearts and cover the dandelion leaves. Season and add 50mls of yoghurt to each. Tear off the dandelion petals, sprinkle all over the yoghurt and lettuce mixture and serve.

Approximate calories per serving: 50

Exotic Sardine Pâté

30 minutes

To serve four people, you will need:

1 x 120g can sardines in oil, drained

Grated rind and juice of 1 small lime or 1/2 a lemon

4 kumquats, halved longways

75ml natural low-fat yoghurt

50g cottage cheese with chives, strained to reduce any liquid

1½ inches of cucumber, skinned and finely chopped

4 dark Ryvita

Garlic salt

Ground black pepper

Preparation:

Remove the tail and spine bones from the sardines and mash with lemon rind and juice until smooth. Add yoghurt, cottage cheese and chives and cucumber. Season with garlic salt and black pepper. Chill and serve on a dark Ryvita garnished with 2 half kumquats.

Approximate calories per serving: 100

Chopped Herring Chunky Pâté

30 minutes

To serve six people, you will need:

3 rollmop herrings (total 200g)

1 large onion

1 large apple (eating apple eg Cox, Granny Smith)

1 teaspoon soft brown sugar

Salt and ground white pepper

4 hard boiled eggs, with 2 yolks discarded

1 tablespoon wine vinegar

1 lemon

Lettuce

Preparation:

Mince the herring, onion, apple and eggs for a chunky texture (if you want them for a pâté then liquidise). Add the vinegar and sugar and season with salt and pepper and refrigerate. Serve each portion sitting on a lettuce leaf, garnished with a slice of lemon and with 2 Ryvita, 2 cream crackers, 2 water biscuits or 4 small table matzas spread with very low-fat spread.

Approximate calories per serving: 250

Vegetarian Coleslaw

30 minutes (veg)

To serve one person, you will need:

250g hard white cabbage, shredded

100g cucumber, thinly sliced and cut

4 medium carrots, shredded or grated

3 tablespoons chives

50mls white wine vinegar

50mls balsamic or cider vinegar

4 teaspoons granulated sweetener

1 large red pepper, diced

2 teaspoons clear honey

Salt and ground black pepper

Preparation:

Dry all the vegetables on kitchen roll. Put in a bowl, mix well and season. Add more sweetener if required. Chill and serve.

Approximate calories per serving: 50

Fluffy Herb Pâté

30 minutes (veg)

To serve four people, you will need:

4 small carrots, washed and sliced

400g Quark or fat-free skimmed milk curd cheese

100g low-fat fromage frais

1 teaspoon Lea and Perrins Worcester Sauce

2 tablespoons Gales clear honey

3 tablespoons chopped chives

3 tablespoons chopped parsley

2 tablespoons any chopped herb of choice, eg. mint, thyme, coriander, rosemary or basil

1 tablespoon sherry vinegar

1 clove garlic, finely chopped

Salt and ground black pepper

Cayenne pepper

Preparation:

Put 1 carrot on each dish. Put all the rest of the ingredients into a liquidiser and blend and season to taste. Chill. Ladle over the carrots and garnish with cayenne pepper. Serve each portion with 2 dry high-baked water biscuits (Jacobs or supermarket own brand).

Approximate calories per serving: 200

Starters and Snacks

Carrot Soup

Melon, Kiwi and Grape Surprise

30 minutes

To serve six people, you will need:

McDougalls Thickening Granules

500g small clean carrots, sliced

1 medium onion, diced

3 sticks celery, finely chopped

Bunch of parsley or watercress, finely chopped – about 1/2 cup

15g butter

15g very low-fat spread

25g plain flour

600mls skimmed milk

600mls chicken stock (made from stock cubes)

3 teaspoons Rose's lime juice

125g carton low-fat natural unsweetened yoghurt

Parsley or chives to garnish

Salt and ground black pepper

Fry Light non-stick cooking spray

Carrot Soup

Preparation:

Boil the carrots in salted water for 12 minutes and drain. Coat a hot saucepan with 4 applications of Fry Light. Add the butter and margarine and sauté the onion and celery until soft, stirring frequently. Stir in the flour vigorously and add all the carrots. Slowly add the stock, milk and yoghurt in equal proportions, stirring. Boil and simmer for 6 minutes. Add the lime juice and chopped parsley or water-cress. Season to taste. Simmer for 90 seconds and allow to cool a little. Now blend in a liquidiser. The soup is now ready to be reheated. If the soup is too thick, blend in a little water or skimmed milk. If the soup is too thin, reboil and blend in a few McDougalls granules. Serve, garnished with pars-ley or chives.

Approximate calories per serving: 250

30 minutes (veg)

To serve four people, you will need:

1 ogen melon or 1 x 350g tin melon balls

1 melon baller

3 Kiwi fruit

16 medium sized black, red or green grapes

Preparation:

Cut and deseed the melon, the seeds are full of calories so throw them away. Scoop out into balls and place in a bowl. If using tinned melons drain off all the juices. Scoop out the Kiwi with the melon baller or slice it. You can leave the peel on or remove it according to your choice. Add to the melon with the grapes, mix gently, chill and serve.

Approximate calories per serving: 100

Borscht and Yoghurt

Watercress, Lychee and Cucumber Soup

30 minutes (veg)

To serve four people, you will need:

225g raw beetroot, not pickled

150g raw apples

100g raw pears

1 medium onion

1 tablespoon cider vinegar

2 tablespoons natural Greek yoghurt

Salt and ground black pepper

30 minutes

To serve four people, you will need:

1 x 425g can tinned lychees supermarket own brand

1 small onion, chopped

1/2 cucumber, chopped finely with the skin left on

Bunch of watercress

3 teaspoons (15 mls) unsweetened lemon juice

Salt and ground black pepper

Ground coriander

Ground nutmeg

300ml skimmed milk

600ml chicken stock made from supermarket cube

3 level teaspoons cornflour

Parsley or chives

Watercress, Lychee and Cucumber Soup

Preparation:

Peel, slice and core the beetroot, onions and the fruit. Add the vinegar, cover with water and simmer, stirring occasionally, until cooked. Liquidise and strain. Season with salt and black pepper, add yoghurt and serve hot or chilled.

Approximate calories per serving: 100

Preparation:

Drain the lychees and put in a saucepan. Add onion, cucumber and stock. Bring to the boil and simmer for 12 minutes. Chop up the watercress coarsely and add. Then add lemon juice, salt, pepper, coriander and nutmeg. Simmer for 8 minutes, stirring occasionally. Allow to cool a little and then blend in a food liquidiser. Return to the washed pan and add the milk and bring back to the boil. Mix cornflour well in a little bit of cold water and add slowly to the soup stirring all the time and boil again. Simmer for 2 minutes adding further salt and pepper to taste. Serve hot or chilled garnished with parsley or chives.

Approximate calories per serving: 100

Starters and Snacks

Green Soup

30 minutes (veg)

To serve four people, you will need:

1.5 litres water

1 large onion, finely sliced

2 cloves garlic, finely sliced

1 level teaspoon shrimp pâté

2 level teaspoons Maggi liquid seasoning or soy sauce

1 level teaspoon salt

250g of mixture of any of the following chopped green leaves: watercress, cabbage, chinese cabbage, sorrel, spinach, lettuce, dandelion or young shoots of nettles (handled with care)

150g white cauliflower heads, finely chopped

Salt and ground black pepper

McDougalls Thickening Granules

Preparation:

Bring water to the boil in a large saucepan. Add the onion, garlic, shrimp pâté, Maggi and cauliflower and simmer for 3 minutes, stirring all the time. If the greens include nettles or dandelion leaves, which should be young, add them now and stir. Then add the chopped greens and simmer for a further 5 minutes and season to taste. The soup is now ready to serve or it can be liquidised. If the soup is very thin, you could simmer it with McDougalls Granules for a minute. However, the cauliflower normally thickens it but if you omit this you will definitely need McDougalls granules.

Approximate calories per serving: 100

Tuna Pâté

30 minutes

To serve four people, you will need:

1 x 200g can tuna fish in brine, well drained

5 tablespoons mango chutney

2 tablespoons lime juice

1 x 75g carton Quark or skimmed milk curd cheese

Salt and ground black pepper

Dried cayenne pepper

4 thin slices of large loaf bread

Preparation:

Put the ingredients in a liquidiser. Blend, season and then chill. Meanwhile, toast the 4 slices of bread until they are slightly burnt and allow them to cool. Spread the chilled pâté on each slice of bread and garnish with cayenne pepper.

Approximate calories per serving: 200

Gefullte Fish

2 hours +

To serve eight people, you will need:

4 small carrots

2 medium onions

450g fresh, skinned, boned, haddock fillet (keep the skins, bones and heads if they are available)

4 teaspoons virgin olive oil

1½ teaspoons caster sugar

Salt and ground white pepper

2 eggs, 1 yolk discarded

3 tablespoons matzo meal or crumbs

1 tablespoon ground almonds

Preparation:

Mince the fish, 1 onion and 2 carrots together. Add the eggs, ground almonds, olive oil, sugar, salt and pepper (you will need about 1 teaspoon of salt and just a pinch of pepper). Add the matzo meal and shape into balls or patties of golf ball size. Boil 750mls of water with the fish skin, bones and head. Add the other 2 carrots and 1 sliced onion, salt and pepper and simmer for 30 minutes and strain. Pour this strained liquid over the patties and boil gently for 45 minutes over a ring or in the oven. Serve hot or cold.

Approximate calories per serving: 100

Chicken Pâté

30 minutes

To serve eight people, you will need:

4 slices bread or 8 cream crackers or water biscuits (supermarket brand)

450g chicken livers, well defrosted if frozen

675g onion, coarsely chopped

Oil for deep frying

5 hard boiled eggs, 2 yolks discarded

2 tablespoons extra virgin olive oil

1 tablespoon very low-fat spread

Salt and ground white pepper

Chopped parsley

Preparation:

Deep fry the onions until burnt and remove. Either grill the livers, turning frequently for 6 minutes, or deep fry at maximum heat for 4 minutes, or cook in a microwave for about 5 minutes. Put into a liquidiser the livers, onions, eggs, olive oil and low-fat spread and blend until smooth. Serve as a starter on 1 large thin slice of toast or with 2 cream crackers or water biscuits and garnish with parsley and green salad.

Approximate calories per serving: 150

Starters and Snacks

Lemon and Mango Borscht

Leek Soup

184

30 minutes (veg)

To serve four people, you will need:

1 stalk lemon grass, the outer 2 layers removed and very finely chopped (if none available a teaspoon of lemon and 2 of lime juice will suffice)

6 medium cooked beetroot, home or supermarket, not pickled

3 teaspoons Dijon mustard

1 x 400g can mangoes

200mls cultured buttermilk or nil percent fat fromage frais

1 tablespoon balsamic or sherry vinegar

1/2 teaspoon dried tarragon

1/2 teaspoon dried mixed herbs

Salt and ground black pepper

McDougalls Thickening Granules

Preparation:

Liquidise all the contents and season to taste. If too thin gently simmer with McDougalls granules. If too thick add water or skimmed milk. Serve hot or cold.

Approximate calories per serving: 150

1 hour

To serve six people, you will need:

3 medium leeks, washed and sliced

2 medium onions, sliced

2 medium potatoes, sliced

2 chicken stock cubes (supermarket, Knorr or similar)

McDougalls Thickening Granules

Salt and ground black pepper

Preparation:

Put all the ingredients, except the stock cubes, into a soup pan. Dissolve the cubes in enough water to cover all the vegetables plus another 1 inch. Boil for 40 minutes. Liquidise and serve. If not thick enough, simmer with McDougalls granules.

Approximate calories per serving: 100

Lemon and Mango Borscht

Leek Soup

Devilled Potato Salad and Celery

Grapefruit and Tomato Soup

30 minutes (veg)

To serve one person, you will need:

3 medium or 6 small new potatoes

1 stick celery

1 tablespoon slimline salad cream, supermarket own brand

Ground cayenne pepper

Lettuce

30 minutes (veg)

To serve six people, you will need:

1 small Kiwi, cut into 6 slices, ends and peel removed

1 litre supermarket tomato juice, chilled

2 teaspoons granulated sweetener

2 tablespoons unsweetened lemon juice

1/2 cucumber, very thinly sliced

Chopped chives to garnish

1 x 125g carton single cream substitute

200mls unsweetened grapefruit juice

1 tablespoon Lea and Perrins Worcester Sauce

Salt and ground black pepper

Preparation:

Whisk in a deep bowl tomato juice, grapefruit juice, granulated sweetener, Lea and Perrins and lemon juice. Season with a little salt and plenty of black pepper. Line 6 glass grapefruit bowls with cucumber slices. Pour in the soup. Float a piece of Kiwi on each and surround with about 1/6 of a carton of cream. Garnish with a ribbon of chives and serve cold or chilled.

Tip: to layer the cream, put a teaspoon upside down at a 40 degree angle to the soup, just touching the surface. Gently pour the cream over the hump of the teaspoon. It will layer and float like magic.

Approximate calories per serving: 100

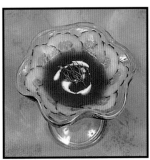

Grapefruit and Tomato Soup

Preparation:

Boil or microwave the potatoes until just soft. Cool and cut into pieces. Slice the celery and mix with the potatoes. Stir in the mayonnaise and wrap up in lettuce leaves. Sprinkle with cayenne pepper to garnish and serve.

Approximate calories per serving: 150

Starters and Snacks

Sweet and Sour Amaranth Chinese Cabbage or Chinese Lettuce

30 minutes (veg)

To serve eight people, you will need:

1 large head Chinese cabbage or Chinese lettuce leaves (amaranth), about 750g

2 tablespoons extra virgin olive oil

Fry Light non-stick cooking spray

1 level teaspoon soft brown sugar

For the sauce, you will need:

3 tablespoons soy sauce

3 tablespoons red wine

3 tablespoons balsamic, sherry or cider vinegar

60mls (4 tablespoons) mango and apple juice or orange juice

4 tablespoons tomato purée

3 tablespoons granulated sweetener

1 tablespoon caster sugar

1 tablespoon cornflour

Salt and ground black pepper

McDougalls Thickening Granules

100ml water or vegetable stock, made from Knorr or supermarket own brand cube

Preparation:

Wash and cut the lettuce leaves into thin strips. Put all the sauce ingredients except the cornflour and the McDougalls granules in a small pan and mix. Mix the cornflour in an eggcup of water and gradually stir in. Coat a hot non-stick pan with 5 applications of Fry Light and add the olive oil. Gradually add the cut Chinese leaves and sauté, stirring for 4 minutes. Add the teaspoon of soft brown sugar and sauté for about 4 minutes more until the leaves are soft. Heat the sauce, stirring all the time to prevent the cornflour getting lumpy. If not thick enough add McDougalls granules. The sauce should be thick and transparent. Put a portion of the leaves into each bowl and spoon over the sauce.

Approximate calories per serving: 150

Exotic Welsh Rarebit

30 minutes (veg)

To serve four people, you will need:

2 kumquats, halved

4 cherry tomatoes, halved

4 slices low calorie bread, toasted lightly

100g low-fat vegetarian cheddar cheese, grated

1 large Granny Smith apple, cored, skin left on and chopped finely

2 spring onions, finely chopped

2 tablespoons lime juice

Tabasco sauce

Salt and ground black pepper

Parsley to garnish

25g flaked almonds

Preparation:

Mix the grated cheese, apple, spring onion, almonds and lime juice with a splash of tabasco and season. Spread over the toast and put under a hot grill until it bubbles. Garnish with 2 halves of cherry tomato, half a kumquat and parsley and serve.

Approximate calories per serving: 225

Devilled Sardines

30 minutes

To serve two people, you will need:

1 small can sardines in oil

1 small can anchovies with capers in oil (John West or supermarket own brand)

1 large wholemeal thin bread slice

Very low-fat spread

Preparation:

Very lightly toast the bread and spread with the low-fat spread. Put 1 sardine on each side of the toast. Put 2 anchovy and capers on each sardine. Toast under a very hot grill for 30 seconds. Divide into 2 portions and serve.

Approximate calories per serving: 100

Starters and Snacks

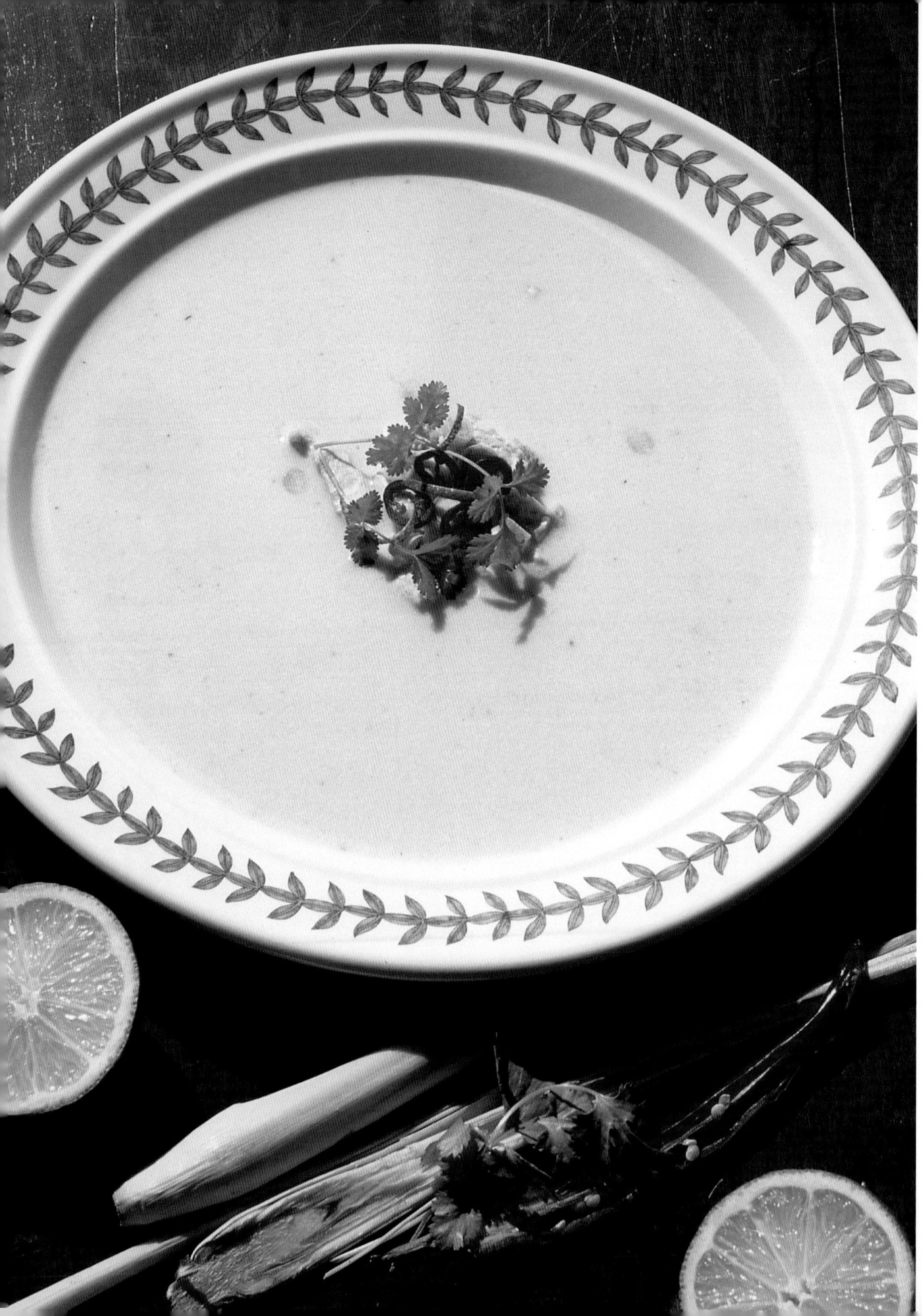

Chicken and Coconut Soup

30 minutes

To serve two people, you will need:

600ml chicken stock made from a supermarket cube

100g boneless, skinless lean chicken, thinly sliced

50g Nestlé or other coconut milk powder

1 stem lemon grass, finely chopped

Rind of 1 lemon, sliced

Juice and pulp of 1 lime, pulverised

1 teaspoon lemon juice

1 teaspoon ground ginger

2 red chillies, deseeded and chopped with fresh coriander leaves, to garnish

Preparation:

Heat the stock in a pan and add the coconut milk powder, ginger, lime peel and pulp and lemon juice. Add the chicken and bring to the boil. Simmer for 8 minutes, stirring to prevent burning. Put into 2 bowls and garnish with chilli and coriander.

Approximate calories per serving: 100

30 minutes (veg)

To serve four people, you will need:

450g scrubbed small new potatoes, cut in half

100g button mushrooms, whole

50ml vegetable stock, made from Knorr or good supermarket own brand cube

2 teaspoons balsamic or sherry vinegar

2 tablespoons chopped chives

100ml carton Greek yoghurt

Salt and ground white pepper

1 Florida starfruit

Preparation:

Put potatoes and onions in a large microwaveable dish. Sprinkle over the stock and vinegar. Cover with Stretch 'n Seal with no vent and cook on maximum for 4 minutes. Cut away the Stretch 'n Seal, being careful not to be scalded by the steam. Stir and season with salt and pepper. Now recover with Stretch 'n Seal with a vent (a slit). Microwave for another 4 minutes until soft. Allow to stand for 10 minutes stirring occasionally. Slice the starfruit into 8 slices and lay 2 on each plate. Spoon the mixture over the starfruit and garnish with yoghurt and chives.

Approximate calories per serving: 150

Starfruit, Potato and Mushroom

Starters and Snacks

Exotic Pears and Mint

30 minutes (veg)

To serve four people, you will need:

4 kumquats, halved longways

100g low-fat cottage cheese with pineapple

1 tablespoon freshly chopped mint

1 x 400g can pear halves, drained

Lettuce

Sprigs of mint

Salt and ground black pepper

Preparation:

Mix the cottage cheese, mint, salt and pepper to taste. Stuff into the pear halves. Put 2 on a bed of lettuce and top each with a half of kumquat and a sprig of mint.

Approximate calories per serving: 75

Pumpkin Soup with Flowers

1 hour (veg)

To serve six people, you will need:

2 medium onions, chopped

4 spring onions, chopped

1 tablespoon sunflower oil

1 x 400g chopped tomatoes

450g pumpkin flesh, deseeded, peeled and sliced

2 tablespoons tomato purée

Salt and ground black pepper

1 litre vegetable stock from good supermarket cube

225g blackberries

4 sprigs sage or 2 of lavender, if available (dried can be used to taste)

2 cloves garlic, crushed

Fry Light non-stick cooking spray

Dandelion, marigold or rose petals to garnish

Preparation:

Put onions, spring onions, garlic and oil in a hot non-stick pan coated with 5 applications of Fry Light. Sauté for 4 minutes, stirring all the time and add the pumpkin, tomatoes, tomato purée and blackberries. Season and cook for a further 4 minutes stirring gently. Add stock and stir for another 10-12 minutes until the pumpkin is soft. Then add the sage or lavender and simmer for a further 3 minutes. Liquidise and serve garnished with contrasting flower petals.

Approximate calories per serving: 150

Exotic Toast

30 minutes (veg)

To serve four people, you will need:

4 slices low calorie bread, lightly toasted

100g fromage frais

100g grated vegetarian cheddar cheese

1 small red pepper, deseeded and finely chopped

4 pineapple rings, fresh or from a can, drained

Salt and ground black pepper

4 strawberries

Preparation:

Mix fromage frais, cheese and peppers and season. Spread on the toast and top with a pineapple ring. Grill gently for about 5 minutes until bubbling and brown. Garnish each with a strawberry and serve.

Approximate calories per serving: 200

Aubergine and Mango Pâté

30 minutes (veg)

To serve eight people, you will need:

2 large aubergines

1 x 400g can mango slices, drained

2 tablespoons extra virgin olive oil

2 teaspoons garlic sauce

2 tablespoons lime juice

1 x 50g can anchovies, drained

4 large thin slices bread, toasted and slightly burnt, cut into fingers, crusts removed

Skimmed milk powder

Preparation:

Roast the aubergines in an oven or microwave until soft. Peel under running warm water and blend in a liquidiser with all the other ingredients. If too runny add skimmed milk powder to thicken. Chill and serve on slightly burnt toast fingers.

Approximate calories per serving: 250

Starters and Snacks

Pumpkin Soup with Prawns

Pea Soup Special

1 hour

To serve six people, you will need:

1 tablespoon extra virgin olive oil

750g pumpkin flesh

1 small onion, chopped

Fry Light non-stick cooking spray

2 stalks celery, chopped

200mls skimmed milk

1 tablespoon coconut powder

125g peeled cooked prawns

2 teaspoons lemon juice

100g low-fat fromage frais

900mls chicken stock, made from supermarket or
Knorr cube

Salt and ground black pepper

Preparation:

Peel and dice the pumpkin flesh.
Remove all seeds. Coat a hot non-stick
pan with 4 applications of Fry Light
and add the olive oil. Sauté the pumpkin, onion and celery for a few minutes
and then place in a saucepan and add
the chicken stock. Simmer for 30 minutes until the pumpkin is soft. Cool
and blend in a liquidiser and return to
the pan. Add the milk, gradually, and
then the coconut powder. Season, add
the prawns, fromage frais and the
lemon juice. Heat to just below boiling
and serve.

Approximate calories per serving: 100

30 minutes (veg)

To serve six people, you will need:

1 medium onion, finely chopped

6 spring onions, finely chopped

2 medium leeks, sliced

500g frozen green peas

300mls skimmed milk

900mls chicken or vegetable stock made from a
good supermarket brand cube

100g cauliflower heads only, finely chopped

Salt and ground black pepper

1/2 level teaspoon dried tarragon

Skimmed milk powder

Preparation:

Put the onions, leeks, spring onions
and peas in a soup pot. Add vegetable
or chicken stock and simmer for 4 minutes, stirring all the time. Now add the
cauliflower heads and tarragon and
season with salt and black pepper.
Simmer for 1 minute and add 300mls
of skimmed milk. Simmer for 2 minutes more and allow to cool a little.
Liquidise and return to the pot. Reheat
and thicken, if necessary, with a little
skimmed milk powder and serve.

Approximate calories per serving: 100

Pumpkin Soup with Prawns

Pea Soup Special

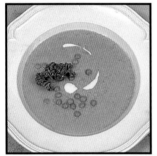

Cauliflower Soup

Fish Soup

1 hour

To serve six people, you will need:

1 large cauliflower, cut into florets and broken up

2 medium onions, sliced

2 chicken stock cubes, Knorr or supermarket own brand cube

Salt and ground black pepper

McDougalls Thickening Granules

1 teaspoon caster sugar

30 minutes

To serve six people, you will need:

450g skinless, boneless white fish of your choice

1 large onion, sliced

4 celery stalks, sliced

4 spring onions, chopped

1 medium leek, sliced

900mls fish stock made with 2 supermarket stock cubes

450mls chicken stock made with 1 Knorr or supermarket own brand cube

1/2 teaspoon dried chilli powder

2 teaspoons dried garlic salt

2 x 400g cans peeled tomatoes

2 small bay leaves

Parsley and chives, chopped for garnish

4 tablespoons skimmed milk powder

Salt and ground black pepper

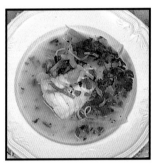

Fish Soup

Preparation:

Put the cauliflower and onions in a soup pan. Dissolve the cube in enough water to cover plus another inch. Add sugar, salt and black pepper to taste. Boil for 30 minutes and liquidise. If too thin, simmer with McDougalls granules. Season and serve.

Approximate calories per serving: 100

Preparation:

Put into a soup pot the onions, spring onions, celery, leek, fish, chicken stock, chilli, garlic salt, bay leaves and tomatoes. Bring to the boil slowly, stirring, and simmer for 18 minutes. Now chop the fish and add to the soup. Add salt and pepper to taste and simmer for a further 8-10 minutes with the lid on, stirring occasionally. Cool, liquidise and reheat. Add the skimmed milk and simmer for a further 2 minutes. Garnish with parsley and chives and serve.

Approximate calories per serving: 150

Exotic Red Borscht

Red Sockeye Salmon Pâté

30 minutes (veg)

To serve four people, you will need:

4 teaspoons extra virgin olive oil

4 kumquats, finely sliced

Fry Light non-stick cooking spray

150g low-fat natural yoghurt

50g Nestlé coconut milk powder

1 onion, chopped

2 sticks celery, chopped

300g raw beetroot, chopped (not pickled)

75g shredded white cabbage

900mls vegetable stock (made with supermarket cube)

1 ½ tablespoons balsamic vinegar

1 bay leaf

4 egg cupfuls boiling water – approximately 100ml

Salt and ground black pepper

Preparation:

Coat a hot non-stick pan with 4 applications of Fry Light and add the olive oil. Sauté the onions and celery until soft, stirring all the time. Stir in the beetroot, cabbage, stock, balsamic vinegar and season with salt and pepper. Simmer for at least 1 hour, stirring frequently. Add the bay leaf halfway through this time and remove it when cooked. Cool and liquidise adding coconut powder dissolved in the 4 eggcups of boiling water. Sieve and, if necessary, add a little water and heat until creamy. Pour into serving bowls, stir in some yoghurt and garnish with kumquats. Serve piping hot or chilled.

Approximate calories per serving: 100

Exotic Red Borscht

30 minutes

To serve four people, you will need:

1 x 200g red salmon (John West, supermarket own or similar), drained and skin and bones removed

4 tablespoons lemon or lime chutney

1 tablespoon Jif lemon or lime juice

1 tablespoon very low-fat spread

75g carton Quark or other skimmed milk curd

1 tablespoon Lea and Perrins Worcester Sauce

Salt and ground black pepper

Dried cayenne pepper

4 thin slices bread from a large loaf, toasted, slightly burnt and left to cool

Preparation:

Put all ingredients except the bread into a liquidiser. Blend and season. Serve chilled. Serve each portion on a large thin slice of slightly burnt toast garnished with cayenne pepper.

Approximate calories per serving: 250

Coconut and Beef Satay or Chicken Satay

30 minutes

To serve four people, you will need:

1 x 200g can sliced peaches

15g (2 tablespoons) Nestlé's coconut milk powder

250g lean rump steak, cut into thin strips

(or 300g skinless breast of chicken cut into strips)

1 teaspoon ground ginger

2 tablespoons lime juice

1 tablespoon lemon juice

1 clove garlic, crushed

Coriander leaves or parsley to garnish

Salt and ground black pepper

Preparation:

Mix all the ingredients together and season to taste. Cover and leave for at least 1 hour, preferably overnight. Thread the meat onto skewers and grill for 10-12 minutes turning 4 times. Heat the peaches in a microwave and serve alongside.

Approximate calories per serving: 150

Stir Fry Vegetables and Chilli

30 minutes (veg)

To serve four people, you will need:

Fry Light non-stick cooking spray

1 tablespoon extra virgin olive oil

1 medium onion, sliced

25g cashew nuts, halved

150mls water

4 spring onions, chopped

60ml Maggi chilli sauce with garlic

100g green beans or mange tout peas, trimmed and blanched for a second in boiling water

100g cauliflower or calabrese, cut into florets

6 tomatoes, peeled and cut in half

1 tablespoon fresh chopped basil or chives

Preparation:

Coat a large hot non-stick pan with 6 applications of Fry Light and add the olive oil. Cook the onion and cashew nuts until the onion is soft. Add the Maggi and garlic and cook for 90 seconds. Stir in the water and the remaining vegetables and simmer for 5 minutes. Garnish with chopped basil or chives and serve.

Approximate calories per serving: 150

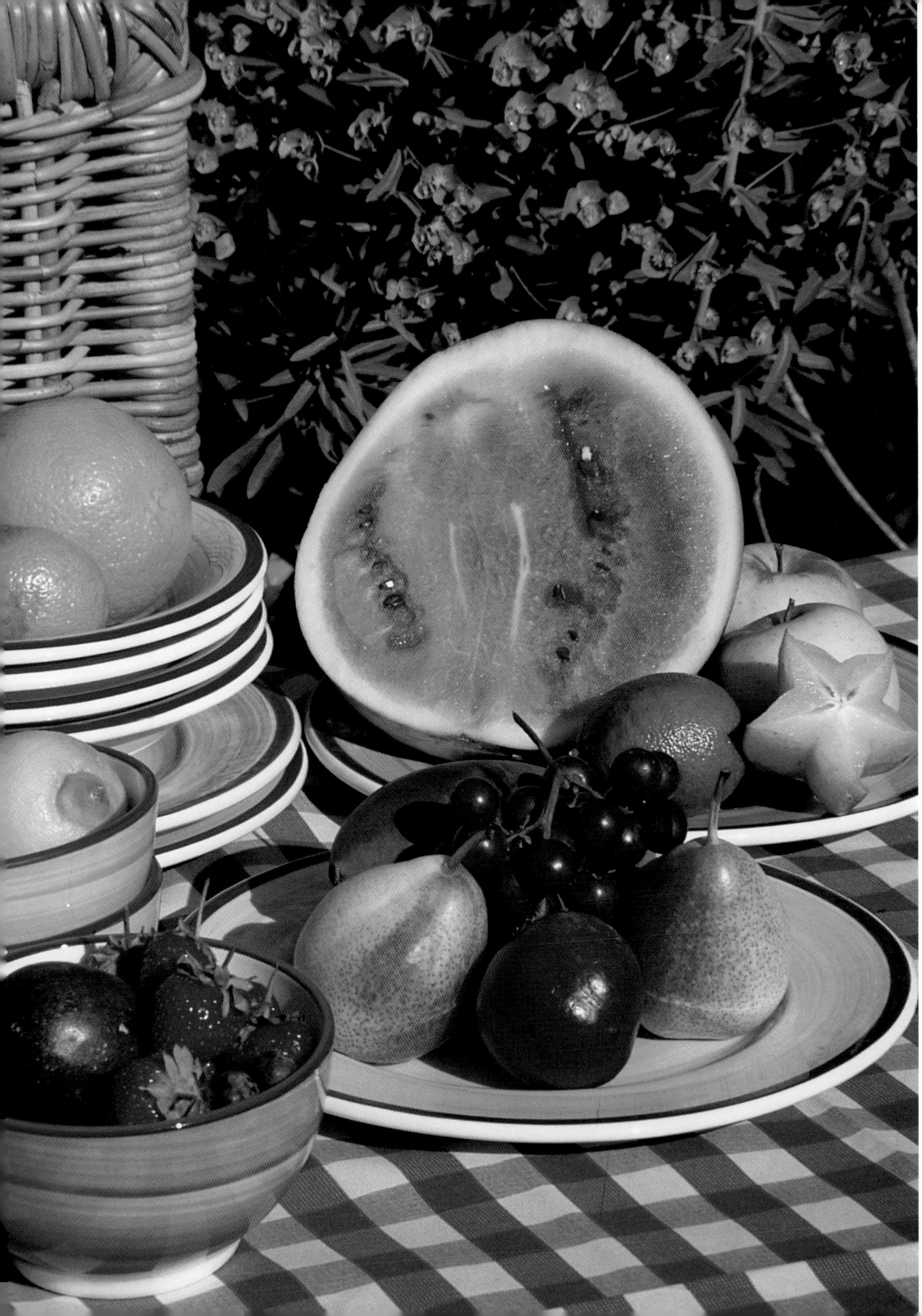

Salad

Make up a salad picnic with lettuce leaves, Chinese leaves and any other leaves or vegetables of your choice including tomatoes, tiny sweetcorn, cucumber and spring onions – but excluding potatoes and other root vegetables. A little celery and apples makes it lovely and crunchy. You can eat as much as you want and are unlikely to exceed 150 calories.

Cottage Cheese

One small carton of low-fat cottage cheese. It can be mixed with pineapple chives or onions as manufactured by most supermarket chains, or you can mix up some celery, pineapple, a few grapes or any other food of your choice into the cottage cheese and have a lovely lunch for under 150 calories.

Vegetable Picnic

Fruit Picnic

Meat

You can take a couple of slices of low-fat ham, of dried venison, salt beef, low-fat salami or pastrami and have them with an apple or three dark Ryvita spread with very low-fat spread. Your lunch will not exceed 200 calories.

Fish

Canned fish make an excellent picnic. Separately pack in your lunch box a couple of drained sardines or a couple of drained tuna or a 100g can of mackerel, salmon, pilchard or any other fish drained; two Ryvita spread with very low-fat spread will make your lunch up to around 200 calories.

Fruit

Why not take with you an apple or a pear or an orange or a satsuma or a banana or a portion of grapes accompanied by one exotic fruit, such as a mango, a kiwango, paw paw, a portion of kumquats or cape gooseberries, 2 passion fruit, 2 Kiwi fruit or whatever you like providing you're sensible and avoid grapes to excess, avocado pear and coconut. Your lunch picnic is unlikely to exceed 200 calories.

Please avoid all nuts.

Vegetable

This is really similar to the salad picnic selection but here you may have for instance a couple of pickled baby beet, a couple of small pickled gherkins, pickled onions, some shredded cabbage, a few whole baby sweetcorn and a couple of boiled new potatoes. If you use a low-fat salad spread such as Crosse and Blackwell or a supermarket's own brand, your vegetable picnic lunch will not exceed 250 calories.

Picnics

Devilled Potato Salad and Celery

30 minutes (veg)

To serve one person, you will need:

3 medium or 6 tiny new potatoes

1 stick celery

1 tablespoonful very low-fat salad cream, Crosse and Blackwell or supermarket own brand

Dry cayenne pepper

Lettuce

Preparation:

Boil or microwave the potatoes until just soft. Cool and cut into pieces. Slice the celery and mix with the potato. Mix with salad cream. Wrap in lettuce to eat. Garnish potato in a sprinkling of cayenne pepper. Put your picnic lunch in a tub with an apple or a pear and two dark Ryvita spread with very low-fat spread.

Approximate calories per serving: 250
(Including fruit and Ryvita)

Ingredients for Devilled Potato Salad

Tomato Cheese and Celery

30 minutes (veg)

To serve one person, you will need:

4 medium tomatoes

4 sticks celery

100g low-fat cottage cheese and pineapple

Salt and ground black pepper

Cream crackers

Water biscuits

Krona low-fat spread

Preparation:

Slice and chop tomatoes and celery. Mix with cottage cheese. Season with salt and pepper and serve or pack for a picnic lunch. Serve with two cream crackers or water biscuits. Lightly spread with Krona.

Approximate calories per serving: 200

Healthy mixed Picnic

Bagel Picnic Selection
Vegetarian optional

30 minutes (veg)

To serve one person, you will need:

1 apple of your choice

1 Kiwi fruit

1 melon baller scoop

50g fresh or strained tinned pineapple

8 seedless grapes – 50g

4 walnuts fresh or dried, in halves

1/4 of a cucumber, finely sliced

25g dried apricots

1 satsuma, peeled and leaved

Granulated sweetener

Preparation:

Line a waterproof picnic container with cucumber slices. Scoop out the kiwi with the melon baller and add. Add the pineapples, the grapes, the walnuts, the apricots and the satsuma and sprinkle lightly with granulated sweetener. Put the top on the box and shake well. To serve just open the box and eat with the apple.

Approximate calories per serving: 300

30 minutes

Sensible portions for filling:

Low-fat fromage frais

Low-fat salami, dried meat or venison

Low-fat cream cheese

1 thin rasher of bacon

Low-fat ham

Any exotic or traditional fruit or berries

Drained tuna fish

25g smoked salmon

A few prawns and a little slimline mayonnaise

25g smoked salmon and low-fat cheese

Low-fat fromage frais

Mushrooms and peppers, as much as you want

Lean chicken or turkey flesh, no skin or fat

Smoked venison

or any sensible combination of the above.

Preparation:

Just toast half a bagel in a pop up toaster and when cool spread with a little very low-fat spread. This represents 80 calories and should be enough for your lunch with one of the above suggested fillings.

Approximate calories per serving: 180
(For a half Bagel fully dressed)

Approximate calories per serving: 260
(For a whole Bagel fully dressed)

We would recommend that a half would be adequate for a snack lunch.

Bagels

Cooking kebabs

Overnight

To serve four people, you will need:

250g lean beef steak (preferably rump), cubed
(venison or turkey may be used in place of beef)

250g lean lamb, cubed

1 green pepper, cut into chunks and deseeded

1 red pepper, cut into chunks and deseeded

1 aubergine, cut into chunks

250g seedless grapes

3 satsumas leaved

1 x 400g can lychees, drained (supermarket brand)

50g of dried apricots

Salt and ground black pepper

For the marinade:

To serve four people, you will need:

1/2 a cup (100mls) extra virgin olive oil

1/4 of a cup (50mls) soya sauce

2 tablespoons of finely chopped ginger

2 cloves of garlic, very finely chopped or crushed

2 tablespoons of tomato purée

A pinch of chilli powder

1 teaspoon of curry powder

1/2 a teaspoon of ground black pepper

Preparation:

Mix the marinade well and marinade
the beef and lamb and dried apricots
preferably overnight, mixing 3 or 4
times during this period. Arrange the
meat, vegetables and fruit artistically
on kebabs and grill or barbeque. Serve
each portion with a 50g (raw weight) of
boiled rice and a seasonal salad.

Approximate calories per serving: 500

Marinading overnight

Traditional Shepherd's Pie

Traditional Shepherd's Pie

2 hours +

To serve four people, you will need:

Fry Light spray cooking oil

500g lean minced beef, pork or lamb or a combination, why not try venison?

1/2 teaspoon dried coriander

1 teaspoon garlic salt

1 tablespoon dried chilli powder

1 teaspoon garlic pepper

2 teaspoons Worcester sauce

1/4 teaspoon dried rosemary

1 teaspoon dried oregano

4 medium carrots, well chopped

4 medium onions, peeled and well chopped

1 pepper, green or red, deseeded and chopped

5 tablespoons tomato purée

1 tub grated Parmesan cheese

600mls chicken stock made from a Knorr, Telmar or good supermarket own brand cube

3 tablespoons of skimmed milk

100g small dried lentils

Salt and ground black pepper

100g instant mashed potato (dry weight)

Dried cyan pepper

2 tablespoons extra virgin olive oil

Preparation:

Coat a hot non-stick saucepan with 5 applications of Fry Light and the extra virgin olive oil. Add the meat, the carrot, the onion and the pepper. Sauté stirring with a wooden spoon until the meat browns and the vegetables just soft. It will take around 8 minutes. Drain off the juices and tip the meat and vegetables into a bowl lined with 3 layers of kitchen towel. Blot off any excess fat with kitchen roll and transfer to an oven casserole dish. Stir in the herbs, Worcester sauce, lentils, the stock and the tomato purée. Now season and bake uncovered at 190 degrees centigrade for 40 minutes or until the lentils are soft. Prepare 100g of instant mashed potatocs and now cover the cooked meat and vegetable with this. Sprinkle over Parmesan cheese and the milk. Garnish with cyan pepper. Grill under a hot grill for 5 minutes until rich, brown and bubbly.

Approximate calories per serving: 500

2 hours +

To serve four people, you will need:

4 x 150g duck breast portions, bone and fat removed with the skin left on

200mls unsweetened orange juice

3 satsumas, leaved

3 tablespoons Grand Marnier

Salt and ground black pepper

1 supermarket chicken stock cube (Knorr, Telma, Maggi or supermarket own brand)

125g natural unsweetened low-fat yoghurt

McDougalls Thickening Granules

2 tablespoons extra virgin olive oil

3 level teaspoons granulated sweetener

2 tablespoons clear honey

20 cherries

20 raspberries

20 strawberries or berries of choice

2 tiger lilies

(a couple more, if available, for decoration)

2 x 400g cans sliced mangoes (supermarket brand)

A selection of Rose, Pansy, Nasturtium and Marigold petals and Dandelion heads and leaves

Preparation:

Brush over the seasoned duck breasts with olive oil. Grill skin side up for 5 minutes over a medium heat. Turn and brush with oil and grill at medium heat for 8 minutes. Turn and grill skin side up under a hot grill for 5 minutes removing the skin with 2 minutes cooking to go. Put aside but keep hot. Heat the orange juice and crumble in the stock cube. Boil and add the granulated sweetener, honey, yoghurt, the chopped up tiger lilies and simmer for 6 minutes. Now add satsuma leaves and Grand Marnier and thicken if required with McDougalls granules. Mix in all the fruit. Lay the duck on a base of flower petals and blanched Dandelion leaves (blanch for a few seconds in boiling water and lemon juice or vinegar) and spoon the sauce over the duck. Decorate with more fresh tiger lilies if available. Serve with a Summer salad, 5 small boiled new potatoes and the mango slices heated in a microwave and drained to make a lovely vegetable. Finally to make this the dish of the year, add some beautiful crystallised flowers as described opposite and on page 327.

Approximate calories per serving: 650

Crystallising Flowers

Almost any flower can be crystallised and used for decoration and eating. Two easy methods are available. The first uses raw white of egg which theoretically could be infected with bacteria although the risk is infinitely small; however flowers crystallised in this way must be used within 48 hours. The second method is more time consuming but rewarding and blooms can be kept for up to a year.

Method 1

Select clean but unwashed flowers, clusters or petals. Remove all the green parts and if using petals, trim off the white base. Coat with a brush or dip in lightly beaten egg white and dust over or dip in caster sugar. Leave to dry preferably on a rack in an airing cupboard until crisp. Put in a good sealed container and use within 48 hours.

Method 2

Dissolve 2 teaspoons of Gum Arabic (from any chemist) in 50mls of a mixture of vodka and white peach liqueur. Paint onto the petals or blooms and dust well or dip in caster sugar. Dry on a rack in a warm airing cupboard until crisp. Store in a sealed container for up to 1 year.

Rosemary Lamb

Mango and Pan Fried Calves Livers

30 minutes

To serve four people, you will need:

8 lean boned lamb chops (or other cuts) to a total of
500g raw weight after trimming excess fat

1 teaspoon extra virgin olive oil

Rosemary sprigs, fresh or dried

Garlic salt

Ground black pepper

Chopped parsley

25g of garlic butter

30 minutes

To serve two people, you will need:

2 x 75g portions fresh calves liver (venison, lamb, pig
or chicken liver may be used in place of calves liver)

Fry Light spray cooking oil

1 tablespoon extra virgin olive oil

1/2 teaspoon dairy butter

6 shallots or small pickling onions, chopped

1 x 400g can sliced mango (provides 8 portions)

Garlic salt

Salt and ground black pepper

Preparation:

Coat a hot non-stick pan with 4 applications of Fry Light and add the olive oil, the dairy butter and some salt. Sauté the onions for 4 minutes over a medium heat, stirring all the time. Remove the onions with a serrated spoon and reserve. Lightly sprinkle each liver with garlic salt and black pepper and sauté in the pan for 6 minutes, turning frequently. Remove from the pan and put the onions back in and sauté for 3 minutes, stirring all the time over a medium heat. Serve with a seasonal salad and 3 small boiled new potatoes and garnish each with a mango slice.

Approximate calories per serving: 350

Mango and Pan Fried Calves Livers

Preparation:

Brush the lamb both sides with olive oil. Season with garlic salt, black pepper and fresh, chopped or dried rosemary. Grill under a medium hot grill for 6 minutes on each side turning once and brushing with olive oil. Turn the heat up to maximum and grill for 40 seconds each side. Garnish with a sprig of parsley or rosemary and 5g (a dot) of garlic butter and serve with four small new potatoes in a seasonal salad.

Approximate calories per serving: 500

Hot Meat or Poultry with Exotic Chunky Sauce

Exotique Pintade Rotir
Guinea Fowl

2 hours +

Exotic Chunky Sauce
To serve ten people, you will need:

2 oranges peeled and chopped

1 x 400g can of mangoes or mango slices with the juice (supermarket own brand)

Pinch of chilli powder

2 tablespoons of lime juice

100mls of orange juice

2 tablespoons of skimmed milk powder

1 tablespoon of chopped nuts of choice

A mixture of mint, parsley, chives, and lemon grass with outer skin removed and, if available, chopped

1 large fennel finely chopped

Salt and ground black pepper

Granulated sweetener

Preparation of sauce:
Mix in a bowl and if necessary, mix with skimmed milk powder.

Approximate calories per serving: 80

To serve one person, you will need:

Either 125g of lean steak or 125g of any other cooked meat or poultry without fat, skin or bone or freshly cooked or warmed up (i.e. supermarket cooked chicken)

Preparation:
Serve meat with 1/10th portion of sauce and heat in the oven or microwave. Serve with 4 small boiled potatoes and a green salad or vegetable such as mange tout peas.

Approximate calories per serving: 450

2 hours +

To serve four people, you will need:

1 ready prepared 1.5kg guinea fowl

2 tablespoons extra virgin olive oil

1 dessert apple, cut in half, skin and core left on

1 onion, cut in half

10 shallots

1 x 400g can of lychees, drained

1 x 400g can of papaya or sliced mango, drained

1 can of asparagus or fresh asparagus

Salt and ground black pepper

Preparation:
Place bird in a non-stick roasting dish with the breast down. Season well and put the apple and onion within the cavity of the bird. Surround with peeled shallots and baste with olive oil. Cover with foil and roast at 180 degrees centigrade for 2 hours basting several times with the rest of the olive oil and the juices. When just 30 minutes to cook, surround with lychees, mango and/or paw paw. Serve with a good portion of fresh or tinned hot asparagus also using the lychees and mango as a vegetable.

Approximate calories per serving: 450

Exotique Pintade Rotir

Hot Meat or Poultry with Chunky Sauce

Meat Dishes **Pork or Turkey in Apple**

Kiwi, Mango and Mushroom

Pork or Turkey in Apple

30 minutes

To serve four people, you will need:

50g very low-fat spread

4 x 100g boneless, fat free pork loin or turkey fillet

1 tablespoon extra virgin olive oil

Paxo golden crumbs or good supermarket own brand

Grated Parmesan cheese

2 eggs with 1 yolk discarded, beaten up with 30mls of skimmed milk (2 tablespoons)

Salt and ground black pepper

2 large Bramley cooking apples, sliced and cored with the skin left on

Dried cinnamon

Watercress

Fry Light spray cooking oil

1 tablespoon granulated low calorie sweetener

Preparation:

Coat a very hot non-stick pan with 5 applications of Fry Light. Lightly coat the apple with cinnamon and granulated sweetener and fry for 2¹/₂ minutes each side. Drain on a kitchen roll. Put the crumbs into a polythene bag. Coat the fillets in beaten egg and milk and shake each individually in a polythene bag with the crumbs. Roll the fillets around the apple and before rolling up, coat the apple with Parmesan cheese. Tie the fillets with the apples and the Parmesan cheese in the middle with string to secure. Grease an oven proof casserole dish with 50g of very low-fat spread and 1 tablespoon of extra virgin olive oil. Bake covered at 190 degrees centigrade for 25 minutes, turning twice and basting. Serve each with 3 small boiled new potatoes and a seasonal salad and Dijon mustard, and decorate with watercress.

Approximate calories per serving: 450

1 hour

To serve four people, you will need:

2 Kiwi fruit, thinly sliced with peel on or off

8 slices tinned mango from a 400g can, drained

Fry Light spray cooking oil

McDougalls Thickening Granules

400g any type of mushroom or edible fungus

100mls vegetable or chicken stock made from a supermarket own brand cube

1 teaspoon Maggi, mixed seasoning or soy sauce

1 teaspoon Lea and Perrins Worcester sauce

4 spring onions chopped

1 medium red onion chopped

2 teaspoons Moutard de Dijon

1 teaspoon dried tarragon

100mls white wine, dry sherry, vermouth or white apple juice

Salt and ground black pepper

Preparation:

Heat a non-stick pan and coat with 5 applications of Fry Light. Sauté the onions and the spring onions for 2 minutes, stirring all the time. Add the mushrooms, stock, Lea and Perrins, Maggi and wine and simmer, stirring all the time until it reduces and thickens. Now add the salt and pepper and tarragon and Moutard de Dijon and continue to simmer until the vegetables feel soft and cooked. It should thicken on its own but if necessary add a few McDougalls granules to thicken. Serve each portion with 50g (raw weight) of boiled rice. Arrange the rice in a pile and surround with mango, mushrooms and Kiwi.

Approximate calories per serving: 350

Stir Fried Liver

Schnitzel Exotic

30 minutes

To serve four people, you will need:

300g of calves liver, fresh and thinly sliced (venison, pig, lamb or chicken liver may be used in place of calves liver)

Fry Light spray cooking oil

2 tablespoons extra virgin olive oil

2 tablespoons cornflour

1 level teaspoon garlic salt

1 large cooking apple diced

1 x 400g can sliced mangoes, strained

1 large onion diced

1 tablespoon soya sauce

1 tablespoon sherry vinegar

Chives or spring onion

Lettuce

Preparation:

Cut the liver into 1 inch squares. Plunge into boiling water for 10 seconds. Drain and sprinkle with cornflour or toss in cornflour in a polythene bag. Spray a large hot non-stick pan or wok with 6 applications of Fry Light and add the olive oil. Add the onion and apple and fry until soft, stirring all the time. Drain from the pan with a serrated spoon leaving the fat behind. Add to the pan the liver, the soya sauce, the garlic salt and the sherry vinegar. Stir fry for 2 minutes and do not over cook. Now re-add the apple and onion. Stir fry for a further minute and serve into a dish lined with lettuce. Quickly warm the drained mango slices in a microwave. Layer over the stir fry and garnish with chopped chive or spring onions. Serve with three small boiled new potatoes or seasonal salad untossed.

Approximate calories per serving: 450

30 minutes

To serve four people, you will need:

4 x 100g of veal, pork, chicken or turkey with fat removed

Paxo or supermarket own brand golden breadcrumbs

1 x 400g can mango slices, use only half. (The other will freeze or keep)

1 x 400g can lychees, use only half. (The other will freeze or keep)

4 red glacé cherries

1 x 125g carton cottage cheese with chives (any good supermarket own brand)

Fry Light spray cooking oil

1 tablespoon extra virgin olive oil

2 eggs with one yolk discarded, beaten and mixed with two tablespoons of skimmed milk

Salt and ground black pepper

1 x 340g can tinned niblets, sweetcorn and peppers

Preparation:

Dip the meat fillets in egg and milk mix. Shake each individually in a polythene bag with golden crumbs until coated. Season liberally with a little salt and black pepper each side. Coat a wide non-stick saucepan with 5 applications of Fry Light and add the virgin olive oil. Fry the fillets turning frequently for 12 minutes until tender and brown. Put each fillet on a plate and decorate with two lychees, with half a glacé cherry in the open end of each lychee. Surround with four mango slices per fillet and serve with a quarter of a portion of the cottage cheese and chives. Serve each portion with 50g (raw weight) of boiled rice and a quarter of a tin of hot sweetcorn and peppers.

Approximate calories per serving: 450
(including corn and rice but excluding the egg)

For an extra 80 calories, you can make this a Holstein Schnitzel by topping with a soft fried egg sunny side up. Fry in Fry Light spray cooking oil. Why not do this and miss your dessert?

Schnitzel Exotic

Stir Fried Liver

Meat Dishes

Veal (or Beef) Roast with Prunes and Rambutans

2 hours +

To serve up to eight people, you will need:

1.5 to 2kg of a lean roasting joint of beef or veal (including the bone). A loin joint is ideal (venison or lean lamb may be used in place of beef or veal)

150g dried prunes

1 x 400g can Rambutans stuffed with pineapple, if these are not available, a 200g tin of pineapple and a 200g tin of lychees will be appropriate

Fry Light spray cooking oil

3 tablespoons extra virgin olive oil

100mls of prune juice (supermarket or other brand)

25g plain flour

300mls red wine (cheap)

Dried rosemary

Parsley to garnish

Sugar

Salt and ground black pepper

Preparation:

Ask your butcher to bone the veal and give you the bones. Simmer these bones in 450mls of water for 1 hour and season. Soak the prunes over night and simmer for 1 hour with a little sugar. Coat a non-stick oven roasting dish with 8 applications of Fry Light and add the veal joint. Season with salt and pepper and sprinkle with rosemary. Baste with the olive oil and cook at 190 degrees centigrade in a hot oven for 1½ to 2 hours basting frequently. Once cooked test that it is soft with a fork and add just 150mls of the bone stock, having discarded the bones. Turn the oven down to 180 degrees and cook and baste for a further 1½ hours. Blend the prune juice and flour in a pan. Add the red wine and the other 150mls of veal stock plus a little fat from the roasting tin. Heat and stir until it thickens and now add the prunes and simmer for a few minutes. Drain off any fat from the veal, top it with the prunes and sauce and garnish with parsley. Heat the rambutans for 3 minutes in a microwave and serve as a vegetable, along with a seasonal salad or 4 small new potatoes.

Approximate calories per serving: 500

Devilled Lamb Steaks

Original Duck à l'Orange

30 minutes

To serve four people, you will need:

4 x 125g of boneless lamb steak with all the fat trimmed off

2 tablespoons Mango chutney

1 teaspoon curry powder

1 tablespoon soft brown sugar

2 teaspoons soya sauce

2 teaspoons balsamic vinegar

1 tablespoon coconut powder – desiccated coconut

Salt and ground black pepper

Preparation:

Place the lamb on a grill tray. Top with a mixture of chutney, curry, sugar, soya sauce and balsamic vinegar. Sprinkle lightly with coconut powder. Cook under a hot grill until tender for 5-8 minutes. Do not turn. Serve each with 4 small boiled new potatoes and mange tout peas and salad.

Approximate calories per serving: 550

30 minutes

To serve four people, you will need:

4 x 100g of duck breast portions, bone and fat removed but skin left on

200mls unsweetened orange juice

2 satsumas, leaved

2 tablespoons Grand Marnier, Cointreau or Brandy

Salt and ground black pepper

1 chicken stock cube (Knorr or good supermarket own brand)

125g natural unsweetened yoghurt

McDougalls Thickening Granules

1 tablespoon extra virgin olive oil

2 level teaspoons granulated sweetener

Preparation:

Brush over seasoned duck breast with virgin olive oil. Grill skin side up for 5 minutes. Turn and brush with oil and grill for 8 minutes. Turn and grill for 5 minutes, removing and discarding the skin before fully cooked. Heat the orange juice and crumble the stock cube in. Boil and stir until the cube dissolves, add the granulated sweetener then the yoghurt, stir well and simmer for 6 minutes. Now add the Grand Marnier, Cointreau or Brandy, stir well and add the satsuma leaves. Simmer and thicken with McDougalls granules if required. Spoon over the duck and serve each portion with four small boiled new potatoes in a seasonal salad.

Approximate calories per serving: 400

Original Duck à l'Orange

Meat Dishes

Chicken Exotique and Dried Venison

2 hours +

To serve four people, you will need:

1 x 400g can mangoes (supermarket own brand)

4 chicken breasts, skinless, boneless and fat free

50g dried venison, cut into 4 pieces (any good supermarket brand)

200mls chicken stock from a Knorr or good supermarket own brand cube

2 tablespoons Nestlé coconut milk powder or other desiccated coconut

1 tablespoon sherry

1 red pepper, deseeded and sliced

2 spring onions, chopped julienne (long ways)

For the stuffing, you will need:

40g bread crumbs

50g grated parmesan cheese

1 small red onion, diced

1 tablespoon chopped parsley

1 tablespoon sherry

1 teaspoon coconut milk powder

1 teaspoon balsamic vinegar

Salt and ground black pepper

Preparation:

Mix together the stuffing ingredients and press into the under side of the chicken. Cover with a slice of dried venison, put in an oven casserole dish and pour over the stock, sherry, and coconut powder. Now add the red pepper. Cover and cook at 170 degrees centigrade for 1hr 15mins. Baste 3 times with the juices during cooking. Garnish with the julienne spring onions. Serve each with quarter of the mango slices heated for 2 minutes in a microwave.

Approximate calories per serving: 350

Mango Cholent

Overnight

To serve six people, you will need:

500g dried prunes

1 x 400g can mango slices (supermarket own brand)

750g lean stewing beef (venison or turkey may be used in place of beef)

1 small turnip

3 small carrots

500g sweet potatoes (ordinary potatoes will do)

1 lime, chopped finely, including the skin

25g brown sugar

1 tablespoon clear honey

Salt and ground black pepper

500g frozen peas

Preparation:

Soak the prunes overnight in plain water (just about cover) and keep the juices. Cube the beef and vegetables and put them in an oven casserole dish with the lime and the prunes. Mix well and pour over the prune juices blended with sugar and honey. You can buy prune juice if you prefer and it gives a much richer flavour than your prune soak. Add water to just cover, mix well and cook at 170 degrees centigrade for 2 to 3 hours until soft and tender. Add more water if required. Heat the peas and mango in a microwave. Serve the Cholent, surrounded by peas and top with strained mango slices.

Approximate calories per serving: 600

Exotique Venison Stew

2 hours +

To serve six people, you will need:

60mls (4 tablespoons) cooking brandy

1kg stewing venison

1 x 400g can mango slices (supermarket own brand)

100g prunes (dried)

100g dried apricots

100g Nestlé coconut milk powder – desiccated coconut

200g can chestnuts

1/2 teaspoon coriander seeds

1 tablespoon plain flour

100g craisins – ocean spray sun dried cranberries

1 large onion sliced

Fry Light non-stick spray cooking oil

2 tablespoons of extra virgin olive oil

1 cinnamon stick

2 strips dried orange peel

McDougalls Thickening Granules

900mls water with 1 Knorr or supermarket chicken stock cube dissolved in it

Salt and ground black pepper

Preparation:

Soak the dried apricots, prunes and craisins in brandy and mango juice for 30 minutes. Pierce the chestnuts with a sharp knife. Place in a pan of water and bring to the boil and simmer for 90 seconds. Remove 1 at a time and peel off the shell and the skin from the chestnuts (easy if hot). Toast the coriander seeds in a hot dry non-stick pan until they pop. Crush when cool and mix with the flour. Cut the venison into pieces about 1 inch x 2 inch. Coat a large, hot non-stick saucepan with 5 applications of Fry Light and add the olive oil. In this, cook the onion until it is soft and remove with a serrated spoon to an oven casserole dish. Turn the heat up to maximum and brown the venison six pieces at a time searing and then transferring to the casserole and sprinkling with flour and coriander. Add the cinnamon stick, strained dried fruits, mango, orange peel and seasoning. In the frying pan in which the venison has been cooked and still containing the juices, add the brandy and the mango juice and stir in the water on maximum heat so as to dissolve all the venison juices. Pour this over the casserole and cook at 170 degrees centigrade for 90 minutes and then stir in the chestnuts. Turn down the heat to 150 degrees centigrade and cook for another 60 minutes. If it dries out add water, if it is too runny then add McDougalls granules 5 minutes before serving. Serve each portion with mashed potatoes (about 100g per person) mashed with very low-fat spread.

Approximate calories per serving: 600

Meat Dishes

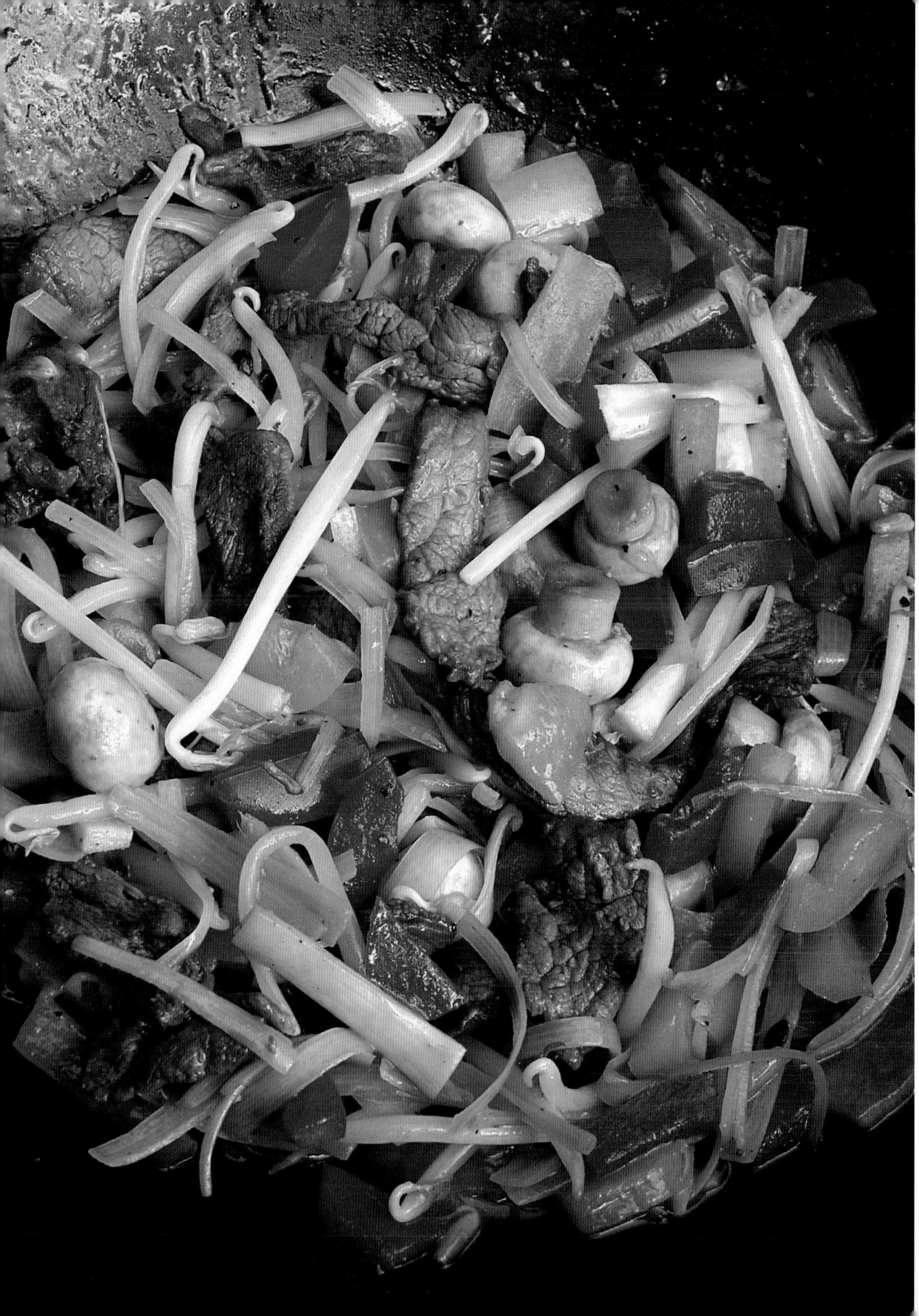

Wok Beef during cooking

1 hour

To serve four people, you will need:

500g lean rump steak, cut into strips

(venison may be used in place of beef but allow a little more cooking time)

1 small red pepper, deseeded and chopped

1 small green or yellow pepper, deseeded and chopped

2 small leeks, cut into thin strips (very thin)

2 small carrots, cut into very thin strips

1 piece peeled root ginger

2 tablespoons extra virgin olive oil

Fry Light non-stick spray cooking oil

100g button mushrooms

75g bean sprouts

3 passion fruits or 1 grenadillo

3 tablespoons Maggi seasoning or soya sauce

Salt and ground black pepper

Preparation:

Coat the beef strips with Maggi or soya sauce. Allow to marinade for about 20 minutes. Coat a very, very hot wok or large non-stick pan with 5 applications of Fry Light and add the virgin olive oil. Drain the beef and sauté for $3^{1}/_{2}$ minutes, stirring all the time and remove with a serrated spoon. Now sauté all the vegetables in the same wok and juices except for the bean sprouts. Sauté for 4 minutes. Re-add the beef, the Maggi marinade, bean sprouts and passion fruit pulp and seeds. Season. Sauté for 3 minutes more and serve with a seasonal salad.

Approximate calories per serving: 350

Red, green, yellow and orange peppers

Meat Dishes

Melon with Dried Wild Venison
or Parma Ham

30 minutes

To serve one person, you will need:

1 sweet ogen melon

100g dried wild venison (or Parma ham) good super-market own brand

Preparation:

Halve and deseed the melon. Serve each half with 50g parma ham or dried wild venison. The two half melons make one portion.

Approximate calories per serving: 300
(including wild venison)
including Parma Ham: 400

Wild venison comes prepacked in six slice 100g packs with a total of 207 calories. It is made by Rannoch Smokery and several good supermarkets.

Chopped Liver Thinner & Richer

1 hour

To serve four people, you will need:

500g chicken, calves or ox liver

3 medium onions, chopped

3 medium hard boiled eggs

1 tablespoon extra virgin olive oil

Salt and ground black pepper

Very low-fat spread

Fry Light spray cooking oil

Lettuce and radishes

Preparation:

Cut and grill the liver under a medium heat for ten minutes, turning occasionally. Alternatively the liver can be cooked in a deep fryer of corn oil for about 5 minutes and drained on a kitchen roll, (alternatively it can be fried in a saucepan with Fry Light cooking spray for about 8 minutes turning frequently or it can be cooked in a microwave dish, coated with 8 applications of Fry Light cooking oil covered with a vented dome or stretch 'n seal and cooked for about 8 minutes on maximum heat turning half way through the cooking time). Once your liver is cooked allow to cool and mince or liquidise along with the hard boiled eggs. Stir in and mix the olive oil and a little Krona until texture and taste are satisfactory. Season with salt and pepper to taste. Serve in balls or scoops on a bed of lettuce, each ball topped with half a radish. Serve each portion with five water biscuits or three cream crackers or three Ryvita or one large slice of Rakusins Matzo.

Approximate calories per serving: 300
(including biscuits or matzos)

Exotique Chicken Satay

30 minutes

To serve four people, you will need:

Fry Light non-stick spray cooking oil

1 tablespoon extra virgin olive oil

4 x 100g skinless, boneless chicken breast fillet

1 teaspoon lemon juice

1 teaspoon lime juice

2 tablespoons peanut butter

100mls apple juice

100mls of coconut liquid (from a tin or made up from powder)

Salt and ground black pepper

McDougalls Thickening Granules

Preparation:

Slice the chicken into long slices. Coat a very hot non-stick pan with 5 applications of Fry Light and add the virgin olive oil. Sauté the chicken strips until white. Lower the heat and add the juices, the peanut butter and the coconut milk powder. Simmer until thickens and add a few McDougalls granules if required. Serve piping hot on a bed of 50g (raw weight) of dried basmati rice.

Approximate calories per serving: 450

Lamb and Paw Paw Corsican Style

1 hour

To serve four people, you will need:

2 tablespoons extra virgin olive oil

500g cooked lamb, lean cut, with all fat removed and sliced

2 medium red onions, sliced

1 x 400g can papaya cubes (supermarket brand)

150g open mushrooms, sliced

4 slices of lean bacon, diced (optional – you can use dried venison or cured beef if you don't wish to use bacon)

1 tablespoon liquid garlic

1 teaspoon ground nutmeg

1 teaspoon soft brown sugar

2 tablespoons brandy

3/4 bottle of cheap red wine

1 or 2 tight cabbages cut into wedges

Fry Light spray cooking oil

Preparation:

Coat a hot non-stick pan with 5 applications of Fry Light and add the virgin olive oil. Sauté the onion, mushrooms and bacon until soft. Pour over the brandy and set alight, shaking until it goes out. Now add the paw paw, the wine, the garlic, the nutmeg, the sugar and season and mix. Arrange the cabbage around the outside of a circular oven casserole dish with the lamb slices in the middle. Pour over the sauce. Cover and bake at 190 degrees centigrade for 45 minutes basting 2 or 3 times during cooking. Serve each portion with a large baked potato cooked in a microwave oven.

Approximate calories per serving: 650

Meat Dishes

Meat Dishes

Exotique Lamb and Papaya or Mango

Overnight & 2hrs +

To serve four people, you will need:

1 x 400 can papaya (paw paw chunks) or mango slices or preferably half a can of each (the rest can be kept or frozen)

1 red onion, finely chopped

4 boneless lamb chops with all excess fat trimmed off

150g low-fat natural Greek yoghurt

2 teaspoons ground paprika

Parsley to garnish

Salt and ground black pepper

To make the Marinade, you will need:

2 tablespoons of white wine

2 tablespoons of balsamic vinegar

1 teaspoon of soft brown sugar

2 teaspoons of clear honey

1/2 a teaspoon of dried dill

1/2 a teaspoon of dried thyme

1/2 a teaspoon of dried rosemary

Preparation:

Mix the marinade with salt and pepper and marinade the lamb for several hours turning twice (preferably left over night). Dry the marinaded chops on kitchen roll but do not rub off the spices. Place in a shallow oven proof dish and sprinkle with onion. Cover with foil and cook at 190 degrees centigrade for 60 minutes. After 1 hour mix the yoghurt and the paprika and spoon over the lamb and cook for a further 20 minutes and serve garnished with paprika and parsley. Heat the mango and papaya for 2 minutes in a microwave and serve as a vegetable with an additional green salad.

Approximate calories per serving: 400
(including salad)

Exotique Lamb and Papaya or Mango

Brandy Fillet Steak/Kiwi Garnish

Brandy Fillet Steak/Kiwi Garnish/Paw Paw/Mango

This delightful meal can be prepared à la table to delight your friends

1 hour

To serve four people, you will need:

8 small thin 50g fat-free fillet steaks
(venison steak may be used in place of beef, but roll thin between grease-proof paper and allow a little longer cooking time)

1 x 400g can papaya cubes (supermarket brand)

1 x 400g can mango slice (supermarket brand)

2 Kiwi fruit, thinly sliced with the peel left on or off

40g seasoned flour

8 very small onions or shallots

3 tablespoons of brandy

300mls of chicken stock made from Knorr or supermarket own brand cube

2 tablespoons of concentrated tomato purée

8 small button mushrooms

1 level teaspoon of dried paprika

4 tablespoons low-fat fromage frais

Salt and ground black pepper

Fry Light spray cooking oil

2 tablespoons extra virgin olive oil

Preparation:

Shake the fillets in a polythene bag with the seasoned flour until coated. Coat a hot non-stick pan with 4 applications of Fry Light and add the olive oil. Toss in the onions (halved if large) and sear the fillets until brown on both sides. Add the brandy – set alight and shake the pan to prevent burning. Blend in stock, tomato purée, mushrooms and season with paprika. Cover and cook on a low heat and simmer for 30 minutes. Just before serving, stir in fromage frais and heat, but do not boil, and serve. Garnish with Kiwi slices. Serve with mango and paw paw heated in a microwave for 3 minutes and serve strained, discarding juices.

Approximate calories per serving: 500

Poultry – Sweet and Sour

Oriental Wok Stir Fry
Venison, Beef, Chicken, Quorn, Plaice or Tuna

Meat Dishes

2 hours +

To serve four people, you will need:

1 x 400g can papaya (paw paw) cubes in syrup – supermarket brand

4 x 125g pieces of poultry, skinless, boneless and fat free

2 peppers, different colours, deseeded and chopped

1 medium onion sliced

1 x 210g can pineapple chunks, drained

1 tablespoon soya sauce

1 tablespoon of coconut milk powder – desiccated coconut

1 tablespoon balsamic vinegar

1 x 220g can whole plum tomatoes

150mls water

1 teaspoon soft brown sugar

Salt and ground black pepper

4 spring onions cut julienne (long ways)

Fry Light non-stick spray cooking oil

Preparation:

Coat a hot non-stick oven casserole with 5 applications of Fry Light. Cook the poultry in this at 190 degrees centigrade for 18 minutes. Put the other ingredients except the spring onions in a pan and season. Boil and simmer for 18 minutes. Pour over the poultry and cook at 180 degrees centigrade for 45 minutes, basting 3 times. Heat the paw paw for 2 minutes in a microwave and serve as a vegetable. Serve garnished with julienne spring onions.

Approximate calories per serving: 300

30 minutes

To serve two people, you will need:

Fry Light non-stick spray cooking oil

2 tablespoons extra virgin olive oil

75g fresh sweetcorn, fresh, frozen or canned

50g mange tout peas

2 tablespoons soya sauce

2 tablespoons clear honey

1 teaspoon ground ginger

4 spring onions, cut julienne (long ways)

2 medium carrots, cut julienne (long ways)

100g (raw weight) rice, cooked according to the manufacturer's instructions

Either 200g lean, thin steak, venison, skinless or boneless chicken, Quorn or firm white fish without skin and bones

Preparation:

Coat a very hot non-stick wok with 5 applications of Fry Light and add the virgin olive oil. The wok must always be kept very hot. Stir fry the carrot, the sweetcorn and the mange touts for 90 seconds. Stir frying in a wok doesn't take so long as it is so hot. Stir in the meat or the Quorn or the fish or the mixture in thin strips and cook for 2 minutes. Add soya sauce, honey and ginger and cook for a further 3 minutes stirring all the time. Stir in the spring onions and rice and cook for a further 5 minutes and serve.

Approximate calories per serving: 600

Oriental Wok Stir Fry

Poultry – Sweet and Sour

Meat Dishes

Tzimmas with Beef, Mango and Prunes

2 hours +

To serve six people, you will need:

Fry Light spray non-stick cooking oil

1kg of lean beef cut into strips 1" x 2" x 3" approx. (venison or turkey may be used in place of beef)

1 medium onion chopped

200g prunes, stoned if possible

4 tablespoons soya sauce

4 tablespoons red wine

4 medium carrots, sliced

1 tablespoon soft brown sugar

1 x 400g can mango slices (supermarket own brand)

Granulated sweetener

1 tablespoon lime juice

2 pinches oregano

1 pinch chilli powder

1 teaspoon salt

Ground black pepper

McDougalls Thickening Granules

1/2 teaspoon coarse ground ginger

400mls chicken stock made from Knorr or supermarket own brand cube

Preparation:

Soak the prunes in boiling water for 15 minutes and drain. Coat a hot non-stick pan with 6 applications of Fry Light and sauté the beef and onions for 7 minutes turning frequently and adding the ginger as it cooks. Now add the soya sauce, the wine, the stock, the mango slices and juices, the prunes, the carrots, the lime juice, the sugar, oregano, chilli, salt and black pepper to taste. Bring to the boil and simmer for about 3 hours adding water if it tends to dry out or bake in an oven casserole dish at 170 degrees centigrade for two and a half hours, adding water as necessary. Taste occasionally and re-season. Add granulated sweetener if you prefer your Tzimmas sweeter. Before serving, if it appears watery, stir in McDougalls granules to thicken. Serve each portion with a 50g dry weight of boiled rice.

Approximate calories per serving: 450
(including the rice)

Steak Diane Exotique prepared at the table

30 minutes

To serve four people, you will need:

25g dairy butter

4 lean minute steaks, 100g each (you may use thin turkey or venison steak, rolled thin between grease-proof paper in place of beef steak)

Fry Light spray non-stick cooking oil

1 tablespoon extra virgin olive oil

3 shallots, skinned and chopped

1 clove garlic, chopped

2 tablespoons brandy

3 tablespoons of beef stock from Telma, Knorr or good supermarket own brand cube

1 tablespoon Worcester sauce

1 tablespoon tomato purée

2 tablespoons chopped parsley

1 tablespoon coconut powder – desiccated coconut

3 Kiwi fruit, balled with a melon baller

Salt and ground black pepper

1 x 400g can rambutans, stuffed with pineapple, paw paw or mango slices

Preparation:

Heat a large non-stick frying pan and coat with 5 applications of Fry Light and add the olive oil and the butter. When foaming, add the steaks and fry for 1 minute each side and season. Add the shallots and the brandy and the garlic. Remove from the heat and set alight and as the flame dies, stir in the stock, the Worcester sauce, tomato purée, parsley, coconut powder and Kiwi. Increase the heat, stirring and shaking and as soon as it boils, serve. Heat the rambutans or the paw paw or the mango (drained) in a microwave and serve as a vegetable.

Approximate calories per serving: 500

Meat Dishes

Cider Chicken Calvados
or Duck or Turkey

Indonesian Pork Satay
you can use Chicken or Lamb

Cider Chicken Calvados

Indonesian Pork Satay

1 hour

To serve four people, you will need:

4 x 100g of boneless, skinless, fat trimmed pieces of chicken, turkey or duck

150mls medium cider

150mls chicken stock, Knorr or supermarket cube

100mls Calvados

100mls Grand Marnier

6 large spring onions, finely chopped including stalks

1 large green (Granny Smith) eating apple, peeled, cored and coarsely chopped

1 tablespoon extra virgin olive oil

Fry Light spray cooking oil

Salt and ground black pepper

McDougalls Thickening Granules

Preparation:

Put the chicken in a hot non-stick pan coated with 5 applications of Fry Light and the olive oil. Add the chopped spring onion and sauté for 2 minutes each side. Add the stock, cider, Calvados and Grand Marnier. Season and boil. Simmer, turning three times for 16 minutes. Add the apple and simmer, stirring frequently. If the chicken is fully cooked i.e. no longer pink and beautifully tender and the juices thick, this is just right for serving. If it has dried out, add a little water or a stock cube. If it is too thin, remove the chicken and simmer the juices with a few McDougalls granules, stirring all the time. Serve the chicken in the sauce, each portion with 4 small boiled new potatoes or 50g dry weight of boiled rice and a seasonal salad.

Approximate calories per serving: 450

Overnight

To serve four people, you will need:
For the Satay:

500g lean pork fillet, chicken or lean lamb

1 clove garlic crushed

2 teaspoons lemon juice

2 teaspoons lime juice

2 tablespoons soya sauce

1 x 400g can mango slices, drained

For the sauce, you will need:

2 tablespoons peanut butter

30g very low-fat spread

2 teaspoons extra virgin olive oil

1/2 tablespoon of soft brown sugar

1/2 tablespoon of tabasco

50g low-fat fromage frais

1 tablespoon coconut milk powder – desiccated coconut

Preparation:

Cut the pork, chicken or lamb into 3/4 inch cubes. Add lemon and lime juices, crushed garlic and soya sauce. Marinade for 3 hours turning occasionally, then leave overnight. Thread the cubes onto skewers (4 per skewer) and grill for 10 to 15 minutes. Serve with hot sauce and serve each portion with 50g (raw weight) of boiled rice and 1 mango slice per portion heated in a microwave.

Preparation of sauce:

In a saucepan, mix the reserved marinade juices in which the meat was marinated with peanut butter, low-fat spread, sugar, tabasco and coconut powder. Heat and stir until thick. Remove from heat. Add fromage frais and pour over the satays.

Approximate calories per serving: 500
(including mango and rice)

Exotic Shepherd's Pie

Citrus Chicken

1 hour

To serve four people, you will need:

1 x 400g can dried paw paw, drained

500g minced lean lamb

2 large onions, sliced

2 large potatoes, thinly sliced

2 small carrots, sliced

1 cup (200mls) fresh or frozen peas

300mls beef stock (supermarket own brand cube)

Mashed potato (enough to cover) you can use instant or your own

Salt and ground black pepper

Mint sauce

50g low-fat grated cheese of any sort

Preparation:

Place the lamb in the oven casserole dish with onion and a layer over of potato, carrots, peas and paw paw. Sprinkle over some mint sauce (about three teaspoons) add stock and grated cheese. Cover with mashed potato and cook at 180 degrees centigrade for about 1 hour or until brown on top.

Approximate calories per serving: 500

30 minutes

To serve two people, you will need:

200g cooked, diced chicken. Skinless, boneless and fat free – can be bought in a good supermarket

75mls unsweetened orange juice

Juice and grated rind of 1 lemon

1 large red pepper, deseeded and chopped

1 medium onion, chopped

200g white cabbage, shredded

Dried thyme and coriander

Maggi liquid seasoning or soya sauce

Salt and ground black pepper

Preparation:

Put chicken in a saucepan with orange juice, lemon juice and rind. Add the pepper, onion, a pinch of thyme and coriander. Season with salt and ground black pepper with half a level teaspoon of Maggi sauce. Simmer for 15 minutes stirring frequently. Add the cabbage and simmer for another 3 minutes. Serve each portion with a 50g (raw weight) portion of boiled rice and a green salad.

Approximate calories per serving: 400

Citrus Chicken

Meat Dishes

Champagne Quail

1 hour

To serve two people, you will need:

2 oven ready quails (supermarket) about 150g each

1 medium onion, chopped

2 small leeks, chopped finely

125g (raw weight) sweet potato or parsnip

2 sticks celery, chopped

100g chopped cauliflower heads

200g fresh brussel sprouts, grated with the outer leaves removed

Half a bottle (350mls) champagne (Brut) or dry vin blanc

100mls Ribena (not low-calorie) blackcurrant cordial

1 satsuma, peeled and leaved

3 tablespoons plain white flour

25g very low-fat spread

1 tablespoon extra virgin olive oil

Fry Light spray cooking oil

Salt and ground black pepper

Preparation:

Peel and halve the sweet potatoes. Boil in lightly salted water, mash and keep warm. Coat a hot, wide saucepan with 5 applications of Fry Light and the virgin olive oil and put in the quails. Sear for 20 seconds, turning and sear for another 20 seconds. Remove from the heat. Now remove the quails from the pan, if necessary adding a little more olive oil if it has dried out. Fry the grated sprouts for 4 minutes with 1 chopped leek, stirring frequently. Strain off the sprouts from the pan and keep warm with the sweet potatoes. Return the quails to the hot pan and juices on a maximum heat. Season again and add chopped onion, the other leek, cauliflower, celery, champagne or vin blanc and Ribena. Simmer for 18 minutes stirring and turning the quails frequently. In a cold bowl, knead the flour and low-fat spread with your fingers. Add to the quails and wine and turn up the heat. Stir vigorously until it thickens. Put the quails on a platter alongside the sweet potato and sprouts and pour over the wine and vegetables. Serve garnished with satsuma leaves.

Approximate calories per serving: 500

Cauliflower au Gratin

30 minutes

To serve four people, you will need:

2 medium or 1 very large cauliflower, broken into florets with 1 inch stalks

2 medium onions, finely chopped

4 tablespoons chopped chives

Garlic salt

Dried chilli powder

Dried paprika

Some vermouth or dried sherry

300mls vegetable or chicken stock made from a good supermarket cube

600mls skimmed milk

4 tablespoons skimmed milk powder

6 tablespoons low-fat cheddar or mozzarella cheese grated

2 tablespoons cornflour

Salt and ground black pepper

Grated powder parmesan cheese

Cyan pepper

McDougalls Thickening Granules

Fry Light spray cooking oil

Preparation:

Mix the cornflour with a little water in an eggcup and then whisk into the skimmed milk. Whisk in the skimmed milk powder and when rich and smooth blend in the cheese. Season with a touch of paprika, a good sprinkle of cyan pepper and a little salt and ground black pepper. Simmer in a saucepan stirring frequently until it thickens. Add McDougalls granules if it refuses to thicken. Put the sauce aside.

Preparation for the cauliflower:

Boil or steam the cauliflower until the stalks just begin to soften. Do not over cook. Put in an oven proof casserole dish and put aside. Coat a hot saucepan with 4 applications of Fry Light cooking oil and gently sauté the onions for two minutes. Now add the chives, vermouth, sherry, 1/2 a teaspoon of chilli powder and 1 teaspoon of garlic salt. Now add the stock and simmer and reduce until thick, using McDougalls granules if required. Now, reheat the sauce and add to the mixture. Mix well and spoon over the cauliflower. Sprinkle with parmesan cheese and grill under a hot grill until it is golden and bubbling or bake in an oven at 190 degrees centigrade until bubbles and golden. Serve alone.

Approximate calories per serving: 300

Meat Dishes

Wild Venison with Ratatouille

Wild Venison with Ratatouille

1 hour

To serve four people, you will need:

4 vacuum packed 100g venison steaks (good supermarket own brand)

1 clove garlic, crushed

1 medium red onion, chopped

1 yellow or red pepper, deseeded and diced

2 small courgettes, sliced finely

4 spring onions, chopped

1 small aubergine, cored, sliced and salted

6 small firm tomatoes, chopped

25g dried walnuts or almond

2 tablespoons balsamic vinegar

1 teaspoon soft brown sugar

Salt and ground black pepper

Garlic salt

Fry Light non-stick spray cooking oil

2 tablespoons extra virgin olive oil

Parsley to garnish

Preparation:

Roll the venison steaks with a rolling pin, between sheets of greaseproof paper to flatten them. Season with salt and black pepper and garlic salt and roll again. Brush over with some virgin olive oil on both sides. Coat a hot non-stick pan with 5 applications of Fry Light and add the remains of the virgin olive oil. Stir fry the onion and garlic for 2 minutes, then add all the other veg, nuts, sugar and vinegar. Stir fry until cooked (about 14 minutes). Meanwhile grill the steaks for 3 minutes turning for rare, 4 minutes turning for medium and 5 minutes turning for well done. Wrap each cooked steak in foil and allow it to stand for 2 minutes whilst serving the veg. Let each person unwrap their own steak. Garnish with parsley.

Approximate calories per serving: 400

Meat Dishes

Meat Dishes

North African Cous Cous

2 hours +

To serve eight people, you will need:

Fry Light non-stick spray cooking oil

500g cous cous made from a 375g (dry weight) supermarket own brand pack

200g fat free steak mince (venison or turkey mince may be used in place of beef)

8 small skinless, boneless chicken or turkey breast portions (about 75g each) cut to make 16 or 32

450mls chicken stock made from a Knorr or supermarket own brand cube

3 small carrots, chopped

1 large red onion, chopped

1 medium turnip, diced

2 sticks of celery, chopped

2 small leeks, chopped

1/4 of an average cauliflower or 2 heads of calibresse, florets only

A good handful of shredded white cabbage

100mls of tomato purée

1 red pepper, deseeded and chopped

1 large potato, finely sliced

2 medium tomatoes, sliced

4 tablespoons extra virgin olive oil

2 tablespoons plain flour

3 tablespoons crumbs or matzo meal

1 teaspoon mixed herbs

3 eggs with 2 yolks discarded

1 can chickpeas

2 teaspoons cornflour

Salt and ground black pepper

Preparation:

Coat a large, hot non-stick saucepan with 6 applications of Fry Light and add 2 of the 4 tablespoons of extra virgin olive oil. Sear the chicken for 4 minutes and put aside. Combine the mince, the flour, the herbs, the crumbs, the matzo meal and the egg. Mix together in a bowl and add more flour if it is too runny. Form into 16 small balls. Add the other 2 tablespoons of extra virgin olive oil to the pan and gently sauté the mince balls for 3 to 4 minutes, turning frequently. Do not worry if some break up. When cooked, remove and put aside. Return to the cooking pan and place in it the chicken, all the vegetables, the chick peas, the stock and all the other ingredients except the cornflour. Stir and simmer for 20 minutes. It should still be runny. Add water if it is not. Season to taste. Now in an eggcup, dissolve the cornflour in about 20mls of water and add slowly to the pot, stirring all the time. Simmer for 3 minutes and put in an oven casserole dish with a lid. Gently press the mince balls onto and just below the surface of the liquid. Put the lid on the casserole and cook at 180 degrees centigrade for 1 hour. Make up the cous cous as per the manufacturer's directions but using 1/2 low-fat spread and 1/2 butter.

Approximate calories per serving: 600

Exotique Beef Soufflé

2 hours +

To serve four people, you will need:

Fry Light non-stick spray cooking oil

4 kumquats, finely sliced

2 tablespoons extra virgin olive oil

500g lean mince beef (minced venison or turkey may be used in place of beef)

1 large red onion, chopped

4 spring onions chopped, julienne (long ways)

75g button mushrooms, chopped

2 small carrots, grated

1 teaspoon sesame seed oil

25g plain flour

2 tablespoons coconut milk powder – desiccated coconut

300mls chicken or beef stock made from supermarket own brand, Knorr or Thelma cube

1 tablespoon Worcester sauce

Salt and ground black pepper

150g frozen mixed cooked vegetables (you can buy them ready cooked or you can cook them yourself from frozen)

150mls Soya milk

3 small eggs, separated with 1 yolk discarded

Preparation:

Coat a hot non-stick pan with 5 applications of Fry Light and add the virgin olive oil. Cook the mince until brown and drain off the fat. Add onion, spring onion, mushroom, carrot and stir fry for 6 minutes. Add flour and Worcester sauce and stir fry for 1 minute. Blend the coconut milk into the stock and add gradually. Boil and simmer for 50 minutes, stirring occasionally, add water if it dries out. Grease an oven proof dish with the sesame seed oil (just a teaspoon is all you need) and add the mixture. In a separate dish, whisk the egg whites until stiff and stir in the 2 yolks and the cooked mixed vegetables. Season and pour over the meat. Cook at 180 degrees centigrade for 20 minutes and serve with hot sweetcorn topped with sliced kumquat.

Approximate calories per serving: 400

Meat Dishes

Meat Dishes

Wild Venison and Mango Exotique

Venison is a delightful meat, slightly stronger than beef and lends itself to exotic fruits. You can now buy lovely lean steaks, vacuum packed at supermarkets.

30 minutes

To serve two people, you will need:

1 pack or 2 supermarket venison steaks to the total of 340g

1 x 400g can of mango slices (supermarket brand)

2 medium tomatoes

2 passionfruits or 1 grenadillo or 1 kiwango

Fry Light spray cooking oil

1 tablespoon extra virgin olive oil

Dried garlic salt

Red currant jelly

Salt and ground black pepper

Mustard pepper

Wild Venison and Mango Exotique

Exotic Liver with Orange

Preparation:

Wipe the steaks with kitchen roll and flatten with a rolling pin between sheets of greaseproof paper. Coat a hot non-stick pan with 4 applications of Fry Light and the virgin olive oil and season. When hot, fry the steaks for about 4 minutes each side and serve. In the meantime, heat the mangoes and juice in an oven or microwave. Cut open the passionfruit or grenadillo or kiwango. Serve the steaks topped with 1 level teaspoon of garlic butter, the flesh of a whole passionfruit and seeds or half the contents of a grenadillo or 1/4 of the contents of a kiwango. Surround each with 3 or 4 hot mango slices, 2 half tomatoes (hot or cold) 1 tablespoon of redcurrant jelly and/or pepper mustard. As an accompaniment asparagus or mange tout peas will finish it off nicely.

Approximate calories per serving: 450
(including mange tout peas or asparagus)

Exotic Liver with Orange, Herbs, Mango and Papaya

1 hour

To serve four people, you will need:

Half a 400g can sliced mangoes – the rest can be frozen or kept

1/2 400g can cubed papaya (paw paw) the rest can be frozen or kept

4 kumquats, finely sliced

Fry Light non-stick spray oil

1 tablespoon extra virgin olive oil

1lb calves, lamb, chicken or pig's liver

1 green pepper, deseed and cut into rings

1 Jaffa orange, peel left on and sliced

Grated rind and juice of another 2 Jaffa oranges

1 chicken stock cube (supermarket own or Knorr etc)

2 tablespoons of coconut milk powder – desiccated coconut

1 teaspoon dried thyme

Salt and ground black pepper.

Preparation:

Coat a hot non-stick saucepan with 5 applications of Fry Light and add the olive oil. Slice the livers and cook until brown, turning all the time. Add the pepper and orange rind and stir for $2^{1/2}$ minutes. Dissolve the chicken cubes in 200mls of hot water and whisk in the coconut powder, a little salt and plenty of ground black pepper. Add to the pan, bring to the boil and simmer for approximately 20 minutes until it is reduced and creamy. Garnish with sliced orange and kumquats. Heat the mango and paw paw for 2 minutes in a microwave and serve as a vegetable.

Approximate calories per serving: 350

Veal Goulash with Lychees

or Venison or Pork

2 hours +

To serve four people, you will need:

Fry Light non-stick spray cooking oil

1 tablespoon extra virgin olive oil

1 x 400g can lychees, drained but juices reserved

1 tablespoon coconut milk powder – desiccated

500g lean veal or venison or lean pork, cubed

1 large onion, sliced

4 spring onions cut julienne (long ways)

3 teaspoons dried paprika

1 small green pepper and 1 small red pepper, both deseeded and chopped

75g button mushrooms

300mls tomato juice

2 tablespoons tomato purée

100mls beef stock from a supermarket cube

1 teaspoon ground nutmeg

1 teaspoon soft brown sugar

1 bayleaf

100mls greek yoghurt, low-fat

1 tablespoon Worcester sauce

Parsley to garnish

Salt and ground black pepper

Preparation:

Coat a hot non-stick pan with 5 applications of Fry Light and add the olive oil. Sauté the veal for 6 or 7 minutes turning all the time. Add the onions, spring onions and stir and fry for 2 minutes. Add peppers, mushrooms, tomato juice and purée, stock, coconut powder, nutmeg, salt and pepper to taste and a bayleaf. Boil, stirring all the time and transfer to an oven casserole dish. Cook at 180 degrees centigrade for 1 hour and stir in the lychees.

If dry, add the lychees juice and if necessary, water. Cook at 170 degrees centigrade for another 30 minutes. Just before serving, stir in the yoghurt and garnish with parsley. Serve each portion with 40g (dry weight) of cooked rice.

Approximate calories per serving: 500
(including rice)

Chicken Pesto

1 hour

To serve four people, you will need:

1 large red pepper, finely chopped

Fry Light non-stick spray cooking oil

200g dried whole earth pasta pots (may be called linguine)

1 large onion, finely chopped

100mls white grape juice

4 small carrots, finely chopped

2 teaspoons dried rosemary

2 teaspoons dried oreganum

2 teaspoons garlic salt

1 teaspoon garlic pepper

1 supermarket or knorr chicken stock cube

5 garlic cloves, finely chopped

200g button mushrooms chopped

2 tablespoons tomato purée

Salt and ground black pepper

Supermarket own or any ready powder of parmesan cheese

200g diced cooked chicken with all the fat, bone and skin removed

1 x 400g can chopped tomatoes.

Preparation:

Coat a large non-stick hot pan with 5 applications of Fry Light and add the peppers, onions, carrots, oreganum, garlic salt, garlic pepper, rosemary and tomato purée. Fry for 3 minutes turning frequently. Add the grape juice and tomato purée and chopped tomatoes. Simmer for 20 minutes, stirring frequently with an open pan. Meanwhile dissolve the chicken cube in half a pint of boiling water and add the chicken, the garlic cloves chopped and the mushrooms. Put this mixture into the simmering vegetables and stir well and simmer for a further 20 minutes. Season with salt and black pepper to taste. Cook the Pesto linguine (pasta pots) in a large pan of lightly salted boiling water for 10 minutes. Strain and put in a large bowl, cover with the vegetable chicken mix, garnish with parmesan cheese and serve.

Approximate calories per serving: 350

Mushroom Flan

Contains Meat

This can be a vegetarian mushroom flan if you use vegetarian stock instead of chicken stock.

1 hour

To serve four people, you will need:

Fry Light spray cooking oil

500g any type of mushroom or edible fungus

120mls vegetable or chicken stock from a good supermarket own brand cube

1 teaspoon Maggi, mixed vegetables or soya sauce

1 teaspoon Lea and Perrins Worcester sauce

4 spring onions, chopped

1 medium red onion, chopped

2 teaspoons Moutard de Dijon

1 teaspoon dried tarragon

120mls white wine, dry sherry, vermouth or white apple juice

Salt and ground black pepper

McDougalls Thickening Granules

For the flan, you will need:

1 teaspoon extra virgin olive oil

4 tablespoons skimmed milk powder

250mls skimmed milk

4 eggs with 3 yolks discarded

75g self raising flour

Salt and ground black pepper

Preparation for the Filling:
In a shallow, hot non-stick saucepan, coat with 4 applications of Fry Light. Sauté the onions and spring onions for 2 minutes stirring frequently. Add the mushrooms, stock, Maggi, Worcester sauce and wine. Simmer until it reduces and thickens. Now season and add tarragon and Moutard de Dijon. Simmer until soft and thick, adding McDougalls granules if required

Preparation for the Flan:
Combine all the flan ingredients in a blender and liquidise until creamy. Pour just over half of this into a large 30cm – 11½ inch flan dish (enough to just cover the base). Cook in an oven at 180 degrees centigrade for 4 minutes until firm. Now add the filling in the middle and pour the rest of the flan mix on top. Bake for another 20 to 30 minutes until firm and golden.

Approximate calories per serving: 250

Meat Dishes

Meat Dishes Chicken and Aubergine

Exotique Turkey and Almond

2 hours +

To serve four people, you will need:

Fry Light non-stick spray cooking oil

8 kumquats, sliced

1 large aubergine, sliced

8 x 75g skinless, boneless chicken breasts

2 cloves garlic, crushed

2 tablespoons coconut milk powder – desiccated coconut

4 small courgettes, sliced

4 medium tomatoes, skin of and chopped

2 tablespoons tomato pure

300mls chicken stock from a cube – supermarket own brand, Knorr etc

2 teaspoons clear honey

3 tablespoons fine chopped fennel

Salt and ground black pepper

Parsley to garnish

Preparation:

Spread out the aubergine slices on kitchen roll and salt. Leave for 20 minutes, salt and leave for another 20 minutes. Rinse thoroughly and drain on a kitchen roll. Coat a hot non-stick oven casserole dish with 5 applications of Fry Light and cook the chicken at 180 degrees centigrade for 35 minutes. Put the aubergine slices in a non-stick pan. Add the garlic, courgettes, tomato purée, honey and the fennel. Now whisk the coconut powder into the chicken stock and add this to the pan. Bring to the boil and simmer and season and cover for 12 minutes while simmering. Pour over the casserole and cook for a further hour. Garnish with parsley and kumquats and serve each portion with 40g (raw weight) of boiled rice.

Approximate calories per serving: 400

1 hour

To serve four people, you will need:

1 x 400g can papaya (paw paw) chunks (good supermarket own brand)

25g dairy butter

3 tablespoons coconut milk powder – desiccated coconut

1 large red onion, sliced

60g button mushrooms or other small mushrooms, sliced (but not oyster mushrooms as they are too slimy)

25g plain flour

1/2 teaspoon brown ginger

1/2 teaspoon ground nutmeg

200mls chicken stock made from Knorr, Telma or supermarket own brand cube

100mls skimmed milk

300g cooked, boneless, skinless turkey meat, cubed

25g flaked almonds, toasted

Parsley to garnish

Salt and ground black pepper

Preparation:

Melt butter in a non-stick pan and stir fry the onions and mushrooms for 4 minutes until soft. Add the flour, the ginger, the nutmeg and cook for a further 90 seconds, stirring all the time. Mix the stock and milk and whisk in the coconut powder. Blend this into the mixture in the pan and bring this to the boil stirring all the time. Now add the turkey and season. Cover for 20-25 minutes, stirring occasionally, and simmer until creamy and reduced. Serve garnished with toasted almonds and parsley. Heat papaya in a microwave for 2 minutes and serve as a vegetable.

Approximate calories per serving: 400

Chicken and Aubergine

Exotique Turkey and Almond

Exotique Venison Casserole

Chicken and Peppers

2 hours +

To serve four people, you will need:

750g of vacuum packed venison for stewing (good supermarket own brand)

1 large onion, chopped

2 medium leeks, chopped

1 clove garlic, crushed

2 teaspoons ground ginger

300mls chicken stock (Knorr, supermarket cube)

1 x 400g can mango slices, drained

1 x 200g can chopped tomatoes

1 tablespoon clear honey

1 tablespoon Worcester sauce

2 tablespoons balsamic vinegar

Salt and ground black pepper

50g plain flour

Fry Light spray non-stick cooking oil

1 tablespoon extra virgin olive oil

Preparation:

Put the venison in a polythene bag with the flour, ground ginger, salt and pepper and shake until coated. Coat a hot, large non-stick pan with 5 applications of Fry Light and add the virgin olive oil. Fry the seasoned venison chunks. Now coat in flour until seared and sealed and remove with a serrated spoon and put aside. Fry the onions and garlic in the same juices until soft and golden. Add any remaining flour from the polythene bag and sauté for 1 minute stirring all the time. Transfer the venison, the onion, the garlic, and flour to a casserole dish and add all the other ingredients. Cook in an oven at 170 degrees centigrade for 2 hours stirring occasionally adding water if it dries out. Serve each portion with four small boiled new potatoes and mange tout peas and salad.

Approximate calories per serving: 500

30 minutes

To serve two people, you will need:

2 x 100g raw, boneless chicken of any cut (all skin and fat removed)

1 red pepper, deseeded, cut into rings and halved

1 green pepper, deseeded, cut into rings and halved

1 purple or yellow pepper, deseeded, cut into rings and halved

Fry Light non-stick cooking spray

2 medium onions, finely chopped

Salt and ground black pepper

2 level teaspoons cornflour

1 tablespoon extra virgin olive oil

Preparation:

Cut the chicken portions into four to make a total of eight. Shake in a polythene bag with the cornflour. Coat a hot saucepan with 5 applications of Fry Light and add the olive oil. Sauté the chicken for 10 minutes, turning and remove and set aside. Sauté the onions for 5 minutes on a hot ring turning frequently. If it becomes dry, add a little more Fry Light spray. Do not remove but now add the peppers, salt and black pepper to taste. Sauté for a further 10 minutes turning all the time. The peppers will provide rich oil for cooking, pour over the chicken and serve with a seasonal salad.

Approximate calories per serving: 350
(including salad)

Chicken and Peppers

Meat Dishes

St Valentine's Day Red Rose Veal Holstein and Tiger Lily

1 hour

To serve four people, you will need:

4 x 100g lean fillet of veal, pork, chicken or turkey, without fat

Paxo golden crumbs or supermarket own brand

1 x 400g can mango slices (use only half and refrigerate or freeze the rest)

1 x 400g can lychees (use only half and refrigerate or freeze the rest)

4 red glacé cherries

125g carton low-fat cottage cheese with chives

Fry Light spray cooking oil

2 tablespoons extra virgin olive oil

2 eggs with 1 yolk discarded, beaten and mixed with 2 tablespoons of skimmed milk

Salt and ground black pepper

1 x 340g can niblets sweetcorn and peppers

4 fresh red roses

4 crystallised red roses if available

4 tiger lilies

To Crystallise your rose:

Dip the whole rose or the petals in freshly beaten egg white and dust or dip in caster sugar. Dry on an airing rack in a cupboard and use within 48 hours. Roses crystallised using Gum Arabica can be kept much longer by Dissolving 2 teaspoons of Gum Arabic (from any chemist) in 50mls of a mixture of vodka and white peach liqueur. Paint onto the petals or blooms and dust well or dip in caster sugar. Dry on a rack in a warm airing cupboard until crisp. Store in a sealed container for up to 1 year.

Preparation:

Dip the meat fillets in egg and milk. Shake each individually in a polythene bag with golden crumbs until coated. Season liberally with a little salt and black pepper each side. Coat a wide non-stick saucepan with 5 applications of Fry Light and add the virgin olive oil. Fry the fillets, turning frequently for 12 minutes until tender and brown. Put each fillet on a plate and top with 2 lychees and half a glacé cherry in the open end of each lychees. Surround with 4 mango slices per fillet and serve with 1/4 of a portion of cottage cheese and chives. Serve each portion with 50g (raw weight) of boiled rice and 1/4 of a tin of the hot sweetcorn and peppers. Surround the plate with red rose potals and top with a crystallised rose if available and a tiger lily. Now to Holstein your steak will cost you 80 calories. To do this, fry a small egg sunny side up in a non-stick pan coated with a few applications of Fry Light and carefully transfer it on top of your steak.

Approximate calories per serving: 550

Exotique Ham and Mango

Stuffed Cabbage

30 minutes

To serve four people, you will need:

1 x 400g can mango slices (supermarket own brand)

4 canned pineapple rings

4 x 75g lean ham steaks

150g low-fat Greek yoghurt

2 teaspoons coarse pepper mustard

1/2 teaspoon yeast extract

Chopped chives (about 2 tablespoons)

Parsley to garnish and some chopped

Salt and ground black pepper

Preparation:

Place the ham in an ovenproof dish. Cover each with a pineapple ring. Mix yoghurt, chive, yeast extract, mustard, salt and ground black pepper. Stir in some chopped parsley and spoon over the ham and pineapple. Cook at 170 degrees centigrade for 30 minutes. Garnish with parsley and serve. Meanwhile, heat the mango slices in a microwave and serve along with a seasonal salad.

Approximate calories per serving: 350

2 hours +

To serve four people, you will need:

200g lean mince beef (venison, turkey or lean lamb or pork may be used in place of beef)

2 tablespoons (raw weight) rice (50g)

2 egg whites

1 medium onion, minced

4 large cabbage leaves

1 x 400g can chopped tomatoes

3 shallots or an additional medium onion, chopped

1 chicken stock cube (Knorr, Telmar or supermarket)

Preparation:

Mix in a bowl the meat, the rice, the egg white and the onion. Dip the cabbage leaves in boiling water for 5 minutes. Roll 1/4 of the meat mixture into each cabbage and tuck in the edges. Place in a casserole dish. Add the tomatoes and shallots (or onion). Dissolve the chicken cube in enough water to just cover. Bake at 180 degrees centigrade for 60 minutes until golden on top. If it dries out, add more water, checking every quarter of an hour. Serve with a seasonal salad and 4 small, boiled new potatoes.

Approximate calories per serving: 400

Meat Dishes

Meat Dishes

Cold Meat Salad with Exotic Chunky Sauce

30 minutes

To serve one person, you will need:

125g lean, cooked poultry or meat (skinless, boneless and fatless)

Exotic Chunky Sauce
To serve ten people, you will need:

2 oranges, peeled and chopped

1 x 400g can mango slices and juices (good supermarket own brand)

Pinch of chilli powder

2 tablespoons lime juice

100mls unsweetened orange juice

2 tablespoons skimmed milk powder

1 tablespoon chopped nuts of your choice

Mixture of mint, parsley, chives and lemon grass if available

1 large fennel, finely chopped

Salt and ground black pepper

Granulated sweetener

Preparation for the sauce:
Mix in bowl and if necessary thicken with skimmed milk powder.

Approximate calories per serving: 80

Preparation for the dish:
Serve the meat with a seasonal salad and a 1/10 portion of the chunky exotic sauce, the remainder of which can be kept in a fridge or frozen.

Approximate calories per serving: 400

Cold Meat Salad with Exotic Chunky Sauce

Chicken and Pasta Thinner & Richer (Cold Dish)

30 minutes

To serve four people, you will need:

300g brown pasta shapes, cooked

250g cooked, skinless, boneless, fatless chicken or turkey, diced

4 medium tomatoes, chopped

1 small bunch of spring onions, chopped

1 green, 1 red or purple and 1 yellow pepper, all deseeded and sliced

1 starfruit, cut into thin stars

8 kumquats, finely sliced with the skin left on

100g low-fat Greek yoghurt mixed with 4 teaspoons of lime juice

Preparation:
Mix in a large bowl, cold cooked pasta, chicken and vegetables. Arrange on a plate, topped with sliced kumquat and surrounded by thin starfruit slices. Spoon over yoghurt and lime and serve.

Approximate calories per serving: 450

Slimmers' Lasagne à la Thinner & Richer

Chicken Curry with Coconut Milk

1 hour

To serve four people, you will need:

Fry Light non-stick spray cooking oil

2 tablespoons extra virgin olive oil

1 medium onion, chopped

1 clove garlic, chopped or crushed

500g lean mince steak (venison or turkey may be used in place of beef)

4 firm medium fresh tomatoes, sliced

50g of spinach, chopped (optional as Chinese leaves will do instead)

1 x 100g can tomato paste

1 jar pasta sauce of your choice (to serve 4)

1 small container Ricotta cheese

1/2 cup (100mls) of grated, dried Parmesan cheese

1 beaten egg

1 packet lasagne noodles (to serve 4)

1/2 cup grated low-fat cheddar cheese

Preparation:

Coat a hot non-stick pan with 5 applications of Fry Light and add the virgin olive oil. Fry the onion and garlic until soft and add the mince. Fry the mince, turning frequently for 3 minutes. Mix together the egg, the spinach and the Ricotta cheese. Layer in an oven casserole dish in the following order, noodles are the base then a layer of mince meat and vegetables and on top a layer of Ricotta cheese mix. This should be followed by a layer of noodles followed by a layer of meat sauce mix followed by Ricotta cheese mix. Then a final layer of noodles topped with fresh tomato slices and grated cheddar cheese. Bake at 180 degrees centigrade for 45 minutes. Sprinkle with Parmesan cheese and serve.

Approximate calories per serving: 600

1 hour

To serve six people, you will need:

50g Nestlé coconut milk powder – desiccated coconut

300mls warm water

Fry Light spray non-stick cooking oil

1 tablespoon extra virgin olive oil

750g skinless, boneless lean chicken, raw and cubed

2 teaspoons Thai red curry Paste

1 stalk lemon grass with the outer skin taken off and split or, if this is not available, 2 teaspoons lime juice

1 teaspoon Maggi liquid seasoning

Coriander and red chilli, chopped to garnish

Preparation:

Reconstitute the coconut milk with warm water. Coat a hot non-stick pan with 5 applications of Fry Light and add the virgin olive oil. Stir fry the chicken until golden. Add the curry paste, the Maggi liquid seasoning and cook for 90 seconds, stirring all the time. Add the coconut milk the lemon grass and simmer for 30 minutes stirring occasionally. Serve each portion with 50g (raw weight) of plain boiled rice or noodles. Garnish with chilli and coriander.

Approximate calories per serving: 400

Chicken Curry with Coconut Milk

Slimmers' Lasagne a la Thinner & Richer

Meat Dishes

Thinner & Richer North African Cous Cous

2 hours +

To serve eight people, you will need:

Fry Light spray cooking oil

500g cous cous made from a 375g pack eg. good supermarket own brand

200g fat free mince steak (venison or turkey may be used in place of steak)

8 boneless chicken portions, skin and fat removed (on average 3 ozs – 75g each)

1 x 200g can chick peas, or if you want to use the dried ones, 4 ozs soaked for 8 hours

3 small carrots, chopped

1 large red onion, chopped

1 medium turnip, diced

3 stick of celery, chopped

2 large leeks, chopped

1/2 cauliflower, florets only

1/2 cabbage, shredded

50mls tomato purée

3 eggs with 2 yolks discarded

1 tablespoon mixed spice

50g very low-fat spread

1 red pepper, deseeded and chopped

4 medium potatoes, sliced

2 tablespoons extra virgin olive oil

Salt and ground black pepper

Preparation:

Mix the mince with eggs and spices and form into balls. Spray a large non-stick hot saucepan with 6 applications of Fry Light and add the virgin olive oil. Brown the chicken turning frequently for 6 minutes. Add the meat balls and fry turning for about 8 minutes until brown. Add the onions, the pepper, the tomato purée, the chick peas and 300mls of water. Stir gently and simmer for 25 minutes. Now add all the other ingredients except the cous cous and stir. Season and put in a casserole dish and cook at 190 degrees centigrade for 1 hour. Make up 500g of cous cous and water from a 375g pack as per directions on the side. Use low-fat spread in place of butter. Mix together with the casserole and serve.

Approximate calories per serving: 400

Meaty Cous Cous

1 hour

To serve four people, you will need:

250g minced lean beef or lamb cooked in a microwave for 5 minutes or fried in low-fat cooking spray or 200g diced cooked chicken or turkey meat, no skin or bone

125g cous cous – semolina type supermarket own brand is excellent

150mls vegetable stock (supermarket cube)

1 courgette, diced

1/4 of a cucumber, diced

2 medium carrots, diced

2 small red onions, very finely sliced

2 medium peppers – green, red or purple, diced

1 x 400g can of chickpeas drained (a low calorie form of these is made by Boots and is excellent value at 80 calories per 100g)

3 tablespoons chopped parsley

3 tablespoons chives

2 tablespoons skimmed milk

Salt and ground black pepper

Fry Light spray cooking oil

1 tablespoon extra virgin olive oil

2 tablespoons lime juice

McDougalls Thickening Granules

Preparation:

Coat a hot large non-stick saucepan with 5 applications of Fry Light and the extra virgin olive oil. Gently sauté the courgettes, carrots, peppers and onions for two minutes. Add all the other ingredients except the cous cous and bring to the boil, season and simmer until the vegetables are soft. Stirring all the time, add in the cous cous and as soon as it is all in remove from the heat, stirring continuously. As soon as it thickens serve and if necessary return to the heat with the McDougalls granules to thicken. If too thick add a little skimmed milk. Serve with seasonal salad or mange tout, peas or similar green veg.

Approximate calories per serving: 500
(including peas or salad)

Meat Dishes

240

Ginger Turkey

30 minutes

To serve four people, you will need:

4 x 100g skinless, boneless, fatless turkey meat

2 tablespoons Maggi liquid seasoning or soya sauce

1 slice peeled fresh ginger

6 small shallots, chopped

3 tablespoons brandy

150mls chicken stock from a Knorr, Telmar or supermarket own brand cube

2 cloves of garlic, finely chopped

A pinch dried coriander

A pinch dried thyme

A pinch dried basil

A pinch dried oregano

1 tablespoon of extra virgin olive oil

Fry Light spray cooking oil

Salt and ground black pepper

McDougalls Thickening Granules

Preparation:

Coat a hot non-stick saucepan with 5 application of Fry Light and add the virgin olive oil. Sear the turkey portions for about 2 minutes each side. Now add the shallots, herbs, garlic, stock, Maggi, ginger, brandy and bring to the boil and season to taste. Simmer for 25 minutes stirring and turning. When the turkey is cooked (tender to fork and not pink) remove from the juices. If it dries out add water or stock. If the juices are thick like syrup then this is just about right. If it is not, simmer with a few McDougalls granules to thicken. Spoon the sauce over the turkey and serve with 4 small boiled new potatoes or 50g (dry weight) of boiled rice and a seasonal salad.

Approximate calories per serving: 350

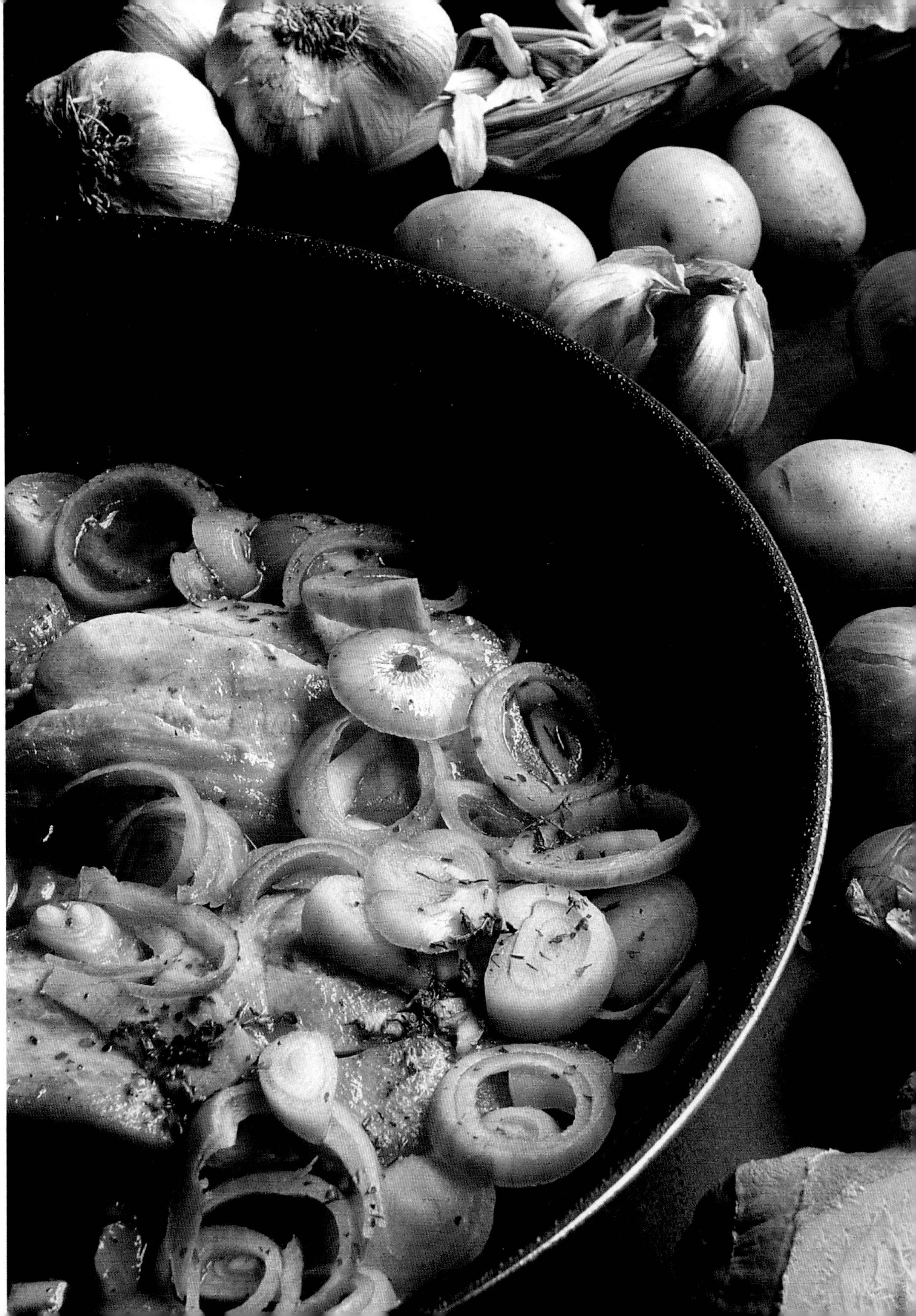

Ginger Turkey in preparation

Meat Dishes

Exotic Turkey Escalopes

30 minutes

To serve four people, you will need:

Fry Light non-stick spray cooking oil

4 boneless, skinless, fatless turkey escalopes (to a total of 500g)

2 tablespoons extra virgin olive oil

3 tablespoons vermouth or white wine

1 tablespoon balsamic vinegar

1 clove garlic, finely chopped or crushed

8 kumquats

Seasoned plain flour

1 x 230g can chopped tomatoes

2 medium onions, sliced

1 red pepper, deseeded and diced

Pinch dried rosemary

Pinch dried oregano

100g stoned olives

1 large aubergine, cubed

100mls chicken cube (any supermarket brand)

Chopped chives

Salt and ground black pepper

Preparation:

Shake the escalopes in seasoned flour in a polythene bag until coated (do these one at a time). Coat a hot non-stick pan with 5 applications of Fry Light and virgin olive oil and sauté the turkey until golden and brown. Remove and set aside in an oven casserole dish. Fry the pepper, onions and aubergines, adding more Fry Light if required until soft. Add tomatoes, olives and herbs and stir in the stock wine, vermouth and balsamic vinegar. Boil, stirring all the time until it thickens. Pour over the escalopes and simmer (covered) for 40 minutes at 180 degrees centigrade. Serve each portion, topped with 4 half kumquats and garnish with chives. Serve each with 3 small boiled new potatoes, mange tout peas and a little hot sweetcorn.

Approximate calories per serving: 400

Mixed Kebab

2 hours +

To serve four people, you will need:

200g raw skinless, boneless chicken or turkey breast

100g lean rump fillet steak or veal or venison

150g button mushrooms

1 red pepper, deseeded and cut into chunks

1 green pepper, deseeded and cut into chunks

8 large spring onions, cut in half

3 tablespoons extra virgin olive oil

1 garlic clove, crushed

4 teaspoons lime juice

1 tablespoon tomato purée

Dried rosemary

Salt and ground black pepper

Maggi liquid seasoning or soya sauce

Preparation:

On 8 long steel skewers, arrange chunks of chicken, peppers, meat, cut spring onion and mushrooms as decoratively as possible. Season with salt and ground black pepper. Mix in a bowl the olive oil, garlic, lime juice, tomato purée and Maggi and brush liberally over the skewered kebabs. Sprinkle with dried rosemary. Cook at 180 degrees centigrade in a grill pan (lined with foil) for 1 hour, basting with the juices 4 times during cooking. Serve with a 50g (dry weight) portion of boiled rice.

Approximate calories per serving: 400

Aubergine Exotique au gratin

2 hours +

To serve four people, you will need:

Fry Light spray cooking oil

1 tablespoon extra virgin olive oil

McDougalls Thickening Granules

600mls skimmed milk

4 tablespoons skimmed milk powder

6 tablespoons of low-fat cheddar or mozzarella cheese, grated

2 tablespoons corn flour

Salt and ground black pepper

2 medium tomatoes, diced

2 large aubergines, trimmed and cut into chip size slices

2 medium onions, chopped

6 tablespoons chopped chives

1 clove garlic, crushed

Garlic salt

Dried chilli powder

300mls vegetable or chicken stock from a supermarket own brand, Knorr, Maggi or Telmar cube

3 tablespoons dry vermouth or dry sherry

1 tub grated Parmesan cheese

Dried paprika

Dried cyan pepper

Directions for the sauce:

Mix the cornflower with a little bit of water in an eggcup and then whisk into the skimmed milk. Into this mixture, whisk in the actual skimmed milk powder and when rich blend in the grated cheese. Season with a pinch of paprika and a good sprinkling of cyan pepper and a little salt and ground black pepper. Simmer in a saucepan stirring frequently until it thickens. Add McDougalls granules if it does not. Allow to cool and put aside.

Aubergine:

Toast the aubergines, on a baking sheet or foil, under a grill until soft (usually 5 minutes). Spread out in an oven casserole dish. Coat a non-stick saucepan with 4 applications of Fry Light and add the virgin olive oil. Sauté the onions and garlic for 3 minutes then add the chives and sauté for a further 1 minute. Add the stock, vermouth or sherry, a pinch of chilli powder, diced tomato and season with garlic salt and pepper. Simmer until all the ingredients are tender and the liquid thickens adding McDougalls granules if required. Spread over the aubergines. Cover with the warm cheese sauce and sprinkle with the Parmesan cheese and cyan pepper. Grill until brown and bubbles, or bake at 190 degrees centigrade until brown and bubbles. Serve alone.

Approximate calories per serving: 350

Meat Dishes

Chicken with Red and Green Peppers

30 minutes

To serve four people, you will need:

Fry Light spray non-stick cooking oil

1 tablespoon extra virgin olive oil

1 medium onion, finely chopped

3 spring onions, chopped Julienne (long ways)

1 tablespoon soya sauce

4 tablespoons Maggi chilli sauce

1 inch ginger root, finely chopped

2 cloves garlic, crushed

1 teaspoon cornflour

1 teaspoon soft brown sugar

1 red, 1 green and 1 other coloured pepper, deseeded and sliced

500g cooked lean skinless, boneless chicken, cut into half-inch pieces

Preparation:

Coat a hot large non-stick sauce pan with 5 applications of Fry Light and add the virgin olive oil. Stir fry the onion, spring onion, ginger, garlic, pepper and soya sauce for 1 minute. Now add the chicken and stir fry until hot. Add the chilli sauce and keep stirring. Mix separately in an eggcup the cornflour with the sugar and a little water. Add to the pan and stir in gradually until it thickens and serve. Serve each portion with 50g (raw weight) of boiled rice per person and a green salad.

Approximate calories per serving: 450

Chicken with Red and Green Peppers

244

Duck Breast Thinner & Richer

30 minutes

To serve four people, you will need:

4 boneless portions duck breast (100g each with the fat and bone removed but the skin left on)

1 tablespoon extra virgin olive oil

Horseradish sauce (supermarket) preferably white

125g carton low-fat unsweetened natural yoghurt

1 tablespoon unsweetened lemon juice

1 large cooking apple, finely sliced and cored with the peel left on

1 x 400g can lychees with the juice discarded (good supermarket own brand)

Salt and ground black pepper

Preparation:

Brush over the seasoned duck breast with extra virgin olive oil on both sides. Grill skin side up for 5 minutes. Turn and brush again with olive oil and grill for 8 minutes. Turn and grill again for 5 minutes removing and discarding the skin just before it is fully cooked. Mix the yoghurt with 3 level teaspoons of white horseradish sauce and lemon juice. Add chopped apple to the yoghurt and spoon the mixture over each duck portion. Serve each with 4 or 5 lychees and a green salad.

Approximate calories per serving: 350

Tandoori Meat

Overnight

To serve four people, you will need:

500g meat cut into 4 or 8 fillets. You can use beef, pork, lamb, chicken or turkey as long as it is boneless, skinless and fat-free

5 tablespoons Tandoori paste (supermarket brand)

300mls low-fat natural yoghurt

Chopped chives

Salt and ground black pepper

1 teaspoon Lea and Perrins Worcester sauce

1 tablespoon extra virgin olive oil

Preparation:

Put yoghurt, Worcester sauce and Tandoori paste in a deep glass bowl. Add the meat and mix well and allow to marinade (overnight if possible) in a fridge. Put the marinaded meat on a grill rack over a grill pan and season. Do not baste yet. Grill under a medium heat for 5 minutes each side and then brush with olive oil and put in an oven at 190 degrees centigrade, still on the grill rack for 30 minutes, turning once and brushing with oil. Serve each with 50g (raw weight) of boiled rice and a green salad.

Approximate calories per serving: 400

Coconut Beef Satay
or Chicken Satay

Overnight

To serve two people, you will need:

1 x 200g can sliced peaches

2 tablespoons Nestlé coconut milk powder – desiccated coconut

250g lean rump steak, cut into thin strips or 300g skinless, fatless, boneless chicken breast cut into strips

1 teaspoon ground ginger

2 tablespoons lime juice

1 tablespoon lemon juice

1 clove garlic, crushed

Coriander leaves or parsley to garnish

Salt and ground black pepper

Preparation:

Mix all the ingredients and season to taste. Cover and leave for 1 hour minimum or preferably overnight. Thread the meat onto skewers and grill for 10 to 12 minutes turning 4 times. Heat the peaches in a microwave and serve alongside. Serve with any green vegetable or a seasonal salad.

Approximate calories per serving: 400

Tandoori Meat

Meat Dishes

New Year's Eve Quail, Champagne and Caviar

2 hours +

To serve four people, you will need:

Fry Light non-stick spray cooking oil

2 tablespoons extra virgin olive oil

4 quails (good supermarkets serve these beautifully and ready prepared)

2 tablespoons dairy butter

10 shallots, halved

250mls champagne

250mls champagne with 1 chicken stock cube crumbled into it

McDougalls Thickening Granules

Salt and ground black pepper

4 sprigs fresh or dried thyme

1 tablespoon dried or fresh lavender flowers

2 medium oranges, seeds and pips removed with the skin left on then grated or finely chopped

Flour

1 jar of real or mock caviar

Preparation:

Coat a deep heavy non-stick pan with 6 applications of Fry Light and add the virgin olive oil and the dairy butter. Put in the quails and keep turning until brown and transfer to an oven casserole dish. Add the shallots to the frying pan and sauté for 3 minutes. Using a serrated spoon, remove these and transfer these to the casserole dish. Gently add the flour a little at a time to the hot juices. Over the heat, stir all the time, until the juices are absorbed. Pour in the champagne chicken stock (but not the other half a bottle of champagne), the thyme, the lavender, the orange and stir to form a thin sauce over a moderate heat. Now remove from the heat and stir in the rest of the champagne. Stir and return to the heat with some McDougalls granules until it just begins to thicken and pour over the quails. Cover the casserole and cook at 180 degrees centigrade for 45 minutes. Add water if it dries out. If it is too thin, add some McDougalls granules. Serve each quail, decorated with caviar on a bed of winter fruits and salad with 5 small boiled new potatoes and a glass of pink champagne.

Have a very happy new year.

Approximate calories per serving: 1000

New Year's Eve Champagne, Venison and Caviar

1 hour

Venison is a delightful meat, slightly stronger than beef, very low in cholesterol and fat and lends itself to exotic fruits. You can now buy lovely lean steaks, vacuum packed in most good supermarkets.

To serve two people, you will need:

Half a bottle of chilled champagne

1 pack of 2 supermarket venison steaks – 340g

1 x 400g can mango slices (supermarket brand)

2 medium tomatoes

2 passionfruit or 1 grenadillo or 1 kiwango

Fry Light spray cooking oil

2 tablespoons extra virgin olive oil

Garlic butter

Redcurrant jelly

Salt and ground black pepper

Mustard pepper

1 jar of real or mock caviar

Preparation:

Wipe the steaks with kitchen roll and flatten with a rolling pin between sheets of greaseproof paper. Marinade in a little champagne for 30 minutes and dry with paper. Coat a hot non-stick pan with 5 applications of Fry Light and add the 2 tablespoons of extra virgin olive oil. Fry the steaks for about 4 minutes each side and put aside keeping hot. Meanwhile, heat the mangoes and juices in a microwave oven with 1 glass of champagne mixed in. Cut open the passionfruit, grenadillo or kiwango. Serve the hot steaks, topped with 1 level teaspoon of garlic butter and a generous portion of caviar and the flesh and seeds of a whole passion fruit or half the contents of a grenadillo or quarter of the contents of a kiwango. Surround each with 3 or 4 hot mango slices, 2 half tomatoes (hot or cold), 1 tablespoon of redcurrant jelly and/or pepper mustard. Asparagus or mange tout peas finish this off nicely. A glass of pink champagne will make your meal.

Have a very happy new year.

Approximate calories per serving: 1000

Chicken Pâté

Sweet and Sour Pork

248

Chicken Pâté

Sweet and Sour Pork

30 minutes

To serve four people, you will need:

500g chicken liver, defrosted if frozen

750g onion, coarsely chopped

A deep fryer of corn oil

5 hard boiled eggs with 2 yolks discarded

1 tablespoon low-fat spread

1 tablespoon olive oil

Salt and ground black pepper

Chopped parsley

Preparation:

Deep fry the onions until almost burnt and remove. Either grill the liver turning frequently for 6 minutes or deep fry at maximum for 4 minutes or coat a microwave dome dish with 4 applications of Fry Light and microwave at maximum heat for 5 minutes turning once during cooking. Put the cooked liver, onions, eggs, olive oil and some low-fat spread in a liquidiser and blend until smooth. Coat a plate with Chinese lettuce leaves. Scoop out the pâté into balls and put onto the lettuce. Garnish with parsley and serve with a large seasonal salad.

Approximate calories per serving: 300

1 hour

To serve four people, you will need:

500g lean pork, cubed

Fry Light spray cooking oil

1 tablespoon extra virgin olive oil

1 tablespoon cornflour

2 tablespoons balsamic vinegar

1 tablespoon soft brown sugar

1 teaspoon soya sauce

1 teaspoon dried ginger

1 teaspoon salt

4 teaspoons mixed spices

1 teaspoon tomato purée

1 teaspoon sherry

1 capsicum, sliced

1 carrot ,shredded

2 sticks of celery, chopped

1 x 200g can pineapple chunks

10 shallots, chopped

1 small tin red kidney beans

Salt and ground black pepper

Preparation:

Coat a hot non-stick pan with 5 applications of Fry Light and the extra virgin olive oil. Fry the cubed pork until cooked (8 to 10 minutes). Put in a saucepan with all the ingredients except the shallots and red kidney beans. Simmer stirring for 10 minutes. Now add the shallots and beans and simmer for a further 10 minutes. Serve with a seasonal salad or a small portion of noodles.

Approximate calories per serving: 600

Chicken and Apricot and Asparagus Thinner & Richer

Turkey and Lychees

This is the ideal Christmas or Thanksgiving dish and on this page it will be considered as part of the Christmas lunch.

2 hours +

To serve four people, you will need:

1 tablespoon of extra virgin olive oil

4 x 150g chicken breast portions, skinless, boneless

1 x 400g can tinned apricots

20g super cook dried onions

16 shallots, peeled and halved

250mls apple juice

McDougalls Thickening Granules

Fry Light spray cooking oil

Salt and ground black pepper

Preparation:

Coat a hot non-stick pan with 5 applications of Fry Light and add the virgin olive oil. Sear the chicken portions for 2 minutes each side and then add the shallots and sauté for 5 minutes turning frequently. Place in an oven proof dish, pour over the apricots (with their juices) and the dried onions. Season. Pour over the apple juice. Cover and cook at 200 degrees centigrade for 1 hour. Add water if it dries out. If the gravy is too thin, add some McDougalls granules for the last 5 minutes of cooking. Serve each portion with some hot, tinned asparagus spears (or fresh) and a 50g portion (raw weight) of boiled brown rice.

Approximate calories per serving: 600

30 minutes

To serve one person, you will need:

2 very generous slices of turkey breast meat cut from a freshly roasted turkey, all skin and bone must be removed

Cranberry sauce

1 x 400g can lychees (good supermarket brand)

Small portion potatoes of your choice

Green vegetables of your choice i.e. broccoli or mange tout peas

For Christmas, proceed as follows...
for other days, **just stop here!**

Preparation:

Today is a very special day and even Thinner & Richer bends the rules a little! We suggest a simple starter i.e. smoked salmon on a slice of brown Ryvita and very low-fat spread. Enjoy your turkey like everyone else, but forego the stuffing, the skin, the gravy and the sauces. Enjoy your turkey breast with lashings of cranberry sauce, 6 lychees, a few potatoes (cooked any way except fried) and some lovely greens (mange tout or broccoli). Everyone else will be jealous. If you want a small portion of Christmas "Pud" then why not! Instead of brandy butter just use 1 squirt of Anchor aerosol dairy whipped cream with brandy or a much larger squirt of Delissimo aerosol whipped cream substitute. One glass of wine and one liqueur will make your day and despite exceeding your calories a little, the fat content remains low. Please try and omit one other meal today.

Approximate calories per serving: 1000

Turkey and Lychees

Chicken and Apricot and Asparagus

Chinese Chicken Salad with Lychees

30 minutes

To serve four people, you will need:

1 x 400g can lychees, drained (good supermarket own brand)

75g easy cook rice of your choice, cooked according to the manufacturer's instructions

300g cooked, boneless, fat free, skinless chicken, shredded

4 spring onions, sliced julienne (long ways)

125g button mushrooms, sliced

50g bean sprouts, blanched in hot water for a few seconds

1/4 cucumber, finely sliced or diced

For the dressing, you will need:

2 tablespoons peanut butter

1 clove garlic, crushed

2 teaspoons grated ginger

1 tablespoon light soya sauce

1 tablespoon balsamic vinegar

1 tablespoon sesame seed oil

2 tablespoons water

2 tablespoons fresh coriander, chopped

Preparation:

Cook the rice to the manufacturer's instructions. To the cooked rice add the spring onions, mushrooms, beansprouts and cucumber. Blend all the dressing ingredients in a blender or using a hand whisk, and pour over the salad. Chill and serve with the lychees.

Approximate calories per serving: 450

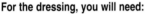

Chinese Chicken Salad with Lychees

Left over Turkey Thinner & Richer

30 minutes

To serve two people, you will need:

200g cooked turkey meat (weighed after removal of all skin, bone and fat)

1 medium onion, thinly sliced

Fry Light non-stick spray cooking oil

1 x 100g can peaches, apricots or mangoes, drained

150mls Knorr garlic chicken stock made from a cube

1 x 125g pack low-fat yoghurt, plain or fruit flavoured

25g plain flour

2 beaten eggwhites mixed with 150mls skimmed milk

Chives or parsley

New potatoes

Green salad

Preparation:

Cut the turkey into slices or cubes and mix in a bowl with beaten egg and milk. Put flour into a small kitchen polythene bag and add the turkey cubes after straining (1/4 at a time and shake to coat them well) and place in a dry bowl. Do not add any salt. Coat a medium non-stick pan with 4 applications of Fry Light and add the sliced onions and fry for 3 minutes. Prevent burning with a wooden spoon. Now add the stock, the turkey and the fruit and bring to the boil and simmer for about 10 minutes. Now add the yoghurt and return to a low heat and cook for 3 minutes but do not allow to boil. Place in a serving dish, garnish with parsley and chives. Serve each portion with 4 small boiled new potatoes and a green un-tossed salad.

Approximate calories per serving: 350

30 minutes

To serve four people, you will need:

4 x 100g skinless, boneless fillet of chicken

150mls chicken stock (Knorr, Telmar or good super-market own brand cube)

100mls sweet, cheap sherry

3 cloves of garlic, finely chopped

6 large spring onions, with the white parts chopped and the green stalks reserved

Salt and ground black pepper

1 x 125g carton low-fat natural unsweetened yoghurt

Fry Light spray cooking oil

1 tablespoon extra virgin olive oil

McDougalls Thickening Granules

Preparation:

Coat a very hot non-stick pan with 5 applications of Fry Light and add the virgin olive oil. Sauté the chicken fillets, turning frequently for 2 minutes each side in order to sear. Add chopped spring onions and garlic and sauté for another 2 minutes. Remove from the heat but do not drain. Add the stock, the sherry and season with salt and black pepper to taste. Boil and simmer for a further 18 minutes, turning the chicken 4 times. As the liquid reduces, the chicken becomes rich and brown. Keep turning and stirring with a wooden spoon. Keep checking the chicken until cooked (not pink and tender to fork). Remove the chicken from the juices. If the juice is not too thick, add some McDougalls granules. Return the chicken to the sauce. Add spring onion leaves to the yoghurt and spoon over the individual portions and serve each with 4 small boiled new potatoes or 50g (dry weight) of boiled rice and a green salad.

Approximate calories per serving: 400

Scallop Seviche

Lobster Salad

Overnight

To serve four people, you will need:

8 large scallops

4 scallop shells

100g peeled cooked prawns

300mls unsweetened lemon juice

150mls Rose's lime cordial

4 small shallots, finely chopped

1 tablespoon finely chopped chives

1 tablespoon finely chopped parsley

1 tablespoon extra virgin olive oil

Salt and ground black pepper

Dried tarragon

Dried thyme

Dried coriander

Preparation:

Clean the scallops under running water. Remove from the shells, take off frill, fringe, guts and any orange flesh (you are left with white flesh only). Wash and dry on kitchen roll and cut into 1/4 inch slices. Clean and scrub shells and dry. Slice scallops into a bowl and pour over the lemon and lime juices. Leave to marinade for 24 hours in the fridge covered with Stretch 'n Seal. Stir 4 or 5 times, if possible, during the marinade. Next day, drain off the juices, add shallots and prawns and mix well. Add olive oil and mix again. Add salt and black pepper. Sprinkle lightly with tarragon, thyme and coriander. Either serve cold and chilled in shells or microwave for 3 minutes, top setting in a microwaveable bowl covered with a dome or perforated Stretch 'n Seal and serve in the shells. Serve each portion with 2 dark Ryvita spread with very low-fat spread.

Approximate calories per serving: 250

30 minutes

To serve one person, you will need:

Approx 500g freshly boiled whole lobster from the fishmonger or 1/2 x 1kg lobster

Preparation:

Most fishmongers boil them for you. Cut the lobster shell from the head to the tail along the back. Carefully crack open the lobster on a chopping board with a hammer and screwdriver (a moulwrench and pliers are good for getting the flesh out of the claws and pincers). Remove meat from claws, legs, pincers tail and body, including any roe. Remove the stomach, intestinal cord, green liver and corral and discard. Discard the head and brain or leave on the shell. Arrange the lobster meat back into an open washed body shell or arrange without the shell on a plate with a large salad of lettuce, tomato, cucumber, radish, red and white peppers, spring onions etc. Sprinkle all with a mixture of lemon and lime juices. Serve with a 50g bowl of Waistline, Crosse and Blackwell or supermarket own brand salad cream or cocktail dressing. Dress salad with a mixture of 3 teaspoons of virgin olive oil, 1 teaspoon of balsamic vinegar, a pinch of mustard powder and black pepper. Serve and enjoy.

Approximate calories per serving: 450
(including dressing)

Lobster Salad

Scallop Seviche

Smoked Salmon Expanded à la Thinner & Richer

Sole in Envelopes

Smoked Salmon Expanded

30 minutes

To serve four people, you will need:

2 medium courgettes, thinly sliced

200g smoked salmon, cut and diced (cheap end pieces will suffice)

2 medium onions, thinly sliced into rings

2 large heads chicory

2 small limes or 1 large lemon, sliced thinly with the peel left on

1 bottle Crosse and Blackwell, supermarket own brand or similar Waistline cocktail dressing

2 tablespoons unsweetened lemon juice

Dried cayenne pepper

Salt

Finely chopped spring onions

Parsley or chives

50ml skimmed milk

2 tablespoons extra virgin olive oil

1/2 cucumber, skin left on and thinly sliced

Preparation:

Line a large serving dish with chicory leaves. In a medium polythene bag mix the following: cocktail dressing, lemon or lime, lemon juice, salt, olive oil, cucumber, courgettes and skimmed milk. Shake the contents thoroughly in the polythene bag until mixed and spoon over the chicory. Cover with diced smoked salmon. Garnish with raw onion rings, cayenne pepper, parsley or chives and spring onions. Serve with 2 water biscuits or cream crackers per portion.

Approximate calories per serving: 300
(including biscuits)

30 minutes

To serve four people, you will need:

4 x 100g fillets boneless sole, plaice, dab or similar white fish

2 tablespoons dry white wine, cider or sherry

1 tablespoon extra virgin olive oil

1 medium onion, finely diced

2 tablespoons shredded root ginger

200g (1/2 tin) drained pineapple chunks

1/4 cucumber, thinly sliced

Chives, well chopped

1 x 125g carton low-fat yoghurt

Salt and ground black pepper

Greaseproof paper

Deep fryer with fresh, or reasonably fresh, Crisp 'n Dry or corn oil

Preparation:

Divide all 4 fillets into 1 inch squares. Sprinkle with a large pinch of salt. Put in a polythene bag with the wine or sherry and shake until well mixed. Now cut out 4 squares from the grease-proof paper 7 x 7 in. Brush each with virgin olive oil. Put a quarter of the fish on each, top equally with onion, cucumber and ginger and add the pineapple chunks. Fold into envelopes and tuck in to secure. (This is easy to do, imagine each square is divided into 2 equal triangles. Put the fish, etc on 1 triangle, fold the corners over, starting with the nearest and tuck in well.) Now deep fry the packets for 4 minutes. Mix the yoghurt with the chives and serve a good portion with an envelope of fish, each accompanied with 4 small new potatoes or a seasonal salad.

Approximate calories per serving: 400
(including salad and potatoes)

Fish Soup with Sweetcorn and Lychees

Salmon and Rice

30 minutes

To serve four people, you will need:

50g smoked salmon, end pieces, chopped and diced

1 x 400g can lychees (supermarket own brand)

250g white fish, skinless and boneless (plaice, haddock, cod, coley, hake)

300mls Stones Ginger Wine

1/2 cucumber, thinly sliced

1 x 225g can unsweetened corn, drained

600mls water

Bunch spring onions

McDougalls Thickening Granules

Salt and pepper

8 finger bread rolls

Very low-fat spread

Preparation:

Steam the white fish over a double boiler or in a steamer for 8 minutes. Mash, add diced smoked salmon and put to one side. Put lychees and juice in a saucepan with ginger wine, add the pint of water, sweetcorn, 1 level teaspoon of salt and a pinch of black pepper. Chop up the white part of the spring onions, reserving the green stalks and add to the pan. Stir and bring to the boil, simmering for 3 minutes. Add the cucumber slices. Now add the fish and the salmon mixture and stir well. After 2 minutes add McDougalls granules until it just begins to thicken. Remove from the heat, garnish with chopped green spring onion and serve. Serve as a main course with 2 small finger bread rolls and very low-fat spread.

Approximate calories per serving: 300

1 hour

To serve four people, you will need:

Fry Light non-stick cooking spray

1 x 410g can red sockeye salmon (John West, Princes, or supermarket own brand)

3 x half-cups dry weight cooked rice, cooked according to the manufacturer's instructions

125g button mushrooms, sliced

Skimmed milk

1 x 300g can Campbells half-fat tomato soup

1 medium onion, sliced

75ml sweet sherry

Salt and ground black pepper

50g flaked almonds

1 x 300g carton low-fat fromage frais

2 tablespoons extra virgin olive oil

Preparation:

Coat a hot large non-stick saucepan with 5 applications of Fry Light and 2 tablespoons of virgin olive oil. Sauté the mushrooms and onions until soft and add the almonds. Line a casserole dish with the cooked rice and cover with the fried mushrooms and almonds. Skin, bone and break up the salmon and add it along with the juices. Dilute the tomato soup with an equal quantity of skimmed milk and mix this in a separate bowl with the fromage frais and the sherry. Season to taste. Now pour this over the rice and salmon and bake at 180 degrees centigrade, covered, for 50 minutes or until the surplus liquid sets. Serve with a seasonal salad.

Approximate calories per serving: 550
(including salad)

Salmon and Rice

Fish Soup with Sweetcorn and Lychees

Fish Dishes **Gefullte Fish**

Prawn and Exotic Salad

Gefullte Fish

Prawn and Exotic Salad

2 hours +

To serve four people, you will need:

2 small carrots

2 medium onions

500g fresh skinned and boned haddock fillets, but retain the skin, bones and heads if possible

4 teaspoons extra virgin olive oil

1½ teaspoons caster sugar

Salt and ground white pepper

2 eggs, 1 yolk discarded

3 tablespoons matzo meal or crumbs

1 tablespoon ground almonds

Preparation:

Mince the fish, 1 onion and 1 carrot together. Now add the eggs, ground almonds, sugar, olive oil, salt and pepper (about 1 teaspoon of salt and a pinch of pepper should be enough). Add the matzo meal and shape into balls or patties of golf ball size. Now boil 750mls of water with the fish skins, bones and heads and add the other carrot and the other onion, sliced. Season with a little salt and pepper, simmer for 30 minutes and strain. Boil the patties gently in this liquid for 45 minutes. Serve hot or cold with a seasonal salad and 4 small boiled new potatoes.

Approximate calories per serving: 300

30 minutes

To serve four people, you will need:

8 kumquats or 1 starfruit, thinly sliced

Chinese leaves, washed and dried

1 x 120g can sweetcorn

250g cooked and peeled prawns

2 tablespoons lime juice

4 tablespoons extra virgin olive oil

100g low-fat fromage frais mixed with 4 teaspoons lime juice

275g pack supermarket frozen, diced vegetables (beans, peas, peppers, etc)

1/2 teaspoon mixed spice

4 spring onions, chopped

1 clove garlic, finely chopped

1 tablespoon balsamic vinegar

Salt and ground black pepper

Preparation:

Cook the supermarket vegetable pack as directed and cool. Mix in the can of sweetcorn and the spring onions. Mix together and whisk the following: olive oil, lime juice, balsamic vinegar, garlic, mixed spice and salt and pepper to form a dressing. Put the prawns in a large bowl and drown in the dressing. Mix well and add the vegetable mixture and serve on a bed of Chinese leaves. Garnish with slices of kumquat or starfruit, dollop on the fromage frais and serve.

Approximate calories per serving: 400

Tomato and Tuna Salad Exotique

30 minutes

To serve four people, you will need:

1 x 200g can tuna in oil, drained and flaked

2 hard boiled eggs, sliced

12 Chinese leaves

4 medium tomatoes, sliced

1 green pepper, deseeded and sliced

4 kumquats, halved longways

1 starfruit, sliced into stars

12 black olives

12 green olives

1 tin anchovies encircles in capers, drained

1 tablespoon extra virgin olive oil

1 teaspoon balsamic vinegar

Salt and ground black pepper

Preparation:

Arrange the sliced tomato and starfruit around the edge of a platter. Lay sliced egg in the centre on a bed of shredded Chinese leaves. Top with flaked tuna. Top this with peppers and kumquats and sprinkle olives all over. Dress with a mixture of olive oil, balsamic vinegar and salt and pepper. Put anchovies on top and serve each portion with 2 dark Ryvita.

Approximate calories per serving: 400

Smoked Rainbow Trout or Smoked Salmon with Exotic Chunky Sauce

30 minutes

To serve one person, you will need:

1 x 125g smoked rainbow trout or 100g smoked salmon

Exotic Chunky Sauce

To serve ten people, you will need:

2 oranges, peeled and chopped

1 x 400g can mango slices with juice

Pinch chilli powder

2 tablespoons lime juice

100ml unsweetened orange juice

2 tablespoons skimmed milk powder

1 tablespoon chopped nuts of choice

Mixture of chopped mint, parsley and lemon grass, if available

1 large fennel, finely chopped

Salt and ground black pepper

Granulated sweetener

Preparation for the sauce:

Mix in a bowl, if necessary thicken with skimmed milk powder. (This sauce can be kept in the fridge or frozen and kept for several months.)

Approximate calories per serving: 80

Preparation for the dish:

Serve a portion of fish with 1 portion of chilled sauce and a large seasonal salad with baby sweetcorn and other vegetables of your choice.

Approximate calories per serving: 400

Fish Dishes

Smoked Rainbow Trout or Smoked Salmon

Tomato and Tuna Salad Exotique

Fish Dishes

Exotic Salmon and Plaice

1 hour

To serve four people, you will need:

1/4 teaspoon dried basil and 1/4 teaspoon dried dill

1 x 410g can red sockeye salmon (John West, Princes or supermarket own brand)

6 plaice fillets, skinned and boned, to a weight of around 75g each

2 tablespoons lime juice

1 tablespoon skimmed milk powder

1 tablespoon Nestlé, or other, coconut milk powder

50g polyunsaturated low-fat margarine

150mls skimmed milk

25g grated low-fat cheddar cheese

25g cornflour

Salt and black pepper

Preparation:
Drain the salmon but put the juices aside and flake the flesh into a bowl. Now season the plaice with basil, dill, salt and pepper and lime juice. On each fillet of plaice put equal amounts of salmon and roll up, skewering with a cocktail stick. Arrange each on an ovenproof dish greased with 25g of the margarine and bake at 180 degrees centigrade for 20 minutes. Meanwhile melt the other 25g of margarine in non-stick pan and gently cook, adding the cornflour. Cook for 1 minute, stirring gradually. Stir in the milk, skimmed milk powder, coconut powder and salmon juices and stir until smooth and season. If it is lumpy, remove any corn-flour lumps and if necessary add water or McDougalls granules. When the fish is fully cooked lather over the sauce and garnish with cheese. Now grill until golden and serve. Serve each with a seasonal salad and 2 dark Ryvita or crackers with very low-fat spread.

Approximate calories per serving: 500

Avocado Salmon

30 minutes

To serve six people, you will need:

Fry Light non-stick spray oil

1 x 210g can red sockeye salmon

1 tablespoon extra virgin olive oil

1 small red onion, finely chopped

1 stick celery, chopped

50g fresh brown breadcrumbs

2 tablespoons low-fat fromage frais

3 medium avocados

1 tablespoon lemon juice

Salt and ground black pepper

Preparation:
Coat a hot shallow non-stick pan with 4 applications of Fry Light and add the olive oil. Sauté the onions and celery until soft. Drain the salmon and flake into a bowl. Now add the cooked onions, celery, breadcrumbs and fromage frais and season. Cut the avocados in half and remove the stones. Scoop out some of the flesh but leave about 1/4 of an inch below the skin to form a support shell. Mix the avocado flesh with lemon juice and stir into the salmon mix. Fill the avocado shells until overflowing with this mixture and pack down. Bake at 190 degrees centigrade for 22 minutes and serve.

Approximate calories per serving: 250

Red Sockeye Salmon Stir Fry

30 minutes

To serve four people, you will need:

1 x 410g can red sockeye salmon (John West, Princes or supermarket own brand)

1 x 250g pack Chinese noodles

2 tablespoons extra virgin olive oil

2 cloves garlic, crushed

1 inch root ginger, grated

1 bunch spring onions, cut julienne (longways)

2 courgettes, thinly sliced

1 small red onion, thinly sliced

2 small carrots, cut julienne

1 red pepper, deseeded and cut into strips

100g mange tout peas, trimmed

100g bean shoots or beansprouts

100g Chinese leaves, shredded

1 x 175g can water chestnuts, drained and sliced

4 tablespoons soy sauce

Preparation:

Drain the salmon, retain the juice, break into chunks and put into a bowl. Cook the noodles according to the manufacturer's instructions. Heat the oil in a wok and add the garlic and ginger. Cook for 30 seconds and add the onion, spring onion, courgette, carrot, pepper and mange tout peas. Stir fry for 4 minutes and add the bean shoots, Chinese leaves and water chestnuts. Stir fry for 3 minutes more. Add 4 tablespoons of salmon juice to this mixture, soy sauce and then the salmon. Cook until the fish chunks are hot, stirring gently. Drain the noodles and make a bed and serve the fish on top.

Approximate calories per serving: 500

Salmon Fillet with Hot Exotic Chunky Sauce

30 minutes

To serve one person, you will need:

Fry Light spray cooking oil

1 teaspoon extra virgin olive oil

1 x 125g boneless fresh salmon or trout fillet, either poached, steamed of fried in Fry Light and virgin olive oil until tender, seasoned with salt and black pepper

Exotic Chunky Sauce
To serve ten people, you will need:

2 oranges, peeled and chopped

1 x 400g can mango slices with juice

Pinch chilli powder

2 tablespoons lime juice

100ml unsweetened orange juice

2 tablespoons skimmed milk powder

1 tablespoon chopped nuts of choice

Mixture of chopped mint, parsley and lemon grass, if available

1 large fennel, finely chopped

Salt and ground black pepper

Granulated sweetener

Preparation for the sauce:

Mix in a bowl, if necessary thicken with skimmed milk powder. (This sauce can be kept in the fridge or frozen and kept for several months.)

Approximate calories per serving: 80

Preparation for the dish:

Serve the fish covered with 1 portion of the sauce, 4 small new potatoes and a seasonal salad or green vegetables of choice.

Approximate calories per serving: 450

Fish Dishes

Oriental Wok Stir Fry

Exotic Kedgeree

30 minutes

To serve two people, you will need:

Fry Light non-stick spray oil

2 tablespoons extra virgin olive oil

75g sweetcorn, fresh, frozen or canned

50g mange tout peas

2 tablespoons soy sauce

2 tablespoons clear honey

1 teaspoon ground ginger

4 spring onions, cut julienne (longways)

2 medium carrots, cut julienne

100g raw weight rice, cooked according to the manu-facturer's instructions

200g any firm white fish or salmon, skinned and boned, cut into thin strips

Oriental Wok Stir Fry

Preparation:

Coat a very hot non-stick wok with 5 applications of Fry Light and add the olive oil. Stir fry the carrot, sweetcorn and mange tout for 90 seconds. Stir in the fish and cook for a further 2 minutes. Add the soy sauce, honey and ginger and cook for 3 minutes. Stir in the spring onions and rice and cook for a further 5 minutes and serve.

**Approximate calories per serving: 600
But what a meal!**

NB In place of fish you may use a similar 200g portion of lean steak, venison or boneless, skinless poultry cut into thin slices or vegetarian Quorn cut into cubes. It is equally delicious.

30 minutes

To serve four people, you will need:

350g smoked fish, haddock or cod, filleted, skinned and cubed

350g cooked basmati rice or long grain rice (made from 100g raw rice boiled or microwaved according to manufacturer's instructions)

25g butter

1 tablespoon chopped parsley

1 tablespoon chopped chives

Pinch dried nutmeg

2 tablespoons lemon juice

1 hard boiled egg, chopped

400g of canned sliced mango

Preparation:

Melt the butter in a non-stick saucepan and add the fish. Stir and cook for 6 minutes. Add the cooked rice, stir and cook for a further 4 minutes. If too dry add a little water. Add parsley, chives, nutmeg and lemon juice. Cook, stirring, until piping hot (about 2-4 minutes). Heat the mangoes in a microwave and serve each portion with mango slices.

Approximate calories per serving: 350

Grapefruit and Red Sockeye Salmon

Smoked Trout

30 minutes

To serve four people, you will need:

1 x 210g can red sockeye salmon (supermarket own brand, John West, Princes etc)

2 small grapefruit

150mls low-fat fromage frais

50g Nestlés coconut milk powder

2 tablespoons lemon juice

Small bunch chives, chopped

1/4 cucumber, chopped

1 tablespoon skimmed milk powder

2 teaspoons soft brown sugar

Salt and ground black pepper

Preparation:

Drain the salmon and flake into a bowl. Cut the grapefruit in half and remove the pulp to leave empty shells. Add half the flesh from one of the grapefruits to the salmon, chopped up. To the fromage frais add the lemon juice, coconut milk powder, skimmed milk powder and sugar. Whisk or liquidise. If this is too thick add water. Now add the salmon and grapefruit mixture and about 2 tablespoons of chopped chives. Mix well and season to taste. Line the grapefruit skins with chopped cucumber and pile in the mixture. Chill before serving.

Approximate calories per serving: 200

30 minutes

To serve four people, you will need:

2 smoked trout fillets, skinned, boned and chopped (to a total of 200g)

1 medium cooking apple, peeled, cored and chopped

2 tablespoons horseradish sauce

4 teaspoons lime juice

2 teaspoons balsamic vinegar

2 sticks celery, chopped

2 tablespoons chopped chives

3 tablespoons (50ml) low-fat fromage frais

Salt and ground black pepper

Lemon or lime, sliced

Parsley to garnish

Lettuce

Preparation:

Mix all the ingredients and season to taste. Split into portions on a lettuce leaf and garnish with sliced lemon or lime and parsley. Serve each portion with 2 high fibre water biscuits.

Approximate calories per serving: 150
(including biscuits)

Grapefruit and Red Sockeye Salmon

NB. If you think this meal is rather on the stingy side there is no reason why you cannot have a double portion, making a total of 300 calories.

Fish Dishes

Quick Hot Prawns

30 minutes

To serve two people, you will need:

1 Fry Light non-stick spray oil

6 tablespoons (90ml) Maggi extra hot chilli sauce

350g shelled prawns

1 inch root ginger, peeled and finely chopped

3 spring onions, chopped julienne (longways)

1 tablespoon extra virgin olive oil

2 cloves garlic, crushed

1 teaspoon soft brown sugar

1 teaspoon cornflour

Preparation:

Coat a hot large non-stick pan with 5 applications of Fry Light and add the virgin olive oil. Add garlic, ginger and spring onions. Then add the Maggi and stir fry for 90 seconds. Add the prawns and continue to stir fry for 4 minutes more. Mix the cornflour with a little water in an eggcup and slowly add, stirring all the time, until it thickens. Then serve piping hot as a main course with 50g (raw weight) of boiled rice.

Approximate calories per serving: 400
(including rice)

Tuna Special

30 minutes

To serve four people, you will need:

Fry Light spray cooking oil

1 x 200g can tuna in brine, drained

2 tablespoons soy sauce

2 tablespoons white wine or vermouth

1/4 teaspoon ground ginger

2 tablespoons extra virgin olive oil

Salt and ground black pepper

1 bunch spring onions or 3 shallots or 1 medium onion, chopped

1 red or green pepper, deseeded and sliced

1 tin French beans or 175g fresh mange tout peas

1 small tin water chestnuts

50g button mushrooms, sliced

Preparation:

Break the tuna into chunks. Place in a bowl and add soy sauce, wine, ginger and black pepper to season. Coat a hot non-stick saucepan with 5 applications of Fry Light and add the virgin olive oil. Sauté the pepper, spring onions and mange tout or beans for 3 minutes. Add the tuna and drained water chestnuts. Stir and cook for a further 3 minutes until soft. Serve each portion with 50g (dry weight) of rice sprinkled with cashew nuts.

Approximate calories per serving: 350
(including rice and nuts)

White Fish Cous Cous

1 hour

To serve two people, you will need:

250g raw boneless white fish, steamed for 20 minutes

125g cous cous (semolina type) supermarket brand

1 courgette, diced

1/4 cucumber, diced

2 medium carrots, diced

2 small red onions, finely sliced

2 medium peppers, green, red or purple, deseeded and diced

1 x 400g can chickpeas, drained (an excellent low calorie form of these is made by Boots or Waters at only 80 calories per 100g)

3 tablespoons chopped parsley

2 tablespoons skimmed milk powder

2 tablespoons extra virgin olive oil

Salt and pepper

Fry Light cooking spray

2 tablespoons lime juice

McDougalls Thickening Granules

Preparation:

Coat a hot large non-stick saucepan with 5 applications of Fry Light and the virgin olive oil. Gently sauté the courgette, carrot, peppers and onions for 2 minutes. Add all the other ingredients, except the cous cous and bring to the boil. Season and simmer until the vegetables are soft. Add in the cous cous, stirring all the time and as soon as it is all in remove from the heat, continuing to stir all the time. As soon as it thickens, serve. If necessary return to the heat with McDougalls granules to thicken. If too thick, add a little water or skimmed milk. Serve with a seasonal salad or mange tout peas.

Approximate calories per serving: 500
(including salad or mange tout peas)

Whole Rainbow Trout à l'Orange

30 minutes

To serve two people, you will need:

2 x 300g rainbow trout, gutted
1 inch root ginger
Grated rind and juice of 1 lime
Grated rind of 1 large orange
1 teaspoon ground cinnamon
1 teaspoon ground nutmeg
2 teaspoons wholegrain mustard
2 cloves garlic
2 additional oranges, peel left on and thinly sliced
75g dairy butter
Salt and ground pepper
Parsley

Preparation:
Wash and dry the trout with kitchen roll. Place each on a lightly buttered piece of foil, large enough to parcel the fish. Make slanting diagonal cuts (about 4) along the exposed side. Now finely chop the garlic, ginger and 50g of butter, lime and orange rind and lime juice. Mix well and beat in the mustard. Spoon the mixture into the cuts on the trout and season with salt and black pepper. Parcel up and bake at 180 degrees centigrade on a tray with a little water for 20 minutes. Serve on a bed of sliced orange and garnish with parsley. Serve each with 4 small new potatoes and a seasonal salad.

Approximate calories per serving: 450

Rainbow Trout

Rainbow Trout

30 minutes

To serve two people, you will need:

2 x 300g (dead weight whole) rainbow trout, gutted
1/2 cucumber, skin removed and sliced
50g dairy butter
10 dried almonds
Salt and ground black pepper
Parsley and chives
A little white wine vinegar

Preparation:
Wash and dry the trout. Place on kitchen foil and season well with salt and a touch of black pepper. Stuff the body of the fish with knobs of butter and then with the sliced cucumber and cut almonds. Sprinkle 2 level teaspoons of white wine vinegar over each fish. Wrap in foil and then double wrap for safety. Place in an oven dish with 1/4 inch of water in the bottom. Cook in a hot oven at 200 degrees centigrade for 20 minutes. Open up your packet, garnish with parsley and chives and drain off any excess butter and juices. Serve with a seasonal salad or 3 small new potatoes per portion.

Approximate calories per serving: 300
(including potatoes and salad)

264

Ingredients for Rainbow Trout

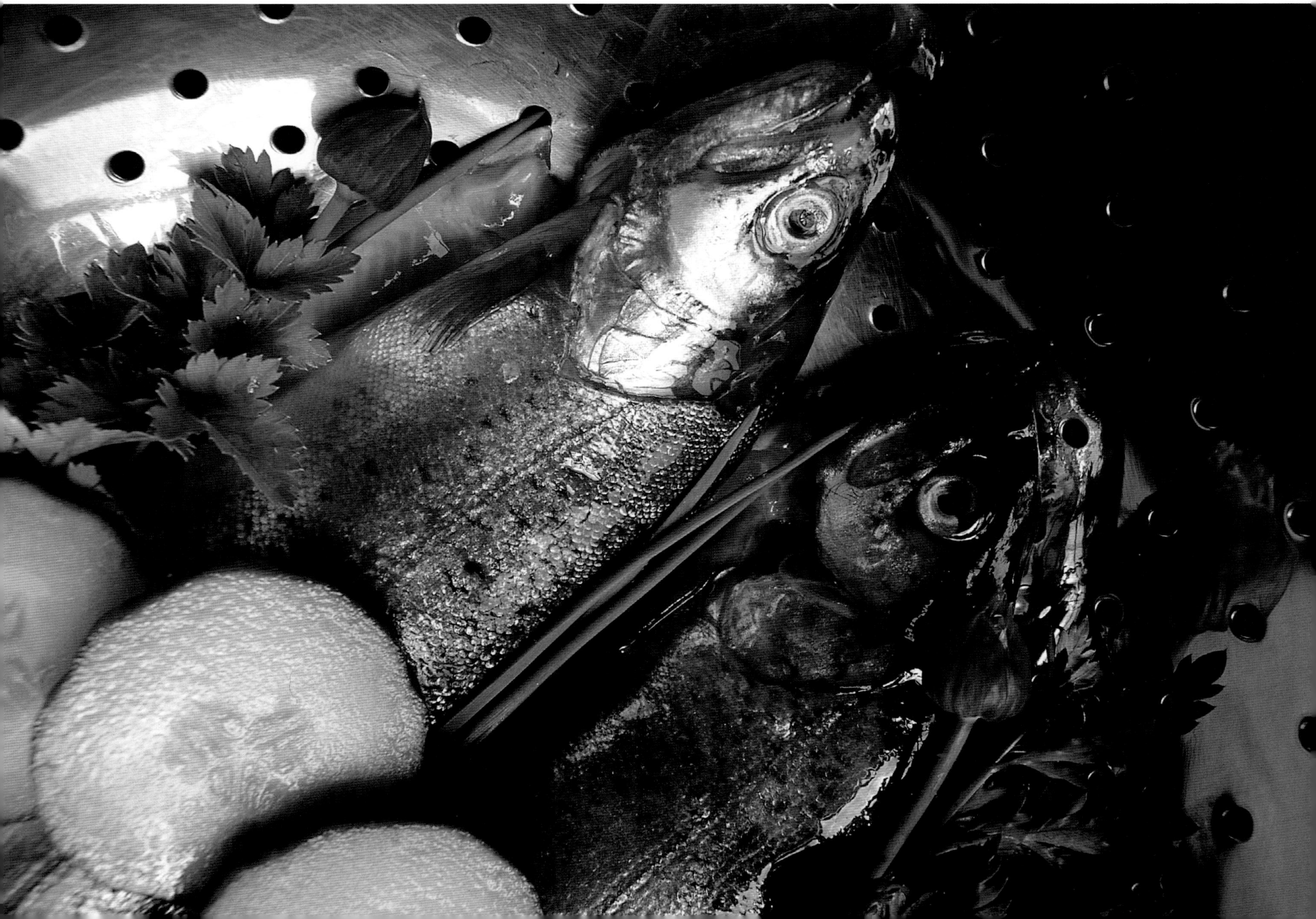

Fish Dishes

Exotic Mackerel

1 hour

To serve four people, you will need:

Half a 400g can tinned mangoes, drained (you can freeze the rest)

4 small sweet mackerel fillets (4 x 100g fillets), or other fish

1 medium onion, thinly sliced

1 small carrot, diced

1 tablespoon plain flour

1 x 400g can tomatoes

1 tablespoon tomato purée

50g coconut milk powder

300mls fish or vegetable stock made from supermarket own brand cube

1 clove garlic, crushed

1 bay leaf, crumbled

75g green stuffed olives

Salt and ground black pepper

Starfruit to garnish

Fry Light spray cooking oil

Preparation:

Coat a hot non-stick pan with 4 applications of Fry Light and sauté the onions and carrots until soft (about 3 minutes). Sprinkle on the flour and stir fry for a further minute. Add the mango, tomato, tomato purée, stock, garlic, bay leaf and coconut powder. Boil and simmer for 40 minutes, stirring occasionally. Now liquidise and sieve into a pan, season and keep warm. Grill or steam the mackerel (or other fish) until cooked for 8-10 minutes. Season the fish well. Stir the olives into the sauce and pour over the fish. Garnish with stars of starfruit. Serve each portion with 4 small boiled new potatoes or a 25g portion (dry weight) of boiled rice.

Approximate calories per serving: 450
(including potatoes or rice)

Potted Herring

2 hours +

To serve four people, you will need:

4 raw herring fillets (75-100g) split lengthways, sprinkled with salt, pepper and onion before rolling them up from the tail and skewering with a cocktail stick

1 large onion, chopped or finely sliced

300mls malt vinegar

150mls water

3 teaspoons granulated sweetener

1 teaspoon sea salt

1 tablespoon black peppercorns

2 bayleaves

1 tablespoon clear golden honey

Salt and ground black pepper

Preparation:

Put the rolled, skewered herrings into a casserole dish. Add the rest of the onions, granulated sweetener and golden syrup. Add salt, peppercorns and bayleaves. Make up the mixture of 2 parts of malt vinegar to 1 part of water pour over the herrings until 3/4 covered. Cover the dish loosely and cook at 170 degrees centigrade for 2 hours until the herrings are soft. Near the end add more sweetener if taste requires. Continue to boil until the liquid is reduced by half. If it boils too vigorously reduce the heat as the herrings will go hard. If they tend to dry out add a little more water. Allow to cool. Chill and serve each with 2 Ryvita portions and very low-fat spread.

Approximate calories per serving: 300

Salmon for a King

30 minutes

To serve four people, you will need:

Fry Light spray cooking oil

1 x 210g can red sockeye salmon (John West, Princes or good supermarket brand)

1 tablespoon balsamic or sherry vinegar

2 teaspoons lime juice

15g dairy butter

100g can sweetcorn, drained

1 small pepper, any colour, deseeded and diced

3 medium leeks, sliced

1 teaspoon dijon mustard

150ml low-fat fromage frais

150mls double cream low-fat substitute

220g hot cooked brown rice (cooked according to the manufacturer's instructions)

Salt and ground black pepper

McDougalls Thickening Granules

Preparation:

Drain, skin and bone the salmon, but keep the juices. To these juices add wine and balsamic vinegar and make up to about 200mls with water. Season with salt and pepper to taste and set aside (this is stock A). Coat a hot large non-stick saucepan with 4 applications of Fry Light and add the butter. Sauté the peppers and leeks until soft and then add the stock A. Add the fromage frais, the cream substitute, Dijon mustard and lime juice. Heat and stir until this thickens. Add McDougalls granules if it does not. Break up the salmon and stir in with the sweetcorn. Arrange a bed of rice on a platter and pour the salmon and sauce into the middle.

Approximate calories per serving: 450

Tuna and Egg Salad Exotique

30 minutes

To serve four people, you will need:

12 Chinese leaves or 1 iceberg lettuce

1 x 200g can tuna in brine, drained

20 cherry tomatoes, any colour

8 kumquats, finely sliced

1 x 120g can sweetcorn

1 small tin butter beans, haricot verts of kidney beans

2 boiled eggs, sliced

4 spring onions, chopped

1 small red onion, sliced finely

1 tablespoon fresh dill and parsley

2 teaspoons lime juice

Salt and ground black pepper

Preparation:

Chop up the lettuce and mix with the onion, spring onions, sweetcorn, beans and cherry tomatoes. Gently mix in the dill or parsley and egg slices. Flake in the tuna and mix again and add the lime juice. Garnish with the kumquats slices and serve. Serve each portion with 4 dark Ryvita or 1 pitta bread or 1 roll or 6 small 15-calorie matzo crackers, spread with very low-fat spread.

Approximate calories per serving: 350
(including bread and spread)

Fish Dishes

268

Salmon à la Greque

1 hour

To serve four people, you will need:

1 x 410g can red sockeye salmon (John West, Princes or good supermarket own brand)

2 tablespoon extra virgin olive oil

1 medium red onion, finely chopped

1 clove garlic, crushed

1 x 400g can chopped tomatoes

2 tablespoons tomato purée

75mls white wine or vermouth

1 x 175g can olives, stuffed with anchovies if possible

Small bunch fresh chopped parsley

Salt and ground black pepper

Fry Light spray cooking oil

Salmon a la Greque

Preparation:

Drain the salmon and retain the juice. Cut into chunks or flakes. Coat a hot non-stick saucepan with 5 applications of Fry Light and add the olive oil. Fry the onions and garlic until soft. Add the tomatoes, tomato purée and wine, bring to the boil and stir. Simmer until about 1 quarter reduced. Add the salmon. olives and half the parsley. Put in an ovenproof casserole and bake at 150 degrees centigrade for 35 minutes. Sprinkle with the remaining parsley and serve each portion with 5 small boiled new potatoes.

Approximate calories per serving: 400
(including potatoes)

Orange Sole

30 minutes

To serve two people, you will need:

2 x 150g fillets boneless lemon or Dover sole

1 Jaffa orange, peeled, depipped and leaved

1/2 teaspoon dried nutmeg

2 tablespoons Grand Marnier

Salt and ground black pepper

2 teaspoons lemon juice

2 teaspoons unsweetened orange cordial or Robinson's Orange and barley cordial

Preparation:

Sprinkle the fish with lemon juice, Grand Marnier, orange cordial, nutmeg, salt and black pepper. Place in a steamer or steam in a wok. Bring water to the boil in the steamer or wok and steam for 10 minutes once it is boiling. Top with orange segments, steam for a further 15 minutes and serve. Serve each with 4 small boiled new potatoes and mange tout peas or a seasonal salad.

Approximate calories per serving: 350

Quick Salmon Steak for One

30 minutes

To serve one person, you will need:

125g salmon steak or fillet

1 tablespoon whole grain mustard

1 teaspoon balsamic vinegar

1 teaspoon dried paprika

Tabasco sauce

2 slices mango or 2 lychees, fresh or canned

Preparation:

Put the salmon on a small ovenproof dish on baking paper. Mix mustard, balsamic vinegar and paprika with a few drops of tabasco sauce and 4 teaspoons of water to make a paste. Pour over the salmon. Cook in a very hot oven (top of an oven at 220 degrees centigrade) for 5-6 minutes until the salmon is cooked. If thick, cook a little longer. Remove the salmon and discard the juices. Garnish with mango or lychees and serve with 6 small new potatoes or a small portion (50g dry weight) of boiled rice and a seasonal salad.

Approximate calories per serving: 400

Pepper, Anchovy and Tomato

30 minutes

To serve four people, you will need:

1 large red pepper, deseeded and sliced

1 large green pepper, deseeded and sliced

1/2 cucumber, sliced

4 medium firm tomatoes, sliced

2 x 50g cans anchovies in oil, drained

Lemon juice

Garlic salt

Ground black pepper

2 medium hard-boiled eggs, sliced

Lettuce

Chives

Preparation:

Arrange a bed of lettuce on each of 4 plates and add the sliced peppers, cucumber and tomato as decoratively as possible. Put 4 slices of boiled egg in the centre of each. Add a pinch of garlic salt and black pepper, layer over the drained anchovies, sprinkle with lemon and garnish with chopped chives. Serve each portion with 3 dark Ryvita, spread with very low-fat spread.

Approximate calories per serving: 200

NB This dish can be warmed in an oven or microwave and served hot.

Pepper, Anchovy and Tomato

Fish Dishes

Smoked Salmon Cous Cous

1 hour

To serve four people, you will need:

200g boneless smoked salmon, chopped (cheap off-cuts are ideal)

125g cous cous (semolina type good supermarket own brand)

175mls vegetable stock made from supermarket own brand cube

1 courgette, diced

1/4 cucumber, diced

2 medium carrots, diced

2 small red onions, very finely sliced

2 medium peppers, green, red or purple, deseeded and diced

1 x 400g can chickpeas, drained (a low calorie form is made by Boots or Waters at 80 calories per 100g and this is ideal)

3 tablespoons chopped parsley

3 tablespoons chopped chives

2 tablespoons skimmed milk powder

Salt and ground black pepper

Fry Light spray cooking oil

2 tablespoons lime juice

McDougalls Thickening Granules

2 tablespoons extra virgin olive oil

Preparation:

Coat a hot non-stick saucepan with 5 applications of Fry Light and the extra virgin olive oil. Gently sauté the courgettes, carrots, peppers and onions for 2 minutes. Add all the other ingredients except the cous cous and bring to the boil. Season and simmer until the vegetables are soft, stirring all the time. Then slowly add in the cous cous. As soon as it is all in remove from the heat, stirring all the time. As soon as it thickens, serve. If necessary return to the heat with McDougalls granules. If too thick add a little skimmed milk or water. Serve with a seasonal salad or mange tout peas.

Approximate calories per serving: 450

Starfruit Salmon Salad

30 minutes

To serve two people, you will need:

1 x 210g can red sockeye salmon (John West, Princes, supermarket own brand etc)

1 small red onion, finely sliced

150mls low-fat fromage frais

2 tablespoons low-fat mayonnaise (supermarket own brand, Waistline)

4 medium tomatoes, sliced

1/2 cucumber, sliced

1 starfruit, thinly sliced into stars

1 x 50g can anchovy fillets, drained

10 stuffed olives

10 grapes

Preparation:

Drain the salmon and flake into a bowl. Add onion, fromage frais and mayonnaise and season to taste. Arrange sliced tomato and cucumber around the outside of a serving platter, pile the salmon mix into the centre and arrange the anchovy fillets in a lattice over the salad. Decorate with olives, grapes and starfruit. Chill and serve. Serve each portion with 3 dark Ryvita, crackers or water biscuits and very low-fat spread.

Approximate calories per serving: 500

Hot Pickled Herring

30 minutes

To serve two people, you will need:

4 small or 2 large rollmop herrings (total of 225g with onions and cucumbers)

1 x 125g carton low-fat natural yoghurt

3 tablespoons freshly chopped chives

4 dark Ryvita

Very low-fat spread

Preparation:

Lightly spread the Ryvita with spread. Place in the bottom of an oven-roasting tray. Arrange 1 small or 1/2 a large rollmop on each with a bit of onion and cucumber. Pour the yoghurt over the rollmop and garnish with chives. Put in an oven at 190 degrees centigrade for 10 minutes and serve.

Approximate calories per serving: 300

NB There is no reason why this cannot be served uncooked. It tastes equally delicious.

Fish Dishes

Lobster Thermidor

Prawn and Mint Dip

30 minutes

To serve four people, you will need:

15g dairy butter

1 tablespoon extra virgin olive oil

2 x 500g or 1kg boiled lobster (cut with a sharp knife from the junction of the head and neck to the tail along the back and separate. Remove the flesh from the body, claws, tail, pincers and legs but discard the green liver, guts and coral)

2 small shallots or 1 small onion, finely chopped

120mls white wine

1 teaspoon Dijon mustard

Dried cayenne pepper

Grated parmesan cheese

1 satsuma, peeled and leaved

Fry Light spray cooking oil

Preparation:

Slice or cut into chunks all the meat. Put the chopped onion or shallots into a hot non-stick pan coated with 5 applications of Fry Light. Sauté for 90 seconds, then add the wine and cook until reduced to half. In another non-stick pan melt the butter and olive oil and heat the lobster meat in this, turning gently. Add the reduced wine and shallots, add mustard and sprinkle lightly with cayenne pepper. Add satsumas and mix again. Return to the lobster shells. Sprinkle with parmesan cheese, brown under a hot grill and serve with a seasonal salad.

Approximate calories per serving: 300

2 hours +

To serve four people, you will need:

4 tablespoons lemon juice

4 tablespoons extra virgin olive oil

2 teaspoons red wine vinegar

Salt and ground black pepper to taste

1 medium onion, finely chopped

2 tablespoons low-fat natural yoghurt

400g peeled cooked prawns (cooked weight)

For Mint Dip, you will need:

3 tablespoons low-fat salad cream (good supermarket brand or Crosse & Blackwell)

3 tablespoons low-fat natural yoghurt

1 teaspoon lime juice

2 tablespoons chopped fresh mint or chives

2 teaspoons liquid honey

Sprig of mint or parsley to garnish

Preparation:

Mix in a bowl the lemon juice, olive oil, wine vinegar, salt, pepper, onion and mint. Add the peeled cooked prawns and stir well. Heat gently in an open pan, stirring all the time until it just begins to boil. Remove from the heat, put in a bowl and refrigerate for 2 hours. Mix the dip ingredients, whisk gently together, stir well or blend in a blender for 15 seconds. Put into a bowl, cover with cling film and chill in the fridge. Split the individual portions and dips and garnish with mint. Serve, dunking prawns well into the dip with a green salad.

Approximate calories per serving: 300

Lobster Thermidor

Prawn and Mint Dip

Shrimp Pilaf Exotique

Fish Soup à la Thinner & Richer Fish Dishes

30 minutes

To serve four people, you will need:

1 x 400g can lychees, drained

1 cup (125g) rice

1.5 litres water

1 tomato, finely sliced

1 x 200g packet frozen prawns or shrimps

1 x 200g packet frozen peas

2 small carrots, shredded

100g mushrooms, sliced

2 tablespoons dairy butter

Salt and ground black pepper

30 minutes

To serve four people, you will need:

500g skinless boneless white fish of choice

1 large onion, sliced

4 celery stalks, sliced

4 spring onions, chopped

1 medium leek, sliced

900mls fish stock, from good supermarket cube

450ml chicken stock, from a supermarket cube

1/2 teaspoon dried chilli powder

1 teaspoons dried garlic salt

2 x 400g cans peeled tomatoes

2 small bayleaves

Chopped parsley and chives to garnish

4 tablespoons skimmed milk powder

Salt and ground black pepper

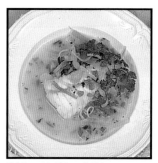

Fish Soup à la Thinner & Richer

Preparation:

Put into a soup pot onions, spring onions, celery, leek, fish and chicken stock, chilli, garlic salt, bayleaves and tomatoes. Bring to the boil slowly and simmer for 18 minutes, stirring frequently. Add the fish, left as whole fillets, salt and pepper to taste and simmer for 8 minutes in a covered pot, stirring occasionally. Now add the skimmed milk powder and simmer for a further 2 minutes and serve garnished with parsley and chives.

Approximate calories per serving: 200

Preparation:

Add the rice to boiling water for 15 minutes until dry. Melt the butter in a non-stick pan until it foams. Season and add all the other ingredients, stirring until piping hot. Mix food with the rice and serve with a seasonal salad.

Approximate calories per serving: 400

Fish Dishes

Plaice, Leek and Lime

1 hour

To serve four people, you will need:

4-6 large filleted boneless plaice

2 small limes, quartered

5 tablespoons vegetable or fish stock made from a supermarket cube

Salt and ground black pepper

2 tablespoons unsweetened lemon juice

4 baby leeks, cleaned, trimmed and cut into rings

1/4 cucumber, thinly sliced

Large bunch parsley

25g dairy butter

3 tablespoons Rose's lime marmalade

McDougalls Thickening Granules

Preparation:

Cook the leeks in a saucepan with the stock. Simmer until tender for about 4 minutes. Add the cucumber. Now place the fish fillets over the cooked leeks and cucumber in a saucepan, sprinkle with lemon juice and add the quartered limes. Add the butter and simmer until the fish is tender and white (about 12 minutes). Cover a serving dish with parsley and put the 4 fillets on it, leaving the juices in the pan. Keep the fish warm in a low oven. Put the marmalade into the juices, leeks, lime and cucumber and boil until it thickens. If necessary add McDougalls granules. As soon as it thickens pour over the fish and serve with 4 small new potatoes.

Approximate calories per serving: 350

Devilled Lobster

30 minutes

To serve one person, you will need:

500g lobster or 1/2 x 1kg lobster, boiled (cut with a sharp knife from the centre of the back at the junction of the head and body towards the tail – this opens into 2 halves. Remove all the flesh from the body, claws, pincers and tail, discard the green liver, guts and corral)

25g dairy butter

1 tablespoon extra virgin olive oil

Paxo Golden Crumbs

1 x 100ml carton low-fat single cream substitute

Dried cayenne pepper

Chopped chives

Preparation:

Remove all the meat as above. Heat the butter and olive oil and pour over the lobster meat. Add 3 tablespoons of golden crumbs, 3 tablespoons single cream substitute, chives and sprinkle liberally with cayenne pepper. Stuff the meat back into the shells and serve with a seasonal salad.

Approximate calories per serving: 450

Prawn Exotique

1 hour

To serve four people, you will need:

1 x 400g can mango slices

450g raw prawns, peeled, deveined, rinsed and dried on kitchen roll

Fry Light non-stick spray cooking oil

1 egg white

2 teaspoons cornflour

1 teaspoon salt

1 teaspoons sesame oil

1/2 teaspoon ground black pepper

350mls water

For the sauce, you will need:

2 inches root ginger, finely chopped

4 cloves garlic, finely chopped

1 medium onion, finely chopped

1 tablespoon groundnut oil

1 teaspoon extra virgin olive oil

2 red chillies, seeded and sliced

1 green chilli, seeded and sliced

4 spring onions, sliced

1 tablespoons dry sherry or vinegar

2 tablespoons soy sauce

2 teaspoons soft brown sugar

60ml chicken stock, made from supermarket cube

2 teaspoons sesame oil

1 tablespoon coarsely chopped black beans

Preparation:

Shake the prawns in a polythene bag with cornflour, egg white, sesame oil, salt and black pepper and leave for 15 minutes. Boil water in a pan, remove from the heat and stir in the prawns for 2-3 minutes until white and drain in a colander. Now in a hot non-stick wok, coated with 5 applications of Fry Light, add the groundnut and olive oil. Stir in the ginger and garlic for 20 seconds. Then add the onion, chillies and stir fry for 90 seconds. Add the black beans, sherry, soy sauce, sugar and chicken stock and cook for 2 minutes. Now add the prawns and stir fry for 1 minute. Stir in the remaining sesame oil and serve. Serve each with a quarter of a tin of mango slices, heated in a microwave.

Approximate calories per serving: 400

Fish Dishes

Sardines

Marinated Red Mullet Exotique

Sardine Exotic Surprise

Overnight

To serve four people, you will need:

4 x 100g boned skinless red mullet fillets (or any fish)

4 tablespoons extra virgin olive oil

Fry Light non-stick spray oil

2 tablespoons lime juice

1 teaspoon soft brown sugar

3 teaspoons dried basil

3 teaspoons dried coriander

1 teaspoon dried thyme

1 large carrot, sliced finely

1 medium onion, sliced

4 spring onions, chopped

Salt and ground black pepper

Preparation:

Coat a hot non-stick pan with 5 applications of Fry Light and 1 tablespoon of extra virgin olive oil. Sear the mullet on both sides for under 30 seconds a side and remove. Now mix all the other ingredients in a bowl and add the fish, making sure the fish is well covered. Allow to marinade for 24 hours in a fridge. Serve with seasonal salad and nil per cent fat fromage frais.

Approximate calories per serving: 400

30 minutes

To serve one person, you will need:

4 fresh gutted sardines

1 starfruit or lime

Lime juice

1 tablespoon extra virgin olive oil

Salt and ground black pepper

1 x 50g carton low-fat fromage frais or 50g from a larger carton

Preparation:

Place the fish on a grill rack, season well with salt and a lot of black pepper, brush with oil and season again. Grill under a moderate heat for 3 minutes. Turn over, brush with oil and season again. Grill for a further 3 minutes. Now turn the heat up to maximum and burn for 1 minute each side. Serve with lime juice and a good portion of fromage frais and garnish with lime or starfruit. Serve each with 2 dark Ryvita to help crunch up and eat the small edible bones.

Approximate calories per serving: 300
(including Ryvita)

Sardine Exotic Surprise

Fish Dishes

Plaice-a-Leekie

30 minutes

To serve two people, you will need:

250g boned plaice fillets

200g leeks, sliced

Juice of 1 large lemon

150mls skimmed milk

4 level teaspoons tomato purée

2 level teaspoons cornflour

Salt and ground black pepper

Preparation:
Layer the fish fillets in a casserole. Add the sliced leeks, tomato purée, lemon juice and seasoning. Add the milk. Slowly dissolve the cornflour in 20ml water in an eggcup and stir in. Cover and cook at 190 degrees centigrade for 25 minutes. Serve with a large jacket potato cooked in a microwave with a knob of low-fat spread.

Approximate calories per serving: 450

Steamed Plaice and Mango

30 minutes

To serve two people, you will need:

2 x 150g boneless plaice fillets

3 teaspoons tomato purée

2 tablespoons lemon juice

1/2 x 400g can drained mango slices

1 teaspoons mixed herbs

Fresh chopped chives

Salt and ground black pepper

Preparation:
Steam the fish in a double boiler or wok with a rack for 3 minutes. Season, sprinkle with lemon juice, top with tomato purée and sprinkle with herbs. Now top with mango slices. Steam for a further 25 minutes and serve each portion with 4 small boiled new potatoes and mange tout or a seasonal salad.

Approximate calories per serving: 350

Salmon For a King in Pitta Bread

30 minutes

To serve four people, you will need:

1 x 210g can red pimento, drained and chopped

1 x 210g can red or pink salmon

2 tablespoons coconut milk powder

6 small eggs, 2 yolks discarded

100g carton low-fat fromage frais

1 tablespoon extra virgin olive oil

100g button mushrooms, sliced

1 Kiwi fruit, sliced thinly and peeled

4 pitta bread, warmed in oven or pop-up toaster

Salt and ground black pepper

Fry Light spray cooking oil

Preparation:

Drain the salmon and flake. Beat the eggs, fromage frais and coconut powder with 2 tablespoons of water and season. Heat a non-stick pan and coat with 4 applications of Fry Light and add the olive oil. Stir in the egg mixture and as it begins to thicken add the salmon, pimento and mushrooms. Cook at a moderately low heat, stirring all the time until thick. Serve in hot pitta bread and garnish with Kiwi.

Approximate calories per serving: 400

Red Salmon Omelette

30 minutes

To serve one person, you will need:

1 x 105g can red sockeye salmon (John West, supermarket own brand, Princes), drained and flaked

2 eggs, 1 yolk discarded

2 tablespoons low-fat fromage frais

Salt and ground black pepper

1/2 teaspoon fresh chopped tarragon, chives or spring onions

Fry Light spray cooking oil

1 teaspoon dairy butter

Preparation:

Coat a hot non-stick omelette pan with 4 applications of Fry Light and add the butter. Beat the eggs, fromage frais, herbs and season. Cook over a moderate heat until the bottom begins to set. Remove from the heat. Flake the salmon over and put under a moderate grill in the pan until it sets. Fold over the edge and serve.

Approximate calories per serving: 350

Fish Dishes

Fish Dishes

New Year's Eve poached Salmon, Caviar, Tiger Lillies and Champagne Thinner & Richer

2 hours +

To serve eight people, you will need:

1 x 400g can mango slices (supermarket brand)

1 whole salmon approx 2 kilo, gutted

1 fish kettle

1 large cucumber

8 tiger lilies

1 jar caviar or mock caviar

Court bouillon

Parsley

A few berry fruits of choice eg blackberry, bilberry etc

250g low-fat salad spread or fromage frais

Extra virgin olive oil

Skimmed milk powder

Salt and ground black pepper

To prepare the Salmon:

Slice half a large cucumber and chop up four tiger lilies. Line the cavity of the salmon with the cucumber and tiger lilies after salting well and wrap in muslin or tea towel and place carefully in a fish kettle, cover with court bouillon, top up with water if required to just cover the fish, bring to the boil and simmer for 8 minutes per 0.5kg plus an additional 8 minutes. Set aside for two hours and then carefully remove and unwrap. Serve the salmon on a platter decorated with four fresh tiger lilies and with a streak of caviar along the salmon from head to tail. Decorate the mouth and the eyes with caviar or fruits of choice. Serve with low-fat mayonnaise or fromage frais, thickened if desired with a little skimmed milk powder and a teaspoon of olive oil and black pepper. Serve with new potatoes and salad of choice and mango slices from a can heated in a microwave.

Court Bouillon

To serve eight people, you will need:

750mls water

125mls dry white wine, dry cider or dry champagne

2 tablespoons vermouth

1 bayleaf

1 large red onion, sliced roughly

1 clove

3 stalks of celery

3 level teaspoons pickling spices

2 level teaspoons salt

1 level teaspoon dried dill weed

1 level tea spoon dried coriander

2 stalks of lemon grass, outer removed and chopped

Sprinkling of black pepper

Directions:

Simmer for one hour and drain. Give everyone a large glass of champagne.

Approximate calories per serving: 600
(including Champagne)

Whole Poached Salmon with Cucumber, Mango, Tiger Lilies and Nettles

2 hours +

To serve eight people, you will need:

1 x 400g can of mango slices
1 whole salmon approx 2kg, gutted
1 fish kettle
1 large cucumber
8 tiger lilies
1 jar of caviar or mock caviar
Court bouillon (see opposite)
Parsley and a few berry fruits of choice eg blackberry, blueberry, bilberry
250g low-fat salad spread or low-fat fromage frais
Olive oil
Skimmed milk powder
Salt and black pepper
Four young nettle shoots picked with a glove

Preparation for Salmon:

Slice half a cucumber and chop the four tiger lilies and the nettles. Line the cavity of the salmon with these and after salting well, wrap in muslin or a tea towel and place in the kettle with the court bouillon. Top up with water if required. Bring to the boil and simmer for 8 minutes per 1/2 kilo plus an additional 8 minutes, then set aside for 2 hours and carefully remove and unwrap. Serve the whole salmon on a platter decorated with caviar and 4 fresh tiger lilies with a streak of caviar running along the salmon from head to tail. Decorate the eyes and the mouth with caviar or fruits of choice. Serve with low-fat mayonnaise or fromage frais, thickened if desired with a little skimmed milk powder and a teaspoon of olive oil and black pepper. Serve with new potatoes and salad of choice mango slices heated in the microwave.

Court Bouillon

To serve eight people, you will need:

750mls of water
125mls dry white wine or cider
2 tablespoons (30mls) of vermouth
1 bayleaf
1 large red onion, sliced roughly
1 whole clove
3 stalks of celery, sliced roughly
3 level teaspoons pickling spices
2 level teaspoons salt
1 level teaspoon dried dill weed
1 level teaspoon dried coriander
2 stalks lemon grass, chopped
Sprinkling of black pepper

Preparation For Court Bouillon:

Simmer all the ingredients for 1 hour and strain before using.

Approximate calories per serving: 600

Fish Dishes

Plaice and Prawn Creole

1 hour

To serve four people, you will need:

1 medium red onion, chopped

1 red pepper, deseeded and chopped

2 spring onions, chopped julienne (longways)

1 x 400g can chopped tomatoes

1/2 teaspoon dried coriander

1/2 teaspoon dried basil

1/2 teaspoon dried oregano

1 teaspoon soft brown sugar

200g skinless boneless plaice, cubed

200g peeled prawns, uncooked

2 teaspoons cornflour

1 tablespoon dry sherry

1 tablespoon balsamic vinegar

1 tablespoon Nestlés coconut milk powder, super-market brand or desiccated coconut

Salt and ground black pepper

Chives to garnish

8 whole cooked prawns

Preparation:
Combine the onions, spring onions, red pepper, tomato juice, basil, oregano, coriander and sugar in a pan. Season and boil for 20 minutes. Add the plaice and peeled prawns and simmer for 15 minutes. Blend together cornflour, sherry and balsamic vinegar in an eggcup. Then stir into the mixture and add the coconut powder and heat until it thickens. Garnish with chives and 8 cooked whole prawns. Serve each portion with 2 dark Ryvita and very low-fat spread.

Approximate calories per serving: 300
(including Ryvita)

St Valentine's Red Rose Salmon Fillet Thinner and Richer and Tiger Lily

30 minutes

To serve four people, you will need:

4 x 125g salmon fillets (good supermarket brand)

50g dairy butter

6 red roses (2 to eat and 4 to decorate)

2 tablespoons chopped chives

Cucumber

Honey

1 x 400g can sliced mango

4 tiger lilies (optional)

Preparation:
Place each fillet on foil. Dot with 12.5g of butter and season well. Put 4 slices of cucumber on each. Sprinkle, finely, chopped chives and petals from 1/2 a rose on top, dot with 1/2 teaspoon of honey, fold over and seal. Bake on a baking sheet at 160 degrees centigrade for 14 minutes. Unwrap and serve with new potatoes (5 per portion) and seasonal salad or green vegetables. Drained mango slices, heated in the microwave are an excellent accompaniment. Decorate each with a whole short stemmed red rose and a tiger lily.

Approximate calories per serving: 500

Midsummer Special Poached Whole Salmon with Flowers

2 hours +

To serve as many as you like, you will need:

1 x 400g can mango slices, drained

1 small whole salmon (approx 2kg), gutted

1 fish kettle

1 large cucumber

Muslin or a tea towel

Court bouillon (see below)

Parsley

Summer flowers in season (dandelion, rose, pansy, nasturtium, marigold leaves and petals, hips etc)

Summer berries (eg raspberry or other)

250g low-fat salad spread or low-fat fromage frais

Extra virgin olive oil

Skimmed milk powder

Salt and ground black pepper

Preparation for Salmon:

Slice half a cucumber and chop four summer flower heads. Line the cavity of the salmon with these and after salting well, wrap in muslin or a tea towel and place in the kettle with the court bouillon. Top up with water if required. Bring to the boil and simmer for 8 minutes per 1/2 kilo plus an additional 8 minutes, then set aside for 2 hours and carefully remove and unwrap. Serve the whole salmon on a platter decorated with caviar and 4 fresh tiger lilies with a streak of caviar running along the salmon from head to tail. Decorate the eyes and the mouth with caviar or fruits of choice. Serve with low-fat mayonnaise or fromage frais, thickened if desired with a little skimmed milk powder and a teaspoon of olive oil and black pepper. Serve with new potatoes and salad of choice mango slices heated in the microwave. Decorate with summer flowers.

NB All the above flowers are edible.

Court Bouillon

To serve eight people, you will need:

750mls water

125mls dry white wine or cider

2 tablespoons (30mls) vermouth

1 bayleaf

1 large red onion, sliced roughly

1 clove

3 stalks of celery, sliced roughly

3 level teaspoons pickling spices

2 level teaspoons salt

1 level teaspoon dried dill weed

1 level teaspoon dried coriander

2 stalks of lemon grass, chopped

Sprinkling of black pepper

Preparation for Court Bouillon:

Simmer all the ingredients for 1 hour and strain before using.

Aproximate calories per serving: 600

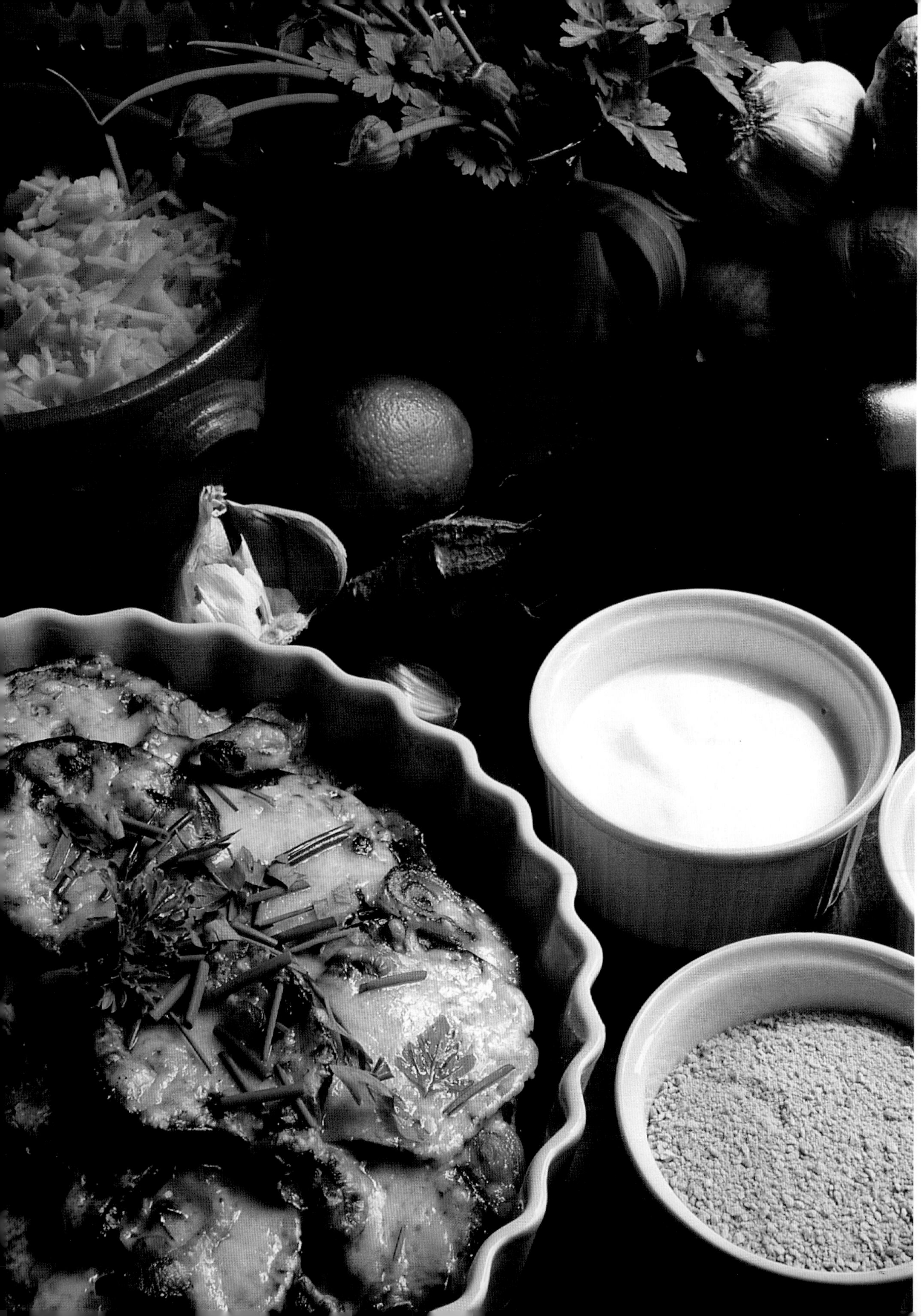

Aubergine Treat

Aubergine Treat

Aubergine au Fromage Frais

2 hours +

To serve four people, you will need:

4 medium aubergines

Fry Light spray cooking oil

1 clove garlic, very finely chopped

1 tablespoon extra virgin olive oil

225g fresh onions, sliced

225g low-fat vegetarian cheddar cheese, grated

Parsley and chives to garnish

2 teaspoons unsweetened lemon juice

Preparation:

Wash, dry and slice the aubergines. Sprinkle with salt and leave for 40 minutes. Wash, drain and dry on kitchen roll. Coat a large hot non-stick pan with 5 applications of Fry Light and the extra virgin olive oil. Fry the aubergine slices, 4 or 5 at a time, for 3 minutes per side until golden brown and drain on a kitchen roll. Fry the onion and garlic in the remaining fat until soft. Arrange the aubergine and onion slices in layers on a greaseproof dish. Season each layer in turn and sprinkle with lemon juice by fingers. Sprinkle with cheese until covered. Cook in a preheated medium oven 190 degrees centigrade for 40 minutes. Garnish with parsley or chives and serve hot with a green salad, if required.

Approximate calories per serving: 350
(including salad)

1 hour

To serve two people, you will need:

Salt and ground black pepper

2 medium aubergines

Fry Light non-stick spray oil

2 tablespoons extra virgin olive oil

1 x 400g can chopped tomatoes

125g carton low-fat fromage frais

50g vegetarian cheddar cheese, grated

Matzo meal or golden crumbs

1 tablespoon lime juice

2 tablespoons chopped chives

Preparation:

Slice the aubergines into long chips, salt lavishly for 10 minutes, wash thoroughly and drain on a kitchen roll. Coat a hot non-stick saucepan with 5 applications of Fry Light and add the virgin olive oil. Sauté the aubergines until golden brown and dry on a kitchen roll. Line a casserole with tomatoes and sprinkle over the grated cheese. Season and add layers of aubergine and tomato, seasoning as you go. Sprinkle with remaining grated cheese. Cover with fromage frais and a layer of golden crumbs. Either bake at 190 degrees centigrade for 25 minutes or for a lesser cooking time toast under a hot grill for 5 minutes before serving. Garnish with chives and serve.

Approximate calories per serving: 250

Aubergine au Fromage Frais

Vegetarian Dishes

Courgette Exotique

30 minutes

To serve four people, you will need:

3 sticks celery, sliced

4 large courgettes, end off and sliced 1/2 inch thick

1 clove garlic, crushed

4 medium tomatoes, thinly sliced

1/4 cucumber, thinly sliced

1 teaspoon dried basil

1/2 teaspoon dried oregano

2 tablespoons chopped chives

2 tablespoons lime juice

1 x 200g can pineapple chunks, drained

1 Kiwi fruit, thinly sliced (skin can be left on or off)

Salt and ground black pepper

1 tablespoon extra virgin olive oil

Preparation:

Place all the ingredients in an oven-proof casserole and mix well. Cover and bake in an oven at 190 degrees centigrade for 20 minutes. Serve with a seasonal salad.

Approximate calories per serving: 150
(including salad)

Aubergine Exotique

30 minutes

To serve four people, you will need:

500g aubergines, peeled and cut into 1 1/2 inch slices

Fry Light non-stick spray oil

1 tablespoon extra virgin olive oil

500g tomatoes, peeled and sliced

2 green or red chillies, diced

200mls tomato juice

4 tablespoons balsamic vinegar

1 tablespoon lime juice

1 tablespoon crushed garlic

150mls thick set low-fat natural yoghurt

6 spring onions, sliced julienne (longways)

1 small red onion, diced

1 tablespoon coconut milk powder

3 Kiwi fruit, peeled and thinly sliced

Salt and ground black pepper

Preparation:

Heat a non-stick pan and coat with 5 applications of Fry Light and the virgin olive oil. Sauté the aubergines for 3 minutes, stirring all the time to prevent burning. Add the tomatoes, tomato juice and lime juice and cook for a further 8 minutes, stirring. Now add the garlic, vinegar, red onion and coconut powder and cook for a further 8 minutes, stirring. Season well and stir in the yoghurt and spring onions. Cook for a further 2 minutes and serve. Serve each portion with a large hot toasted pitta bread.

Approximate calories per serving: 250
(including pitta bread)

Mushroom Flan

1 hour

The filling:
To serve four people, you will need:

Fry Light spray cooking oil

450g any type of mushroom or edible fungus

120ml vegetable, or if not vegetarian, chicken stock made from good supermarket cube

1 teaspoon Maggi mixed seasoning or soy sauce

1 teaspoon Lea and Perrins Worcester Sauce

4 spring onions, chopped

1 medium red onion, chopped

2 teaspoons Dijon mustard

1 teaspoon dried tarragon

100mls white wine, dry sherry, vermouth or apple juice

Salt and ground black pepper

McDougalls Thickening Granules

Preparation for the filling:
Coat a hot non-stick saucepan with 4 applications of Fry Light. Sauté the onions and spring onions for 2 minutes, stirring frequently. Add the mushrooms, stock, Maggi, Lea and Perrins and wine and simmer, stirring all the time until it reduces and thickens. Now season and add tarragon and Dijon mustard. Simmer until soft and thick. Add McDougalls granules if required.

The flan
To serve four people, you will need:

1 teaspoon extra virgin olive oil

4 tablespoons skimmed milk powder

230mls skimmed milk

4 eggs, 3 yolks discarded, (4 egg whites and 1 yolk)

75g self raising flour

Salt and ground black pepper

Preparation for the flan:
Combine all the flan ingredients in a blender and liquidise until creamy. Pour just over half into a large 30cm flan dish, enough to just cover the base. Cook in the oven at 180 degrees centigrade for 4 minutes or until firm. Now put the filling in the middle and pour the rest of the flan mixture on top. Bake for another 20-30 minutes until firm and golden.

Approximate calories per serving: 250

Vegetarian Dishes

Vegetarian Dishes

Aubergine Exotique au Gratin

1 hour

To serve four people, you will need:

Fry Light spray cooking oil

1 tablespoon extra virgin olive oil

McDougalls Thickening Granules

600mls skimmed milk

4 tablespoons skimmed milk powder

6 tablespoons low-fat (can be vegetarian) cheddar or mozzarella cheese, grated

2 tablespoons cornflour

Salt and ground black pepper

2 medium tomatoes, diced

2 large aubergines, trimmed and cut into chip-sized slices

2 medium onions, chopped

6 tablespoons chopped chives

1 clove garlic, crushed

Garlic salt

Dried chilli powder

300mls vegetable or chicken stock if not vegetarian, made from good supermarket, Knorr or other cube

3 tablespoons dry vermouth or dry sherry

1 tub grated parmesan cheese

Dried paprika

Dried cayenne pepper

Preparation for the sauce:

Mix the cornflour with a little water in an eggcup and then whisk into the skimmed milk. Now slowly whisk in the skimmed milk powder and when rich blend in the grated cheese. Season with a pinch of paprika, a good sprinkling of cayenne pepper and a little salt and pepper. Simmer in a saucepan, stirring all the time, until it thickens (add McDougalls granules if not thick enough) and put the sauce aside.

Preparation for the Aubergines:

Toast the aubergines on a baking sheet or foil under a grill until soft. Spread out in an oven-casserole dish. Coat a non-stick saucepan with 4 applications of Fry Light and the virgin olive oil and sauté the onions and garlic for 3 minutes. Then add the chives and sauté for a further 1 minute. Add the stock, vermouth or sherry, a pinch of chilli powder and the diced tomato and season with garlic salt and pepper. Simmer until all tender and the liquid thickens (add McDougalls granules if required). Spread over the aubergines. Cover with warm cheese sauce and sprinkle with parmesan cheese and pepper. Grill or bake at 190 degrees centigrade until brown and bubbles.

Approximate calories per serving: 350

Greek Dip Exotique

Vegetarian Curry with Lychees

30 minutes

To serve three people, you will need:

6 kumquats, thinly sliced

1 Florida starfruit, thinly sliced into stars

20 black olives

20 cherry tomatoes

10 Chinese leaves, torn up and shredded

4 basil leaves, torn up and shredded

100g vegetarian mozzarella cheese, diced

1/2 cucumber, skin left on and finely sliced

4 spring onions, chopped

100g Greek low-fat yoghurt, mixed with 4 teaspoons lime juice

200g houmus or 100g taramasalata (the former being vegetarian and the latter being fish roe)

Preparation:

Combine the torn up Chinese leaves, cucumber, basil, spring onions, tomatoes and cheese. Add the olives and yoghurt and lime and mix well. Serve with 50 grams of houmus for vegetarians (or 25 grams of taramasalata) for each portion. Garnish with starfruit and kumquats. For a main meal we suggest you serve this with 1 large whole pitta bread.

Approximate calories per serving: 450
(including pitta bread)

1 hour

To serve four people, you will need:

50ml low-fat Greek yoghurt

75g bran cereal, Kelloggs or supermarket All Bran

1 x 400g can lychees (supermarket own or other brand)

1 large red onion, chopped

1 tablespoon medium, mild or hot curry paste, according to taste

1 teaspoon dried paprika

1 tablespoon tomato purée

2 teaspoons lime juice

1 heaped tablespoon mango chutney

300mls skimmed milk

450mls vegetable stock made from Knorr or good supermarket own brand cube

Pinch of garlic powder

2 heads calabrese, cut into florets

4 medium carrots, chopped

4 medium potatoes, chopped

1 small cooking apple, chopped

Fry Light non-stick spray oil

1 tablespoon extra virgin olive oil

Preparation:

Coat a hot non-stick pan with 5 applications of Fry Light and add the olive oil. Stir fry the onions and then stir in the curry paste, paprika, tomato purée, lime juice, chutney, garlic, milk and stock. Boil and simmer for 25 minutes. In a separate pan boil the calabrese, carrots and potatoes for 10 minutes. Then add the apple and cook for a further 3-4 minutes. Now drain and add to the curry mixture. Stir in the bran cereal, yoghurt and drained lychees and serve each portion with 50 grams (raw weight) of boiled rice.

Approximate calories per serving: 400

Vegetarian Curry with Lychees

Greek Dip Exotique

Vegetarian Dishes

1 hour

To serve two people, you will need:

1 x 175g packet Quorn cubes (good supermarket own brand)

75g mushrooms, sliced

3 small carrots, sliced

4 large spring onions, sliced

1 x 250g pack rolled puff pastry

2 sticks celery, sliced

About 150g spinach, chopped

50g sun-dried tomatoes, soaked

1 tablespoon lime juice

4 teaspoons extra virgin olive oil

Fry Light non-stick cooking spray

2 teaspoons freshly chopped coriander or 1/2 teaspoon of dried

1/2 teaspoon dried oregano

1/2 teaspoon dried chilli powder

2 teaspoons fresh chopped mint or 1/2 teaspoon of dried

1 clove garlic, finely chopped or crushed

About 1 inch root ginger, diced or 1 teaspoon of dried

Cheap white wine or vermouth

4 tablespoons low-fat fromage frais

3 tablespoons low-fat Greek natural yoghurt

Sesame seeds

4 fresh or canned lychees

Salt and ground black pepper

2 pinches nutmeg

McDougalls Thickening Granules

Preparation:

Cut out 4 large circles of puff pastry and cook on a baking sheet at 220 degrees until it rises. Coat a hot non-stick saucepan with 4 applications of Fry Light and 1 tablespoon of extra virgin olive oil. Add the carrots, celery and chilli powder and stir fry until soft and keep gently simmering and season. In another large non-stick pan heat and coat liberally with 5 applications of Fry Light and 1 teaspoon of virgin olive oil. Add the Quorn, garlic, spring onions, sun-dried tomatoes and ginger and sauté for 3 minutes. Now add the mushrooms and 50mls of wine or vermouth. Add the spinach, stir and sauté for 3 minutes. Stir in the fromage frais and yoghurt and season with 2 pinches of nutmeg, salt and pepper to taste and simmer for a further minute. If it is too runny add McDougalls granules and simmer and stir until thick. Now put the carrots, celery and chilli on a plate. Cut the puffs in half to give a top and a bottom. Put 4 bottoms on top of the celery and carrot mixture. Spoon the Quorn mix onto each and top with remaining pastry. Garnish with sesame seeds and 1 lychee per puff. Serve alone, 2 per person.

Approximate calories per serving: 500

NB In place of Quorn you can use 175g of cubed lean chicken, beef, pork or turkey, but, of course, this is no longer vegetarian.

Tofu with Exotic Chunky Sauce

1 hour

To serve four people, you will need:

125g carton low-fat fromage frais

450g tofu, cut into strips

Fry Light spray cooking oil

2 tablespoons extra virgin olive oil

1 medium onion, finely chopped

1 clove garlic, crushed

225g button mushrooms, sliced

1 medium pepper, any colour, deseeded, finely chopped

1 tablespoon lime juice

1 teaspoon dried oregano

1 teaspoon dried chilli powder

1 teaspoon dried marjoram

3 tablespoons tomato purée

1 tablespoon wholemeal flour

100ml dry white wine, white grape juice or vermouth

Maggi liquid seasoning or soy sauce

Salt and ground black pepper

Preparation for the dish:

Coat a large non-stick saucepan with Fry Light spray cooking oil and 1 tablespoon virgin olive oil. Fry the tofu for 6 minutes until it is brown and drain on kitchen roll. Add the remaining olive oil and some more Fry Light. Add the vegetables, mushrooms, garlic and herbs (but not tomato purée, flour, wine or soy sauce). Cook, stirring until the vegetables are tender. Now add the tomato purée and flour and stir, simmering, for 30 seconds. Now add the wine and a dash of soy sauce, stir and simmer for a further 3 minutes. Add the tofu and cook for 3 minutes more. Add the fromage frais. Heat and serve with a portion of Chunky Exotic Sauce and a salad.

Approximate calories per serving: 450
(including sauce and salad)

Exotic Chunky Sauce
To serve ten people, you will need:

2 oranges, peeled and chopped

1 x 400g can mango slices with juice

Pinch of chilli powder

2 tablespoons lime juice

100ml unsweetened orange juice

2 tablespoons skimmed milk powder

1 tablespoon chopped nuts of your choice

Mixture of chopped mint, parsley, chives and lemon grass if available

1 large fennel, finely chopped

Salt and ground black pepper

Granulated sweetener

Preparation:

Mix all ingredients in a bowl and, if necessary, thicken with skimmed milk powder.

Approximate calories per serving of this lovely sauce: 80

Vegetarian Dishes

Subtle Kebabs

Kiwi, Mango and Lychee Beans

Subtle Kebabs

Kiwi, Mango and Lychee Beans

30 minutes

To serve four people, you will need:

450g clean, washed, small new potatoes

1 medium green pepper, seeded

1 medium red pepper, seeded

450g onions

20 small button mushrooms

4 tablespoons extra virgin olive oil

1 tablespoon unsweetened lemon juice

Garlic pepper

1 teaspoon concentrated tomato purée

Dried basil and rosemary

1 large aubergine, cubed

Preparation:

Boil the potatoes for 8 minutes in salted water and drain. Cut the peppers into oblong pieces and skewer alternating with potatoes, aubergine and mushrooms to make the kebabs. Mix the oil, lemon juice and tomato purée and season with garlic pepper, basil and rosemary to taste. Brush this mixture over the kebabs and either barbecue or cook under a moderate grill for 10 minutes, turning twice. Serve with a seasonal salad, untossed.

Approximate calories per serving: 350
(including salad)

1 hour

To serve four people, you will need:

Fry Light spray cooking oil

1/2 x 400g can tinned lychees, drained

1/2 x 400g can tinned mangoes, drained

2 Kiwi fruit, sliced with the peel left on

200g haricot beans, soaked overnight or from a tin

1 litre vegetable stock, home made or from good supermarket cube

1 tablespoon extra virgin olive oil

2 medium onions, diced

4 ozs of cucumber, medium sliced

4 ozs of courgettes, medium sliced

1 medium aubergine, seeded, halved and sliced

1 medium red pepper, seeded and sliced

1 medium green or purple pepper, seeded and sliced

150ml unsweetened apple juice

150g long grain brown or white rice (dry weight)

Preparation:

Boil and simmer the beans in salt water until tender (about 1 hour) but the tinned variety can be used immediately. Coat a hot non-stick saucepan with 4 or 5 applications of Fry Light and add the olive oil, onion, cucumber, courgette and peppers. Sauté for 3 minutes, turning occasionally or stirring. Now add the aubergine and sauté for another 6 minutes, stirring. Put beans in a casserole dish, add the sautéed vegetables, fruit, rice and grape juice. Mix well and put the casserole in a medium oven at 190 degrees for 50 minutes or until the rice is tender. If it dries out during cooking add a small amount of water. Season to taste and serve alone.

Approximate calories per serving: 450

Peas Exotique

30 minutes

To serve four people, you will need:

1lb frozen peas

1 x 400g can mango or papaya, drained

50g dairy butter

10 spring onions, chopped julienne (longways)

1 teaspoon soft brown sugar

1 teaspoon clear honey

120ml vegetable stock made from supermarket cube

Handful chopped fresh parsley and mint

Salt and ground black pepper

Preparation:

Place all the ingredients in a saucepan and season. Boil and stir. Simmer for 15 minutes, adding water if it dries out. Serve as a main course with 5 small boiled new potatoes.

Approximate calories per serving: 400
(including potatoes)

Crunchy Kutchie-Fyky

30 minutes

To serve four people, you will need:

450g fresh onions, finely chopped

4 medium hard boiled eggs

1 x 200g tin unsweetened sweetcorn

1 tablespoon extra virgin olive oil

Low-fat spread

Salt and ground black pepper

Lettuce

Radish

Preparation:

Mash the eggs in a large bowl. Add the onions, sweet corn and oil. If required, further soften with a little low-fat spread. Season with salt and ground black pepper and chill. Serve on a bed of lettuce, garnished with half radishes. Serve each portion with 5 water biscuits or 3 cream crackers or 3 Ryvita or 1 large slice of Rakusens Matzo.

Approximate calories per serving: 200

Crunchy Kutchie-Fyky

Vegetarian Dishes

Budgie Millet Exotique
a very sustaining vegetarian main dish

1 hour

To serve two people, you will need:

1 x 400g can mango slices, supermarket brand

75g millet (pet shop, specialist or health food shop)

300ml vegetable stock, using supermarket own cube

3 small leeks, cut into rings

150g calabrese (sprouting broccoli), split into small florets

2 tablespoons extra virgin olive oil

3 tablespoons low-fat fromage frais

25g Nestlés coconut milk powder

2 teaspoons lime juice

Preparation:

Rinse the millet with boiling water and boil in the vegetable stock for 25 minutes. Stir fry all the vegetables in a hot wok coated with virgin olive oil, until soft. Mix the coconut milk powder with an eggcup of boiling water, cool and add the lime juice. Whisk this into the fromage frais. Heat the mango slices in a microwave and drain and serve with the main dish.

Approximate calories per serving: 500

Pumpkin Fritters

1 hour

To serve four people, you will need:

450g pumpkin flesh, deseeded, cut into large chip-sized pieces

1 tablespoon seasoned flour

1 egg, beaten with 2 tablespoons (30ml) skimmed milk

1 packet Paxo Golden Crumbs

2 x 125g cartons unsweetened natural Greek low-fat yoghurt or other low-fat yoghurt

4 tablespoons fresh chopped chives or spring onions

Dried cayenne pepper

Dried paprika

Deep fat fryer with Crisp 'n Dry oil

Salt

Preparation:

Put all the yoghurt in a bowl and add the chives. Sprinkle with cayenne pepper and chill. Steam the pumpkin flesh for 30 minutes and dry on kitchen roll. Salt well. Put seasoned flour in a polythene bag, add pumpkin, a little at a time, and shake until coated. Coat the floured pumpkin with beaten egg mixture by dipping or again using a polythene bag to shake. Put plenty of crumbs in another polythene bag and add the now egg-soaked pumpkin a little at a time. Shake well and lay out on kitchen roll. Deep fry for 3 minutes, drain on more kitchen roll and serve with lashings of yoghurt dip and seasonal salad.

Approximate calories per serving: 200
(including salad)

Bulghar Wheat Exotique

1 hour

To serve four people, you will need:

225g bulghar wheat from supermarket or health food shop

5 spring onions, sliced julienne (longways)

1 bunch parsley, chopped

3 fresh mint leaves, chopped or 2 teaspoons of dried mint

20 cherry tomatoes

8 kumquats, finely sliced

4 tablespoons extra virgin olive oil

2 tablespoons lime juice

1 tablespoon lemon juice

1 teaspoon balsamic vinegar

50g Nestlés coconut milk powder, dissolved in 3 egg-cups of boiling water

1 Florida starfruit, thinly sliced

Salt and ground black pepper

Preparation:

Soak the wheat in a large bowl of cold water until it swells (about 1 hour) and drain well. Combine in a bowl the kumquats, parsley, julienned spring onions, mint and tomatoes. Add the coconut milk and then mix with the wheat. Make a dressing from lemon and lime juices, balsamic vinegar and olive oil. Whisk together and season. Toss, chill and serve.

Approximate calories per serving: 500

Vegetarian Quorn Chilli Stir Fry

30 minutes

To serve four people, you will need:

Fry Light non-stick spray oil

2 tablespoons extra virgin olive oil

3 cloves garlic, crushed

1/2 root ginger, grated

1 red pepper, deseeded and sliced

6 spring onions, sliced

350g Quorn pieces

2 tablespoons dry sherry

For the sauce, you will need:

2 tablespoons soy sauce

1 tablespoon balsamic vinegar

1 tablespoon chilli sauce

1 tablespoon soft brown sugar

1 tablespoon cornflour

200ml vegetable stock made from supermarket cube

McDougalls Thickening Granules

Preparation:

Coat a hot non-stick wok with 5 applications of Fry Light and add the virgin olive oil. Fry the garlic, ginger and red pepper for 3 minutes. Add the Quorn and spring onions and gently fry, stirring all the time, for 5 minutes. Add the sherry and stir well. Now in a separate jug, blend sauce ingredients and if not thick enough add a few McDougalls granules. Stir the sauce into the mixture and stir fry for 4 minutes until thick. Serve each portion with 50g (raw weight) of boiled rice.

Approximate calories per serving: 350

NB This dish can be a little difficult to thicken. If the sauce does not thicken with the cornflour McDougalls granules can be added. However, it is probably better to wait until the mixture is cooking in the wok and then if it is not thick enough add the McDougalls granules near the end of the cooking time.

Vegetarian Dishes

Vegetarian Dishes

Vegetable Curry

1 hour

To serve six people, you will need:

3 medium peppers, any colour, deseeded and sliced

8 small carrots, sliced

Cut cabbage to the same volume of peppers and carrots in total

3 courgettes, sliced

200g turnip or sweet potato, finely chopped

6 spring onions, chopped

2 cloves garlic, finely chopped or crushed

120ml vegetable stock made with supermarket own brand cube

2 x 400g cans whole tomatoes

1/2 teaspoon dried chilli

Pinch mixed spices

1 teaspoon ground ginger

1 teaspoon ground cinnamon

1 tablespoon ground coriander

1 teaspoon ground oregano

1 teaspoon turmeric

1 teaspoon brown sugar

4 sprigs fresh mint if available, shredded or 1 teaspoon dried mint

30ml (2 tablespoons) lime juice

1 tablespoon lemon juice

2 satsumas, peeled and leaved

Salt and ground black pepper

McDougalls Thickening Granules

Hot curry powder

Preparation:

Drain the tomatoes but save the juice. Cut up the tomatoes and put aside. Mix tomato juice, stock, lime juice with spring onions, spices, carrots and sugar in a stewing pot. Cover and boil. Simmer for 6 minutes. Uncover and simmer, stirring, until it thickens. Then stir in all the vegetables, tomatoes, lemon juice, sugar, satsumas and left over ingredients. If you want it hot add hot curry powder. If you wish to thicken it simmer with McDougalls granules. Serve each portion with 2 ounces (raw weight) of boiled rice (a very convenient method is to use Uncle Ben's Microwaveable Rice).

Approximate calories per serving: 350
(including rice)

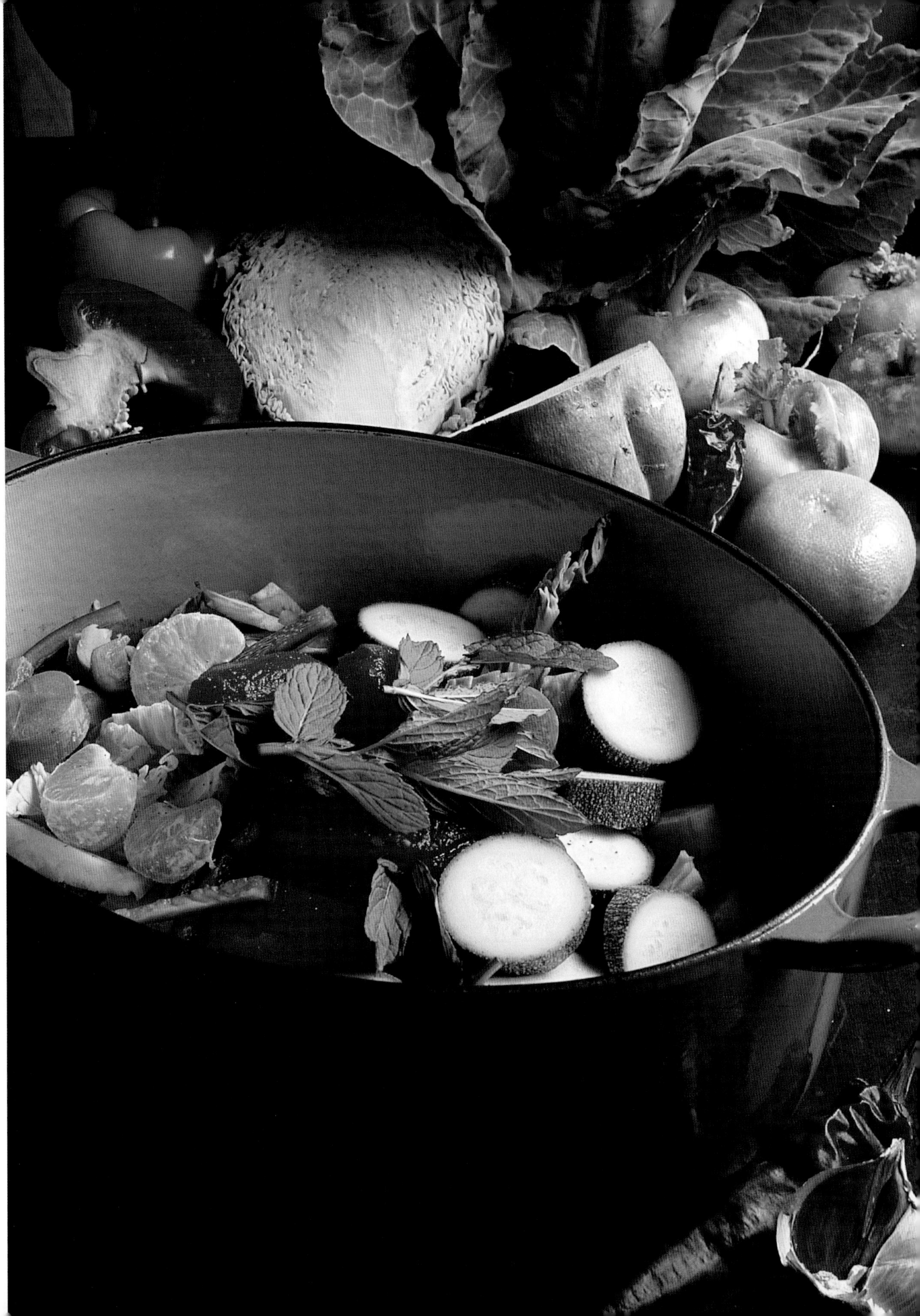

Vegetable Curry ingredients

Vegetarian Dishes

Quorn with Exotic Chunky Sauce

30 minutes

To serve two people, you will need:

McDougalls Thickening Granules

175g Quorn pieces

1 clove garlic, chopped or crushed

1 medium red pepper, deseeded and sliced

4 spring onions, chopped

1 tablespoon dry sherry or vermouth

100g bean sprouts, canned or fresh

100g broccoli or cauliflower, florets only

1 tablespoon extra virgin olive oil

Fry Light spray cooking oil

Salt and ground black pepper

Soy sauce

Exotic Chunky Sauce (see right)

Skimmed milk

Preparation:

Coat a hot non-stick pan or wok with 5 applications of Fry Light and add the olive oil. Fry the Quorn pieces until they are brown, turning occasionally to prevent burning. Now add the peppers, spring onions and garlic and stir fry for 5 minutes. Add the sherry and stir well. Add the bean sprouts and the broccoli or cauliflower heads. Season with salt and ground black pepper and a splash of soy sauce. Add 4 portions of Exotic Chunky Sauce and stir fry for a further 5 minutes. If the mixture is too thick add skimmed milk, if too thin McDougalls granules. Serve each portion with 50g, dry weight, of rice or a small portion of noodles and salad.

Total approximate calories per serving: 450
(including rice or noodles and salad and Exotic Chunky Sauce)

Exotic Chunky Sauce
To serve ten people, you will need:

2 oranges, peeled and chopped

1 x 400g can mango slices and juice

Pinch of chilli powder

2 tablespoons lime juice

100ml unsweetened orange juice

2 tablespoons skimmed milk powder

1 tablespoon chopped nuts of your choice

A mixture of mint, parsley, chives and lemon grass if available (outer layer removed and finely chopped)

1 large fennel, finely chopped

Salt and ground black pepper

Granulated sweetener

Preparation:

Simply mix all the ingredients in a bowl. Thicken with milk powder.

Approximate calories per serving: 80

Rice Exotique

Coconut Vegetables

1 hour

30 minutes

To serve four people, you will need:

200g raw weight whole grain or basmati rice

1 x 400g can guava halves or rambutans (if you cannot get rambutans use lychees and pineapple chunks to a total of 400g)

1 x 400g can mango slices, drained

1 x 200g can pineapple chunks, drained

50g seedless grapes

50g flaked almonds

3 tablespoons extra virgin olive oil

25g Nestlés, or other coconut milk powder

2 tablespoons lime juice

2 teaspoons lemon juice

Pinch of ground cloves

Salt and ground black pepper

Preparation:

Cook the rice according to the manufacturer's instructions. Drain and cool. Make up coconut milk in 1 eggcup of boiling water and blend with the lemon and lime juices. Drain all the exotic fruit and reserve the juices. Coarsely chop the fruit and mix with nuts, rice and grapes. Now blend together the coconut, lemon and lime juices with olive oil and cloves to make a dressing. If it is too thick add some of the reserved fruit juices. Add to the rice mixture. Chill and serve.

Approximate calories per serving: 500

To serve four people, you will need:

Fry Light non-stick spray oil

1 tablespoon extra virgin olive oil

1 large onion, sliced

1 orange or yellow pepper, deseeded and sliced

2 chillies, deseeded and sliced

1/2 teaspoon ground coriander

2 tablespoons lime juice

50g Nestlés or supermarket brand coconut milk powder (or desiccated coconut)

200g broccoli florets, quickly blanched in boiling water

200g shredded cabbage

Preparation:

Heat a large non-stick wok and coat with 4 applications of Fry Light and add the virgin olive oil. Fry the onions, pepper and chillies for 2 minutes. Add the coriander and cook for 1 minute. Stir in the coconut milk powder, lime juice, broccoli and cabbage and stir for 5 minutes. If too thick add a little water. Season and serve.

Approximate calories per serving: 150

Vegetarian Dishes

Vegetarian Dishes

Cherry Tomato, Pineapple and Mango Salad

Cherry Tomato, Pineapple and Mango Salad

30 minutes

To serve four people, you will need:

1lb cherry tomatoes, any colour – green, red, yellow or mixture

1 x 400g can mango slices or fresh mangoes

1 x 400g can of pineapple chunks or fresh pineapple

2 Kiwi fruit

2 satsumas, leaved

12 berries (strawberry, raspberry, gooseberry, loganberry or mixture)

3 tablespoons (50ml) low-fat fromage frais

1 bunch calabrese

2 tablespoons sherry vinegar

1 tablespoon natural yoghurt

Worcester Sauce

Old English mustard

2 teaspoons soft brown sugar

1 melon baller scoop

2 tablespoons skimmed milk powder

Preparation:

Put in a liquidiser and blend the following: half the mango slices, all the juice from the mango and pineapple, fromage frais, yoghurt, sherry vinegar, a dash of Worcester Sauce, a pinch of mustard powder. Blend until smooth. Add sugar, blend again and refrigerate. Now arrange on a platter the tomatoes, the other half of the mangoes (now chopped), pineapple chunks, Kiwi balls (made with the melon baller scoop). Trim off the long stalks from the calabrese and add the florets, divided if required and finally add the berries and satsuma leaves. Now pour over the mango sauce and serve each portion with 2 dark Ryvita and very low-fat spread.

Approximate calories per serving: 300
(including Ryvita)

Mixed Exotic Salad and Yoghurt Dressing

30 minutes

The dressing
To serve four people, you will need:

225ml low-fat Greek yoghurt

125ml skimmed milk

1 oz Nestlés coconut milk powder or supermarket own brand

1 clove garlic, crushed

2 teaspoons maple syrup or clear honey

Salt and ground black pepper

Preparation:

Mix all the ingredients and season. Use to dress a salad of any mixture of lettuce, Chinese leaves, cherry tomatoes, spring onions, raw carrots, shredded cabbage, bean sprouts, red or green peppers, deseeded, and any other non-root vegetables of your choice including baby sweetcorn. Garnish with 2 stars of starfruit and thin slices of lime. Top with 2 or 3 lychees, either fresh ones or canned, or other exotic fruit. Lather on the dressing.

Approximate calories per large salad: 350
(including dressing and exotic fruit)

Coconut Rice

Dressed Seasonal Salad

30 minutes

To serve four people, you will need:

75g Nestlés or other brand coconut milk powder or desiccated coconut

500mls warm water

350g basmati rice, well washed and drained

2 tablespoons lime juice

A few cashew nuts

8 lychees, fresh or canned

30 minutes

Prepare a large platter of green salad, peppers, tomatoes, carrots, broccoli spears, boiled beetroot, radish and any other stem, not root vegetable of your choice (but spring onions are okay). You can put in a little fruit.

The dressing

To serve six people, you will need:

300mls low-fat fromage frais

3 tablespoons skimmed milk

1 tablespoon balsamic or sherry vinegar

1 teaspoon Dijon mustard

1 teaspoon German mustard or 2 teaspoons of either

1 whole cucumber, diced

4 tablespoons chopped chives

15g ground or flaked nuts of your choice

Salt and ground black pepper

Preparation:

Put the sliced cucumber and chives in a bowl. Blend the rest of the ingredients in a liquidiser. If too thin add skimmed milk powder. Season to taste and mix with chives and cucumber. Chill for a few minutes and pour over 6 individual portions of salad.

Approximate calories per serving: 250
(including dressing)

Dressed Seasonal Salad

Preparation:

In a large non-stick saucepan place the coconut milk powder and warm water and stir. Bring to the boil, add the rice and simmer over a low heat for 10 minutes, stirring occasionally, keeping covered all the time. Just before serving stir in the lime juice. Serve each portion garnished with 2 lychees and 6 cashew nuts.

Approximate calories per serving: 400

Vegetarian Dishes

Baby Parsnips, Breadcrumbs and Corn

1 hour

To serve four people, you will need:

2 x 400g cans sweet corn and peppers, unsweetened (Green Giant, supermarket own brand)
450g small parsnips, washed and scrubbed
100g Paxo or other golden breadcrumbs
2 tablespoons extra virgin olive oil
100g grated low-fat vegetarian cheddar cheese or cheese of choice
Dried cayenne pepper
Chopped fresh parsley
Fry Light non-stick spray oil
Salt and ground black pepper

Preparation:

Cook the parsnips in lightly salted boiling water for 8 minutes and drain. Coat a hot, large non-stick saucepan with 5 applications of Fry Light and add the virgin olive oil and plenty of black pepper. Stir in the parsnips and sauté lightly, stirring well, for 2 minutes. Remove from the heat and stir in the breadcrumbs, cheese and a pinch of salt. Put in a casserole dish and cook at 220 degrees centigrade for 15 minutes. Sprinkle with parsley and cayenne pepper and serve each portion with 200 grams or half a can of hot sweetcorn and peppers.

Approximate calories per serving: 450

Wok Quorn

30 minutes

To serve four people, you will need:

200g Quorn chunks
2 medium onions, sliced
4 spring onions, chopped
2 small leeks, sliced
1 clove garlic, finely chopped
3 stalks celery, sliced
2 tablespoons extra virgin olive oil
Fry Light non-stick cooking spray
1 x 400g can chopped tomatoes
4 medium courgettes, sliced
Salt and ground black pepper
Dried oregano
1 inch stem ginger

Preparation:

Spray a hot wok with 5 applications of Fry Light and add the olive oil. Add the onions, garlic, celery and cook until softened but crisp. Add chopped tomatoes, courgettes, spring onions and ginger. Season with oregano. Cover the wok and cook until soft. Serve each portion with 3 small boiled new potatoes, mange tout peas and a green salad.

Approximate calories per serving: 350
(including potatoes and salad)

Vegetarian Lasagne

1 hour

To serve four people, you will need:

Fry Light non-stick spray oil

1 tablespoon extra virgin olive oil

2 zucchini, sliced

2 cloves garlic, crushed

1 x 400g can tomatoes, drained

1 medium onion, chopped

1/2 teaspoon capsicum, chopped

1 x 200g carton low-fat yoghurt

1 cup or 200mls grated low-fat vegetarian cheddar cheese

1/2 teaspoon cumin

2 eggs

Lasagne sheets

1x 100g can tomato purée

Salt and ground black pepper

Preparation:

Heat a non-stick pan and coat with 4 applications of Fry Light and the olive oil. Sauté the onions and garlic for 2 minutes. Add zucchini, capsicum, tomatoes and tomato purée and cook until all soft. Beat together the eggs, yoghurt, cumin, half of the cheese and salt and black pepper. Now, in a casserole dish, layer lasagne, tomato mix and yoghurt in layers and sprinkle with cheese. Cook at 180 degrees centigrade for 40 minutes and serve.

Approximate calories per serving: 350

Cranberry Rice Salad

30 minutes

To serve four people, you will need:

2 satsumas, leaved and coarsely chopped

225g raw weight easy cook rice

50g dried stoned dates, chopped

50g dried apricots, chopped

50g Ocean Spray dried cranberries or craisins

50g dried apple, chopped

4 spring onions, sliced

25g mixed nuts, chopped

2 firm small tomatoes, chopped

1 tablespoon fresh rosemary, finely chopped

2 tablespoons virgin olive oil

1 tablespoon unsweetened orange juice

1 teaspoon lime juice

1/4 teaspoon ground nutmeg

Salt and ground black pepper

Preparation:

Cook the rice in boiling salted water for 15 minutes or microwave according to manufacturer's instructions. Drain well. Mix with all the other ingredients and serve with a seasonal salad.

Approximate calories per serving: 400

Vegetarian Dishes

Vegetarian Dishes

Chicory, Pineapple, Kiwi and Mushrooms

30 minutes

To serve four people, you will need:

Fry Light non-stick cooking spray

2 large halved or 4 small chicory 300g in total

2 medium onions, chopped

100g button mushrooms, fresh or canned

120ml vegetable stock, cube or home made

120ml double cream substitute (supermarket brand)

1/2 x 400g can pineapple chunks, drained

1 large Kiwi fruit, skin left on and finely sliced

Parsley

Salt and ground black pepper

Preparation:

Spray a hot non-stick saucepan with 4 applications of Fry Light. Sauté the onions for 2 minutes. Now add the chicory, pineapple and mushrooms and sauté for 5 minutes, stirring occasionally. Now add the vegetable juice or stock and simmer for 7 minutes, stirring frequently. Remove from the heat, season to taste and stir in the cream substitute. Reheat, stirring all the time, until almost boiling. Put onto a serving dish, surround with Kiwi, garnish with parsley and serve alone.

Approximate calories per serving: 150

Chicory, Pineapple, Kiwi and Mushrooms

Kiwi, Mango and Mushroom Treat

Kiwi, Mango and Mushroom Treat

30 minutes

To serve four people, you will need:

2 Kiwi fruit, thinly sliced, peel on or off

8 slices tinned mango from a 400g can, drained

Fry Light spray cooking oil

McDougalls Thickening Granules

450g any type of mushroom or edible fungus

120ml vegetable, or chicken if non-vegetarian, stock from good supermarket cube

1 teaspoon Maggi mixed seasoning or soy sauce

1 teaspoon Lea and Perrins Worcester Sauce

4 spring onions, chopped

1 medium red onion, chopped

2 teaspoons Dijon mustard

1 teaspoon dried tarragon

100mls white wine, dry sherry, vermouth or apple juice

Salt and ground black pepper

Preparation:

Coat a hot non-stick pan with 5 applications of Fry Light. Sauté the onions and spring onions for 2 minutes, stirring all the time. Add the mushrooms, stock, Maggi, Lea and Perrins and wine and simmer, stirring all the time, until it reduces and thickens. Now season with salt and pepper and add the tarragon and Dijon mustard. Simmer until soft and thickens again, adding McDougalls granules if necessary. Serve each portion with 50g, raw weight, of boiled rice (or Uncle Ben's Microwaveable Rice). Arrange on a plate a pile of rice in the centre surrounded by mango slices. Then put the mushroom mixture round the outside and finally surround with Kiwi fruit.

Approximate calories per serving: 300
(including rice)

Cauliflower au Gratin

1 hour

To serve four people, you will need:

2 medium or 1 very large cauliflower, broken into florets with 1 inch stalks

2 medium onions, finely chopped

4 tablespoons chives, chopped

Garlic salt

Dried chilli powder

Dried paprika

50ml vermouth or dry sherry

300mls vegetable, or if non-vegetarian chicken stock made from good supermarket cube

1 pint skimmed milk

4 tablespoons skimmed milk powder

6 tablespoons low-fat vegetarian cheddar or mozzarella cheese, grated

2 tablespoons cornflour

Salt and ground black pepper

Grated or powdered parmesan cheese

Cayenne pepper

McDougalls Thickening Granules

Fry Light spray cooking oil

Preparation For the Sauce:

Mix the cornflour with a little water in an eggcup and then whisk into the skimmed milk. Whisk in the skimmed milk powder and when rich and smooth blend in the cheese. Season with a touch of paprika, a good sprinkling of cayenne pepper and a little salt and ground black pepper. Simmer in a saucepan, stirring frequently, until it thickens. Add McDougalls granules if it does not thicken. Put the sauce aside.

Preparation For the Cauliflower:

Boil or steam the cauliflower until the stalks just begin to soften but do not overcook. Put in an oven-proof casserole dish and put aside. Coat a hot saucepan with 4 applications of Fry Light and gently sauté the onions for 2 minutes. Now add the chives, vermouth, sherry, 1/2 teaspoon of chilli powder and 1 teaspoon of garlic salt and stir well. Add the stock and simmer, stirring all the time, reducing until thick. If required you can use McDougalls granules. Now reheat the sauce and add to this mixture.

Mix well and spoon over the cauliflower. Sprinkle with parmesan cheese and grill under a hot grill until golden. Alternatively, bake at 190 degrees centigrade until it bubbles and is golden.

Approximate calories per serving: 300

Vegetarian Dishes

Sweet and Sour Amaranth Chinese Lettuce

30 minutes

To serve four people, you will need:

1 large head amaranth (Chinese lettuce), about 750g

2 tablespoons extra virgin olive oil

Fry Light spray cooking oil

1 teaspoon soft brown sugar

For the suace, you will need:

3 tablespoons soy sauce

3 tablespoons red wine

3 tablespoons balsamic, sherry or cider vinegar

4 tablespoons mango and apple juice or orange juice

4 tablespoons tomato purée

3 tablespoons granulated sweetener

1 tablespoon caster sugar

1 tablespoon cornflour

Salt and ground black pepper

McDougalls Thickening Granules

100mls water or vegetable stock made from good
supermarket own brand or other stock cube

Preparation:
Wash and cut the Chinese leaves into thin strips. Put all the sauce ingredients, except the cornflour and McDougalls granules, in a small pan and mix well. Mix the cornflour in an eggcup of water and gradually stir in. Coat a hot non-stick pan with 5 applications of Fry Light and add the olive oil. Gradually add the Chinese leaves and sauté, stirring, for 3-4 minutes. Add the teaspoon of soft brown sugar and sauté for a further 4 minutes until soft. Heat the sauce, stirring all the time to prevent cornflour lumping. If it is not thick enough add McDougalls granules. The sauce should be thick and transparent. Stir whilst cooling. Spread the leaves over a serving bowl and spoon over the sauce. Serve hot or cold with 50g (raw weight) per portion of boiled rice.

Approximate calories per serving: 350
(including rice)

Exotic Leeks

1 hour

To serve four people, you will need:

300g small leeks, outer leaves off, washed and cut into 1 inch slices

1 tablespoon extra virgin olive oil

8 kumquats, halved

1 clove garlic, crushed

8 medium tomatoes, skinned and chopped

1 tablespoon tomato purée

Chopped parsley and chives to garnish

75g Nestlés or a good supermarket own brand coconut milk powder

Salt and ground black pepper

Preparation:

Place the sliced leeks into 2 litres of boiling water and add the coconut milk powder. Reserve the parsley, chives and kumquats and add all the other ingredients to the leeks. Simmer for 25 minutes. Drain and serve. Garnish with parsley, chives and kumquats. Serve with a seasonal salad.

Approximate calories per serving: 150
(including salad)

Sesame Seed and Caraway Salad

30 minutes

To serve two people, you will need:

500g white or red cabbage, shredded

1 medium red onion, chopped

1/2 teaspoon caraway seeds

1 tablespoon sesame seed oil

1 small red pepper, deseeded and sliced

1 satsuma, leaved

20 thin slices cucumber, peel left on

Salt and ground black pepper

Preparation:

Place the cabbage, onion and caraway seeds in boiling salted water. Simmer for 10 minutes and drain. Return to the pan and add the sesame oil and all the other ingredients. Toss over a low heat for 2 minutes, season and serve.

Approximate calories per serving: 200

Vegetarian Dishes

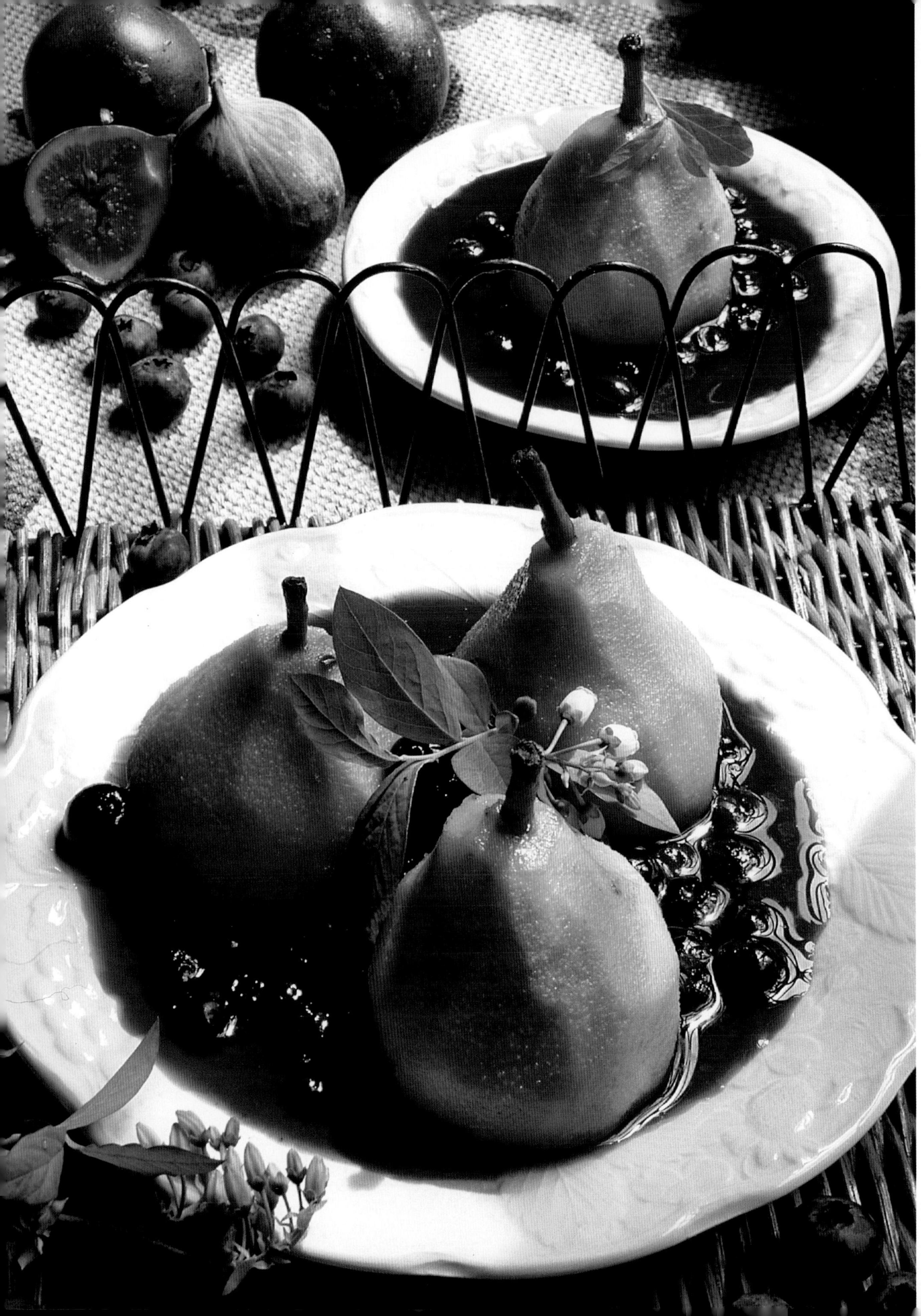

Pears in Berry Sauce

Pears in Berry Sauce

30 minutes

To serve four people, you will need:
4 small hard cooking pears (about 1 pound), peeled and a slice off the bottom to make them stand up, leave the stalks on for decoration
1 litre unsweetened apple juice
1 tablespoon balsamic vinegar
1 stick cinnamon
200g berries of your choice eg. strawberries, black-berries, blueberries, loganberries, tayberries, goose-berries.

Preparation:
Boil the pears in apple juice, balsamic vinegar and cinnamon. Simmer until cooked but not too soft. Remove the pears and stand them upright in a bowl. Discard the cinnamon stick and continue to boil the juices until they are reduced by half. Add the berries and cook for a further 4 minutes, stirring gently. Remove from the heat and either pour straight over the pears and serve or if you prefer the sauce to be smoother either sieve it or liquidise.

Approximate calories per serving: 200

Pears Grand Marnier

1 hour

To serve three people, you will need:
3 hard pears to a total of 700g
1 tablespoon unsweetened lemon juice
3 tablespoons Grand Marnier
250ml unsweetened grape juice
50g granulated sweetener
2 teaspoons clear honey
1/2 teaspoon ground cinnamon
Angelica
Green marzipan or lime rind

Preparation:
Peel the pears but leave the stalks on. Quickly brush with lemon juice to prevent oxidation. Slowly heat in a non-stick pan the Grand Marnier, grape juice and granulated sweetener and bring to the boil. Add the honey and cinnamon and stir. Add the pears and cook until soft, basting with the juices every 5 minutes. It may take up to 30 minutes depending upon the size of the pears. When cooked, remove the pears and decorate with green marzipan or angelica or lime rind. Reduce the remaining juices in the pan stirring until it becomes syrupy. Pour over the hot pears and serve.

Approximate calories per serving: 150

Desserts

Rambutans and Pineapple Chantilly

30 minutes

To serve six people, you will need:

1 x 410g can (good supermarket brand) rambutans stuffed with pineapple and passionfruit (if these are not available lychees can be substituted with equal portions of pineapple chunks)

3 tablespoons Gales clear honey

2 or 3 strips angelica, cut into 1cm squares

300ml low-fat fromage frais

1 sachet gelatine, dissolved in 50ml apple juice

150ml double whipped cream substitute or whipped cream substitute from an aerosol spray eg. Anchor or Delissimo

12 red glacé cherries

Preparation:

Slice each rambutan (or lychee) and line the bottom of 6 grapefruit bowls. Decorate with cut angelica and diced glacé cherries. Chop up the rest of the rambutans and mix with the fromage frais in a bowl. Add honey and mix well. Add the dissolved gelatine and mix again. Pour into the grapefruit bowls of rambutans and chill for 1 hour. Top with whipped cream substitute and serve.

Approximate calories per serving: 150

Kiwango Ice

30 minutes

To serve four people, you will need:

1 kiwango

250g (1/2 litre) vanilla, low-fat, soft-scoop ice cream

3 tablespoons clear honey

Preparation:

Either: scoop out a quarter of the ice cream into each of 4 glass grapefruit dishes. Cover with a quarter of the kiwango seeds and flesh and spoon over the honey and serve.

Or: proceed as above but then mash together all the ingredients in a bowl and return to the freezer for 15 minutes and serve.

Approximate calories per serving: 150

NB Kiwangoes are relatively new exotic fruit. They are oblong with round ends and covered in spines. The colour is orange to gold. To use, cut in half and scoop out all the seeds, which are green, and discard the skin. The seeds are edible.

Stuffed Pineapple

Berry Omelette Exotique

30 minutes

30 minutes

To serve four people, you will need:

1 medium sized fresh pineapple

3 fresh passionfruits

1/2 x 400g can mango slices, drained, each slice cut into 3 pieces

2 Kiwi fruit

1 melon baller scoop

2 satsumas, peeled and leaved

Granulated sweetener

1/4 cucumber, finely diced

2 tablespoons Cointreau

Lemon juice

Low-fat vanilla soft scoop ice cream

Preparation:

Cut the pineapple in half longways. Remove the flesh with a sharp pointed knife and cut it all into cubes. Scoop out the Kiwis with a melon baller scoop. Mix in a large bowl the mango, kiwi balls, satsumas, cucumber and the Cointreau. Sprinkle with lemon juice granulated sweetener to taste. Spoon back into the 2 pineapple halves. Cut the passionfruit in half, watching your fingers (the knife may slip) and teaspoon the flesh over the fruit. Serve each portion with a scoop of low-fat vanilla ice cream.

Approximate calories per serving: 150

To serve two people, you will need:

4 tablespoons berries of your choice

4 eggs, separated and 2 yolks discarded

1 tablespoon caster sugar

1 tablespoon icing sugar

2 tablespoons apple juice

100g low-fat fromage frais

1 Kiwi fruit, sliced with the peel left on

Preparation:

Whisk the 2 egg yolks with sugar and apple juice. Whisk, in a separate bowl, the 4 egg whites until stiff and cover the egg yolks with it. Place the berries in an ovenproof dish, pour the egg mixture over and cook at 180 degrees centigrade for 15 minutes. Sprinkle over the icing sugar. Top with Kiwi slices and serve with fromage frais.

Approximate calories per serving: 300

Desserts

Cranberry Ice Cream

Melon, Orange, Mango and Mint Chantilly

30 minutes

To serve ten people, you will need:

1 litre soft scoop low-fat vanilla ice cream

50g Ocean Spray Craisins (dried cranberries available from most supermarkets)

Preparation:
Remove the ice cream from the container. Mix in the cranberries, refreeze and serve.

Approximate calories per serving: 150

30 minutes

To serve four people, you will need:

1 honeydew melon

1 x 400g can mango slices, drained

2 oranges, peeled and leaved

Mint leaves, diced

A sprig of mint

Low-fat aerosol cream substitute (eg. Anchor)

Melon baller

Preparation:
Ball the melon with the melon baller and place in a dish with slices of mango and orange. Sprinkle with mint. Chantilly with the cream substitute and decorate with pieces of mint sprig. Add low-fat ice cream, if hungry.

Approximate calories per serving: 180
If you add a generous scoop of low-fat soft scoop ice cream this will add an additional 100 calories to make a total of 280 calories.

Super Low Microwaveable Pears

Mango and Lychee Mousse

30 minutes

30 minutes

To serve four people, you will need:

4 ripe dessert pears, stalks left on

100ml mango and apple or apple and orange juice

2 pinches ground cinnamon

2 pinches ground nutmeg

Candarel granulated sweetener

150g carton low-fat natural yoghurt

4 teaspoons clear honey

2 passionfruit

Deep microwave dish

Stretch 'n Seal

To serve eight people, you will need:

1 x 400g can mango slices in juices

1 x 400g can lychees in juices

2 tablespoons low-fat natural yoghurt

4 tablespoons (60ml) low-fat fromage frais

1/2 teaspoon lime juice

Skimmed milk powder

1/4 teaspoon vanilla essence

Granulated sweetener

2 teaspoons clear honey

Preparation:

Peel the pears and core from the base leaving the stalks. Sit them upright in the microwave dish, sprinkle with the juices, cinnamon, nutmeg and Candarel to taste. Cover with Stretch 'n Seal leaving a vent and cook on high in a microwave until they are fork-tender (8-12 minutes in a 650 watt microwave, 6-8 minutes in a 850 watt microwave). Serve each with a teaspoon of honey or a quarter of a pot of yoghurt.

Approximate calories per serving: 100

Preparation:

Blend the ingredients in a liquidiser. Sweeten to taste with granulated sweetener. Thicken, if required, with skimmed milk powder. Chill and serve.

Approximate calories per serving: 100

Desserts

Ice Cream Grand Marnier

1 hour

To serve four people, you will need:

1 x 400g (1/2 litre) carton low-fat soft scoop vanilla ice cream

3 tablespoons coarse marmalade

1 teaspoon lime juice

2 tablespoons Grand Marnier

Preparation:

Coarsely mix or mash the ingredients. Refreeze for an hour and serve.

Approximate calories per serving: 250

Quince Thinner & Richer

1 hour

To serve four people, you will need:

1 cardamon pod

1 large quince (about 500g)

200ml or 200g carton low-fat fromage frais

2 tablespoons caster sugar

1 tablespoon granulated sweetener

Very low-fat spread

8 green glacé cherries

8 red glacé cherries (or other colour)

4 teaspoons mixed fruit peel

60ml apple juice

Preparation:

Cut the quince in half horizontally (ie divide it into a top and a bottom). Cut out the core and take a thin slice off the top and bottom. Take an ovenproof dish and grease with low-fat spread. Sit the quince, top and bottom down (ie the cut half up). Cut open the cardamon pod and you will find it full of tiny black seeds. Crush these seeds together with sugar and granulated sweetener and sprinkle over the quince. Dot liberally with low-fat spread and top with the cherries and the peel. Spoon 4 tablespoons of water or apple juice over the top. Cover and bake at 190 degrees centigrade for about an hour until tender. Spoon over the fromage frais and serve as 4 portions.

Approximate calories per serving: 100

Melon and Berries

30 minutes

To serve four people, you will need:

1 sweet melon (ogen or honeydew) or 1 x 400g can melon balls

200g berries (blackberries, loganberries, tayberries, strawberries, raspberries or any of your choice)

Roses lime cordial

Granulated sweetener

100ml unsweetened orange juice

Melon baller

Preparation:

Deseed the melon and shape into balls with the melon baller to get a total weight of balls of 400 grams. Sprinkle lightly with granulated sweetener. Spoon over the berries and gently mix. Serve into 4 glass grapefruit dishes. Mix the orange juice with 2 tablespoons lime cordial, sprinkle over the fruit, chill and serve.

Approximate calories per serving: 80

Pears, Apple and Ginger Hot Chantilly

1 hour

To serve six people, you will need:

1 spray aerosol can whipped cream substitute (Anchor, Delissimo or similar)

250g cooking apples (Bramley)

500g hard cooking pears

450mls Stone's Ginger Wine

1 level teaspoon ground cinnamon

1 tablespoon golden syrup

4 level teaspoons granulated sweetener

12 green glacé cherries

McDougalls Thickening Granules

Unsweetened lemon juice

Preparation:

Peel the pears and leave whole. Core and slice the apples, leaving the skin on. Brush the fruit with lemon juice to prevent oxidation. Put wine in a saucepan and slowly bring to the boil. Add apples, cinnamon, granulated sweetener, golden syrup and the pears. Simmer for 30-45 minutes until the pears are soft, turning or basting occasionally. Remove the pears. Boil the remaining wine and juices for 10-15 minutes until it thickens. Add McDougalls granules if required. Cut the pears in half, spoon the liquid over the pears and decorate with green cherries. Top the Chantilly with whipped cream substitute and serve hot.

Approximate calories per serving: 150

Chocolate Treat with Mangoes | **Mango and Peach Brulée**

30 minutes

To serve six people, you will need:

1/2 x 400g can mango slices, drained and mashed

2 large over-ripe bananas, peeled and mashed

100g caster sugar

1 vanilla pod or 1 teaspoon vanilla essence

Pinch of salt

50ml skimmed milk

1 tablespoon skimmed milk powder

75ml low-fat fromage frais

1 tablespoon white wine, cider or sherry vinegar

1¼ tablespoons cocoa powder

50ml apple juice

50ml water

1 tablespoon golden syrup

125g self raising sponge flour

Preparation:

Mix and sift the flour, sugar, skimmed milk powder, salt and cocoa onto a large 10 inch to 12 inch flan oven dish. Mix the milk, fromage frais and vanilla essence (or pod, cut in 2) and pour over the flan dish and the contents. Spoon over the bananas and mango, mix well with a plastic or wooden spoon into a thick and lumpy mixture. Bake in a preheated oven at 180 degrees centigrade for 12–18 minutes until it just begins to set and has a skin on top. Do not overcook. Allow to cool a little and serve.

Approximate calories per serving: 200

Chocolate Treat with Mangoes

30 minutes

To serve six people, you will need:

1 x 400g can mangoes, sliced and drained

1 x 400g can sliced peaches, drained

150ml unsweetened low-fat natural yoghurt or buttermilk

200ml double cream substitute

1/2 teaspoon grated nutmeg

1 teaspoon vanilla essence

100g soft brown sugar

4 tablespoons Grand Marnier

1 tablespoon concentrated low-sugar orange cordial

Preparation:

Put the drained fruit in an ovenproof casserole. Sprinkle over 2 tablespoons of Grand Marnier. Beat in a large bowl the yoghurt or buttermilk with the double cream substitute, nutmeg, vanilla essence and the other 2 tablespoons of Grand Marnier. Whisk until blended and smooth and spoon over the fruit. Sprinkle over the brown sugar. Grill under a hot grill until it caramelises (about 4 minutes) and serve.

Approximate calories per serving: 250

Fruit Jelly

Fruit Flan

2 hours +

To serve eight people, you will need:

2 x 15g sachets gelatine powder

200mls boiling water

2 level tablespoons granulated sweetener

50ml unsweetened lemon juice

1 bottle hock (Liebfraumilch or Reisling)

1 x 400g can fruit cocktail

1 x 400g can pineapple chunks

1 Anchor, Delissimo or similar aerosol whipped cream substitute

Preparation:

Put gelatine into a bowl with boiling water and stir until dissolved, heating if necessary. Then add the granulated sweetener, lemon juice and the wine. Stir and allow to cool until it begins to set. Layer the fruit and jelly in a large bowl or jelly mould. Pour in the jelly and chill for several hours in a fridge until set. Score the edge of the jelly right around with a sharp pointed knife about 1 inch deep. Gently lower the mould into hot water (do not get any water in the jelly) for 20 seconds. Remove and quickly turn over onto a plate. Serve alone or Chantilly with whipped cream substitute.

Approximate calories per serving: 200
(including Chantilly)

1 hour

To serve eight people, you will need:

4 eggs, 2 yolks discarded

50g caster sugar

2 tablespoons granulated sweetener

25g dairy butter

25g low-fat spread

50g plain flour

25g ground nuts, any type

3 tablespoons Amaretto (almond liqueur)

15 strawberries, halved

75g blueberries or blackcurrants

100g raspberries

100g green seedless grapes

1 x 200g can mandarin segments

3 tablespoons apricot jam

1 passionfruit

Preparation:

Grease a cake tin (preferably round, 9 inch in diameter) with a little low-fat spread. Put the eggs, sugar and sweetener in a bowl and whisk over a bowl of very hot water until creamy and cool. Or alternatively whisk in an electric mixer. Gradually add flour to the egg mixture, add melted butter, the remains of the spread and the nuts. Stir well with a spoon, pour into the cake tin and bake at 180 degrees centigrade for 30-40 minutes until well risen. Turn out and cool. Sprinkle with Amaretto and arrange decorative circles of fruit with the passionfruit pulp and seeds in the centre of the design. Put jam and 2 tablespoons water or apple juice into a pan, bring to the boil and simmer for 1 minute. Sieve and brush over the fruit to glaze. Cool and serve.

Approximate calories per serving: 200

Fruit Jelly

Fruit Flan

Desserts

Baked Fruit

1 hour

To serve six people, you will need:

1 x 400g can sliced mangoes

1 x 400g can sliced lychees

1 large Kiwi fruit

2 grapefruits, peeled and leaved

3 medium oranges, peeled and leaved

1 Cox apple, skin left on and chopped

4 ounces dried apricots

600ml unsweetened orange juice

Granulated sweetener

1 tablespoon golden syrup

Preparation:

Drain the mangoes and lychees and put in an oven proof casserole. Add the dried apricots, grapefruit, orange, syrup and apple. Sprinkle lightly with granulated sweetener. Pour over the orange juice and cover. Bake at 190 degrees centigrade for 25-30 minutes. Serve cold.

Approximate calories per serving: 250

Slimmer Fruit Ice Cream

1 hour

To serve eight people, you will need:

500g (raw weight, not containing stones) berries or fruit flesh, cut into cubes, spread out on a tray and frozen for at least 4 hours

255g low-fat fromage frais

50mls skimmed milk

Granulated sweetener to taste

1 teaspoon lime juice

3 teaspoons clear honey

Vanilla essence to taste

Skimmed milk powder

Preparation:

Put fruit (still frozen) into a large bowl. Add all the other ingredients and mix well. Sweeten and add vanilla essence to taste. Blend in a liquidiser until creamy. Add skimmed milk powder if too thin and reblend. Freeze for 50 minutes and serve.

Approximate calories per serving: 75

NB This preparation will not keep. If over frozen it becomes solid and loses its texture. However, it is still delicious defrosted but does not look very appetising.

Exotique Banana Dessert

30 minutes

To serve two people, you will need:

100g low-fat fromage frais

2 bananas, thinly sliced

3 teaspoons lime juice

25g chopped dates

2 teaspoons clear honey

2 teaspoons flaked almonds

1 Kiwi fruit, peeled and thinly sliced

1 satsuma, leaved

1 tablespoon water or apple juice

Preparation:

Place the banana in an ovenproof dish, sprinkle with lime juice and add the dates. Separately blend together the honey, almonds, and the water or apple juice and spoon over the banana. Cook at 180 degrees centigrade for 2 minutes. Serve with fromage frais, garnished with Kiwi and satsumas (flesh – not cooked).

Approximate calories per serving: 250

Peach and Papaya (or Passion) Chantilly

30 minutes

To serve four people, you will need:

1 x 400g tin peach halves, drained (retain syrup)

Either 4 passionfruit or 1/4 x 400g can papaya chunks (pawpaw), drained

1 aerosol can spray whipped cream substitute (Anchor or Delissimo)

50ml unsweetened orange juice

Preparation:

Mix the peach syrup with 50ml of unsweetened orange juice. Put 2 peach halves, cut side uppermost, into each of 4 glass bowls. Cut the passionfruit in half, being careful not to cut your fingers, and spoon and contents of half a passionfruit over each peach half (ie 1 passionfruit per portion). Alternatively, cover the peach halves with a quarter of the papaya chunks. Ladle over the peach and orange syrup. Top Chantilly with cream substitute. Serve chilled.

Approximate calories per serving: 200

Desserts

Witches Blackberry Sorbet

30 minutes

To serve four people, you will need:

500g blackberries (or other of choice), frozen or fresh

3 tablespoons lime juice

3 tablespoons shredded mint

8 tablespoons clear honey

8 large ice cubes

Preparation:

Freeze fresh berries or use frozen berries. Place the ingredients in a food processor all and blend until smooth or roughly granular. Refreeze if too runny. Scoop out with an ice cream scoop and serve.

Approximate calories per serving: 100

Strawberry (or any other fruits) Mousse

1 hour

To serve six people, you will need:

500g strawberries, raspberries or any berry fruit

4 tablespoons low-fat yoghurt

8 tablespoons (120ml) low-fat fromage frais

1 teaspoon lime juice

Skimmed milk powder

1/2 teaspoon vanilla essence

4 teaspoons clear honey

Granulated sweetener

Preparation:

Blend the ingredients in a liquidiser. Sweeten to taste with granulated sweetener. Add more vanilla essence to taste. Thicken, if required, with skimmed milk powder. Chill and serve.

Approximate calories per serving: 100

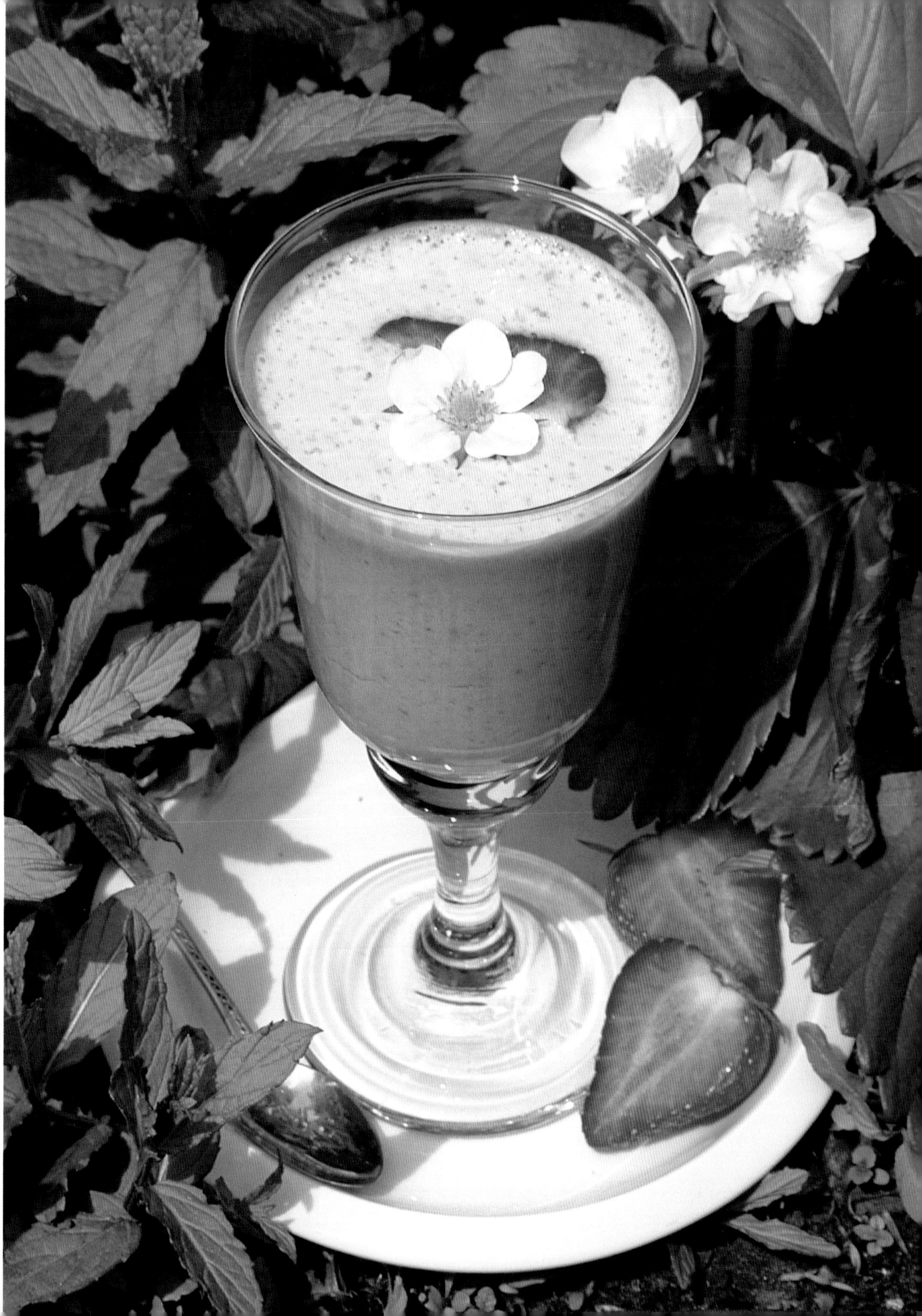

Strawberry Mousse

Desserts

Midsummer Fruits with Flowers and Crystallised Flowers

30 minutes

Preparation:
Just make a mixture of best midsummer fruits and crystallised or fresh flowers of your choice. Calories are automatically controlled and a squirt of Anchor or Delissimo whipped cream aerosol substitute will make your meal.

Don't worry about the calories, It is almost impossible to exceed 150 calories per serving.

Crystallising Flowers:
Almost any flower can be crystallised and used for decoration and eating. Two easy methods are available. The first uses raw white of egg which theoretically could be infected with bacteria although the risk is infinitely small; however flowers crystallised in this way must be used within 48 hours. The second method is more time consuming but rewarding and blooms can be kept for up to a year.

Method 1
Select clean but unwashed flowers, clusters or petals. Remove all the green parts and if using petals, trim off the white base. Coat with a brush or dip in lightly beaten egg white and dust over or dip in caster sugar. Leave to dry preferably on a rack in an airing cupboard until crisp. Put in a good sealed container and use within 48 hours.

Method 2
Dissolve 2 teaspoons of Gum Arabic (from any chemist) in 50mls of a mixture of vodka and white peach liqueur. Paint onto the petals or blooms and dust well or dip in caster sugar. Dry on a rack in a warm airing cupboard until crisp. Store in a sealed container for up to 1 year.

Hot Winter Fruits and Champagne

30 minutes

Preparation:
Just select any winter or exotic fruits. Put in an oven-proof casserole with 2 tablespoons clear honey per portion. Crystallised flowers can be added now or as a decoration. Serve topped with a squirt of Delissimo or Anchor low-fat cream substitute. Top each portion with fresh or crystallised rose petals or roses.

Don't worry about the calories, it is almost impossible to exceed 200 calories per serving.

Flowers suitable for crystallising:

Lavender

Violets or Pansies

Rose Petals

Nasturtiums

Primroses

English Cowslips (not American variety)

Marigolds

Dandelions

Carnations

Chives

any herb flowers

Honeysuckle

Tiger lilies

Chrysanthemums

Blackberry, Lychee and Cape Gooseberry Dessert

30 minutes

To serve four people, you will need:

1 x 400g can blackberries, drained, or 200g fresh berries

8 fresh or canned lychees, drained

8 physalis (cape gooseberry), if none available small kumquats will do

1 x 200g can low-fat greek yoghurt

Caster sugar

Preparation:

Place the mixed fruit in a deep oven-proof dish. Fill to half or three-quarters full and cover with yoghurt. Sprinkle with caster sugar and cook under a hot grill until the sugar caramelises. Serve hot or cold with a scoop of low-fat soft scoop ice cream.

Approximate calories per serving: 250

Banana Bake Exotique

1 hour

To serve two people, you will need:

2 medium bananas, peeled and sliced

25g raisins or craisins (dried cranberries)

2 tablespoons lime juice

2 tablespoons orange juice

1 Kiwi fruit, peeled and sliced

1 passionfruit

Granulated sweetener

Preparation:

Soak the raisins or craisins in a mixture of lime and orange juice for about 40 minutes. Slice the bananas longways and arrange in a casserole in 4 half moon crescents. Sprinkle over the raisins and the juices. Top with sliced Kiwi, sprinkle with granulated sweetener and bake at 150 degrees centigrade for 20 minutes. Scoop out the passionfruit flesh and put on top of the banana mixture. Serve hot.

Approximate calories per serving: 100

NB For an extra treat you can have a 50g scoop of low-fat ice cream and the total now becomes 200 calories.

Desserts

Honey and Apple Crisp

1 hour

To serve four people, you will need:

4 cups dessert apples, sliced

1/4 cup (50mls) soft brown sugar

1 tablespoon lime juice

1/2 cup (100mls) clear honey

1/2 cup (100mls) plain flour

4 tablespoons granulated sweetener

Pinch of salt

1/4 cup (50mls) low-fat margarine

1/4 cup (50mls) nuts, preferably chestnuts

NB – Solids shown as liquid measures

Preparation:
Spread apples in a baking dish.
Sprinkle with granulated sweetener,
lime juice and pour over the honey.
Mix, in a separate bowl, the flour,
brown sugar, salt and work in the margarine (a small blender will help).
Spread over the apples and bake at 180
degrees centigrade for 30-40 minutes
until brown.

Approximate calories per serving: 300

Guava Ice Cream

30 minutes

To serve eight people, you will need:

500g (1/2 litre) pack low-fat soft scoop ice cream

1 x 400g can guava halves in syrup (good supermarket brand)

2 tablespoons clear honey

Preparation:
Liquidise the contents of the tin of
guava halves and juice and add the ice
cream. Do not blend too much as
chunks and seeds are good. Put back
into an ice cream container and
refreeze. Delicious.

Approximate calories per serving: 200

NB In place of guava you can use mango, lychees,
paw paw, sharon fruit, rambutans or any canned soft
fruit to a weight of about 400 grams.

Banana Split

Exotic Caramel Custard

30 minutes

To serve one person you will need:

1 banana

Low-fat soft scoop ice cream

Supermarket brand toffee, chocolate or fudge syrup

Low-fat aerosol whipped cream substitute (Delissimo or Anchor)

1 glacé cherry

Preparation:

Slice the banana in half lengthways to give 2 half moon crescents and lay on a plate. Put a ball of ice cream in the middle, cover with a little syrup, squirt over the cream substitute and crown with a glacé cherry and serve.

Approximate calories per serving: 250

1 hour

To serve four people, you will need:

400ml skimmed milk

4 teaspoons fructose (fruit sugar)

60ml apple juice

3 or 4 drops vanilla essence

6 small eggs, 2 yolks discarded

1 tablespoon coconut milk powder

4 fresh or tinned lychees or rambutans stuffed with pineapple

Preparation:

Heat the fructose in a pan until brown and syrupy. Pour into a small dish and put aside. Gently heat the skimmed milk, vanilla and coconut powder until it boils, stirring all the time. Pour over the beaten eggs and mix well. Put the fructose syrup into 4 small individual pie dishes and pour the mixture on top. Bake at 150 degrees centigrade for 30 minutes. Chill, turn out and serve. Top each with a lychee or a rambutan.

Approximate calories per serving: 180

Desserts

Red Rose Petal Sorbet

Overnight

To serve six people, you will need:

200g reduced calorie sugar

5 x 50g granulated sweetener

275ml water

275ml white wine or champagne

3 tablespoons lime juice

1 tablespoon lemon juice

Petals of 3 or 4 large scented red roses

A few extra roses if you want to crystallise them

Gum Arabic (from chemist)

Vodka

Clear peach liqueur

Preparation:

Dissolve the sugar and granulated sweetener in the water and boil for approximately 5 minutes until syrupy. Add the white wine, rose petals, lemon and lime juices and liquidise. Pour into a freezer tray and freeze until it begins to set. Now whisk or beat well and freeze overnight. Serve decorated with crystallised rose petals or whole crystallises roses made as follows: dissolve a teaspoon of gum Arabic in 25mls of vodka or peach liqueur mixture. Paint each rose petal or dip them in the mixture and sprinkle or dust with caster sugar. Dry overnight on a rack and store in a sealed container.

Approximate calories per serving: 200

Independence Day Sweet Dessert Flag

1 hour

This dessert is meant to be a copy of the American flag with the 50 states in the square in the top left hand corner and red and white stripes throughout.

To serve ten people, you will need:

500g blackberries or bilberries

1kg raspberries or strawberries

5 bananas

1 x 340g tub low-fat plain cottage cheese

Preparation:

On a flat oblong tray or platter reproduce the Stars and Stripes as opposite. Either glaze the banana or paint with lemon juice to prevent it oxidising. Chill and serve.

Approximate calories per serving: 200

NB In place of the banana you can use any other white fruit (eg white grapes, apple or pear)

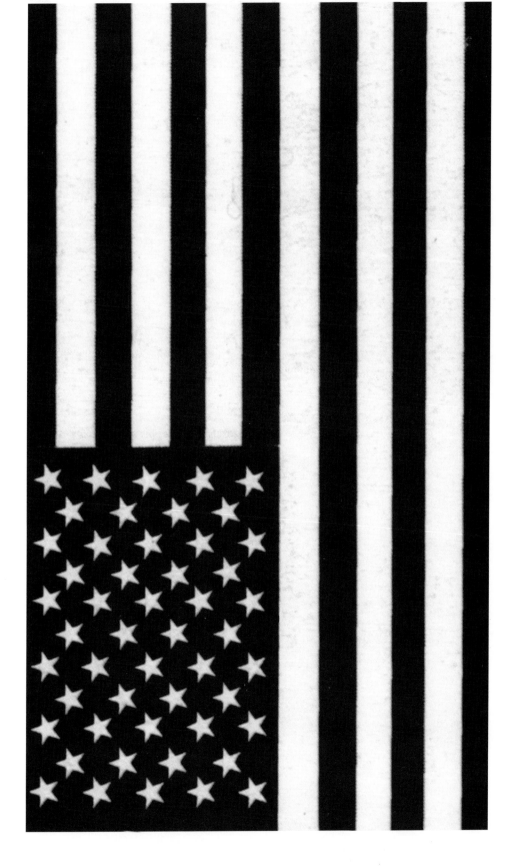

Desserts

Red stripes – Raspberries or Strawberries
White stripes – Bananas or white fruit
Blue square – Blackberries or Bilberries
White stars – cottage cheese

Mango and Orange Drink

To serve six people, you will need:

1 x 400g can sliced mango

200mls unsweetened orange juice

2 teaspoons (10ml) clear honey

4 teaspoons (20ml) lime juice

3 tablespoons (45ml) Candarel granulated sweetener

500ml water

Preparation:
Blend, chill and serve.

Approximate calories per serving: 100

Banana Thrill

To serve six people, you will need:

3 scoops low-fat vanilla ice cream

450ml skimmed milk

2 tablespoons clear honey

2 small bananas, peeled and chopped

1 tablespoon coconut milk powder

Preparation:
Blend until frothy and serve.

Approximate calories per glass: 125

Coconut and Papaya Surprise

To serve six people, you will need:

1 x 400g can supermarket papaya (paw paw)

1 x 400g can coconut milk

5 teaspoons lime juice

1 teaspoon vanilla essence

2 tablespoons clear honey

Preparation:
Blend, chill and serve.

Approximate calories per glass: 100
(Can be served with crushed ice)

Hot Pineapple Treat

To serve six people, you will need:

1 litre unsweetened pineapple juice

1 cinnamon stick

3 cloves, whole

2 tablespoons/30ml clear honey

Preparation:
Boil together the juice, cinnamon and cloves and simmer for 20 minutes. Remove the cinnamon and cloves. Stir in the honey. Serve hot.

Approximate calories per glass: 100

Thinner and Richer Head Banger

To serve six people, you will need:

1 litre unsweetened orange, pineapple, mango or other juice

180ml Ribena Lite cordial

3 teaspoons dried cayenne pepper

Pinch of salt

Preparation:
Combine, refrigerate and serve.

Approximate calories per glass: 100

Other Drinks

You can enjoy a very large glass of any unsweetened fruit juice for 100 calories – even better, squeeze your own fruit (electric squeezers are not expensive). You may also make delicious milkshakes using 200mls of skimmed milk or soya milk, one scoop of low-calorie ice cream, 8 ice cubes and any milkshake cordial, just liquidise and serve. This will cost you 200 cals and you should omit your starter or dessert. You may however enjoy a diet or low-calorie drink without penalty.

Coconut and Papaya Surprise

Mango and Orange Drink

RNIs (reference nutrient intakes) represent our daily requirement of vitamins and other nutrients which help regulate our body processes, to grow and to resist infection. The amount we need varies according to our age and sex.

Nutritionalists particularly emphasise the importance of anti-oxidant vitamins A,C and E. A healthy intake of these in the diet, with certain minerals and trace elements, may increase resistance to heart disease and certain cancers. However, all nutrients are important, and a diet which lacks, for instance, B-vitamins, can lead to multiple deficiency diseases within months. The body can synthesise some vitamin D from sunlight, but if it isn't getting much sun (for instance, if you're wrapped up from head to toe and live in Bootle) dairy products or fish liver oils are essential sources of vitamin D. The recipes in this book have been designed to provide you with all the food you need to keep you healthy.

Anti-oxidants (found mostly in fruit and vegetables, which is why you should eat lots) counter the effects of free radicals which, if allowed to accumulate, can damage DNA molecules and may make cells more likely to become cancerous. Like all nutrients, anti-oxidants must be absorbed in conjunction with other vitamins and minerals to be fully effective.

Nutrient	Sources	Function
Vitamin A	Fish liver oils, eggs, liver; dark green, orange & yellow vegetables; red capsicums.	Skin, night vision. Pregnant women should not eat liver or take extra vitamin A.
B1/Thiamin	Milk, offal, eggs, wholegrain & fortified cereals, vegetables.	Nervous system & release of energy from carbohydrates.
B2/Riboflavin	Dairy products, liver, kidneys, Marmite, eggs, mushrooms, beef.	Repair and maintenance of body tissue.
Niacin	Beef, pork, chicken, fish, wholemeal bread.	Efficient functioning of brain and nervous system.
B6/Pyridoxine	Liver, wholegrain cereals, meat, fish, bananas, walnuts, avocados, potatoes.	Growth & maintenance of nervous system. Works together with niacin & vitamin B 2. Too much (i.e. over 50mg a day) is dangerous; it can affect sensory nerve function.
B12/Cobalamin	Liver & other animal products such as eggs, cheese, milk, meat & fish. Also from fortified cereals.	Healthy nervous system.
Vitamin C	All fruit & vegetables particularly citrus fruits, capsicums, leafy green vegetables, especially when eaten fresh & raw.	Skin, teeth & nervous system; helps iron absorption. Smokers may need an extra 80mg a day.
Folic Acid	Foliates can be obtained from fresh green leafy vegetables, liver, most pulses, peanuts, bread almonds & fortified cereals.	Works with B12. An extra 4mg a day should be taken by women planning a pregnancy, to avoid neural defects in babies.
Vitamin D	Dairy products & the action of sunlight on the skin; fortified margarines & spreads; herrings, kippers, salmon.	Helps calcium and phosphorus to be absorbed in order to maintain healthy bones & teeth. Too much may be deposited in the kidneys & liver with damaging results.
Vitamin E	Vegetable oils, olives, avocados, nuts, seeds, some fortified cereals.	Anti-oxidant.
Iron	Leafy green vegetables, liver, dried apricots, beef, eggs and cocoa powder, whole grains.	Red blood cells.
Calcium	Dairy produce & white bread, canned salmon & sardines with bones.	Strong bones & teeth.
Zinc	Cheese, eggs, beef and wholemeal bread.	Immune system, wound healing, growth.
Sodium	Table salt – but don't add it to infants' diets. Too much tends to increase blood pressure in susceptible individuals. One level teaspoonful is about 4 gms.	Intake should not exceed 6g daily. Sodium is in almost all processed food, notably yeast extract and stock cubes, so read labels and avoid adding salt at the table.
Potassium	Lo-salt contains potassium; other sources include bananas.	Works with sodium.
Magnesium	Unrefined cereals and greens.	May help to lower blood pressure.
Trace Elements	Iodine is found particularly in seafood, and copper in shellfish and liver	All these are essential, and adequate quantities are available from the recipes in this book

Steaming vegetables	Light steaming reduces nutrients such as Vitamin C, thiamin, pantothenic acid, B6, folic acid, riboflavin, biotin and niacin, but losses are less significant than from boiling.
Boiling vegetables	Boiling vegetables for more than a few seconds reduces vitamin C and long cooking can boil it right away. The water-soluble B vitamins, riboflavin and so on, leach into the water.
Boiling cereals	40%-50% of thiamin, pantothenic acid, B6, folic acid, riboflavin, biotin and niacin are lost – but have you tried raw rice? The point is don't over cook it.
Frying	Use the barest minimum of oil. Stir-fry fast; some vitamin A is lost in air and with heat, and vitamin C is heat sensitive.
Grilling	This is generally healthier than frying since less fat is used. However, prolonged exposure to heat makes certain proteins harder to digest and 25% of the thiamin is lost from bread when you toast it.
Microwaving	Since little water is necessary, the microwave oven is quite good at retaining water-soluble vitamins other than those destroyed by heat.
Roasting	Roast with as little fat as possible and drain off the surplus.
Bought dried fruit and vegetables	Thiamin is destroyed by exposure to sulphur dioxide, widely used as a preservative; check labels. Storage allows changes to occur so check sell-by dates.
Canned vegetables and fruit	Some of the vitamin and mineral content (primarily B1/thiamin, vitamin C and folic acid, with minerals) of canned fruit and vegetables leaches into the water, so use it as stock or fruit juice where you can and buy fruit in juice, rather than syrup, wherever possible.
Bought fruit juice	Use quickly. Vitamin C diminishes once cans, packs and bottles are opened.
Frozen food	Check labels for added sugar and salt, store according to instruction and don't re-freeze once thawed. If you are freezing your own fruit and vegetables, do so as soon as possible after harvesting, label for rapid turnover, and allow blanched food to cool completely before freezing (so that it doesn't raise the freezer temperature as it goes in). Blanched food looses some of its Vitamin C and thiamin – but less than it might have lost had it been stored. Freezing generally retains nutrients well.
Almost any processed or preserved food from wine to sausages	Check label for preservation by sulphur dioxide. This preserves vitamin C well, but destroys thiamin (vitamin B1) completely.
Fresh vegetables	Keep in a cool dark place. Use greens only while green and never use green potatoes; they are poisonous.
Milk	Keep in a cold dark place to retain vitamins. Do not leave milk on the doorstep; sunlight destroys vitamin C and riboflavin.

Charts '**Normal' Quantities and Measurements**

Normal Quantities

Bread (wholemeal)	Small slice **25g** – Medium slice **38g** – Large slice **55g**
Porridge	Small portion made with one sixth of a pint of milk **130g** made up weight – Medium (1/4 pint milk) **180g** – Large (1/3 pint milk) **225g**
Flaked cereals	Small portion 20g – Medium portion **30g** – Large portion **50g**
Butter	Scrape **7g** – Moderate serving **10g** – Thick serving **12g** – Knob **12g**
Eggs	Scrambled **2 size 3 eggs** – Omelette **2 size 3 egg whites and 1size 3 yolk**
Cheese	Small portion **20g** – Medium portion **30g** – Large portion **50g**
Venison	Average serving **120g**
Dried herbs	1 teaspoonful **1g**
Cod fillet	Small **50g** – Medium **120g** – Large **175g**
Cod Steak	Average **50g**
Herring (filleted)	Small **85g** – Medium – **120g**
Mackerel	Average portion **160g**
Plaice	Small **75g** – Medium **130g** – Large **180g**
Fish paste	Average spread **10g**
Green Beans, Cauliflower or leafy vegetables	Small portion **60g** – Medium portion **90g** – Large portion **120g**
Peas (frozen or fresh)	Small portion **40g** – Medium portion **70g** – Large portion **100g**
Baked potatoes (with skin)	Small **100g** – Medium **180g** – Large **220g**
Apple (eating) with core	Small **75g** – Medium **110g** – Large **170g**
Avocado (flesh only)	Half **75g**
Canned fruit with juice	Average portion **90-135g**
Honey	Average spread on bread **20g** (a teaspoon piled high)
Marmite	A thin scrape **1g** – Thickly spread **4g**
Fish paste	Average spread **10g**
Whole milk	A serving in tea or coffee (per cup) **25g** – (per mug) **30g**
Semi-skimmed milk	A serving in tea or coffee (per cup) **30g** – (per mug) **40g**
Skimmed milk	A serving in tea or coffee (per cup) **35g** – (per mug) **50g**
Aerosol cream	An average serving **10g**
Wine	An average glass **125ml**
Fruit juice	An average glass **160ml**
Coffee or tea	A cup **190ml** – A mug **260ml**
Cocoa	One heaped teaspoon **6g**

Measurements and Temperatures

These are the approximate measures used in the recipes:

1oz = 25g
4oz = 100g
8oz = 1/2lb = 225g
16oz = 1lb = 450g
2lbs = 1kilo
2fluid oz = 50ml
5 fluid oz = 1/4 pint = 150ml
10 fluid oz = 1/2 pint = 300ml
15 fluid oz = 3/4pint = 450ml
20 fluid oz = 1 pint = 600ml
13/4 pint = 1litre
1 cup = 1/3 pint = 200ml
1breakfast cup = 1/2pint = 300ml

There are various variations throughout the world. The US pint is only 16 fluid ounces, their tablespoons are smaller and Australian tablespoons are bigger. However, standard measurements have been adopted through this book:

Pint = 20 fluid oz
Teaspoon = 5ml
Tablespoon = 15ml
Dessertspoon = 10ml
Large can = 400/500g
Small can = 200/250g
Mini can = 125/150g

Oven Temperatures:

Gas1/2 = 275ºF = 100ºC = very cool
Gas 2 – 325ºF = 120ºC = cool or slow
Gas 3 = 360ºF = 185ºC = moderate
Gas 6 = 400ºF = 200ºC = moderately hot
Gas 8 = 450ºF = 230ºC = hot
Gas 9 = 475ºF = 240ºC = very hot

NB Reduce fan oven temperatures by 10 or 15%

Carbohydrates and Proteins

About half our daily food intake should consist of carbohydrates from starchy foods and fruit and vegetables, supplemented by milk products or soya milk. (which contain a good deal of carbohydrate). They should not come, as 29% do at present, from non-milk extrinsic sugars – that is, the nutritionally redundant sugar in sweets, in the sugarbowl and in processed foods. Always read labels. Baked beans and many other canned vegetables contain sugar; so do frozen peas, sometimes. Try to find brands which don't. Anything with added glucose, fructose, corn syrup, maltose, lactose, dextrose or galactose is to be avoided.

Bread	Wholemeal contains 92% of the vitamin-rich wheat berry and white bread, 72%; everything else is in between. White bread contains fractionally less protein than wholemeal and far fewer of the B vitamins (which are lost in milling). However white bread is fortified by law (in the UK with calcium, B1 and niacin). Bread that's just called brown is probably white bread coloured with caramel.
Beans and Pulses	Beneficial on cholesterol levels.
Potatoes, carrots and other starchy root vegetables	Leave the skin on potatoes when you can.
Breakfast cereal	Oats may have a beneficial effect in lowering harmful cholesterol.
Dried fruit	Avoid any which have been rolled in sugar and try to avoid those preserved by sulphur dioxide; it destroys thiamin.
Nuts	Some nuts are very high in fat, so where they are found in the recipes don't exceed the amount stated.
Sugar, syrup and sweets	Empty calories, that is they provide instant energy as a drug might, but no nutritional value. Widely used as a preservative and bulking agent; read labels and avoid altogether. Some authorities link sugar with heart disease and obesity and all link with dental carles. Dark Muscovado alone contains unidentified trace elements. There is no physiological requirement for sugar; hardly anybody in Europe had tasted it until four hundred year ago. Of the non-sugar sweeteners, xyilto, sorbitol and maltitol don't rot your teeth but they are no less fattening than sugar. Less calorific are sweeteners such as saccharin, aspartame and acesulfame K. Some granulated sweeteners contain sugar so read labels before you buy.
Fruit drinks and squashes	Avoid altogether – these contain little fruit and lots of preservatives, colourings and sugar (besides water). Buy fruit juice instead and read the label to make sure it contains no added sugar; better still make your own.
Cakes and biscuits	Avoid altogether.
Honey, malt and treacle	Honeycomb contains trace elements and sugars. Most honey has no added sugar; read the label. Malt and treacle contain some trace element and minerals but none you can't obtain from other sources.
Alcohol	Alcoholic drinks are made by fermenting sugars in one form or another. They contain no nutrients that you can't find elsewhere.

Protein-rich food
Proteins convert into aminoacids for growth and repair. They can also be converted into energy. There's no such thing as pure-protein food – and like other foods, everything on this list is a mixture. Cheese, for instance, is high in saturated animal fat. In general proteins should make up just under 15% of your daily food intake. Excessively high intake increases the rate at which kidney function is lost with age, so you should not exceed twice the recommended level.

Cheese
Eggs
Beans and pulses
Meat
Offal (liver, kidneys)
Fish and shell fish
Quorn (Mycoprotein)
Tofu and meso
TVP (textured vegetable protein)
Nuts

Charts Fats and Fibre

Fat is more fattening than anything else – weight for weight, more than twice as calorific as carbohydrate or protein and, of course, invisible in foods such as milk, chocolate or pastry. It also converts more easily into body fat.

Fats

Although by following the recipes you will avoid eating too much, at least a fifth of your daily food intake will consist of fat, since it helps the fat-soluble vitamins to work and contains some properties unavailable from other sources. Just as almost every food is a mixture of carbohydrates, fats and proteins in varying proportions, so most fatty foods contain fats of more than one kind – butter, for instance, is two-thirds saturated fat. Saturated fat contains more of the kind of cholesterol that furs up your arteries (and yes, just to complicate matters, there is beneficial cholesterol too). The average British diet is 40% fat, of which half is saturated. This is unhealthy; the recommended fat level is 25%. Fat is easily available energy, however, and the fat intake of children under 5 should not be restricted.

Poly-unsaturated	Corn oil, sunflower, soya and safflower oils; almonds, brazil nuts, hazelnuts; oily fish. Omega 3 oils are particularly important for a healthy heart and you can get them from herrings, mackerel and salmon	Eat more poly-unsaturated than saturated fat.
Mono-unsaturated	Olive oil, peanuts, peanut butter, avocados, almonds, hazelnuts and barcelona nuts	About half your daily fat intake should be mono-unsaturated
Saturated (solid at room temperature)	Lard, cheese, cream, butter, some margarines, coconut cream, fresh and desiccated coconut, peanut butter, brazil nuts, bacon fat, fat meat and bacon, eggs and bought pastries and pies	Adults in Britain consume, on average, half their daily fat intake as saturates – far too much. If your overall fat intake is currently too high you can cut it to the correct level by sticking to the recipes in this book. Remember that children under five need whole milk, not skimmed, and all children should have at least half a pint of milk a day, as long as it agrees with them. Adults, however, can cut down on saturated fat by drinking skimmed or soya milk.

Fibre

Most foods (except sugar) contain some fibre, either available, that is soluble and nutritionally useful, or non-available – simply cellulose which passes through the system and helps to keep it moving. The recipes in this book contain enough fibre. Remember that absorption of iron, zinc and calcium can be reduced by excessive consumption of whole grain cereals over a long period.

Bread	Wholemeal has more of the husk (roughage) than wheatmeal or granary bread; brown bread is white bread coloured with caramel. White bread has more calcium than wholemeal, though less vitamins B6 and E. It contains bleaches and improvers – though if you buy soft, open-textured wholemeal from a supermarket you may be getting flour improvers with that too. They are not known to do you any harm.
Rice	Again, brown rice has more roughage, and also more B vitamins.
Potatoes in skins	Leave the skin on where you can. Much of the potato's vitamin C content is just beneath the skin, and the skin contains valuable fibre.
Beans and Pulses	Beans, dried peas and lentils are a rich source of protein and contain soluble fibre which can lower cholesterol.
Dried fruit	Raisins, apricots and so on are a delightful source of sweetness to anyone who has rejected sugar. They taste of naturally occurring fruit sugar (fructose) which does not shock the pancreas into action as sucrose does. If you wish to avoid dried fruit preserved by sulphur dioxide, read the labels.
Porridge or Muesli	Read the label. Oats contain soluble fibre and are an excellent food. However, some proprietary mueslis are high in sugar and its easy to make your own using fresh and dried fruit and nuts.
All-bran	High in sugar.
Fruit and vegetables	Fruit and vegetables contain valuable anti-oxidant vitamins and trace elements for protection against heart disease and many cancers. The WHO recommends a minimum of 5 portion a day.

Long-term alcohol abuse causes brain and liver damage and is linked to many cancers. A man should drink no more than 21 units of alcohol a week and a woman no more than 14. Drinking during pregnancy is out.	**Tea**	High in tannin and has some caffeine (a stimulant).	Nutrients: fluoride and manganese.
	Coffee	High in caffeine.	Instant coffee has potassium. Coffee has a diuretic and stimulant effect, but irritates the stomach. Its unwise to drink more than 2 cups or real coffee a day.
	Alcohol	Red wine contains tannin and all alcohols except neat spirit retain some of the sugars they're made from, in unfermented form – from 2% in the least sweet beers, to 30% in liqueurs.	Certain wines contain iron. Beers and stouts give you B vitamins. On the other hand, remember that Diet Pils is no less fattening than any other alcoholic drink, and beer gives you a beer-gut quickly. It is possible to find low-alcohol or no-alcohol drinks which taste okay and contain very few calories: read labels.
	One unit of alcohol is...	Half a pint/250ml	Ordinary beer or lager
		1 x 125ml glass	Wine or vermouth (about 7 glasses from a bottle)
		25ml pub measure	Spirits (about 30 units from a bottle)
		A third of a can	Strong cider
		A quarter of a can or two-fifths of a bottle	Strong larger

Obesity Jargon

CALORIE	The amount of heat required to raise 1g of water by 1 degree centigrade.
Calorie	This calorie with a capital 'C' is 1000 calories or more – correctly a kilo calorie or a K cal (do not bother to count them) – just look for low calorie and low fat products.
Fat	This is what makes us obese. Each stone of fat contains 37,000 Calories and 35,000,000 CALORIES. We all need some fat but most of us eat far too much. Polysaturated fats (dairy and animal) are thought to be injurious to our hearts, arteries and other organs. Polyunsaturated fats (corn and some other vegetable oils) are probably better. In *Thinner & Richer*, we have a low-fat diet. Where we do use fat, it is in the form of polyunsaturated such as Krona low calorie spread, Flora, cornflour or sunflower oil and Fry Light non-stick cooking spray. When we do use oil, it is usually virgin olive oil which is a monounsaturated fat, thought to be protective to the heart and responsible for the low incidents of coronary heart disease in the Mediterranean countries: however if a recipe requires a little butter, we shall tell you. Remember a little fat is essential and the occasional use of butter is probably not disadvantageous.

Charts   Body Mass Index Ready Reckoner

Measuring yourself

For the information of the vain amongst us, we are at our tallest when we wake up. Weigh yourself with as few clothes as possible to assess whether your weight to height ratio on the body mass index is too low, acceptable, too high or dangerously obese. Never weigh yourself more than once a week – you're supposed to be learning to eat normally, not worrying obsessively about your weight – and when you do stand on the scales, do so at the same time of day wearing the same sparse clothing (and no shoes).

42 – 59
Very Obese
Health is seriously at risk. Losing weight **immediately** is essential.

31 – 41
Obese
Health is at risk. Losing weight **now** should be seriously considered.

26 – 30
Overweight
Health could suffer. Some weight loss should now be considered.

19 – 25
Healthy
A desirable BMI figure indicating a healthy weight.

11 – 18
Underweight

Height (feet and inches)

Weight (kg)	4'6"	7"	8"	9"	10"	11"	5'	1"	2"	3"	4"	5"	6"	7"	8"	9"	10"	11"	6'	1"	2"	3"	4"	5"	6"	7"
110	59	57	55	53	51	50	48	47	45	44	42	41	40	39	37	36	35	34	33	32	32	31	30	29	28	28
109	59	57	55	53	51	49	48	46	45	43	42	41	39	38	37	36	35	34	33	32	31	30	30	29	28	27
108	58	56	54	52	51	49	47	46	44	43	41	40	39	38	37	36	35	34	33	32	31	30	29	29	28	27
107	58	56	54	52	50	48	47	45	44	42	41	40	39	37	36	35	34	33	32	32	31	30	29	28	28	27
106	57	55	53	51	50	48	46	45	43	42	41	39	38	37	36	35	34	33	32	31	30	30	29	28	27	27
105	57	55	53	51	49	47	46	44	43	42	40	39	38	37	36	35	34	33	32	31	30	29	29	28	27	26
104	56	54	52	50	49	47	45	44	43	41	40	39	38	36	35	34	33	32	31	31	30	29	28	28	27	26
103	56	54	52	50	48	47	45	44	42	41	40	38	37	36	35	34	33	32	31	30	30	29	28	27	27	26
102	55	53	51	49	48	46	45	43	42	40	39	38	37	36	35	34	33	32	31	30	29	28	28	27	26	26
101	55	53	51	49	47	46	44	43	41	40	39	38	36	35	34	33	32	31	31	30	29	28	27	27	26	25
100	54	52	50	48	47	45	44	42	41	40	38	37	36	35	34	33	32	31	30	29	29	28	27	26	26	25
99	54	52	50	48	46	45	43	42	41	39	38	37	36	35	34	33	32	31	30	29	28	28	27	26	26	25
98	53	51	49	48	46	44	43	41	40	39	38	36	35	34	33	32	31	31	30	29	28	27	27	26	25	25
97	52	51	49	47	45	44	42	41	40	38	37	36	35	34	33	32	31	30	29	29	28	27	26	26	25	24
96	52	50	48	47	45	43	42	41	39	38	37	36	35	34	33	32	31	30	29	28	28	27	26	25	25	24
95	51	50	48	46	44	43	42	40	39	38	36	35	34	33	32	31	30	30	29	28	27	27	26	25	24	24
94	51	49	47	46	44	43	41	40	38	37	36	35	34	33	32	31	30	29	28	28	27	26	26	25	24	24
93	50	48	47	45	44	42	41	39	38	37	36	35	34	33	32	31	30	29	28	27	27	26	25	25	24	23
92	50	48	46	45	43	42	40	39	38	36	35	34	33	32	31	30	29	29	28	27	26	26	25	24	24	23
91	49	47	46	44	43	41	40	38	37	36	35	34	33	32	31	30	29	28	28	27	26	25	25	24	23	23
90	49	47	45	44	42	41	39	38	37	36	35	33	32	32	31	30	29	28	27	27	26	25	24	24	23	23
89	48	46	45	43	42	40	39	38	36	35	34	33	32	31	30	29	29	28	27	26	26	25	24	24	23	22
88	48	46	44	43	41	40	38	37	36	35	34	33	32	31	30	29	28	27	27	26	25	25	24	23	23	22
87	47	45	44	42	41	39	38	37	36	34	33	32	31	30	30	29	28	27	26	26	25	24	24	23	22	22
86	47	45	43	42	40	39	38	36	35	34	33	32	31	30	29	28	28	27	26	25	25	24	23	23	22	22
85	46	44	43	41	40	38	37	36	35	34	33	32	31	30	29	28	27	26	26	25	24	24	23	22	22	21
84	45	44	42	41	39	38	37	36	34	33	32	31	30	29	29	28	27	26	25	25	24	23	23	22	22	21
83	45	43	42	40	39	38	36	35	34	33	32	31	30	29	28	27	27	26	25	24	24	23	23	22	21	21
82	44	43	41	40	38	37	36	35	34	32	31	31	30	29	28	27	26	26	25	24	24	23	22	22	21	21
81	44	42	41	39	38	37	35	34	33	32	31	30	29	28	28	27	26	25	25	24	23	23	22	21	21	20
80	43	42	40	39	37	36	35	34	33	32	31	30	29	28	27	26	26	25	24	24	23	22	22	21	21	20
79	43	41	40	38	37	36	35	33	32	31	30	29	29	28	27	26	25	25	24	23	23	22	21	21	20	20
78	42	41	39	38	37	35	34	33	32	31	30	29	28	27	27	26	25	24	24	23	22	22	21	21	20	20
77	42	40	39	37	36	35	34	33	32	31	30	29	28	27	26	25	25	24	23	23	22	21	21	20	20	19
76	41	40	38	37	36	34	33	32	31	30	29	28	27	27	26	25	24	24	23	22	22	21	21	20	20	19
75	41	39	38	36	35	34	33	32	31	30	29	28	27	26	25	25	24	23	23	22	21	21	20	20	19	19
74	40	39	37	36	35	33	32	31	30	29	28	28	27	26	25	24	24	23	22	22	21	21	20	20	19	19
73	39	38	37	35	34	33	32	31	30	29	28	27	26	26	25	24	23	23	22	22	21	20	20	19	19	18
72	39	38	36	35	34	33	31	30	29	29	28	27	26	25	24	24	23	22	22	21	21	20	20	19	19	18
71	38	37	36	34	33	32	31	30	29	28	27	26	26	25	24	23	23	22	22	21	20	20	19	19	18	18
70	38	36	35	34	33	32	31	30	29	28	27	26	25	25	24	23	22	22	21	21	20	20	19	19	18	18
69	37	36	35	33	32	31	30	29	28	27	26	26	25	24	23	23	22	21	21	20	20	19	19	18	18	17
68	37	35	34	33	32	31	30	29	28	27	26	25	25	24	23	22	22	21	21	20	19	19	18	18	18	17
67	36	35	34	32	31	30	29	28	27	27	26	25	24	23	23	22	21	21	20	20	19	19	18	18	17	17
66	36	34	33	32	31	30	29	28	27	26	25	25	24	23	22	22	21	21	20	19	19	18	18	17	17	17
65	35	34	33	32	30	29	28	27	27	26	25	24	23	23	22	21	21	20	20	19	19	18	18	17	17	16
64	35	33	32	31	30	29	28	27	26	25	25	24	23	22	22	21	21	20	19	19	18	18	17	17	17	16
63	34	33	32	31	29	28	28	27	26	25	24	23	23	22	21	21	20	20	19	19	18	18	17	17	16	16
62	34	32	31	30	29	28	27	26	25	25	24	23	22	22	21	20	20	19	19	18	18	17	17	16	16	16
61	33	32	31	30	29	28	27	26	25	24	23	23	22	21	21	20	20	19	18	18	17	17	17	16	16	15
60	32	31	30	29	28	27	26	25	25	24	23	22	22	21	20	20	19	19	18	18	17	17	16	16	15	15
59	32	31	30	29	28	27	26	25	24	23	23	22	21	21	20	19	19	18	18	17	17	16	16	16	15	15
58	31	30	29	28	27	26	25	25	24	23	22	22	21	20	20	19	19	18	18	17	17	16	16	15	15	15
57	31	30	29	28	27	26	25	24	23	23	22	21	21	20	19	19	18	18	17	17	16	16	15	15	15	14
56	30	29	28	27	26	25	24	24	23	22	22	21	20	20	19	18	18	17	17	16	16	16	15	15	14	14
55	30	29	28	27	26	25	24	23	23	22	21	20	20	19	19	18	18	17	17	16	16	15	15	15	14	14
54	29	28	27	26	25	24	24	23	22	21	21	20	19	19	18	18	17	17	16	16	15	15	15	14	14	14
53	29	28	27	26	25	24	23	22	22	21	20	20	19	19	18	17	17	17	16	16	15	15	14	14	14	13
52	28	27	26	25	24	24	23	22	21	21	20	19	19	18	18	17	17	16	16	15	15	15	14	14	13	13
51	28	27	26	25	24	23	22	22	21	20	20	19	18	18	17	17	16	16	15	15	15	14	14	13	13	13
50	27	26	25	24	23	23	22	21	20	20	19	19	18	18	17	17	16	16	15	15	14	14	14	13	13	13
49	26	26	25	24	23	22	21	21	20	19	19	18	18	17	17	16	16	15	15	14	14	14	13	13	13	12
48	26	25	24	23	22	22	21	20	20	19	18	18	17	17	16	16	15	15	15	14	14	13	13	13	12	12
47	25	24	24	23	22	21	21	20	19	19	18	17	17	16	16	16	15	15	14	14	13	13	13	12	12	12
46	25	24	23	22	22	21	20	19	19	18	18	17	17	16	16	15	15	14	14	14	13	13	12	12	12	12
45	24	23	23	22	21	20	20	19	18	18	17	17	16	16	15	15	14	14	14	13	13	13	12	12	12	11
44	24	23	22	21	21	20	19	19	18	17	17	16	16	15	15	15	14	14	13	13	13	12	12	12	11	11

Height (metres): 1.36 1.40 1.44 1.48 1.52 1.56 1.60 1.64 1.68 1.72 1.76 1.80 1.84 1.88 1.92 1.96 2.00

Weight (stones and pounds) — side scale: 17st, 7lbs, 16st, 7lbs, 15st, 7lbs, 14st, 7lbs, 13st, 7lbs, 12st, 7lbs, 11st, 7lbs, 10st, 7lbs, 9st, 7lbs, 8st, 7lbs, 7st